AROUND TADLEY
fact and fable

Tadley and District History Society

Published by Tadley and District History Society (TADS)
PO Box 7264, Tadley RG26 3FA, United Kingdom.

First published November 1999; second impression
December 1999; third impression (with minor alterations)
April 2000; fourth impression September 2000.

Layout, design and pre-press Ian Burn and Alan Cooke.

Picture research Carol Stevens, Ian Burn and Alan Cooke.

Illustrations Carol Pope.

Maps Peggy Anscombe and Ian Burn.

Software The text for this publication was compiled in
a database using FileMaker Pro. Pages were made-up
using Adobe PageMaker. Maps were drawn using
Adobe Illustrator.

Typefaces The main text is set in 9 on 10 point Minion.
Headings are set in 8 on 10 point Futura and captions
set in 8 on 9 point Futura.

Cover design The project committee (many thanks to
James Lambden for making the task easier).

Printing and binding produced through AB Print,
Wokingham, Berkshire.

*Further copies of this and other TADS publications
may be obtained by writing to Tadley and District
History Society, PO Box 7264, Tadley RG26 3FA,
United Kingdom.*

ISBN 0 9537043 0 0

Front cover picture

Tadley Band, about 1907. The picture was taken
outside the Primitive Methodist Chapel, Main Road,
Tadley. Band members: 1/Albert Smith, 2/Sidney
Jury, 3/Arthur Kimber, 4/Charles Lambden, 5/
Ernest Stamp, 6/Thomas Lambden, 7/George Smith,
8/David Norrise, 9/John Kimber, 10/Arthur
Monger, 11/Ted Saunders, 12/George Sears.

**This project is part of Stage 2000,
Basingstoke and Deane Borough Council's
Millennium Initiative.**

Basingstoke and Deane Borough Council are not
responsible for any inaccuracies that may be
contained within this publication.

Tadley God help us! Back of beyond!
Broom-maker's cottage, heather and pond,
Acres of gorse flame, hills keeping guard,
Goats on the common and geese in the yard.
Smother of blossomin' apple and pear,
Coco-nut shies and the fun of the fair.
Work polished off without grumble and fuss,
Trips to the town on the top of the bus.
Trifles put by 'gainst a rainier day.
Mornings for thrift and the evenings for play.
Lined honest faces all tanned by the sun,
Lamplight in windows ere supper is done.
Threshing machines and the flying of chaff,
Lads who can bargain and labour and laugh.
Pitches for cricket, and pubs for a drink,
Tadley ain't nearly so bad as you think.

Poem printed in *Berkshire Chronicle*
and written by S.E. Collins, probably in the 1930s

Foreword

Welcome to *AROUND TADLEY – fact and fable*; we hope that you will enjoy it.

This is a book for browsing through. It is about the history of the locality; we hope it will prompt the memories of the older generation and stimulate the interest of the young and newcomers to the area.

Tadley and District History Society (TADS) the local history group, as their millennium project, set out to provide a reference source of places, events and people that seemed significant in the history of Tadley and the surrounding area.

During the last 50 years the local population has become less indigenous. Most of the TADS members involved in compiling this book are 'foreign' to the area, but have grown to appreciate the people and countryside of this beautiful part of north Hampshire.

In the course of our research we have learned of many events that have taken place. Some small but interesting, others of national and even international importance. A great deal of information is available about some events, little about others. Amongst the latter we include matters that may be fable, but which are part of the local folklore.

We have not set out to produce a publication of a high academic standard; this would have taken more time and resources than we had available. We have done our best, within these limitations, to verify the information gathered.

Much of what is included has, because of space restrictions, had to be in less detail than we would have wished. Additional information that has been collected is maintained on our database and in our archives. If you, the reader, wish to investigate further any particular subject please contact the Society.

And remember reader, **history** is everything that has happened up to the moment you are reading these words and **you** are part of it.

Millennium Project Team

Tadley and District History Society (TADS)

Tadley and District History Society (TADS) was founded in 1984 for people with an interest in local social history, and in the broader scope of history and natural history. Monthly evening talks are arranged, usually on the third Wednesday of each month, except August, at St Paul's Church Hall, Tadley. There is also an annual coach outing and occasional local walks.

Current membership numbers seventy and meetings are open to visitors.

The society has published a number of local history booklets, and reproduced several older out-of-print publications of significance to the area. A list of all current TADS publications, together with ordering details may be obtained by writing to: Tadley and District History Society, PO Box 7264, Tadley RG26 3FA, United Kingdom.

TADS is a member of Hampshire Archives Trust which is associated with Hampshire Public Record Office.

For further information and programme details contact: Bob Brown tel: 0118 981 6109 or Derek Ward tel: 0118 981 2626; email: derekgeorgeward@cs.com

Acknowledgements

A book of this kind could not have been produced without the support of numerous people and the Project Team (Peggy Anscombe, Bob Brown, Lorna Brocks, Ian Burn, Alan Cooke, Pat Galvin, Malcolm Isted, Carol Stevens, Mike Targett and Derek Ward) owe a considerable debt to all those who have given so generously of their time and knowledge. Without their contribution the book would have been the poorer. We hope it does credit to the wealth of fascinating information and photographs they so freely supplied. It will be obvious to many of them that we have only been able to include a fraction of what they contributed. We hope to use some of the photographs, which did not make it to the book, in displays produced for the 'Millennium Year'.

It is impossible to individually thank everyone who helped collect and supply information. We would, however, like to offer our thanks to Ann Broad, Dr Peter Brough, Philip Cooper, Marcus Hall, James Lisney, John Locke, Alan Caiger-Smith, David Hawkings, Gordon Rollinson and Dr Michael Speight who wrote entries. Special thanks also go to the members of Tadley and District Society who helped and supported the project from its inception.

Despite our best efforts we realise that errors and mistakes are still likely to remain. Please advise of any, in case we ever foolishly decide to go through all the effort again and produce a second edition! If any copyright has been infringed, we apologise and will do our best to correct the matter.

We gratefully record the ready assistance from the staff at the following libraries and archival repositories: British Library, Public Record Office, Hampshire Record Office, Berkshire Record Office, Reading University Library, Post Office Archives, Guildhall Library, Family Record Centre, Basingstoke Library, Willis Museum, Winchester Local Studies Library, Tadley Library, BT Archives, Newbury Library, Reading Local Studies Library, York Railway Museum, Dr Williams Library, Probate Office (London), National Portrait Gallery Library

Most of the line drawings in the book were done by Carol Pope, whilst the maps and diagrams were drawn by Peggy Anscombe and Ian Burn, with help and comment from the rest of the Project Team. Our thanks also go to Jean Burn for all her help with the typing.

Many people helped with the checking and proofing of the book. Our thanks in particular to Frank Anning, Isla Barlow, Margaret Cross, Sue Rayner, Harold Shell and Vickie Ward who at various stages spent time checking for errors – spelling, grammatical and factual. Any mistakes that still remain after all their efforts are the responsibility of the Project Team!

Finally, our grateful thanks go to AWE/Hunting-BRAE for printing the book, and Basingstoke and Deane Borough Council (Stage 2000) for their grant.

TADS would like to be informed of the existence and location of any items relevant to the area: e.g. documents, photographs, implements, musical instruments, flags, collections.

How to use the book

Entries are printed in alphabetic sequence, using what we consider to be the most familiar or most up-to-date heading for each subject entry; e.g. the entry for The New Inn public house in Baughurst is found under its current title of The Badgers Wood.

Cross references to associated subjects, or where more detail is given, are printed in bold text. The alphabetical reference word is in bold; e.g. the entry heading for Ernie Kimber would be **Kimber, Ernie** whilst a cross reference within the text would be Ernie **Kimber.**

Entries that start with a number are sorted by the alpha-equivalent of the number; e.g. the entry for the **2403 Aldermaston Squadron** is under 'T' (two thousand four hundred and three).

We have used several abbreviations in the book. The majority are standard abbreviations in common use elsewhere; e.g. USAAF (United States Army Air Force), but, in order to save space, we have adopted a few of our own. These have been kept to a minimum to avoid confusion. Abbreviations we have used are: 'AWE' & 'AWRE' for AWE Aldermaston; 'Some Account…' for Daniel Benham's book *Some Account of the Village of Tadley in Hampshire, and of the Independent Church there*; 'Tadley School' for Tadley Community Primary School.

Where possible, the location of places is given in brackets immediately after the appropriate entry heading, using standard Ordnance Survey six-figure grid reference. We have not included the sheet reference square as all the locations are within the same 100 km grid square (SU).

Building or hut reference numbers are quoted in places. These refer to the wartime buildings on, or near, Aldermaston Airfield and are identified on the 1945 Aldermaston record site plans 263/45 and 264/45, available from TADS and other sources.

A detailed map showing the area is included as a guide. It is intended to show the location of, in particular, places that no longer exist, e.g The Red House, Pamber Heath, and of pro-

posed constructions that were not pursued e.g. Berkshire and Hampshire Junction Canal.

At an early stage the project team decided that our area of interest should be within a four mile (6 km) radius from Tadley Library. Where we knew that other villages were producing millennium publications we have tried not to duplicate information.

Map showing the area covered by the book

A few topics did not easily fit into the format chosen by the project team. Additional information on education, health care and medical services, war memorials and enclosure acts is included in Appendices i to iv after the alphabetical entries, at the back of the book.

When quoting from other sources in an entry, the source is, wherever possible, given in the text; a bibliography of sources consulted together with references for further reading is also given at the back of the book.

Where the location is in Tadley we have not included 'Tadley' in the entry heading or text. However, for non-Tadley locations, or where there is the possibility of any confusion, we have included a location; e.g. St Saviour's Church, Tadley and St Saviour's Church, Mortimer West End.

A

A340 (Aldermaston Road) The main road through Tadley, linking Basingstoke with the A4 (Bath Road) at Aldermaston. Its importance as a communications route has long been recognised; in 1771-72 an Act of Parliament created the **Aldermaston and Basingstoke Turnpike Trust**. Ernie Kimber, writing in *Tadley During My Time and Before*, describes the road as being, at one time, little more than an unmetalled muddy cart track, ending at the top of Tadley Hill, by The **Green**. Early twentieth century photographs of Mulfords Hill reinforce this impression. In 1926, the road was metalled from the county boundary (by Lloyds Bank) to **Park Prewett Hospital**.

Acorn picking Mentioned in the Report of His Majesty's Inspector of Schools in 1906 as one of many reasons for the wholesale absence of children from **Tadley School** at various times throughout the year. The most likely use for the acorns was to feed pigs, many families keeping one as a source of meat. See **Butchers; Pig butchers; Silchester School**.

Act of Uniformity (1662), The During the **Civil War** the Puritans replaced many church ministers. With the Restoration of Charles II, they were ejected and there was a promise of religious tolerance. Unfortunately this failed to materialise. After 1661 a number of Acts were passed designed to exclude Nonconformists from office, or any position of influence. Troublesome preachers were dealt with by the Act of Uniformity of 1662, which required all beneficed clergy to conform to the Prayer Book, and deprived of their livings any who refused to give their unfeigned assent to everything the book contained. This marked the beginning of that great social and religious division between 'church' and 'chapel' that persisted almost to the present day. See **Puritan Ejection; United Reformed Church; St Peter's Church**.

AEI Research Laboratory, Aldermaston (594 649) Associated Electrical Industries Ltd (AEI) bought **Aldermaston Court** for £17,000 in the first weeks of World War II to act as an emergency headquarters for their London offices in the event of air raid damage. However, the house and grounds were requisitioned by the government in 1941, and not returned until after the war ended. In 1947 AEI decided to establish a research laboratory devoted to long-term fundamental research. Initially the laboratory was based in the house and wartime army huts in the grounds and later in purpose-built buildings. Early research included work into the usefulness of the recently developed electron microscope and from 1951 into the behaviour of very high current discharges in gases. Nuclear research had been undertaken from the foundation of the laboratory in 1947. Two particle accelerators were installed before 1950: one 500,000 volts and the other 4,000,000 volts. This led to the building of 'Merlin', Britain's first privately owned research reactor. Situated beside the lake, near where **Portland House** is today, the reactor was commissioned on 16 July 1959. Science teachers from local schools remember taking parties of school children on educational visits to see the reactor. The hope that AEI's pioneer research at Aldermaston would bring valuable business to the remainder of the AEI Group proved mistaken and the Aldermaston laboratory was closed down and eventually sold to the Cleaver-Hume Group of Correspondence Colleges who moved onto the site on 23 September 1965.

Air Training Corps The cadet force of the RAF. The Air Training Corps was founded in 1941 under a Warrant from King George VI. 2403 Aldermaston Squadron was formed in September 1963 after a short period as a detached flight of 211 Newbury Squadron. The squadron's headquarters have been located at the Medway Hut, Aldermaston Road (beside Barclays Bank) since its foundation. Cadets, aged 13 to 22, meet twice a week and most weekends to learn aviation subjects; fly to solo standard in Grob Gliders; fly in Bulldog aircraft; become skilled on the range and in the art of fieldcraft; to survive in the wild and, take part in the Duke of Edinburgh Scheme. A distinguished former cadet is Squadron Leader P.H. Rosental RAF who received the Queen's Commendation for valuable service in the air. This was gained when he was attached to the Hong Kong Defence Force Helicopter Wing. He was responsible for a courageous rescue from a ship in dangerous seas off Hong Kong harbour.

Airways Training Ltd After World War II, British Overseas Airways Corporation (BOAC), the forerunner of British Airways, suffered from a shortage of suitably trained aircrews and ground engineers. They opened their Central Training School at **Aldermaston Airfield** in March 1946 to provide suitable training for new recruits and ex-RAF crews on a wide range of civil aircraft including Tudors, Haltons, Plymouths, Yorks, Lancastrians, Hythes and Dakotas. During the 1946-7 financial year a total of 847 students passed through the school. The school's name changed to Airways Training Ltd from 1 April 1947 and was run by both BOAC and British European Airways (BEA). The school worked to capacity until the end of 1947 by which time the training programme to meet the immediate postwar requirements of BOAC and BEA was completed. In December 1947, the staff establishment was reduced with most training being transferred to the companies' line bases. Expenditure on the school at Aldermaston could no longer be justified and training ceased on 30 September 1948. During the 1947-48 financial year 2,973 students passed through the school. See **Eagle Aviation**; **Alf Woodall**.

Aldermaston (591 653) A village in Berkshire two miles north of Tadley. The name Aldermaston was originally derived from Heldremanestone (Alderman's Town). During the 1950s and 1960s it became synonymous with **AWRE** but was almost untouched by the development of the site and remains a small country village. See **Aldermaston Court**; **Aldermaston Estate**.

Aldermaston Airfield (595 630) In 1941 the higher part of the **Aldermaston Court** estate was chosen by the government as a site for development as a Bomber Operations Training Unit (OTU). The woodland was cleared and a standard 'A Class' airfield with three concrete runways was built. The workshops and administration buildings were on the south side, near the main entrance at **Falcon Gate**. There were five hangars. Four were built to take the largest RAF aircraft. The fifth, just off the airfield, was for the Ministry of Production where Spitfire fighter planes were assembled by Vickers

Supermarine. The Spitfires were flight tested from the airfield. On the east side of the airfield there was a large bomb dump which covered nearly half the site. The airfield was opened by No 92 Group of the RAF on 1 July 1942, but was never used by the intended Wellington bombers because, by then, it had been earmarked for the United States Army Air Force (USAAF). It was allocated to the 8th US-AAF as an air transport base and became USAAF station No 467 in October. The airfield was relinquished to the Air Ministry on 15 June 1945. The RAF's Technical Training Command took over and a Canadian Aircrew Holding Unit (a personnel unit) occupied the airfield for six months in case of a need to send airmen out to the war against Japan. By December 1945 the airfield was put on 'care and maintenance', although Vickers Supermarine still retained their Spitfire test facilities at the southern corner of the airfield. In spring 1946 the Ministry of Civil Aviation took over. British Overseas Airways Corporation (BOAC) used it as a training site between March 1946 and September 1948. The Ministry of Civil Aviation departed in April 1950 when it was handed over to the Ministry of Works for the construction of **AWRE**. See **Airways Training Ltd**; **D-Day**; **Hangar 5**; **Operation Market Garden**; **Operation Torch**; **United States Army Air Force (USAAF)**.

Aldermaston and Basingstoke Turnpike Trust By the eighteenth century traffic on roads had increased so much that the statutory labour system of parishes and townships being responsible for their maintenance could no longer cope. One solution was to form turnpike trusts, empowered to levy tolls for the upkeep and improvement of named stretches of highway. The first turnpike trust was established by a private Act of Parliament in 1663 and by 1750 most of the major through routes in England were turnpike roads. The Aldermaston and Basingstoke Turnpike Trust was formed by an Act of Parliament in 1771-72. It ran from **Aldermaston** to Basingstoke via **Tadley**, **Pamber End** and Sherborne St John. It would have been a route for getting goods to and from the **River Kennet Navigation**, opened in 1723. Tolls were levied for the upkeep of the road. Toll keepers are recorded in the census at Pamber End, next to the **Queen's College Arms**, as late as 1871. A normal toll would be a farthing for a head of cattle and 6d for a carriage horse. Local carts and those going to church or to a funeral were exempt. During Victorian times, when turnpike roads were less hazardous places, the job of collecting the tolls was often done by women. In 1841 Dinah Foster (aged 60) and in 1871 Jane Stokes (aged 57) appear in the census as Toll Collectors at Pamber Gate. They were both widows and lived alone. This was probably their only form of livelihood and without it they may have been paupers living off the parish. Turnpike roads are largely associated with the stage-coach era. They ceased to

View of Aldermaston Court from the south west

be profitable with the coming of the railways to which the long-distance trade transferred and the turnpike tolls declined remorselessly. During the 1850s and 1860s the condition of many turnpike roads deteriorated and trusts tried to pay off their debts. Most trusts were dissolved in the 1870s and 1880s and in 1888 responsibility for main roads passed to the newly created county councils. Papers in the Hampshire Record Office detail the closure of the toll house at Pamber End and its sale to **Queen's College, Oxford**. Census records also give details of toll booths on other local turnpike roads: one in Baughurst next to The **Wellington Arms** and one adjacent to The **Pineapple** at **Ashford Hill**. See **Kennet & Avon Canal**; **Roads**.

Aldermaston Arm (602 672) A cut on the **Kennet & Avon Canal**, to **Aldermaston Station** at **Aldermaston Wharf**. It was built by the Great Western Railway, after they bought the canal in 1852, to enable goods to be transferred from it to the railway. Most of the arm has now been filled in but its original line may still be seen from the nearby railway bridge. See **Railways**.

Aldermaston Brewery See W.J. **Strange & Son Ltd**.

Aldermaston Bridge (602 672) Originally a swing bridge, over the **Kennet & Avon Canal** at **Aldermaston Wharf**, it was replaced by a lift bridge in 1984.

Aldermaston Charities The bequests of charitable gifts to the village of Aldermaston are recorded on an ancient board in the porch at **St Mary the Virgin Church, Aldermaston**. In 1703 the Revd Robert Dixon gave two houses by Coopers Bridge for four widows; these houses have since been restored for continued use. In 1732 Richard Hollyman gave £10 and stipulated that the interest should be distributed at set times to the poor of the village. The church received a piece of land behind Fisherman's Cottage, known as 'Church Acre'. See **Candle Auction, Aldermaston**; **Charities**; **Almshouses**.

Aldermaston Court (596 648) The original manor house, built in 1636 by Sir Humphrey Forster, was badly damaged by fire in 1843. In 1849 Daniel Higford Davall Burr purchased the estate and commissioned architect Philip C. Hardwick RA to supervise the building of the present house, called Aldermaston Court. Many of the best features of the original house which had survived the fire were incorporated in the new one (chimneys, entrance hall, staircase, gallery and much of the oak panelling and stained glass). Situated close to the lake the new house was very similar in design to Sandringham.

In September 1939 **Aldermaston Estate** was broken up and sold in lots at auction. The house and its immediate grounds were purchased for £17,000 by Associated Electrical Industries Ltd for possible use as an evacuation centre for London staff, but before long it was requisitioned by the government. Initially it was used to accommodate women of the Auxiliary Territorial Service (ATS); in early June 1940 exhausted ATS women arrived from the Dunkirk evacuation. In November 1943 the American IXth Air Support Command (ASC) moved in, becoming the XIXth ASC in February 1944.

Photo: J.W. and C.A. Stevens

The house and grounds were returned to AEI in 1947 and they established a research laboratory, where they built a reactor. On 23 September 1965, two years after the departure of AEI, Cleaver-Hume, a correspondence company, moved in. Soon afterwards, the house, now known as Aldermaston Manor, became a commercial residential centre. In 1971 the house was purchased by an American publishing company, Macmillan Schools Ltd. It was primarily intended to be their commercial office and research base, together with the ancillary uses of storage and printing. In 1981 Blue Circle became the new owners and the house was further developed as a conference and residential centre, whilst elsewhere on the estate a new group headquarters was constructed. In 1998 ownership passed to Richcliff Securities. The house itself is now a hotel known as The Manor House Hotel. See **AEI Research Laboratory; Aldermaston Estate; Portland House.**

Aldermaston Decoy (607 634) Also known as Decoy Pond or Coy Pond, Aldermaston Decoy was a stretch of water, about two acres in size (0.8 ha), which originally acted as a trap for wildfowl. The name 'decoy' is a corruption of eende (de) from the Dutch for duck and kooi (coy), Latin for hollow place or cage, hence de-kooi or decoy. From the lake a number of small pipes, called canals, led off. The wildfowl were enticed to enter the pipes where they were netted and killed at the other end. The decoy was worked by a decoyman and his dog. The decoyman would carry a piece of burning peat to disguise his scent. The dog, a trained water spaniel, usually red in colour – sometimes dressed up in a fox's brush and coat – acted like a 'pied-piper', having an hypnotic effect on the birds which followed it to their slaughter.

The Aldermaston Decoy was possibly the work of the Skelton family of Lincolnshire in the mid eighteenth century, during the Congreve occupation of **Aldermaston Estate.** However, during Daniel Higford Davall Burr's ownership (1849-85) it had already disappeared. Mary Rose Newham in her book, *Notes on the History of the Parish of Aldermaston,* comments that 'the Decoy Pond was used a great deal by visitors as a bathing pool with diving board and cemented bottom placed there by Mr Keyser.' The remains of the decoy are within the part of the estate now occupied by **AWE.**

Aldermaston Estate Aldermaston (Heldremanestone) consisted of a mill, worth twenty shillings (£1), and two fisheries, worth five shillings (25p), in the **Domesday Survey** and was held by William the Conqueror. Prior to that, the land and properties had formed part of the estates of Earl (King) Harold. William and his army are believed to have camped on the estate on their way north from their victory at Hastings to cross the Thames at Wallingford before advancing on London. During the remainder of the reign of William and later his son

William Rufus, Aldermaston was owned by the crown. There is no evidence of there being a large house at that time. In 1100 Henry I granted the estate to Sir Robert Achard, a distinguished Norman soldier whose son built the transept of the chapel in the church. It remained in the family for over 250 years until Peter Achard died in 1361 without a male heir, when it passed to Thomas de la Mare. In 1490 Sir Thomas died. John, his son, had died before his father, so his daughter Elizabeth inherited the estate; she married Sir George Forster, son of Sir Humphrey Forster. Elizabeth I visited Aldermaston twice (1566 and 1592). The fifth Forster, also called Sir Humphrey, and his wife Anne built the mansion in 1636. Aldermaston saw a lot of activity during the **Civil War.** In 1644 Parliamentary troops camped in the park. After the war all the estates were sequestered because of suspected Royalist sympathies and were not returned until 1660. In 1752 the Forster male line died out and the estate passed to the Congreve family. Many changes to the estate occurred during the family's ownership. The lake by the house was created by damming the stream. The **Eagle Gates** were won at a game of cards and moved to their present location from Midgham. The **Kennet & Avon Canal** was built along the northern edge of the estate.

On 13 January 1843 a serious fire destroyed more than a third of the house. William Congreve never recovered from the fire and died within three months. The property passed into Chancery, eventually being purchased in 1849 by Daniel Higford Davall Burr. Architect Philip Hardwick was commissioned to build a new manor house, **Aldermaston Court,** using as much of the old material as possible that had been saved from the fire. Daniel Higford Davall Burr died in 1885 and the estate passed to his son who only lived there for a few years before putting it up for sale. It was bought for £16,000 in 1893 by Charles Edward Keyser, a stockbroker. Keyser was obsessed with the idea of keeping the village unchanged, which in his definition meant unspoilt. He forbade advertisements, opposed all modernisation, and refused to allow any expansion by the building of houses. On his death in 1929 estate duties were high and the estate was put on a 'care and maintenance' basis. After the death of Mrs Charles Keyser in 1938 the whole estate was sold by her son, Norman, to a syndicate Messers Cribble, Booth and Shepherd who auctioned it off in separate lots at Reading Town Hall on 20 and 21 September 1939. Many of the lots were bought by their occupants. The house and its immediate grounds were bought by Associated Electrical Industries Ltd but subsequently requisitioned by the government. The extensive parkland was also sold, but very soon afterwards was chosen by the government as a site for a military airfield (**Aldermaston Airfield**). After the war the airfield had several occupants before being taken over by AWRE.

See **AEI Research Laboratory, Aldermaston; Aldermaston Court**.

Aldermaston Lock (601 671) Lock on the **Kennet & Avon Canal** at **Aldermaston Wharf**. Prior to its current name it was called Hag Pit Lock (after the nearby 'hag' or clay pit, which was transformed into the **Aldermaston Arm** during the nineteenth century) and later Brewhouse Lock (after the nearby brewery of W.J. **Strange and Son Ltd**). Aldermaston Lock was originally a 'turf sided' type of design. In the 1760s it was enlarged, together with the others on the **River Kennet Navigation,** to take the Newbury barges. An unusual scalloped form of lock wall construction was adopted at Aldermaston. After years of neglect the lock was restored in 1983 and is now a Grade II listed structure. See **Railways**.

Aldermaston Manor See **Aldermaston Court**.

Aldermaston Marches The Campaign for Nuclear Disarmament (CND) was founded in London in 1958, the year after Britain had tested its first H-bomb in the Pacific Ocean. In April 1958 the first Aldermaston March took place. 9,000 people walked all, or part of, the 50 miles (80 km) from London to Aldermaston, some 5,000 of them eventually gathering outside **AWRE**. The CND Aldermaston March became an annual event for several subsequent years under the cry of 'Ban the Bomb' and to the movement's theme tune 'We Shall Not Be Moved'. By 1963 the March had swelled its numbers to 70,000. The last Aldermaston March was in 1964. In April of that year Canon Collins resigned as Chair of CND and the movement began to languish as other causes (e.g. the Vietnam War) and other means of protest (e.g. street demonstrations) had a higher profile. During the 1970s and 1980s AWE (and Greenham Common Airbase) again became the centre of attention with demonstrations against cruise missiles, culminating in a 'thirtieth anniversary' march in 1988 and a symbolic holding of hands around Greenham Common Airbase and AWE. See **Greenham Peace Women**.

Aldermaston Methodist Church (591 621) See Tadley Common Methodist Church.

Aldermaston Mill See Old Mill, Aldermaston.

Aldermaston Nativity Play See York Nativity Play.

Aldermaston Nomads Motor Cycle Club Founded in 1962 by Mike Slatter, Roy Brett and Joe Stennett as part of the AWRE **Rec Soc**, with AWRE apprentices making-up the membership. In 1963 they organised competitive events and the first Pathfinder trials around North Hampshire; Air Vice Marshall Bennett presented the awards at The Hind's Head public house, Aldermaston. Events continued in that form until 1981 when changes in rally rules made it impracticable to run them, but Army three stage training trials were commenced. In 1970 a side-car event was introduced at Pickling Yard, Mortimer. Still running today, the club has a steady membership of around 40 involved in trials, classic road racing and, more recently, motor-

cross. The club helps to organise, and take part in, the Motor Cycle Club's (MMC) Lands End to Exeter Classic Trials.

Aldermaston Parish Hall Built in 1897 by Charles Keyser, owner of **Aldermaston Estate**. His interest in things medieval probably influenced the unusual 'mock gothic' design of the hall. Surprisingly, when the estate was sold in 1939, so was the hall, leaving the village community without a public building. Action by a group of parishioners and the dowager Lady Mount of **Wasing Park** enabled the property to be purchased back on behalf of the parish in 1948.

Aldermaston Pottery (591 652) Aldermaston Pottery, situated in the centre of the village, was founded in 1955 by Alan Caiger-Smith. It became widely acclaimed for pottery known as tin-glaze earthenware, made from red clay, thrown on the wheel, covered with a glaze whitened with tin oxide and painted by hand in a variety of colours including lustre. Once the Pottery was established, it was maintained by a changing team of seven or eight potters. Each potter learnt all the processes: throwing, painting, making glazes and colours and firing the kiln. The large kiln was fired with reject wood from the local willow cricket-bat industry. In the course of time many Aldermaston potters, having learnt the trade, set-up studios of their own in other parts of the British Isles. The Pottery was a busy place, well known locally but also visited by people from all over the world. As well as supplying local demand and private commissions it held exhibitions in the UK and overseas, including Japan, USA, Scandinavia, Australia and New Zealand. Examples of the work are to be seen in the Victoria and Albert Museum and in many collections at home and abroad. The Pottery closed in May 1993 with a well-remembered final exhibition on the premises. Alan Caiger-Smith is now retired. From 1999 a permanent collection of his work will be on view in the Museum of Reading. The premises now operates on a shared studio basis, known as The Pottery, Aldermaston.

Aldermaston Recreational Society See AWE **Rec Soc.**

Aldermaston School (598 653) Aldermaston School is a Church of England (Voluntary Controlled) Primary School. An educational establishment of some kind existed in the village in the eighteenth century. Aldermaston School opened on 3 October 1836 and was built at the sole charge of William Congreve of **Aldermaston Estate**. The first stone of the schoolroom in Church Road was laid on 30 June 1838. The school is famous for the dessert pear Williams Bon Chrétien. In 1988 the school moved to new buildings in Wasing Lane and in 1992 the old buildings were reopened as the Cedars School (593 651). The school houses are named after the former owners of Aldermaston Estate – Achard, Congreve, Forster and Keyser. See **Williams Pear**.

Aldermaston Soke (617 632) See **Soke**.

Aldermaston Station (601 673) Railway station to the north of Aldermaston village, on the Reading-Newbury line. Although outside the parish, the land was owned by Daniel Higford Davall Burr, owner of **Aldermaston Estate**. He gave the land for a station to be built, on the proviso it would be called Aldermaston. During the mid to late nineteenth century it was an important route for transporting the produce of the local woodland industries to London. See **Besoms; Broomyards; Railways**.

Aldermaston Wharf (603 672) Wharf on the **Kennet & Avon Canal**. In 1740, because of its central position on the **River Kennet Navigation**, Aldermaston was chosen as the the site of the canal's main carpentry depot. It became an important outlet for the export of 'very considerable quantities of round and hewed timber, hoops, brooms etc, as well as of malt and flour'. With the arrival of the railways canal trade from Aldermaston Wharf gradually declined, despite the opening of **Aldermaston Arm**, linking the canal to the railway. After years of neglect the largely derelict canal was closed to navigation in 1951. Restoration in Berkshire began in 1962 and in September 1986 Aldermaston Lock was officially reopened. A small Visitor Centre (originally a canalman's cottage dating back to the turn of the nineteenth century) was opened at Aldermaston Wharf in 1992. See Richard **Aldington; Aldermaston Lock; Besoms; Broomyards; Hoops.**

Aldermaston Witch Maria (or Martha) Hale was known as the Aldermaston Witch. It was believed she roamed the **Aldermaston Estate** as a hare and sat outside The **Falcon** public house, watching the comings and goings. She, whilst a supposed hare, was shot by a gamekeeper. The hare escaped but Maria had a nasty limp the following day. Fond of practical jokes and putting curses on people, she made several people ill and no one recovered until she died. When Maria was buried the grave digger made sure she would not reappear, burying her underneath a yew tree and filling the grave with bricks and heavy stones. See Maria **Hale; Tadley Witch.**

Aldington, Richard Novelist and poet (1892-1962), born in Portsmouth. He first came to be noticed through his poems, but after serving at the Western Front during World War I he used the experiences in his war novel *Death of a Hero*. For eight years during the 1920s he lived in Malthouse Cottage, **Aldermaston Wharf**, renting it from local resident Brigadier General George Mills. Aldington based, Georgina, the heroine of his novel *The Colonel's Daughter* (1931), on Mills' daughter, Helen. The village depicted in the book is clearly **Padworth** and several other characters were based on locals. Aldington referred to Padworth in his autobiography *Life For Life's Sake* as a refuge for a shell-shocked survivor of World War I.

Allen, Ambrose A Town Councillor, affectionately known by some as 'The Mayor of Tadley'. Ambrose

was born in Mortimer in 1884, the son of Frederick and Priscilla, but lived in Tadley all his life. As a young man he was apprenticed to a blacksmith in Basingstoke. By 1915 he is listed in **Kelly's Directory** as a blacksmith in Tadley. The business expanded to include the repairing and selling of motor cycles and by 1923 he is listed as a motor engineer. The business had by then moved to its Tadley Hill site using an ex-army hut as its premises. Such huts were in common use in the 1920s, the War Department having sold them off at the end of World War I. Ambrose continued to run the garage well into the 1950s; in the later years he was greatly assisted by Arthur Martin. Ambrose was also the local organiser of a pre- National Health scheme run by the **Royal Berkshire Hospital**, enabling people paying a small weekly sum to receive free hospital treatment. Ambrose Allen died in 1968, aged 84, and bequeathed his house and property 'to be used for the accommodation and benefit of elderly and needy folk' The income from this bequest enabled the **Ambrose Allen Centre** in Franklin Avenue to be built. Ambrose Road is named after him. See **Allen's Garage; Charities**.

Allen's Garage (605 609) Located at the junction of Tadley Hill and Fairlawn Road and named after Ambrose **Allen**. When ownership passed to the **Kent family**, John Kent initially continued using the existing ex-army building but later redeveloped the site. Throughout the 1950s and 1960s Thames Valley Transport housed a double decker and a single decker bus in large sheds to the rear of the site, where Linton Close is today. The bus crews were local people and could be seen early mornings washing and preparing their buses for the day's work. One of the drivers was Bill Helyar, Des Helyar's father, who conveniently lived next door. The site today is divided between Allen's Motor Repairs, a petrol station and a convenience store. See **Bus and Coach Services**.

Allotments Areas of ground, each a quarter of an acre (0.1 ha) in size, which can be rented from a local authority. The idea of providing land on which poor families could grow their own vegetables goes back several centuries. In the late nineteenth century it became a statutory obligation on local authorities to make such plots available, a process culminating in the Allotments Act of 1908. Tadley's allotments (at Spiers Green, Giles Green and West Heath) date back to the 1800s – an Enclosure Act of 1851 granted six acres of land as 'allotments for the labouring poor of Tadley and neighbourhood'. See **Enclosure Acts; Appendix iii**.

Alms-houses Originally the part of a monastery in which alms (charity for the poor) were distributed. After the dissolution of the monasteries it became the custom for rich men to build alms-houses, intended mainly as homes for the elderly poor, which would bear their names. **Kingsclere and Whitchurch Rural District Council** referred to Alms

House Road, Tadley, in a Register of Local Land Charges held in the files of **Mothe's Charity**. See **Browne's Charity; Aldermaston Charities**.

Alton Town 14 miles (23 km) south of Basingstoke, situated in an area where the water is particularly suitable for the brewing of pale ale. In the nineteenth and early twentieth century, much of the land around the town was given over to growing hops for the brewing industry. Up until World War II many Tadley families would go down to Alton for the **hop-picking** harvest. See Albert **West**.

Ambassador Club (588 624) Social club based in a single storey building beside the **Bishopswood shops**. The club was founded in 1966. The northwest corner of the present building was part of the canteen adjacent to **Hangar 5**, the Ministry of Aircraft Production building used during World War II for the assembly of Spitfire fighter aircraft. After the war and prior to becoming a social club it was the AWRE Police Club. Also during the 1950s a weekly baby clinic was held there.

Ambrose Allen Centre (595 624) A day centre catering for the needs of the elderly of Tadley. The centre was formally opened on 21 September 1993 by Jimmy Perry, OBE, co-writer of the 'Dad's Army' television series. It was built on a site in Franklin Avenue, between **Holmwood Health Centre** and **Tadley Town Council** offices, and financed with money from Ambrose **Allen**'s will. It is currently used by Age Concern, who run a lunch club on two days a week, and by **Loddon Valley Lions** as a respite day care centre for the frail on two days. Social activities for the over 60s are provided at the Monday Club. See **Charities**.

Amphitheatre (644 626) Part of the Roman town of **Calleva Atrebatum**, located just outside the perimeter walls at the north-east corner near **St Mary the Virgin Church, Silchester**. It was excavated during the 1980s.

APACE During the mid-1960s, whilst Tony Wedgewood Benn was Ministry of Technology, AWRE established a centre at the low security site at **Blacknest** to provide consultancy and training facilities for industry, using the expertise of AWRE scientists and engineers. The centre was called APACE (Aldermaston Project for the Application of Computers to Engineering) and opened in October 1966. Much research was done into engineering production management techniques, including group technology. The centre was gradually run down after the demise of the Ministry of Technology in 1970.

Ashford Hill (555 620) A small village three miles (5 km) west of Tadley on the B3051 road. Before the common was enclosed there were only two houses, Brook Farm and Woodhouse Farm, a few squatters' cottages and a tiny wooden church on Tucker's Hill. The church was burnt down in the late 1700s or early 1800s. A brick kiln belonging to this early settlement period was, in the 1600s,

owned by the Goddard's of **Blacknest**, Brimpton. Ashford Hill became part of the newly formed parish of Kingsclere Woodlands in 1846. The present village began in the Old Cow Pen Lane (now Old Lane) area where thatched cottages date from 1800-1810. In 1847-48 the present church of St Paul's was begun. The building of a Wesleyan Methodist Chapel in 1838 had prompted Lord Bolton, the Duke of Wellington, aided by **Queen Anne's Bounty**, to replace the burnt down church. The *Victoria County History* reported 'three **Primitive Methodist** Chapels in the modern parish…at Plastow Green, Ashford Hill and Wolverton End'. See **Enborne Valley Reservoir Scheme; Aldermaston and Basingstoke Turnpike Trust**.

Ashford Hill Meadows (558 622) 50 acre (20 ha) nature reserve, owned and run by English Nature, comprising the valley bottom running along the course of Baughurst Brook behind The Ship Inn. It is a site of national botanical importance because of the mixture of differing habitats and over 300 higher plant species existing in the meadows. Still very much in an undeveloped state, the only time the area was ploughed, thereby losing valuable plants and seeds, was during World War II when corn was grown under instructions from the Ministry of Agriculture. The area is bordered by a Site of Special Scientific Interest (SSSI) thus making the reserve more 'naturally' valuable.

Ashford Hill Primary School (554 620) Opened in October 1863 as Kingsclere Woodlands (CE) School, with 45 pupils and space for 123. Enlarged in 1895, the school transferred to new buildings close by in 1984, and another classroom was added in 1995. By the 1920s the County Council had taken full responsibility for the running of the school. It is interesting to note that, when the Education (Provision of Meals) Act of 1926 came into effect, the Headmaster's wife began providing 'school meals' and not the Local Education Authority. The old school is now known as Bell House.

Ashford Hill Reservoir See **Enborne Valley Reservoir Scheme**.

Atom(ic) Parson, The See **Great St Mary's Church, North Tadley**.

Atom town The nickname Tadley was given in 1957 by the national and local press following the growth and development of **AWRE**.

Atomic weapons Since 1950, all Britain's nuclear weapons have been designed at **AWE**. The parts were also mostly manufactured there, but the weapons were assembled at **AWE Burghfield**.

Atomic Weapons Establishment See **AWE, Aldermaston**.

Atomic Weapons Research Establishment See **AWE, Aldermaston**.

Atrebates The Atrebates were a Belgic tribe who lived in Ancient Gaul, in the area around the modern town of Arras. Following the Roman conquest of Gaul, some of the tribe led by their king

Atomic Weapons Research Establishment housing – Plantation Road between the 1950s and the early-1960s

Commius, crossed the English Channel in 57 BC. They established a small kingdom south of the Thames with its capital, **Calleva Atrebatum**, being founded between 50 and 10 BC. However, the Atrebates had been virtually overrun by the Catevellauni tribe by the time of the Roman invasion of Britain in 43 AD. It is thought that the settlement was used as a fortress by allied British tribes during the resistance to the Roman attacks.

Attwood, Arthur Basingstoke born journalist whose early career was as a printer. In recent years he has become well known for his local history column in the *Basingstoke Gazette*, which has included several articles on aspects of Tadley's local history. He was the speaker at the first **Tadley and District Society** meeting in November 1984 and was invited back to the tenth anniversary meeting in November 1994. See Local **Newspapers**.

AWE Aldermaston (599 630) A government decision in January 1947, that Britain should develop it own atom bomb, resulted in the setting-up of a separate establishment to co-ordinate research and construction work on the new weapon. For the first three years the small team of scientists and engineers, led by physicist William **Penney**, was based partly at the Armament Research Establishment at Fort Halstead in Kent and partly at the Woolwich Arsenal in London. After a great deal of searching for a suitable site throughout much of southern England, a permanent home – the Atomic Weapons Research Establishment (AWRE) – was formally opened on 1 April 1950 on 880 acres of land at **Aldermaston Airfield**. The existing airfield buildings were used as accommodation while con-

struction began. A workforce of 4,000 people was assembled and work proceeded with the first new building being completed by December 1951. By April 1952 the main warhead fabrication plant was ready to begin operations, together with the Health Physics block and the first radioactive effluent processing plant with its 12.5 mile (20 km) pipeline to the Thames.

The first British nuclear weapon trial, **Operation Hurricane**, took place on 3 October 1952. Further atmospheric tests were carried out during the 1950s at Maralinga in the Australian desert and Christmas Island in the Pacific Ocean. In 1958 an agreement on the uses of atomic energy for mutual defence purposes was signed with the United States. Part of this agreement was the provision of facilities for Britain to test its nuclear devices at the United States underground test site in the Nevada Desert and no further British atmospheric tests were conducted. In total, Britain conducted 21 atmospheric and 25 underground tests, last one was held on 26 November 1991. In 1996, the world's nuclear powers agreed to a Comprehensive Nuclear Test Ban Treaty. Since then, AWE's scientists and engineers have had to validate nuclear weapons without nuclear testing. Today AWE's main task is to provide and support the warheads for the **Trident** weapons system, which is now Britain's sole nuclear deterrent. Work on Trident is accompanied by an increasing emphasis on de-commissioning, e.g. the Royal Navy's Polaris system and the Royal Air Force's **WE177 free-fall bomb**. AWE is required to support Trident and to maintain the capability to design and build a future nuclear weapon, should it be required. This will involve AWE in complex computer modelling and non-nuclear experiments using simulators and simulated materials and the data from earlier tests.

Initially run directly by the Ministry of Supply, Aldermaston became part of the newly formed United Kingdom Atomic Energy Authority in 1954 and from that date became the site of all UK nuclear weapons research and development – 'The Weapons Group'. In 1974 it became part of the Ministry of Defence. Called the Atomic Weapons Research Establishment (AWRE) between 1951 and 1987, the name was altered, in 1987, to the Atomic Weapons Establishment (AWE). During the 1990s management passed from being solely government to a partnership between government and **Hunting-BRAE**, a consortium of Hunting Engineering Ltd, Brown and Root Ltd and AEA Technology plc.

AWE Burghfield Originally an ordnance factory manufacturing munitions during World War II, it was built in 1939-40 following the relocation of the Woolwich Arsenal from London. During the war the factory was operated by the War Department and run by the Imperial Tobacco Company as an agency factory manufacturing 20 mm ammunition.

At the end of the war the factory ceased its manufactory role, becoming a storage depot run by the Ministry of Works. In 1954 it was reopened specifically for the production of atomic weapons. From 1964 it was administered by the Ministry of Defence as ROF Burghfield. It became AWE Burghfield in 1987, in line with **AWE Aldermaston**.

AWE Community Link A magazine first published by AWE in the 1990s. Distributed to local residents, it covers various aspects of the work done at AWE. See **AWE News-Link**.

AWE News-Link The internal staff magazine for AWE employees. A previous magazine was published under the title of 'AWRE News'. Over the years it has included several articles of local historical interest. See **AWE Community Link**.

AWRE See **AWE, Aldermaston**.

AWRE housing When AWRE opened in the early 1950s hundreds of specialist staff were recruited from all parts of the country. They had to be found somewhere to live. Running in tandem with the task of building the research facilities on site was the building of accommodation for the employees. Between 1951 and 1960 over 2300 houses were built for AWRE, with over 1000 of them being in the Tadley area. One of the first estates to be built, the Oakridge Estate, was in Basingstoke. Several experimental designs were incorporated in the housing there and all classes of personnel working at AWRE were offered them.

Houses in Priors Road and Almswood Road, on the Tadley Common Estate, were among the first built locally, mainly to house the Ministry of Defence (MoD) police. The first eight houses, 10-24 Priors Road, were handed over in the second half of March 1951 and occupied soon after, at a rent of £1 5s 3d (£1.27p) a week. The rest of this estate, Calcot Estate in Reading, Valley Road Estate in Newbury and Baughurst Common Estate all followed swiftly over the next few years. Houses were also purchased in small developments in Thatcham and Earley for staff to rent. The houses were mainly built to specific designs in well laid out roads with open spaces and mature trees left standing. During the 1960s tenants were given the option of buying the houses they occupied. The properties in the surrounding towns were quickly sold, together with many of those in Tadley and Baughurst. Over the next decade, the remainder of the local holding was sold to Newbury District Council, and the rest to various housing associations. Only a few were retained for the use of the MoD police. See W.E. **Chivers & Sons Ltd**.

B

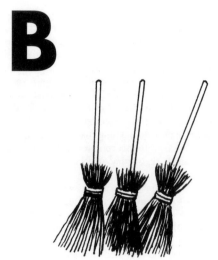

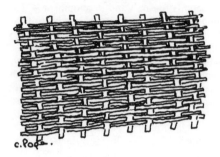

c. Poo̴o̴.

Back Lane (607 608) Former name of Winston Avenue. It forms part of the parish boundary between Tadley and Pamber. Renamed in 1951 as part of the street-naming scheme for Tadley. Failure to consult **Pamber Parish Council** about the name change resulted in letters of protest to **Kingsclere and Whitchurch Rural District Council**. Early maps show Back Lane to be the continuation of the main route from Basingstoke to what was, in the eighteenth and nineteenth centuries, the village of Tadley. Many older 'locals' still prefer to use this name believing it to more aptly describe the location than the modern name. See **Street names**.

Badgers Wood, The (579 618) A public house, at one time called The New Inn, on the junction of Wolverton and Brimpton Roads in Baughurst. In 1841 it is recorded as being run by Stephen Taylor and later, in 1871, as being kept by his widow Patience Taylor. The building was originally a barn that was part of Inhurst Farm.

Bakeries The art of a master baker, like that of the blacksmith, is a skill learned over many years. This, together with the fact that most householders would undoubtedly have made their own bread, results in few bakers or baker's assistants being listed in the early census returns. In 1851 only one per parish is listed: Martin Palmer near the Manse, Tadley, Joseph Partridge at The Brook, Little London, and John Boman at Inhurst. By 1891 Tadley had three (Fanny Hedges at Heath End and Daniel and Frederick Faulkner at Tadley Hill). Pamber two (Fredrick Kimber at Pamber Green and Samuel Englefield at Little London), and Baughurst one (Pearce's Stores). As a family tradition the names of local bakers changed little over the years – the secrets and skills being passed from generation to generation. The equipment required to bake bread,

and the need to have suitable storage for the flour, prevented the easy establishment or relocation of premises. Things changed little during the first half of the twentieth century. With the addition of Benhams bakery at Pamber Heath the area was served by the same four bakeries throughout the first half of the century; Roger's becoming Thick's, Kimber's, and Pearce's. There was also a bakery at the junction of Soke Road and Pamber Road, in the premises now called 'Corner House'. See **Kimber's Shop; Oaktree Cottage; Pamber Heath Stores; Pearce's Stores; Thick's Bakery; King's Bakery**.

Ban the Bomb See **Aldermaston Marches**.

Band of Hope A **Temperance Movement** for children, founded in 1847; many local villages (including Tadley, Charter Alley, Baughurst and Silchester) held meetings.

Bands The area has a long tradition of bands, many of which started during the nineteenth century out of the temperance movement and local churches. See **Baughurst Gospel Temperance Band; Haughurst Hill Drum and Fife Band; Tadley Bands**.

Banks Prior to the construction of **AWRE** no bank had a branch in Tadley, the nearest was in Basingstoke. As Tadley grew, so did the demand for local banking facilities and several companies opened branches. During the early AWRE construction work there was a bank near **Chivers Hostel**, in a hut next to that of the Industrial Manager (Bob Weston).

Barclays Bank opened its premises in Aldermaston Road on 11 August 1952 as a sub-branch of Basingstoke. It eventually became a full branch on 12 May 1958. In 1994 it became a sub-branch of Barclays Basingstoke Business Centre. It is currently part of Barclays North Hampshire Group. During the early years of AWRE, Barclays operated a 'lunchtime' only branch on site.

Lloyds Bank in Tadley opened as a sub-branch to Basingstoke in November 1956, becoming a full branch in September 1962. It was originally located in a caravan near the Falcon Fields estate, before moving to its present building opposite the junction of Mulfords Hill and Silchester Road. The first cashpoint was installed inside the branch in April 1975 and a 'hole in the wall' in April 1984.

Midland Bank (now HSBC) originally opened an office in Tadley on 1 June 1964 in a 'portacabin' at 2 Franklin Avenue. On 3 March 1975 it relocated to 2 The Parade, Mulfords Hill, premises previously occupied by Beryl Weston's haberdashery, wool and baby clothing shop. A cash dispenser was installed at the bank in late 1989. The original 'portacabin' building served as **Tadley Parish**, then **Town**, **Council** offices until it was demolished in 1996.

Barclays Bank plc (596 625) See **Banks**.

Bark picking Before the introduction of chemical dyes, oak bark was used for the tanning of leather. The bark was stripped in 'planks' from trees during the spring months; it could be removed more easily then because the sap was rising. The bark, which contains a quantity of tannin, was dried and then reduced to powder before being made into tan liquor. Men from this area would travel throughout Southern England to carry out this work. In some areas (e.g. Sussex) large areas of trees were grown exclusively for their bark. Bark pickers were paid by the weight of bark removed, but often it was left to dry for long periods before being weighed, so reducing the amount they were paid. Tadley men were known to complain of the money lost through this unfair method of payment.

Barn Close House (596 609) Situated on the west side of Church Road this now quite substantially sized house began as a small cottage. In 1878 Revd **Saulez**, who was by then installed as first rector of Tadley, made extensions and alterations prior to its use as a vicarage. Florence **Davidson** refers to its state, saying that 'before this time it was only a very poor place'. It is possible that it was used as a cottage by visiting curates from Overton as early as 1850 or before, although it is also thought they 'put-up' at **Bishopswood House**, later known as **Elmhurst**. See **Barn Close Laundry**.

Barn Close Laundry (597 608) Rosemary Drive, Church Road, Tadley now occupies the site that once was Barn Close Laundry. Run by Miss Marshall and Miss Paine it is first listed in **Kelly's Directory** in 1907. By 1915 Miss May Marshall was still living at **Barn Close House** but the laundry was under the management of Miss Maggie New. An old photograph shows 19 people working there, of whom four were men. By 1923 the laundry is no longer listed in **Kelly's Directory**. See **Laundries; Scouting**.

Barrows Ancient burial sites dating from the Bronze Age. Five 'round' or 'bell' barrows, dating from the Early to Middle Bronze Age (2000–1500 BC), are to be found in the area. Four are in the field(s) on the north side of the **Hurst Community School**, while the fifth outlying barrow is further north on the road to **Brimpton**.

Bartlett's Corner (610 625) The local name for the junction of Pamber Heath and Silchester Roads. It probably originated from when George Bartlett, publican of The **Pelican**, and his son Charles lived at the junction of the two roads in the 1870s. A reference to Bartlett Corner in Peter Pugh's book 'The Manor Reborn' mistakenly links the origin of the name to the **Williams Pear** at Aldermaston.

Basingstoke and Deane Borough Council The current local authority covering affairs in **Baughurst**, **Little London**, **Pamber**, Silchester and **Tadley**. The Council was formed on 1st April 1974 following the Local Government Act of 1972 and took in, among others, both the **Kingsclere and Whitchurch Rural District Council** and the Basingstoke Rural District Council. A shadow council operated in the year leading up to the creation of the new body. When formed, it was agreed that its name should reflect equal importance of town and country. With this in mind, the name Basingstoke and Deane was chosen, Basingstoke being the largest conurbation and Deane the smallest hamlet in the newly formed borough. Today it looks after almost 150,000 residents living within its 245 square miles. There are 57 councillors spread over 25 wards. The council staff include almost 500 within four departments: Chief Executive, Planning and Transportation, Community Services and Finance. See **Local government; Hampshire County Council**.

Basingstoke Area Local Plan See Tadley Local Plan.

Basingstoke Canal The 34 mile (55 km) long canal ran from Basingstoke to its junction with the River Wey Navigation at Byfleet. Completed in 1794, at a cost of £153,463, the canal was intended to increase the development of central Hampshire's agricultural trade – barges loaded with coal and fertilisers coming down from London and returning with timber, chalk and farm produce. Never very successful financially, it was not as significant to Tadley life and trade as the **Kennet & Avon Canal**. At one time there were proposals to link the Basingstoke Canal with the Kennet & Avon Canal. The route of that proposal (the **Berkshire & Hampshire Junction Canal**), which was never built, passed through Tadley and would have had a significant effect on the local economy.

Basingstoke Cottage Hospital (640 517) The Cottage Hospital movement, established in the 1860s, was intended to provide residential care for village people who had no other hospital available. The hospitals were usually converted cottages with room for 6-8 patients with regular visits from a general practitioner. Some funds for the upkeep of the hospital came from the patients, the rest from charity. Basingstoke Cottage Hospital was situated in the town, at the junction of Hackwood and

Photo: HSBC Archives

Midland Bank (later Tadley Town Council Offices), sited in Franklin Avenue between 1964 and 1975

Southern Roads. Built in 1879, at a cost of £600, it had three wards: ladies', men's and children's. It was closely connected with the Royal Hampshire County Hospital at Winchester and operations were generally carried out by surgeons from Winchester. Before The **Shrubbery** was used as a maternity hospital, many mothers had their babies delivered either at the Cottage Hospital or at home. See **Health care and medical services; Hospitals.**

Basingstoke Council See **Basingstoke and Deane District Council.**

Basingstoke Gazette See Local **newspapers.**

Basingstoke Hospital (612 538) See **North Hampshire Hospital.**

Baughurst (549 618) Spellings of the name and particularly their interpretation have over the years been very varied. The Anglo Saxon 'Beaggan hurst' is believed to mean 'The hurst (wood) occupied by Beagg'. By the fifteenth century it was written Baghurst. In the mid 1800s two people are held responsible for the addition of the 'u', one of whom was the Duke of **Wellington**, giving us the spelling we use today. Alternative interpretations have been 'Bog wood' and 'Badgers wood'. The **Domesday Survey** of 1086 does not specifically mention Baughurst, although other tithings in the Manor of Hurstbourne Priors were. It was part of the Evingar Hundred. It is said the tenants of Baughurst objected to travelling to Hurstbourne to swear their fealty to the Bishop of Winchester each year and were granted a transfer to the Manor of Manydown in 1440. At the dissolution this manor passed to

the Dean and Chapter of Winchester in 1541. Although included in the sale of the Manor of Manydown in 1649, Baughurst was restored to the Dean and Chapter of Winchester in 1660. The land, however, came under the ownership of the Duke of Wellington from 1817 to 1943. Over the past 100 years the village of Baughurst, like its neighbour **Tadley**, has extended northward and settlement on the heathland of Baughurst Common has occurred. See **Inhurst.**

Baughurst Cricket Club See **Cricket.**

Baughurst Gospel Temperance Band Formed in the 1870s as a result of 'revival' meetings in Baughurst, the Baughurst Gospel Temperance Band held open-air meetings in Shyshack Lane, Heath End on Sunday afternoons, and at 5.30 pm at the **Poplar tree.** In winter a lamp was carried on a pole to give light to the musicians. The band also played at the indoor services at **Baughurst Primitive Methodist Chapel**, as well as at Camp Meetings and **Hospital Sunday** parades. Because of the death of many of its older members, together with too few younger people wanting to join, the band was wound-up during World War II. The musical tradition is still carried on today by the Hannington Band within Methodist Chapels in the area. They still use the drum carried by Robert Carter who was with the Baughurst Band for very many years. See **Baughurst Methodists.**

Baughurst House (573 595) Many major alterations and additions to this house disguise its origins as James **Potter**'s simple copyhold tenement.

It was first redeveloped in 1694 by James Potter when it resembled the newly extended **Brown's Farm** opposite. During the early nineteenth century it was rebuilt to resemble a small mansion. Extra wings were added and it was given the grandiose title of Baughurst House. The 1911 Ordnance Survey map marks **fishponds** in the grounds. See **Baughurst Quakers**.

Baughurst Methodists William May, in the tithing of **Inhurst**, was granted a Dissenters' Meeting House Certificate in 1795. His house is where the first Wesleyan Methodist Meetings took place – **Chapel House** in the Baughurst Road. A property on this site in 1839, and occupied by James Stacey, is described in the Tithe Roll as a 'house, chapel and garden'. In 1810 the house of John Stair was registered; no details are available but it was in that year that the Society of **Primitive Methodists** was formed – possibly the first sign of a split in Baughurst. The Preaching Plan of the Reading Circuit of 1824 shows the Wesleyans in Baughurst held services each Sunday at 10.30 am and 2.30 pm in a 'rented preaching place or dwelling house'. The registration of the home of James West in 1841 in conjunction with a Joseph Williamite, a Primitive Methodist preacher, clearly led to the first Primitive Methodist chapel being built in 1845 on land owned by John Treacher. Primitive Methodism was the dominant movement in North Hampshire. By 1868 a second minister had been appointed to the **Silchester Primitive Methodist Circuit**, the Revd J.W. Normandale. It was planned that he should come to live in Baughurst and a new chapel was built and opened on Sunday 22 December 1872. The old chapel became the village Reading Room. For many years Revival Meetings were a regular feature of the chapel year. Known as camp meetings, they were still held in the Silchester Circuit in the 1970s with the Hannington Band taking the lead after the **Baughurst Gospel Temperance Band** finished during World War II. See **Baughurst Reading Room; Blacksmiths**; Susan **Jones; Methodists; Salvation Army**; John **Wesley**.

Baughurst Parish Council A meeting held at Baughurst School on 4 November 1894 was called to elect the councillors who would form the Parish Council. The election was conducted by a show of hands and was restricted to men who owned property within the parish. The chairman, however, was Wallace Walker of Wolverton House who did not live within the parish boundary. The treasurer, Mr Lazenby, was also the appointed treasurer for Pamber Parish Council. The first meeting of Baughurst Parish Council took place on Monday 31 December 1894. In 1932 the council amalgamated with Ewhurst and Wolverton under the Local Government Act 1929. The new parish was divided into two wards with four councillors for Baughurst and three for Wolverton. In the early 1930s six council houses were built at Wolverton Common, Basingstoke Corporation was approached to extend their electricity supply to the surrounding villages and a water supply was requested. In fact it was 1956 before supplies of either electricity or water came to Baughurst. That same year Baughurst Common Estate was started and two years later became a ward of the parish with four representatives on the Council. Also at that time the Hurst Secondary Modern School was built. In the 1960s street lighting schemes were approved, a play area in Long Grove built and Heath End telephone exchange changed its name to Tadley. By the 1970s a new sewage scheme was announced and a new mains drainage scheme authorised. However, there are still quite a few houses in Baughurst that are still not on mains drainage. In the 1980s a speed limit of 40 mph was introduced in Heath End Road, a new village hall built at Heath End and a 'village appraisal' agreed. In the 1990s the Hurst Community Centre became a reality. See **Hurst Community School**.

Baughurst Primitive Methodist Chapel The second **Primitive Methodist** chapel in Baughurst. The construction is mostly in brick under a steeply pitched slate roof; the buttresses and corners are faced with stone. Built in 1872 the Chapel was closed on 25 October 1987. It became a private house, called The Old Chapel, in the 1990s. See **Baughurst Methodists; Silchester Primitive Methodist Circuit**.

Baughurst Quakers Brown's Farm was established as the first Quaker meeting-house and burial ground in the parish in 1662. It was the home of Richard Potter, brother of James **Potter**. By his 70th year Richard was less inclined to open his house for weekly Quaker meetings and so in 1695 James Potter's house opposite officially became the second Quaker meeting-house. A second burial ground was established in the meadow adjoining Forge Fields in Town's End. Upon James Potter's death the Baughurst Meeting declined in importance and a new meeting-house eventually had to be found. In 1728 Leonard Cole's house (now known as Rose Cottage) in the north of the parish became the third Quaker meeting-house and burial ground. The last recorded Quaker burial there was in 1791 and the existence of the Baughurst Meeting ceased shortly after this date. See **Baughurst House; Brown's Farm; Quakers**.

Baughurst Reading Room (584 610) Originally Baughurst's first Primitive Methodist Chapel, next to the forge, on the west side of the Baughurst Road. It became the Parish Reading Room following the move of the Chapel to larger premises in 1872. Records in the *Hants & Berks Gazette* show it was often closed in the summer months when farming, hop-picking and rod-stripping took precedence, reopening in October or November. Eventually falling into disuse, its dilapidated structure, together with that of the smithy beside it, could, however, still be seen in the 1960s. It is now the site of three properties. See **Blacksmiths**.

Baughurst School (581 601) Situated on the Baughurst Road at Church Green, Baughurst **National School** opened in 1843 with room for 105 children. From 1 November 1872 it was regulated by the Charity Commissioners. At the time the school closed in 1962 there were 19 children and two teachers: Head Mistress, Miss K.C. Flatt and Miss M. Cambridge. With numbers low and the school's fabric in poor condition (the cost of installing modern sanitation was too great) it was decided to close and transfer the children to Aldermaston and Burnham Copse Schools. See **Aldermaston School; Burnham Copse Infant School; Burnham Copse Junior School**.

Baughurst Village Hall (580 620) See **Heath End Village Hall**.

BEA British European Airways. See **Airways Training Ltd**.

Beach family The Hampshire landowning family of Oakley Hall and Manor. In 1856 the family estates covered much of Hampshire, over 6000 acres (9600 ha) including land at Tadley, Little London, Pamber and Monk Sherborne. The Rt Hon William Wither Bramston Beach MP and Privy Councillor was probably the best known member of the family due in part to his untimely death in 1901 at the age of 49. While travelling from the House of Commons he was thrown from a hansom cab and later died from his injuries. His name was associated with the sale by auction of much land in Pamber Heath and Little London in 1897, thereby allowing plots of land to pass into the hands of local families. Due to bankruptcy debts the whole estate was auctioned in 1933. In the 1950s the last remaining piece of land in the parish of Pamber owned by the family became Beach's Crescent in memory of this once important local land-owning family.

Beale, Dr Stanley Medical doctor who practised in the Tadley area during the 1920s and 1930s. On his retirement in 1933 he sold his practice to Dr Lionel **Holmwood** for £4915 10s 0d (£4915.50p). See **Health care and medical services; Hospitals**.

Beating the Bounds A ceremony carried out during Ascension Week to walk and redefine the boundaries of the ecclesiastical parish. The custom is known to date from the end of the ninth century or before. Chairmen of the **vestry meetings**, parish officers, and prominent vestrymen armed with the authority of a wand of office checked that boundary stones were in position and that no buildings encroached, unrated, on parish territory. The custom continued well into the second half of the nineteenth century, long after maps made the occasion irrelevant. Since the 1920s the custom has only been revived on a few occasions. It is also known as Perambulations of Bounds or Possessioning, Processioning or Bannering. During the 1970s Roger **Searing** organised Beating the Bounds involving pupils from **Burnham Copse Junior School**.

Beavers, George Ex-councillor and Chairman of **Kingsclere and Whitchurch Rural District Council**. He and his wife, Elsie, were closely involved with Tadley Community Centre and in recognition of this the Beavers Room in the new **Community Centre** is named after him, as is Beavers Close.

Benham, Daniel B Author of *Some Account...*, Daniel Benham (1789–1870) was born in London. Little is known of his connections with Tadley, although it is thought that he probably spent time here with relatives since there are several Benham families in the area. A Joan Benham is recorded as possessing land in Tadley as early as 1189-90. Research has shown that in one of his books he admitted that 'from boyhood to the age of 22, I was engaged in Naval Service for the Country, before becoming involved in commercial pursuits'. The 1861 Census shows him to be a retired Secretary of the City Gas Company living in fashionable Regent Square, London with his wife Charlotte and two servants. Upon reading his nine books (available in the British Library), it is obvious that almost all of them have a religious theme and were written during his retirement. By 1839 he was a member of the Sunday School Union to whom he gave lectures, and was later a follower of the United Brethren sect. All of his books, including the one about Tadley, show that he was methodical in researching his subject thoroughly before putting pen to paper.

Benyon family The present owners of **Pamber Forest** (under the title of the Benyon Trust). The family are significant local landowners and their family seat is at Englefield House, Theale. Successive male inheritors of Englefield House have taken the name Benyon to perpetuate the name. The first Richard Benyon, an orphan, was born in 1698. He entered the East India Company at the age of 12 and rose to be Governor of Madras. He returned to England with a fortune of £75,000. Widowed twice, he was married for the third time in 1745 to Mary, the widow of Powlett Wrighte, descendant of The Lord Winchester, famous for his gallant defence of Basing House during the Civil War and owner of the Englefield estates. See Richard **Benyon; Englefield Estate**.

Benyon, Richard Richard Fellowes (1811–1897) inherited **Englefield Estate** in 1854 from his uncle, on condition that he took the name Benyon. It is this Richard Benyon, philanthropist and MP for Berkshire for 25 years, who instigated an extensive building programme, providing new schools, churches and houses throughout the estate and modernising cottages and farm buildings. See **Benyon family; Mortimer West End School; Pamber Heath School; Royal Berkshire Hospital; St Saviour's Church, Mortimer West End; St Stephen's Church, Little London**.

Berkshire & Hampshire Junction Canal A proposed canal, which was never built, that would have run through Tadley (see map at the back for route).

The **Basingstoke Canal**, completed in 1794, was never economically successful and during the early 1800s it was thought that the solution was to make it part of a through waterway. The opening of the **Kennet & Avon Canal** in 1810 gave an impetus to building a link between the two canals. Engineer John Rennie surveyed a 21 mile (34 km) route from Enborne to Old Basing via Brimpton and Kingsclere Common. It included a 1500 yard (1.4 km) tunnel in Tadley parish. Local opposition prevented the proposals being accepted and the depressed state of trade prevented them being revived until 1824. A new shorter 13 mile (21 km) route was surveyed by Francis Giles between Midgham and Old Basing. It involved 6.5 miles (10 km) of deep cutting and embanking, a half-mile (0.8 km) tunnel under Tadley Hill (topographical), an inclined plane at Sherborne, 3 aqueducts, 38 bridges and some 12 or 13 locks. Despite the proposals reaching Parliament in 1825-26 the Berkshire & Hampshire Junction Canal Bill failed to receive approval and when new communications links were next being planned railways were the preferred form of transport and Tadley's canal became a historical curiosity. Good communications (e.g. the Kennet & Avon Canal) were important to the success of local industries like besom-making; what effect a canal running right through Tadley would have had on the local woodland trades must remain conjecture.

Berkshire County Council The Council came into being on 1 April 1889, together with **Hampshire County Council**, as a result of the Local Government Act of 1888. At the same time Reading became a County Borough in its own right while Bradfield Rural District Council was set up to administer the parishes along the Kennet Valley such as **Aldermaston** and **Brimpton**. Functions of the County Council included social services, licensing laws, highways, etc. The passing of the Local Government Act of 1972 resulted in the creation of a new Berkshire from 1 April 1974, smaller in area but more populous than old Berkshire, and the new County Council soon moved into its Shire Hall headquarters at Shinfield. At the same time, Reading rejoined the administrative part of the county and Newbury District Council was set up. From the 1 April 1998, all districts within Berkshire were given unitary status and Berkshire County Council ceased to exist. Areas west of Reading, including Aldermaston and Brimpton are now administered by West Berkshire Council, formed from most of the old Newbury District Council. See **Kingsclere and Whitchurch Rural District Council; Basingstoke and Deane Borough Council; Vestry Meetings.**

Berkshire Record Office See **Hampshire Record Office.**

Besoms Derived from the Old English (pre 1150) word 'besema'. By definition it means a 'bunch of twigs for sweeping'. Local besom makers will give you a more derogatory description of the word, meaning 'a wayward woman', which they believe comes from a Scottish or Dutch word.

Birch-brooms (or besoms as they are more familiarly known) were one of several local trades based on wood from the surrounding forests (others include: **Hoops** and **Rakes**). Besoms are made from birch and heather and it is possible the local industry stretches back to the Middle Ages. Heather is mentioned in the Close Rolls of Henry III (1252), relating to Pamber Forest, as being used for thatching. The softer heath brooms were used in flour-mills and for domestic purposes, whilst the birch brooms found a growing market in a variety of uses throughout the nineteenth century. From a peak at the end of the nineteenth and early part of the twentieth centuries, the industry declined until today Arthur **Nash** and 'Wilf' Gundry are the only commercial broom makers in the area.

The besom-maker, or broom squire, generally buys standing birch by the acre in the autumn (see **Coppicing**), cutting going on throughout the winter months. The cut bundles of twigs are piled in huge 14 feet (4.2 m) high stacks in the workshop yard, where they season for several months. The pliability of the broom is essential for it to do its job properly; too little seasoning and the finished broom will be brittle and useless. The stacks are built in a special way – open enough to let the wind penetrate and help the seasoning process, while still preventing rain and melting snow from reaching the centre of the pile and causing rot. The bundles of brushwood are built up in layers, lengthways and crossways alternately, each bundle head to tail with the next. The layers must be perfectly level and square, so that the stack does not collapse in a high wind. When complete, it is thatched over with more bundles of bush, steeply pitched so that the rain runs off easily. The birch is ready for use when the twigs have become both hard and pliable. Large numbers of handles are also needed. A variety of woods may be used, but the commonly used ones are hazel, ash, lime or chestnut. As the handles need not be perfectly straight, wood not good enough for other craftsmen can often be bought cheaply. These are selected, cut and stacked for months in thatched-over piles.

The broom-making season starts in the spring. When the handles are seasoned the broom squire holds them in a 'broom-horse', similar to that used by many woodland craftsmen, and strips away the bark with a double-handled draw-knife. He then uses a semicircular draw-shave to smooth them, and chips their ends to a point with an axe. Making the besom heads starts with opening up a seasoned stack, trimming the bundles with a short-handled billhook or axe, then sorting them for quality and length. In the past this task was often done by women and children, who rebundled unsuitable twigs for sale as firewood. Twigs selected for brooms

West's Broom Yard, Mulfords Hill, about 1910

Photo: Tadley WI Scrapbook

are tied into separate bundles – longer, rougher brushwood for the core and the smoother shorter twigs for the outside. The broom squire sits astride his 'broom horse'. Grabbing a handful of the longer, rougher twigs, he rolls them into a circular shape, then arranges another handful of shorter, smoother ones around them. Besom heads are made in two sizes, measuring 30 cm or 25 cm around the base of the head. The broom squire judges this entirely by hand and eye; when the tips of the fingers of both hands meet around the base, it is a 30 cm one; when they just overlap, it is the smaller size. Once he is satisfied with its size and shape, the head is ready for binding. Traditionally willow twigs, thin strips of ash, oak and chestnut – even bramble – were used for the binding. Later, strips of imported cane were used, but as supplies dried up during World War II, galvanised wire became the usual material. When he is satisfied with the size and shape of the broom, the broom squire binds it about 10 cm from the top of the head. He repeats the process with another length of wire just below the first. Finally he chops the top of the head off square with a short-handled axe on a chopping block beside him. The head is then ready to be fitted to the handle, the pointed end of which is pushed into the exact centre of the broom head, then driven in about 23 cm with sharp blows. It is held in place by a nail hammered through it between the two bindings. No family or yard would make a broom exactly the same as another. Variety could occur in

length and thickness of handles or birch and in the way they were 'bonded'.

Finished besoms are sold in bundles of a dozen (12); a skilled broom squire was able to turn out up to 12 dozen (144) brooms a day. Apart from their use sweeping garden lawns and paths they had other surprising uses. Steel workers found them ideal for brushing off the coatings of impurities from the surface of newly made steel plate directly it was removed from the furnace. In vinegar brewing the bottoms of vats were lined with handleless brooms known as swales to filter the vinegar; the birch also added colour to the vinegar and helped to create an acetic acid content.

Bethany (609 619) A residential home for elderly Christians built in 1992 to the rear of the **Gospel Hall**, Pamber Heath Road. It is managed by The Bethany Care Trust and has close links with the Gospel Hall.

Bevan, Aneurin 'Nye' See **Lane End Cottage, Brimpton Common**.

Big Arch (602 615) **Bishopswood Stream** was liable to flooding, which is why the area around New Road was so suitable for withy beds (**willow osiers**). To eliminate this problem at **Mulfords Bridge** a large culvert was built in 1969-70 by **Kingsclere and Whitchurch Rural District Council**. Local children enjoyed playing there and it was soon given the name 'The Big Arch'.

Bishops Wood Bishops Wood or Bishopswood was the Bishop of Winchester's land-holding in **Tad-**

ley. It was part of the manor of Overton granted to him in a Charter of 909 AD. King Edward the Elder confirmed in law, 'to my beloved bishop Fridestan', and in the presence of the royal family, peers and bishops, 'land in several places; 20 measures at Uferantun with the wood at Tadanleage' (i.e. Tadley). This was thought more important than the lands at 'Overton' as Tadley was written in capital letters. The grant of land in the charter covered an approximate area between Wyeford, Church Road, Bishopswood Lane and back along the eastern Baughurst parish boundary. The bishop had permission to fence this little wood in the middle of the royal game forest of Pamber, and put in his own bailiff to manage it. Bishops Wood is now given over to housing.

Bishopswood Court (589 623) A £2.5 million housing project near the **Bishopswood shops**, which opened in March 1993, comprising 44 one-bedroom self-contained flats for the elderly.

Bishopswood Golf Course (588 615) Built on land which was formerly Bishopswood Farm, it was opened in April 1975. The clubhouse stands on the site of the old farm buildings and house, while the first green is on the site of the World War II **Aldermaston Airfield** sick quarters (Buildings 491/492). It was developed by **Blake's Builders**. It is a 9 hole, Par 72 course with a 12 bay floodlit driving range and a resident PGA professional. The first club president was Peter West and the first club captain Gareth Owen.

Bishopswood House (602 614) See **Elmhurst**.

Bishopswood Infant School (598 615) Designed and built as a First School to cater for the age group 5 to 9 years. It was to form part of a new three-tier system: First Middle and Secondary. However, when it opened in April 1972 with Mrs C. Gibb as Headteacher, it had reverted to being an Infant school, taking 5 to 7 year-olds. When it first opened the flooding of the **Bishopswood Stream** resulted in water 1.8–2.5 m deep on one occasion, leaving the infant school marooned. Council workmen had to come with bricks and planks to enable staff and children to get out of the building. The stream was unfenced and at flood times was incredibly dangerous. Teams of parents escorted groups of 4 or 5 year olds along the edge of the stream, between the school and **Elmhurst**. The Infant school was built without a playground because the County ran out of money and did not consider a playground essential for infant children. The school was given the car park to use as a playground. As the Tarmac had been laid on heather it sank when delivery lorries used it. The Infant school was also not allocated any playing fields. The headteachers of the Infant and Junior schools arranged between them that the infant school should have exclusive use of one of the football pitches during the day. The pitch returned to junior use after school hours. The school now has the advantage of managing its own funds

and it has undertaken various building modifications including a patio enhancement and an adventure playground. Much needed land drains have been added giving greater use of the school field. As the school was built on the old withy beds, frogs still return every year to spawn. The school has been admitting four year olds since 1994, but despite this the Greenacre Playgroup, a pre-school unit also at this site, continues to flourish. See **Education; Appendix i.**

Bishopswood Junior School Built as a Middle School to take 9 to 13 year olds, it opened in January 1972 as Tadley's third Junior School taking 7 to 11 year olds. The Headteacher was Miss Wendy Over who became Mrs Rawlings following her marriage in 1979.

Bishopswood Shops (588 622) Built for the United Kingdom Atomic Energy Authority in 1957, at a cost of £25,000, to supply the rapidly growing **AWRE housing** estates. The complex, known as Halstead House, comprises shops and flats. Frank Harris, the hairdresser, was the first shop to open in 1957 and is still there today. Swift's Dry-cleaners have also been there since those early days. Another early occupant of the shops was Simon's Stores, a general stores and post office operating after the war (1940s and early 1950s) in a converted wooden wartime hut where the Bishopswood Road bus stop is today. When the shops were built Simon's did not move in immediately because of the high rents being charged. They eventually moved into the corner unit, next to Swift's Dry-cleaners. Initial plans were for the building of ten shops, with space for a further ten which were never constructed. See **Fort Halstead**; Tadley **Post Offices.**

Bishopswood Stream Small stream running through Tadley into Pamber Forest. It is known by various names along its course: on the 1914 Ordnance Survey map it is shown as Bishopswood Stream east and west of Gutteridge Lane. See **Bowmont's Brook**; Reuben **Hicks; Sewage; Silchester Brook; Willow osiers.**

Black Death The Black Death, probably bubonic plague, reached England in 1348 and lasted until 1357. It was at its height in Hampshire during the winter of 1348-49; although this initial outbreak diminished by the end of 1349, there were further severe outbreaks in 1361-62, 1369 and 1379 and it remained endemic in Britain until 1660. All available evidence suggests that the plague of 1348-49 hit the agrarian economy of much of Hampshire, diminishing the population by about one half, leading to a scarcity of labour and a change in the management of farms. Major landowners enclosed their lands, turning them into large farms with tenant farmers or else the Lord of the Manor used the land for pasturing sheep or cattle. Some villages were practically wiped out, especially if they suffered in a later attack. Its actual effect on **Tadley** and the surrounding area has not been researched. Florence

Davidson mentions it in *The History of Tadley*, but not in any great detail. Some have suggested that it might offer a possible explanation for the abandonment of the original village of Tadley next to **Tadley Place**: the effects of plague forcing the villagers to relocate their houses. See **Pamber Priory**; **St Mary the Virgin, Silchester**.

Black Fans An old local name, common in the nineteenth century, appearing in Pamber census returns between 1841 and 1891. It covered the land and properties skirting the edge of **Pamber Forest** from behind Burney Bit and up the south side of Sandy Lane and Winston Avenue. It also included some properties along the main Basingstoke Road at Pamber Green. Locals had a variety of pronunciation of 'Fans' from 'Vals' to 'Fews'. There is no agreed explanation for the name.

Black's Cafe (591 623) A cafe and greengrocers in Franklin Avenue run by William 'Sonner' Black. It closed in 1956 after being bought by Basingstoke Co-operative Society for the site of their shop. Generally referred to as 'Sonner', William Black was born in Wiltshire in 1898, a member of a family of showmen who often wintered in Shyshack Lane. He won the Croix de Guerre and Mons Star for his service to France during World War I. He enlisted at the age of 16 but was discharged in 1916 as a result of wounds received. During World War II he organised the Tadley Home Guard, training his men with broomsticks because of the lack of guns. He was reputed to have been the only **Home Guard** sergeant-major in the country. He died on 1 January 1968. See **Co-op**; **Fairgrounds**; **Williams family.**.

Blacknest (567 630) Situated at **Brimpton Common** near The **Pineapple** public house. The existing Victorian house, with later additions, was preceded by a much older property of the same name. Originally possibly a farm house to which a Georgian frontage may have later been added (reference a print of the post-1750 period). The house formed part of a large estate known to have been occupied by the Goddard family from the early part of the eighteenth century and possibly the seventeenth century. There is reference to the brick kiln at Ashford Hill being owned by the Goddards in the 1600s.

It remained in private hands until the 1920s, later becoming the headquarters of the London Metropolitan Water Board, probably in view of the proposals for the **Enborne Valley Reservoir Scheme**. Return visits by **World War II** Canadian pilots has prompted suggestions that it was also used as an officers mess in the 1940s. During the 'setting-up' of **AWRE** in the early 1950s it was occupied by the Chief Administrations Officer. Following the building of additional accommodation it was used as a hostel for AWRE apprentices until they moved to **Boundary Hall**.

The Forensic Seismology unit attached to AWE moved into the property in March 1961 under the directorship of Dr Hal Thirlaway and have continuously occupied the site ever since. Lord Sherfield, Chairman of the UKAEA at the time, established the seismology group (made up of scientists from both on and off the AWRE site) to monitor nuclear testing. The centre's specific brief is now to analyse seismic data for the verification of the Test Ban Treaty, 1963. In addition they aim to develop ways of improving the detection of atomic explosions as separate from naturally occurring earthquakes. Periodically other, non related groups, have shared the site, one of which was **APACE** (**A**ldermaston **P**roject for the **A**pplication of **C**omputers to **E**ngineering).

Blacksmiths Prior to the 1930s, when motor transport gradually replaced the horse, the blacksmith was one of the most important trades in village life. The blacksmith was next to the vicar in village hierarchy, being responsible for making essential everyday items. It was also a good place to gather gossip and possibly the one warm place to be. They forged ploughshares and spades, produced the working tools for other craftsmen (hooks and shears for thatchers, saws and adzes for carpenters) and many other implements like cauldrons, knives, tankards and toys, made fittings for wagons and shoes for horses and stirrups for their riders. Blacksmiths who specialised in shoeing horses were known as farriers. At first blacksmiths were itinerant, touting for work where they could get it. Then as demand for their skills grew they set up their forges in towns and villages, generally near woodland so that they were assured of ready supplies of wood for firing their hearths and smelting the iron. As with many local trades, the blacksmith's skills were usually handed down from generation to generation.

A large rural parish often required more than one smith or forge. Locally, all three parishes record a forge at two sites; Tadley along the common on Pamber Heath Road, this also served as Pamber Heath Forge. The first positive census reference to this site is in 1891 when it was operated by John James, remaining in the hands of the **James family** until it closed. Central to the early village of Tadley was the Tadley Hill forge situated (approximately) in what is now the bus lay-by. From 1841-61 Daniel Soundy is the smith, later William Ford and subsequently his sons. Edward and Harry were apprenticed in the late 1800s but it is Leonard whom most older locals remember. Ambrose **Allen** was also a blacksmith, but who, from the 1920s, lists his business as 'motor engineer – all kinds of agricultural implements repaired'. The Tadley Hill forge is thought to have ceased to be operational in the 1920s, the site later used as the Tadley Sorting Office. To serve the southern and eastern ends of Pamber parish there was a forge at **Pamber End** at the junction of Bramley Road and Aldermaston Road. William, and later Francis Follett (1871), are the only recorded blacksmiths there.

The principle Baughurst forge was located on the western side of Baughurst Road just north of its junction with Shaw Lane (now Bankfield). John Treacher was blacksmith and owner of both the forge and its surrounding land in the 1840s and at that time he employed George Jacob. From the mid 1800s to almost the end of the nineteenth century the smithing there continued to be carried out by the Jacobs family. George and his son Charles in 1861 and later his grandson Frank working alongside his father in 1881. By 1903 Herbert Attwood had moved from Woolhampton and, renting the site from George Appleton, became the last Baughurst blacksmith. He gave up smithing in 1941-42 and took on the job of village postman (age 70) delivering letters and parcels by bicycle until January 1948.

Arthur Kernutt was an apprenticed blacksmith in 1891, at the age of 19, but whether at Baughurst or Heath End is uncertain. By 1907 however he was operating a forge on Heath End Road, now a parade of shops. He was still listed as blacksmith in the 1939 **Kelly's Directory**.

Wolverton Forge, built in 1750, was in the Wiggins family for many years, employing, at its busiest, six men working two forges. Throughout the nineteenth century the forge on **Silchester Common** was in the hands of the Ford family. In 1851 Thomas and his brother Charles who in 1871 is working with his son William, who then continued to operate it until the 1890s. By 1935 the forge had however closed, but John Wigley had worked it for over 30 years prior to this time. See **Baughurst Methodists; Elm Farm; Rest Shelter.**

Blake, Noah Father of Albert 'Albie' **Blake** and grandfather of George and Albert 'Bert' **Blake**. Born in 1854 and died in 1947, aged 93. The founder of **Blake's Builders.**

Blake, Albert 'Albie' Father of Albert 'Bert' and George Blake. Prior to taking over his father's building business he and his wife kept a small shop on the north side in Honeybottom, Mount Pleasant. With the purchase of the shop came a carrier van and business which he did not operate but sold to Edith Kent. Albert later kept the shop at Mulfords Hill, the site of which is **Budgens** car park. On his leaving the shop it was run by Yorke Lowe and later J.S. **Whatmore & Sons**. See **Blake's Builders; Carriers; Kent family; Lowe family.**

Blake's Builders Local builders who were based in Blakes Lane during the early part of this century – the lane is named after them. One of the earliest brick builders in the area, the company's origins date back to 1899 when Noah Blake carried out his first contract in Old Basing under the distinguished architect Sir Edwin Lutyens. In the early days the company centred around Basingstoke and consisted of Noah and seven sons. In 1906 the business moved to Blakes Lane, Tadley. Amongst the work they carried out during this time was the **Salvation Army** hall near the bottom of Mulfords Hill. Noah retired in 1924 and one of his sons Albert 'Albie' continued the business. In 1932 the firm moved to the A4 at Padworth. 'Albie' kept the business going throughout **World War II** with only one man. He handed it over to his sons in 1945. With post-war development the business prospered and was responsible for much local authority housing in the area. Between 1959-62 they built the Millers Road estate. In addition they rebuilt **Wasing Place** after it was destroyed by fire. The last project carried out by George and Albert 'Bert' before they retired was the **Bishopswood Golf Course** and clubhouse. See **Blake's Building Profiles.**

Blake's Building Profiles Developed by George Blake in 1965 upon his retirement from **Blake's Builders**. After many years in the building trade he saw the need for a modern version of the 'gauging rods' used to square and level up brickwork corners.

Blue Bus See **Bus and coach services.**

Blue Circle See **Aldermaston Court; Portland House.**

Blue Gown The 1868 Derby winner, owned by Sir Joseph **Hawley**, trained locally by John Porter and ridden by John 'Tiny' **Wells**. Eighteen horses ran in the race and Blue Gown's starting price was 7-2. See **Hawley Farm.**

Blue Star Coaches, Mortimer See **Bus and coach services.**

BOAC See **Airways Training Ltd.**

Board Schools Board Schools were established after the 1870 Education Act. The country was divided into School Board Districts and the Boards were empowered to build new schools in areas of poor provision or to absorb existing schools. Initially the schools were secular and non-denominational but an amendment in the statute allowed School Boards to provide religious instruction if they wished. In 1902 School Boards were abolished and the schools became Council Schools under the control of the County Councils. See **Ramsdell School; Tadley School; Wootton and Tadley School Board.**

Bombs During World War II there were several incidents where bombs fell locally. In September 1940 a stray German bomber, possibly looking for **Bramley Camp**, dropped several bombs across Pamber Heath, one falling in Clapps Gate Road, one in The Glen and others in the pine trees. Two people were killed – a lady in Clapps Gate Road who was hanging out her washing and a young girl who worked in Andrew Broadhurst's shop in The Glen. Other occurrences of bombs dropping appear to coincide with the raids on Reading, Newbury and Basingstoke. The aircraft may have been lost and wanted to ditch their bombs before being caught by the fighters. On the night of 2 July 1940, four bombs were dropped near Rawlins Farm, **Monk Sherborne**. Nobody was injured but part of the house where Sir Alistair and Lady Gibbs lived was demolished and part of the farmhouse was also demolished. Another bomb fell in Sherborne Wood leaving a large crater which is still visible today; some small incendiary bombs were also dropped which started small fires in fields beyond Rookery Dell. Several bombs are known to have fallen in the Baughurst area with one fatality. One, which landed near the **Calleva Park** roundabout, was reputedly a V1 flying bomb.

Bottom Farm (607 616) The old name for **Rowan Farm**.

Boundary Hall (595 625) Residential complex for staff working at **AWRE**, situated by the **A340** near **Falcon Gate**. Inaugurated in September 1950, it was one of the earliest AWRE buildings to be erected. It was named Boundary Hall by AWRE's first Resident Engineer, Mr D.I. Aronsberg, because of its proximity to the Hampshire-Berkshire border. In the early days (1950s and 1960s) AWRE had to offer accommodation to attract staff, but by the 1980s Boundary Hall had outlived its original purpose and it was demolished in the summer of 1995. The names of the individual blocks that made up Boundary Hall were (south [left] to north [right]) Argyle, Buckingham, Cumberland, Dorset, Essex, Flint, Gloucester, Hereford, Jersey and Kent. See **Blacknest**.

Boundary Players The Boundary Players was originally the Dramatics Section of the Ministry of Supply Recreational Association (Aldermaston). Its first performance, in a hall in Tadley in February 1952, was the play 'Jane Steps Out'. The Dramatics Section was then given the use of a small building (Building 203) adjacent to the **Den**, which had a seating capacity of 78. Fourteen productions were put on in this tiny theatre, starting with 'Message for Margaret'. In 1955 the Dramatics Section was renamed the Boundary Players under the leadership of Peter Todd. A year later the company moved to the clubhouse of the Recreational Society complex at AWRE, and on 10 October 1956 opened with two Terence Rattigan plays 'The Browning Version' and 'Harlequinade'. By 1959 the Players had over 270 season ticket holders. In December of that year they became the first amateur company to perform John Osborne's 'Look Back in Anger'. In 1965 the **William Penney Theatre** was formed within the club buildings. To celebrate the opening of the new theatre the Boundary Players, in conjunction with the Berkshire Shakespeare Players, presented 'The Taming of the Shrew'. The same play and cast opened The Watermill Theatre, Newbury. In 1995, electrical system and building construction problems were discovered and the theatre was closed for repairs, reopening in 1996. The Boundary Players continue to perform three productions every season and provide excellent entertainment.

Bowmont's Bridge (607 616) Bridge over **Bowmont's Brook** at the junction of Fairlawn, Rowan and Pamber Heath roads. In 1928 a parish council meeting agreed to build a bridge over the ford. The

iron barriers by the side of the road are all that remains of the original bridge. The name is believed to have originated from the Bowman family who lived in the farm on the corner of Sandy Lane adjacent to the ford: Bowman has at some time become corrupted into Bowmont.

Bowmont's Brook (617 616) Small stream running through Tadley into Pamber Forest. It is known by various names along its course: within Pamber Forest it is marked on maps as Silchester Brook, while some locals know it as Tadley Brook. East of Mulfords Hill into **Pamber Forest** it is commonly known as Bowmont's Brook.

Boy Scouts See Scouting.

Bradfield Rural District Council See Berkshire County Council.

Bramcot (607 617) A seventeenth century two storey brick cottage in West Street with a tiled roof and double casement windows. The beam in the dining room is said to have been hewn from a tree in the garden. In October 1911 it was sold at auction and the sale particulars describe a property of two reception rooms and four bedrooms somewhat larger than a simple cottage. It was set in 2.5 acres with a considerable number of outbuildings and, very importantly, 'standing at a considerable elevation above sea level well away from a main road'. In 1987 the orchard was built upon and the development of six properties was aptly called 'The Orchard'.

Bramley Camp Bramley Ammunition Depot was founded in 1917, a 1,000 acres site being requisitioned. As well as being used as a top secret ammunition store the site very soon developed as a prisoner of war camp. There were 3,500 Germans, in what later became known as South Camp, by 1918. During the war ammunition was dispatched day and night. After the Armistice the prisoner of war Camp slowly emptied. From 1922 the RAOC School of Ammunition was based there and it was the centre for the Explosive Ordnance Disposal Training, preparing troops for work in Hong Kong, Aden, Cyprus and Northern Ireland. During World War II there was an enormous expansion in the camp; by 1944 the total military and civilian staff was about 4,400 and the depot handled an average monthly rate of 35,000 tons of ammunition. After the war European Voluntary Workers came to Bramley Camp. The future of the camp was reviewed during the sixties. In 1974 the RAOC School of Ammunition moved to Kineton and the camp began to contract, finally closing on 1 September 1978. Between 1978 and February 1987 the camp became Ammunition Depot Bramley, acting as an ammunition store for the United States Army. After the Americans left, the camp was wound down and the land was gradually developed for private housing and commercial development. There have been two major projects to clear the site. In 1987 'Operation Apple' discovered 400 cases of munitions and in 1995 'Operation Cornelius' dug up about 1,750 shells and bombs, 250 suspected chemical munitions and 5,000 smoke bombs. See **World War I & II.**

Brant family Denis (1927–1993) first came to Tadley in the 1950s from Monk Sherborne. In partnership with his mother they started **Peg's Cafe.** Denis soon left the running of the cafe to his mother and sister, Peggy, and began to expand his own business on the same site. From a wood round and one lorry he built the thriving haulage and demolition company of D. Brant Ltd, later moving the business to White House Farm, Silchester Road. When BMX racing became popular in the 1970s Denis generously provided an area on the site for the locally based BMX club. He owned and maintained vintage vehicles which were often to be seen at local events. In later years Denis bought land at Brimpton Common and began the Lakeside Garden Centre but unfortunately never lived to see it become the success it is today. Julie, the eldest of his three daughters, now runs D. Brant Reclamation Ltd and perpetuates his name. See **Reading Hawks.**

Brass Bands See **Baughurst Gospel Temperance Band; Haughurst Hill Drum and Fife Band; Tadley Bands.**

Brewer's cycle shop (614 624) Located in Clapps Gate Road, Pamber Heath, it traded as a cycle shop between 1941-1957. It was well-known because of the penny-farthing cycle on the roof of the shop. The wooden building was previously a railway carriage placed on the site of **Brown's Cottage.** See Sidney A. **Knight.**

Brewery or Brewhouse Lock (601 671) Old names for **Aldermaston Lock.**

Brewing and licensing laws Throughout history licensing control has always been a conflict between raising taxes from beer sales and the accompanying drunkenness and disorder. In the thirteenth century control was vested in followers of the monarch in return for their allegiance. Between the fourteenth and sixteenth centuries the local sheriff or alderman controlled ale houses and inns to preserve public order. However, in those times of poor water supplies, beer was considered an essential dietary supplement, and as such it called for a delicate balance between the health of the population and the wealth of the brewers and the country. In the seventeenth century licensing became the job of the courts giving magistrates more influence over the local community, inns and beer sellers, while opening hours were set by the Watch Committee which generally comprised church elders and the lord of the manor.

The Beer Act of 1830 created a free trade in the sale of beer. Inns, taverns and ale houses were still controlled by the magistrates but another outlet, the beer house, came onto the scene. Generally a private house or building that was purely for the sale of beer, sometimes brewed on the premises but more likely to have been bought from a bigger brewer and sold on. Any householder who paid rates could apply for the two-guinea (£2.10p) excise license to brew and sell beer. Many such beer houses existed in and around Tadley. Often only a part-time occupation or as a second income with the woman of the house running the beer sales while the man carried out another occupation. By 1838 nearly 46,000 beer houses were added to the existing 51,000 licenses premises. Gradually local breweries took the place of small village malthouses. The Tadley area was served by H & G **Simonds Ltd** from Reading, W.J. **Strange** & Son Ltd from Aldermaston and John **May & Co Ltd** from Basingstoke.

From the Industrial Revolution through Victorian times there was much migration of people from the country to the towns accompanied by much social and drunken disorder. The new, often wealthy, middle class of factory owners, realising that a drunk workforce was of little use, financed various temperance movements and other nonconformist religious societies such as The **Band Of Hope, Salvation Army** etc. From World War I to fairly recent times opening hours were laid down nationally, again to maintain a balance between 'drunken disorder' and revenue taxes. These fixed hours (10.00 am to 2.00 pm and 6.00 pm to 10.00 pm) remained with us until the 1980s when all-day opening was allowed. See A **British Workman;** The **Old Malthouse** and individual public houses.

Brick and tile making From Victorian times until quite recently the production of bricks and tiles was an important local industry. With the increasing use of bricks and tiles as the primary building materials during the nineteenth century, replacing wattle and daub and thatch, and with the suitability of local materials like clay, several kilns sprang up to meet the demand. Whereas in the late nineteenth century there were more than a hundred kilns operating in Hampshire, by 1975 there were only five locally and today there are none. See **Inhurst Brickyard; Little London Brick Works; Pond Farm; Ramsdell Brick Works; Tadley Brickyard.**

Bridges Bridges were not common prior to the development of mechanised road transport after World War I. Unless a river or stream was very deep or fast moving, there tended only to be a ford. Between the wars many fords were replaced with bridges; e.g. **Bowmont's Bridge.**

Bridge House (601 616) A house on the northern corner of Mulfords Hill and Stephens Road. It takes its name from the nearby **Mulfords Bridge** over the Bishopswood Stream. Originally the house had extensive grounds bordering the stream, land which now forms the surrounding housing estate. Over the years it was home to many well regarded people; e.g. I.G. Symes (see **Rest shelter**) and the Huntleys who in the 1939 Kelly's Directory are listed as mushroom growers. Miss Huntley cultivated the house's orchard by under-planting with daffodils which she then sold. In 1952 Mrs Richard Wallis and her children moved to Bridge House from Baughurst after the death of her husband, grandson of the founder of **Wallis & Steevens**.

Brimpton (559 647) The parish of Brimpton lies between the A4 (Bath Road) in the north and the Hampshire/Berkshire border in the south. The village of Brimpton, about 3 miles (5 km) northwest of Tadley, is situated near the centre of the parish, between the rivers Enborne and Kennet. In 944 it was written as Byrningtune but was recorded in the Domesday Survey as Brintone. Evidence to support the existence of a pre-Roman settlement in or near the village comes from five burial mounds (**Barrows**) at **Brimpton Common**, while a hypocaust found near The Forge Stores is evidence of Roman occupation. At the north end of the parish, in the grounds of Manor Farm, is the Knights Hospitallers' Chapel of St Leonard, a fourteenth century building still in good repair. The southwest corner of the parish was on an old drover's trail. Oak Cottage at Hyde End, which is at least fifteenth century in origin, was formerly an inn frequented by drovers. Nearby Smithy Cottage, once a forge, is reputed to be where the horse of Charles I was shod on his retreat from the first battle of Newbury. See **Civil War; Ghosts; Lane End Cottage**.

Brimpton Common (568 631) Situated in the south-eastern corner of Brimpton Parish, it lies to the west of Tadley and is bordered by The **Hurst Community School** to the south, The **Pineapple** public house to the west and Larkwhistle Farm to the east. It was originally an extension of the north Hampshire heathland. See **Blacknest; Brimpton; Barrows; Brant family; Lane End Cottage**.

British European Airways Corporation See Airways Training Ltd.

British Overseas Airways Corporation Forerunner of British Airways. British Overseas Airways Corporation (BOAC) and British European Airways Corporation (BEAC) ran **Airways Training Ltd** at **Aldermaston Airfield** after World War II.

British Red Cross The Tadley 'First Aid' group was founded in 1962, although it had been meeting since the previous year. Margaret Price was the founder of the group. Nursing as well as First Aid was taught in the early years and most of the activities were held in Wigmore Hall that, before it was demolished, used to be on the path between Wigmore Road and Shyshack Lane. The group closed in April 1997. Following the restructuring of the Red Cross in Hampshire, it amalgamated with the Kingsclere group. The last leaders were Ronald and Sheila Needham. The group had its first meeting in **Heath End Village Hall**, and its last in the **Ambrose Allen Centre**. The Red Cross Medical Loan section currently operates from the **Holmwood Health Centre**.

British Schools The British and Foreign School Society, backed mainly by Nonconformists (that is not conforming to the Church of England) was set up in 1808 by Joseph Lancaster, to run weekday schools, based on ideas he had started to use in 1798. There could be more than two hundred children in one room, with only one paid master, divided up into small groups taught by older children, called 'monitors'. The monitor may have been only just ahead of the group in the subject being taught. In the 1871 census Esther Allen, living at The Malthouse, was recorded as a British school teacher. She probably taught at the Day School begun in the 1840s and opening alongside the Sabbath School, in the Old Meeting house (United Reformed Church). The Sabbath School was started by the Revd Samuel **Browne**'s daughters in 1810. See **Education; National Schools; Appendix i**.

British Workman, A (595 577) Officially opened in Charter Alley in January 1881 and believed to be one of a number of such premises born out of the **Temperance Movement** of the time. The idea to build what was described as an 'eating house' may have been prompted by the number of men employed at the **Ramsdell Brickworks** with nowhere to go in their free time but the local public houses. The degree of support for such projects was shown by the attendance of over 200 persons at the opening, and with well-known people like Thomas **Burberry** and Richard Wallis making speeches. The project was instigated and funded by the Bonney family; William Bonney owned the house but the idea was conceived by his son. The building has since become a private dwelling called 'Crossways'. See **Wallis & Steevens**.

Broom Squire Local name for a besom broom maker. See **Besoms**.

Broomyards The term may conjure up in the mind the idea of a large commercial enterprise employing a number of men. Rarely was this so until the late nineteenth and early twentieth centuries when it is known for example that Billy 'Stumpy' West and his son Alfred 'Stumpy' West employed three women and at least four men to work in their yard on Mulfords Hill (now the site of Hillcrest) and who, in their best season had 22,000 bavins to use (1 bavin made 4 brooms). It is difficult to assess the numbers of broom makers and yards at any one time because toward the end of the nineteenth century the term 'agricultural labourer' was often used instead of 'broom maker' in the census. Undoubtedly you would have found brooms being made along any lane in Tadley, yet the 1881 census records only four men listing this as their occupation. Even with its nucleus of broom makers, **West Street** did not have a single major yard. The majority were part-time workers comprising a family unit: brothers, father and son, women and small children, working adjacent to the home. In the early part of the century brooms were sold wholesale for 1s 6d (8p) a dozen and an experienced man could make between 8-12 dozen a day.

The market for brooms would vary from family to family. In the main they were probably sold to a local wood dealer. Others dealt direct with the London merchants (e.g. Bennett, Francis and Annett) who sent out agents to inspect and buy brooms on the spot or place advance orders. Others would sell their brooms from wagons. Loads of 50-60 dozen would be hawked over a wide area; as far as Oxford, Aldershot, Uxbridge and Watford. Prior to the mid nineteenth century this was the only way they were sold.

The broom trade began to decline in the 1920s and 1930s but the names more recently associated with broomyards (Appleton, Gundry, Nash, Saunders, Staceys, West, Wigley) are a reflection of the much larger trade that existed not only in Tadley but at Heath End and Pamber throughout the centuries. In 1999 Arthur **Nash**, supplied by the Gundry brothers of Little Aldershot and occasionally by Albert **West**, is the only commercial broomyard in the area, possibly in the country. See **Tadley Memorial Hall**.

Brown's Cottage, Pamber Heath (614 624) At 10.00 am on a Monday morning in September 1940 one of three **bombs** fell on this cottage in Clapps Gate Road, tragically killing a neighbour who was putting her washing on the line. The cottage, built in 1920, was subsequently demolished and for some time **Brewer's cycle shop** was run from a wooden building on the site.

Brown's Farm, Baughurst (572 593) Originally a yeoman's cottage dating from at least 1611. It was rebuilt in 1693 during Richard Potter's occupancy. The original cottage was not demolished, merely encased in new, matching, brick and plasterwork, making it three times as large. The bricks came from **Ramsdell Brickworks**. Its name relates to the Brown family who, by the marriage of John Brown to Mary Potter (Quaker) in January 1697, eventually became the owners of what was the first Quaker Meeting House in Baughurst. See James **Potter**; **Quakers**.

Brown's Rod Yard (586 623) Situated at the end of Shyshack Lane, then a cul-de-sac, Brown's Rod Yard was owned by Brown's of Woolhampton. **Willow osiers** were stripped at the yard, by local women, before being taken by horse and cart to Woolhampton Station where they were sent to London for basket making. Work at the yard declined during the 1950s and it eventually closed.

Browne, Samuel Minister at Tadley Old Meeting during the early 1800s, Samuel Browne (1753-1826) was one of the earliest known local authors. In 1805 he wrote a book entitled *Travels of a Seek-Truth*, printed by J. Lucas of Basingstoke. The book is an allegory, comparable to Bunyan's *Pilgrim's Progress*, '...in which the work of the Spirit in conversation is represented setting forth the Sinner's miserable state by nature and the Saint's recovery through Grace by the Work of the Spirit'. Village names in

the book bear only a faint resemblance to local places: Dancer's Green, May Gain, Opera Street, Revel Green are all in the neighbourhood of Vain Delight. The printing of the book, like many early books, was 'sponsored'. A list near the beginning records over 200 'subscribers' including several local residents such as Mr Hasker, Miss May, Mr D. Prior and Mr Andrews all from Tadley, together with others from Aldermaston and Padworth. A copy of the book can be seen in the Rare Books section of the British Library. There are no known loan copies available. An earlier work, *The Protestant Youth's Instructor*, was published in London 1798 with a second edition being published in 1819. See **British Schools**; **Tadley Revel**; **United Reformed Church**.

Browne's Charity, Sir George Sir George Browne was a resident of Wolverton until his death in 1685. He bequeathed four houses, Poor's Cottages, and 15 acres of land, the rent from which (then £20-22) was to be divided between the poor of the parish to pay for clothing and fuel. See **Charities**; **Wolverton Manor**.

Brownies See **Guiding**.

Browning Hill (585 600) Situated to the south west of Tadley, Browning Hill is one of the highest points locally (372 feet/113 metres).

Browning Hill Beer House A beer house near **St Stephen's Church, Baughurst**. In the 1841 census the keeper is listed as Benjamin Spicer. It is now a private property called 'The Bell House'.

Budgens (599 622) John Budgen opened his first shop in Maidenhead in 1872 and by the early part of the twentieth century had opened stores throughout the Thames Valley. Budgens, Tadley had previously been J.S. **Whatmore & Sons**. The store was purchased in 1965 by Murdoch Norton, a subsidiary of Kinlochs, who in 1977 were taken over by Bookers whose retail chain was Budgens. On 31 October 1989 a new purpose-built supermarket was officially opened by Heidi White and Laura Butler, two children from **Bishopswood Junior School**.

Burberry, Thomas Founder/inventor of the Burberry weatherproof coat. By 1856 at the age of 21 Thomas Burberry had opened his first outfitters shop on the north side of Winchester Street, Basingstoke. It expanded rapidly due to his ability to design and make clothes for specific purposes. By 1871 the shop employed 80 staff. However, a tragic accident on Monday 17 April 1905 resulted in the shop being severely damaged by fire. The shop was rebuilt as an 'Emporium', the remains of which are now 'Chicago's' night club and previously Maples furnishing store. Burberry's are probably best known for their gabardine cloth, a waterproof material that does not tear and is cool and comfortable to wear. Burberry's were tailors to Lord Kitchener and Lord Baden-Powell, designed uniforms for British officers and manufactured the tent that Roald Amundsen used on his journey to the

South Pole. Thomas Burberry was an ardent Baptist and at the Hackwood Road workroom employees would gather for prayers to begin each day. He was generous to charities and as a Temperance worker was strongly in support of Sunday closing. He died in 1926 and the business was continued by his son Arthur. By now the majority of Burberry's business was carried out from the Haymarket store in London although their Basingstoke tailor's shop continued until much later. Throughout this period of expansion the company's advertising was designed by Major George **Roller** who lived in Tadley and acknowledged his association with the company by naming his horse **Gabardine**. See A **British Workman; Temperance movement**.

Burghfield Royal Ordnance Factory See AWE **Burghfield**.

Burney Bit (610 619) Originally part of Pamber Common. The area became inhabited possibly as a result of enclosure. Much of the area was owned by William Beach of Oakley Hall and sold as individual plots on 5 October 1897. See **Beach family**.

Burnham Copse Infants School (592 622) Originally part of the annex of **Tadley School**, held in The **Den** in the 1950s, to cope with the dramatic increase in population as **AWRE** was being built. As the need for additional accommodation grew those over 7 years of age were transferred to form **Burnham Copse Junior School** in 1955. The Infant School continued in The Den, under the control of Berkshire Education Authority until 1960 when it moved to the site vacated by the Junior School. The official opening of both the Infant and Junior Schools took place in The **Royal** cinema on 15 November 1956. When the present buildings were built in 1984 it became known as the 'Wigwam School'. Kathy **Cook**, an ex-pupil of the school, was at the official opening and was guest of honour at the 10th anniversary celebrations in 1995. The new school won a design award: the architect was Ian Templeton. See **Education; Appendix i**.

Burnham Copse Junior School (592 622) Formed from the older pupils at **Tadley School**'s annex in The **Den**. It opened on 5 September 1955 with 155 children in part of **Chivers Hostel** (where Searing Way is now), opposite the old **Community Centre** in Newchurch Road. Roger **Searing** was headmaster for the next 24 years. The official opening of the two schools, Infant and Junior, by J.F. Wolfenden, Vice-Chancellor of The University of Reading, was on 15 November 1956. In June 1960 the present Burnham Copse Junior School buildings were occupied leaving the old buildings in Newchurch Road for the Infant School. See **Education; Appendix i**.

Burnham Copse Plantation (589 629) A copse on the **Aldermaston Estate** that was behind The **Falcon** public house. Much of it was destroyed when **Aldermaston Airfield** was built in the 1940s – runways, hangars and taxiing areas were con-structed on it. Today it is part of **AWE**. The name, however, is kept alive with both a road and a school named after it.

Burrell's Farm (605 606) A two storey cottage in Main Road. It is a Grade II listed building with two storeys, irregular fenestration and a central brick chimney. The structure is a timber box frame with brick infill and a Norfolk reed scalloped ridge thatched roof. It has a single storey south end extension with tiled roof. The cottage, reputed to be over 600 years old, is considered by some to be the oldest in Tadley. It is often referred to as Grants Farm due to its long association (over 70 years) with the Grant family.

Bus and coach services Local bus and coach services developed, mainly, from the carrier services of the nineteenth and early twentieth centuries. They generally began as family concerns, often one man and a bus or coach operating a single route. The development of mechanised transport, in particular, after the end of World War I when there was an influx of qualified drivers and surplus vehicles, led to a dramatic growth in services between the wars. Being almost equidistant from three major towns (Basingstoke, Newbury and Reading) Tadley and the surrounding area was well-served by companies. Routes and services were dictated by demand. Most villages would have a had at least one service a week on market day, whilst others would have benefited from a more frequent service, being on the route between larger villages and a town. The 1930 Road Traffic Act and competition from larger firms in the towns led to many smaller companies being taken over, a process that accelerated after World War II.

Over twenty firms have run buses to and from Tadley for private hire or as service buses. These have included Thames Valley Transport, Venture, Bee Line and, today, Stagecoach and Reading Buses.

The local name most synonymous with bus and coach services is Kent. During the twentieth century various members of the **Kent family** have operated services in the area. W.E. 'Billy' Kent started business as a carrier in 1911, developing bus services between the wars before selling out to Venture company in 1937, to concentrate on coach work. Blue Bus was an inter-war company started in 1924-26 by Billy's brother, Fred, which ran between Baughurst and Basingstoke via Charter Alley and Ramsdell. Based in Charter Alley, the service was taken over by Billy in 1935. Billy and Fred's mother, Edith, started her own coach firm in 1923. She developed the business, running a bus service between Kingsclere and Newbury and, in 1936, buying the business of another local firm, Vincent's of Ashford Hill. Although called Kingsclere Coaches, the firm was in fact based in Baughurst. She sold the business in 1937, to Newbury & District Motor Services.

Staff outside Barker's butchers shop on Tadley Hill in the early-1930s.

Photo: Brian Gooch

Fords of Silchester was another local company. Albert 'Bert' and Reginald Ford of Coombelands, Silchester ran a bus service from 1922 until the late 1950s when the business was sold to Kent's Coaches. Albert was a cab proprietor as early as 1912, but it was in 1922 that the bus operation began, when he and Reginald bought a second-hand 14-seater Ford T. Initially, the service ran between Reading and Silchester; at a later date also running to Newbury on Thursdays. Between the wars Bert ran a cycle shop and garage along the Pamber Road; today it is called Bob's Garage. Another Silchester firm, Lovegrove, ran a bus service between Silchester and Reading until 1926, when they sold out to the Reading based firm, Thames Valley Transport, in order to concentrate on coach work.

In 1924, Thames Valley Transport extended their bus service between Reading and Mortimer on to Tadley, via Silchester. Two crews, living in Tadley, operated the bus which was stored overnight in a large green shed adjacent to Fairlawn Road, beside **Allen's Garage**. Jack Lambden drove the No 9 double decker service for about 20 years. See **Carriers**.

Bus shelter See **Rest shelter**.

Butchers In the early nineteenth century butchers obtained their supplies directly from the farm, slaughtering the animals on their premises. Most butchers slaughtered an average of only one cow, and perhaps two sheep a day, even in busy times. The census returns for all three local parishes record only five butchers for the period 1841-91, all but one being in Tadley. In 1841 and 1851 the Elliott family; Gideon, Brother William and son William. Gideon is also listed in 1861. None are recorded in 1871 and only a William Clarke at Pamber Heath in 1881. Barnet Barlow, who in Ernie **Kimber**'s book, *Tadley During My Time and Before*, is referred to in his tale of the pig butcher, makes the fifth in 1891. This might therefore be seen as a reflection of the limited amount of meat, other than pig, that was eaten prior to the twentieth century.

Pamber Heath continued to have its own butcher, George Middleton, throughout the early 1900s. His business was located on Pamber Heath Road at the junction with Burney Bit, now Georgina Gardens. By the inter-war years most local butchers got their meat supplies from Reading slaughterhouses (Barkers was an exception, still having its own slaughterhouse on site). Brian Gooch recalls that after World War II he collected pigs (sometimes six to eight a week) from **Inhurst House**, a pig farm before it became a school. By the 1930s the butcher's trade consisted of both shop and delivery sales. The advent of motorised delivery vans gave butchers a far wider catchment area and butchers from surrounding villages made local deliveries, and vice versa. For example Capels from Mortimer, Trotman's from Newbury and Lansley's from Basingstoke all had local customers.

Tadley butcher Frederick Hussey is first recorded in the 1903 **Kelly's Directory** and continued to be listed until 1939 by which time it has become 'Hussey & Sons'. In 1910 a butchers, owned by Frederick Hussey is known to be operating at Tadley

Hill, in the premises later known as Barkers. The most well remembered Hussey's butchers shop was in New Road now occupied by **Morland Surgery**. Tommy Marks, not a local man, bought the business a few years after World War II, running it right up until his retirement in 1977. When the Bishopswood shops opened in 1957 he also had premises there, which were later run by Fred Curtis and now by Ray Klatt. Tommy Marks sold the New Road business to Brian Gooch, who had been working in the shop since 1956. Brian ran it for several years until he retired in 1988. W. Barker & Co, later part of Anstee's of Reading, operated the shop on the eastern side of Tadley Hill until its closure in 1935. Although closed, the shop, slaughterhouse and relevant equipment remained for some years before the building was eventually pulled down. The site has never been redeveloped and is now overgrown. See **Pig Butcher**.

Butt Inn, The (600 670) A public house near **Aldermaston Lock** serving both the canal and railway users, local industry and the new housing development close by. It was possibly an outlet for the nearby brewery of W.J.**Strange & Son Ltd** when it was in operation. It was refurbished in 1997.

C

CAB See **Citizens' Advice Bureau**.

Calleva Arms, The (627 621) The public house on Silchester Common. Originally called 'The Crown' it was owned by Courage Brewery until the 1980s. Deeds of the site, dated 1779, show it passing to the Rector, John Coles, in 1832. He supposedly acquired the land and built the beer house there prior to 1839, not only for the use of the local inhabitants, but to prevent the Methodist Chapel being built on the site and being too close to his rectory. In 1851 it was kept by John Charlton whose occupation was given as 'carpenter/beer seller'.

Calleva Atrebatum (640 625) Calleva, meaning place or town in the woods of the **Atrebates**, was an Iron Age, and then Roman settlement, founded by the Atrebates tribe probably between 50 and 20 BC. It is a significant archaeological site because, unlike most other Roman towns in Britain, it was completely abandoned after the Romans left and so was never built over. The site may originally have been chosen because it was hidden and protected by its environment, a gravel spur overlooking the Loddon Valley, about 90 metres above sea level, with commanding views to the east and south and the only access over level ground from the west.

The original Iron Age settlement consisted of round huts and grain stores casually grouped in the Celtic manner. By around 100 AD these had been replaced by a formally planned Roman town with a regular street grid and town blocks (insulae). Calleva was not a military town, its main function being the administrative centre of the territory (civitas) of the Atrebates. From their base in the town, officials collected taxes and oversaw the implementation of justice in the surrounding area. Calleva was also the principal market town of the region. With a maximum population of around 4,000, Calleva Atrebatum owed its importance to its position on the ancient trackway that went from the Imperial capital, Londinium (London), to the south-west. Five important routes to various parts of Roman Britain converged on the town. Inside the walls were the forum, a basilica, baths, temples and an early Christian church and outside, an amphitheatre. Calleva prospered without defences until the end of the second century AD when a rampart of gravel and clay was built. This was replaced by a stone wall 1.5 miles (2.5 km) around 260-280 AD which survives today; at its highest it was about 4.5 metres (by the south gate) and 3 metres thick at its base.

Following the departure of Roman troops from Britain, in the early fifth century, Calleva went into a decline. Its main purpose of administering the region for the Romans had disappeared, and the inhabitants were no longer able to exert control over the surrounding countryside from which they had previously acquired the resources they needed. Although a small community remained, the population had dropped so much that after about 450 AD it cannot really be called a town. Until recently, little was known about post-Roman Calleva because early Victorian excavations destroyed important evidence about buildings that may have come after the solid masonry houses of the late fourth and fifth centuries. **Grim's Bank** earthwork, running from Ufton through Padworth to near **Decoy Pond**, was probably a defensive fortification built by the residual inhabitants against the threat of Saxon aggression.

The earliest description of the site was by John Leland, the King's Antiquary, in about 1540. Excavations only began to reveal the site's secrets during late Victorian times, the most notable of these was by The Society of Antiquaries between 1890 and 1909. They uncovered the plans of buildings with stone foundations but were unable to tackle the chronology of the settlement. George Boon undertook a series of excavations between 1954-58 and in 1961, together with Professor Sir Ian Richmond, he re-examined the site of the early Christian church. No further excavations were done until the early 1970s when Professor Michael Fulford and members of the Archaeology Department from The University of Reading began excavating. Between 1974 and 1978, and from 1991, they excavated the defences, including the town wall and its gates; between 1979 and 1985, the amphitheatre and forum basilica. Since 1997 the work has concentrated on an area known as Insula IX – the area that does not have any major public buildings – which should allow the excavations to shed light on the daily life of the ordinary inhabitants of a residential district of the town.

Hampshire County Council owns the interior of the walled town and the land is leased on an agricultural tenancy. The town walls and amphitheatre are in the care of English Heritage and can be visited at any reasonable time, free of charge. There is a public car park and guided trail, allowing public access to the walls and amphitheatre. Background information may be found in the **Calleva Museum**, Bramley Road, Silchester, the **Silchester Gallery** in Reading Museum and 'The Museum of the Iron Age' in Andover Museum. The majority of the finds from the Victorian excavations are kept in Reading Museum. See **Amphitheatre; Devil's Highway, Impstone; Little London Brickworks; Portway; St Mary the Virgin Church, Silchester.**

Calleva Football Club In 1970 a group calling itself MRE (Millers Road Estate) formed a boys' football club, but decided to change its name when more lads from all round the area wanted to join. Matches were played at Silchester. In 1971, a competition held to name the club resulted in 'Calleva' as the popular choice. The club originally catered for boys up to 13 years of age and ran mixed teams for the under 10 year olds. Later, in 1977, girls up to 12 years old were admitted. It now has 15 teams aged from 7 years upwards. The men's team play in the Basingstoke Sunday League and the juniors play in the Peter Houseman Youth League and the South Chilterns Youth League. Home fixtures are played at Silchester, AWE or the field by The **Pineapple**. The club is now affiliated with **Tadley Football Club** which, it is hoped, will be beneficial to them both. See **Pamber Forest Football Club.**

Calleva Museum (629 624) A small hut in the Recory grounds in Bramley Road which houses a permanent exhibition about the Roman town of **Calleva Atrebatum**. It is a memorial to Lt-Col J.B.P. **Karslake** who died in 1942 and whose collection formed the nucleus of the original display. It was established at a meeting on 26 February 1949, attended by nearly 30 people including the Duke of Wellington and Mrs Leonora Karslake. To further the establishment of the museum Mrs Karslake had, on 4 December 1947, offered her late husband's 'den', to house the exhibits. In addition she gave a gift of £50 towards the expense of setting it up. The *Hants & Berks Gazette* reported the official opening on 7 July 1951, by the Chairman of **Hampshire County Council**, Mr Charles L. Chute. It is believed the museum was a contribution to the 1951 Festival of Britain. Today it is open daily during daylight hours, admission free. Most of the artefacts excavated from Calleva Atrebatum over the years are housed in the Museum of Reading; a selection of them are on display in their **Silchester Gallery**.

Calleva Park (583 627) A modern commercial park of small industrial units on the A340, off the Heath End roundabout. It started in the mid 1980s on what was the western end of a former **Aldermaston Airfield** runway. The site was used as a 100 yard (92 m) and 50 yard (46 m) rifle range by the AWRE Rifle and Pistol Club between 1962-80. The range was dismantled and the site declared safe by the Ministry of Defence before being sold to Newbury Council. The latest phase of the park's construction was completed in 1998. Situated in West Berkshire and owned by Country Estates Ltd it has attracted various types of industry including electronics, computing, printing and the service sector. It was designed to blend in with the surrounding wooded rural area and has received the Mars Award for Environmental Improvement. The park name was taken from the Roman town of **Calleva Atrebatum** in nearby Silchester.

Campbell Gill, Revd Dugald Benefactor of **Little St Mary's Church, Heath End**. On his death his will (proved on 4 October 1890) established a charity for the maintenance of the church. On 1 October 1939 a contract was drawn up stating that 'the trustees of this charity shall pay the income of the fund to the incumbent of Baughurst Parish Church for holding one ordinary service with a sermon in the Church once every Sunday and to celebrate Holy Communion there once a month'. The trustees were also to pay the churchwarden for cleaning, lighting, heating and insurance of the church.

Candle Auction, Aldermaston The Aldermaston Candle Auction is held every three years, on St Lucy's Eve (13 December). An iron horseshoe nail is stuck into a candle one inch from the top and the candle is lit. As the candle burns away bidding begins and the last person to make a bid before the nail drops rents the piece of land known as 'Church Acre' for the next three years. 'Church Acre' is in fact two acres, one rod and thirty-three poles and is situated just behind 'Fisherman's Cottage'. The auctioneer is always the vicar of Aldermaston but the auction is presided over by the Lord of the Manor (in modern times the current owner of **Aldermaston Estate**). The amount bid is the rent per year and this money is used for the support of the church. In 1801 the highest bid was £7.00, but nowadays it is generally over £100.00. Made in 1965 the current tallow candle will last until 2005. In the past, candle auctions were common elsewhere in the country, but Aldermaston's is one of the few still held today. Whilst Aldermaston uses a horse-shoe nail in the candle, traditionally a pin was used, hence the origin of the phrase 'you could hear a pin drop'. See **Aldermaston charities**.

Carnival and Sports During the 1920s an annual 'carnival and sports' day was held at Hawley Park (now known as **Hawley Farm**). As well as side-shows and competitions there was a comprehensive programme of athletics. One of its objectives was to raise money to build **Tadley Main Road Methodist Church** and for the maintenance of the **Tadley Bands**. After the church was completed in 1931 the event ceased. Many villages have a tradition of carnivals and fairs. Tadley is no exception. Other similar events over the years have included **Tadley Revel** and, more recently, the **Treacle Fayre**.

Carriers In the days before cars and public transport, people rarely travelled far from where they lived. A few people had their own transport such as a pony or donkey and cart but the majority depended on 'carriers' wagons'. The local carrier would transport people to and from the local towns or collect orders from shops in the towns for their customers. Originally, the carrier wagon would have been a horse drawn covered cart; Ernie **Kimber** likened it to a 'wild-west wagon'. They ran services from Tadley and the surrounding villages to the local major towns of Basingstoke, Reading and Newbury. The carrier would put-up and stable his horses at public houses in the towns, and place their customers' orders with the shops who would deliver the goods to the wagons. Meanwhile any passengers would be doing their own shopping. Anyone who wanted the carrier to call to collect an order would leave a board outside their home with the relevant initials on it (e.g. 'K' for Kents). The arrival of the motor car and bus in the early to mid-1920s led to the decline and eventual disappearance of carriers. Many carriers however developed their businesses into the rapidly expanding **bus and coach services**.

Alfred Lipscombe ran a local carrier business from a yard where Churchill Close is today. In **Kelly's Directory** he is listed, between 1899 and 1915, as running a service to Basingstoke on Wednesdays and Saturdays, carrying passengers and goods and also doing shopping for customers. Another local carrier was Tom Wakefield, amongst whose customers was the **Barn Close Laundry**. Thomas Bowman is listed in Kelly's Directory 1903-11 as running a service to Reading on Tuesday and Saturday. William Kent, from Heath End, Baughurst, started a horse drawn carrier service in 1911, serving Baughurst, Tadley, Pamber and Sherborne St John and travelling to Basingstoke. By the beginning of the

war in 1914 the service had become mechanised; after the war he expanded the business into buses. In Pamber Heath, Mr Bailey ran a carrier service from Shirley Cottage in Pamber Heath Road. At the time it was said his motorised service far outshone the nearest rivals who still operated a horse and cart. Nearby, Henry Pontin ran a service to Reading on Tuesdays and Saturdays from his yard in Silchester Road on Tadley Common. Kelly's Directory lists him between 1907-15; by 1923 it lists the business as being run by George Pontin. See **Kent family**.

Cat, The (605 610) A small beer house that was situated on the north side of Fairlawn Road, about 100 yards from the junction with Tadley Hill. The 1871 census lists George Sumpter as being the 'beer house keeper'. How long The Cat was in use is unclear but it is known that the site was cleared by John Stacey and Sons in the 1970s to allow the building of several chalet bungalows. During groundwork alterations in the early 1990s a plaque was found marking the site. See **Brewing and licensing laws**.

Cedars School See **Aldermaston School**.

Census A census of the population of England and Wales has been taken every ten years since 1801, except 1941 (because of World War II). Until 1841 it was conducted by the **overseers of the poor** and clergy. It consisted merely of a count of the number of people (male and female), houses and families in each parish or township, with a simple attempt at occupational analysis. The establishment of the General Register Office in 1837 made it possible to conduct a more sophisticated census, using the local officials of this department, plus a large number of temporary employees (enumerators). Since 1841 each householder has been required by law to supply information on everyone who spent 'census night' in the house. In 1841 the census form asked for name, address, approximate age, occupation and whether or not the person was born in the same county as that in which he was then living. In 1851 the form was refined to include a column for marital status, the relationship of each person to the head of the household, exact age, and parish and county of birth. The schedule of 1851 remained virtually unchanged until 1891 when an additional question concerning the number of rooms occupied was added. Since the records contain personal details they are closed for a hundred years from the date of the census, instead of the 30 years now normal for public records.

In general terms the census provides a snapshot picture of those who lived in the area during Victorian times – the sort of people they were, their families, ages, work and where they came from – which when used in conjunction with other local information (e.g. **Kelly's Directory**) helps to build up a picture of the local history. For example, the 1861 census was taken in the middle of probably the most prosperous twenty years in Tadley's history, when both agriculture and the wood trades were at their peak. Unlike most parishes of the time, Tadley's population figure of 900 was high and still rising. April, when the census was taken, was the one month of the year when the maximum number of inhabitants was likely to be found in the parish; owing to the nature of employment for most of the year the parish was comparatively empty. From late November until the end of March most of the men and many of the women were employed either **coppicing** in the nearby woods, or working in the withy beds; in early spring the men, and very often the whole family, would be employed hoeing and from late April until the early autumn in bark picking; in the summer they would be taking the harvest across the southern counties and then in the autumn hop-picking around Alton. The information contained in the census is sometimes difficult to interpret. For example, the term 'agricultural labourer' hid a multiplicity of skills, such as thatching, which was not regarded as an extraordinary craft in those days. Similarly, of the thirty-nine broom-makers, only a few would have been full-time masters; the majority would have been making brooms part-time for these master broom-makers. This trait was evident among the most prosperous of these people, the wood-dealers. Wood-dealers bought and transported the standing underwood and timber, employing others to cut it and then selling it to the various craftsmen and timber merchants. Although their living and small wealth came from wood, they described themselves as small-farmers, since they needed to buy land to keep and feed the considerable numbers of draught horses they used. The average family size was less than expected but this may have been accounted for by the prosperity of the time. In 1841 in less prosperous times, the family sizes, particularly among the broom-makers, were much larger. In an age of high infant mortality, an extra child was seen as another wage earner and families of from ten to fifteen children were common.

Central Training School See Airways Training Ltd.

Chandler, Maria See Tadley Witch.

Chandler, Thomas Said to be the ghost at the **Queen's College Arms**. He died in July 1880, after working for nearly 50 years as a woodsman and handyman at the public house. He is buried in the grounds of **Pamber Priory**. See Ghosts.

Chapel House, Baughurst (583 611) Situated on the Baughurst Road, it was for a while the residence of George Whitefield (1714-70). The Wesley brothers, John and Charles, visited regularly and the house eventually became the first, and, possibly, the only Baughurst Wesleyan Methodist Chapel and was registered in 1795. By 1747 Whitefield had established 31 separate societies following a Calvinistic tradition. Baughurst, and the surrounding area, however, came under the influence of **Primitive Methodists**. See John **Wesley**.

Charcoal burning Charcoal, the most efficient and cleanest of fuels, has a long history. Charcoal-making is very skilful and demanding work, each stack of wood needing constant attention day and night to achieve the conditions necessary to allow the burning of the wood without complete combustion. Any wood was used and it was convenient for using up all the loppings and misshapen wood. However, for certain uses, some woods were preferred to others. For example, alder, willow and dogwood were used for the finer musket gunpowder. Charcoal burning is one of the oldest documented industries in **Pamber Forest**, being first mentioned in the thirteenth century and the connection is marked by local names like Charcoal Gully. These gullies are common in north Hampshire and the wood growing in them was often inaccessible. The most convenient way to bring it out was as sacks of charcoal. The trade of charcoal burning was passed from father to son, evidence of which appears throughout the 1841-81 census returns: William and son Benjamin, Thomas and son Thomas Benham also Thomas and son John, John and son Joseph Englefield. Other local names, Bowman and Saunders, are also listed as (charcoal) coal burners. The industry went into slow decline after 1870 due in main to the increasing importation of wood products. By 1891 only one Tadley man is listed as a coal burner. More recently, between World War II and 1970, charcoal burning was carried out at **Soke Road** by Joseph **Michnik**. See **Heather House; Tadley Court**.

Charities From 1786 the Clerk of the Peace had to send returns of charities to Parliament, receive their accounts and register their objectives, trustees etc. Many charitable gifts were made well before these 1786 regulations e.g. Adam de Port's charity was established in the twelfth century. Today Town and Parish Councils still make claims on these early bequests to the poor and needy. See **Browne's Charity; Hyde's Charity; Mothe's Charity;** Adam **de Port Charity; Sympson's Charity; Wheat's Charity**.

Charter Alley In some documents it is written Charter 'Ley' but the Methodist Circuit records refer to it as 'Chatter Alley'. In the *Oxford Dictionary of English Place Names* 'Chart' is defined as the Anglo Saxon word 'Ceart' meaning rough common overrun with gorse and bracken. See A **British Workman; The White Hart**.

Charter Alley Methodist Chapel Prior to the building of the chapel in 1852, at a cost of £234, the earlier meetings were held in a nearby house for about 20 years. Shortly after 1988 the church closed and was taken over by the Brethren whose chapel, next to the school in Ramsdell, had fallen into decay.

Chine Cottage (606 610) A semi-detached cottage (with **Rose Cottage**) in **Malthouse Lane**, within the **Tadley Conservation Area**. Both properties are Grade II listed buildings, Chine Cottage being the older of the two. During the 1770s it was leased to two thatchers. It has a thatched roof with two eyebrow dormers, painted brick walling, cambered openings and casement windows. It has a modern gabled brick porch and a tiled extension on the west side of the building.

Chivers Hostel (591 622) W.E. **Chivers & Sons Ltd**, major contractors during the construction of **AWRE** in the 1950s established a hostel to house and feed the hundreds of building workers employed on the site. The main headquarters of the hostel were in what became the (old) **Community Centre** in Newchurch Road.

Chivers & Sons Ltd, W.E. The building and civil engineering firm of Chivers will always be associated with the early development of AWRE. The firm was founded in Devizes in 1884. In 1908 it was placed on the Government list for War Department work, benefiting from the military build-up before World War I. Further growth followed with re-armament in the 1930s prior to World War II. In 1947 the firm won a contract to convert the pre-war RAF station at Harwell into an Atomic Energy Research Establishment. When in 1949 the government decided the United Kingdom should develop its own nuclear deterrent weapons system and started construction at Aldermaston, Chivers were ideally placed to tender for work, negotiating an extension to their Harwell contract. At the peak of construction in the early 1950s, out of about 4,000 men employed on site, approximately 1,600 were Chivers employees – including 150 bricklayers, 120 painters, 50 steel fixers, 220 carpenters, 700 labourers, 70 plasterers and 40 plumbers. During construction the old wartime buildings around Franklin Avenue became a labour camp where some 1,600 men lived. As an example of the scale of the workforce, fleets of buses were used at lunchtime to ferry men to the Chivers canteen which served some 6,000 meals a day. In those early days of AWRE Chivers had a crucial role in the rapid development of Tadley from a small rural community into a modern village. As construction at AWRE was completed Chivers role declined and the labour camp disappeared. As well as AWRE the firm had other local links, building both **St Paul's Church** and Basingstoke District Hospital (**North Hampshire Hospital**). Recession and difficult business conditions in the early 1980s forced the firm into receivership in 1985.

Christ Church, Ramsdell (589 574) Ramsdell village church was built in 1867 at a cost of £1,000 and was consecrated on 23 November of that year by Revd Charles Spencer Sumner, Bishop of Winchester. Faced in flint with brick dressings it consists of a chancel and nave with a small bell turret containing one bell. It was built so that the long walk to Wootton and the village chapel would not stop the villagers going to Church of England services. The first vicar was the Revd Joseph Fuller

(1867-92). A plaque inside the church states: 'The Incorporated Society for Buildings & Churches granted £35 AD 1867 towards building this church on condition that all sittings are free and unappropriated'. In 1953 the Vicar of Baughurst looked after the two parishes and in 1999 it forms part of the 'Benefice of Baughurst and Ramsdell and Wolverton with Ewhurst and Hannington', with the Revd Dr Andrew Barton living at The Rectory, Wolverton.

Church Acre See **Aldermaston charities**; **Candle auction**.

Cinema See The **Royal**.

Circus Farm Between 1955 and 1966 Circus Farm's postal address was 'Caravan opposite Main Gates' and it was occupied by Mr and Mrs McGarrigle. During the post-war years the Raymer's family circus regularly visited Tadley, wintering their circus equipment and caravans at Fox Farm which is now part of the gravel and land-fill workings behind Whitehouse Farm, next to the McGarrigle's land. Because of changes in family circumstances in 1966 the circus equipment was moved next-door and the 'Caravan opposite Main Gates' became Circus Farm.

Citadel, The The inner security area of **AWE** where missile warhead components are manufactured.

Citizens' Advice Bureau (CAB) (595 624) Tadley & District CAB opened on 7 October 1985 after local councillors and residents recognised the need for an advice centre in the area. The chairman of the steering committee and, later, of the management committee was Councillor Bob **O'Bee**. The Bureau started with a part-time manager, Sue Cutler, and seven volunteers: in the first full year they dealt with 2518 enquiries. In 1998 there were 14 volunteer advisers, 7 volunteer clerical staff, and two part-time paid staff, dealing with over 6,000 enquiries. The first premises were in the vacant semi-detached police house in Mulfords Hill. Two years later the Bureau moved next door to allow the police house to be re-opened as a police station. By 1993 the accommodation was inadequate and the Bureau moved in December to a new building in Franklin Avenue, sharing it with Tadley Town Council. The Bureau was formally opened by the Mayor of Basingstoke, Councillor John Shears, on 25 May 1994. Councillor Jo Slimin was the Bureau chairman at this time. 1997 the chairman, Bob O'Bee, died and Jo Slimin again took up the post. The original manager, Sue Cutler, is still in charge and one of the advisers, Susan Adams, was awarded an MBE in 1998, in recognition of her work in the Bureau despite many painful disabilities. The CAB organisation celebrates its 60th anniversary in 1999.

Civil War The area surrounding Tadley was quite significant during the English Civil War of 1642–46, since it was close to the divide between Royalist and Parliamentary controlled territory, and therefore in close proximity to military action. The village lay between the Parliamentary-held London, Windsor and Basingstoke and the Royalist capital of Oxford, stronghold of Newbury and powerbase of the West Country. Because of the strategic importance of the Thames Valley the two armies had a significant impact on Tadley and nearby villages. The war came closest following the First Battle of Newbury in September 1643, when, on the road between **Aldermaston** and **Padworth**, Prince Rupert launched an attack on the Parliamentary army that was retreating to Reading, leading to 300 fatalities. The site of this attack is remembered in the name 'Red Lane', purported to be named after the blood that ran down the road. In the days before the Second Battle of Newbury in October 1644, Parliamentary armies camped in **Aldermaston Estate**, with their commander, the Earl of Manchester, staying in Aldermaston Manor. The preceding month had seen a confrontation at Aldermaston between about 700 Royalist troops (disguised as Parliamentarians) and a genuine Parliamentary cavalry troop.

Local notables, like the Marquis of Winchester at Basing House, and Sir Humphrey Forster of **Aldermaston Manor**, were Royalists and their political views may have influenced the sympathies of Tadley's inhabitants – but in the latter stages of the war Parliamentary troops were stationed at Aldermaston Manor and at The Vyne and this may also have had some effect on the locals' sympathies. Whilst Tadley itself did not see any military confrontation, the presence of combatants in the area must have had some impact on the local villages. In addition to the breakdown of justice and the limitation of the Church's activity, the armies demanded recruits (volunteers or otherwise), food and other supplies and money, and it is entirely possible that Tadley and surrounding villages suffered – Parliament voted assistance to Berkshire in 1645. To the south of Tadley was the two-year siege of Basing House, which ended in October 1645 when the fortress was finally stormed by Cromwell. The Marquis of Winchester was sent to the Tower of London, and his estates were confiscated, but after the war he regained them, and moved to Englefield House. See **Benyon family**; **Ghosts**; **Padworth House**.

Climate See **Weather and climate**.

CND Campaign for Nuclear Disarmament. See **Aldermaston Marches**.

College Arms See **Queen's College Arms**.

Common land An integral part of the rural economy. Under the early medieval open-field system, local people held in common the right to graze cattle, catch fish or collect wood and peat on any land not under cultivation. While tenants worked arable fields in strips they supplemented their livelihood by grazing their cattle on the common pasture. Common land consisted of meadows, wasteland and roadside strips. Cattle were not allowed to graze on the common meadows from Candlemas (2 February) until Lammas Day (1 August) when the meadows were cropped. In the 1235 Statute of Merton, Tadley had a large amount of common land because of the lack of a lord of the manor and therefore no one in authority to arrange enclosure. Powerful lords of the manor in Norman times began to claim that the lords actually owned common land, while the peasants had only specific rights to use it. An inevitable next step was for each lord to attempt to frustrate these rights by physically enclosing his land. Beginning in the thirteenth century, enclosure reached its peak in the eighteenth and nineteenth centuries, until steps were taken to prevent it in the Enclosure Act of 1850 (1852) and the Commons Act of 1876. Even today commons frequently remain under threat from development and other demands, in spite of the supposedly final Commons Registration Act of 1965. See **Enclosure Acts**; **Tadley Common**; **Turbary Allotment Trust**; **Appendix iii**.

Community Centre (new) (591 622) The new community centre was built in the car-park to the rear of the old one. It comprises one large hall which can be converted into two smaller ones, and four smaller meeting and counselling rooms. It cost £800,000 and was opened on 26 November 1994 by John Shears, Mayor of Basingstoke. Three of the small rooms are named after prominent Tadley & District Community Association members in recognition of their hard work and support – namely the Beavers Room, the Newley Room and the Talbot Room.

Community Centre (old) (591 622) Built during the early 1940s, as the **Aldermaston Airfield** gymnasium and chapel (Building 223), it was located in what is now Newchurch Road. During the 1950s it served as part of **Chivers Hostel**, after which it became Tadley's community centre. The building was demolished in 1993 to make way for a new Community Centre.

Community Church In 1908 a group of Christians in Basingstoke started the town's first Baptist Church in a former school on Sarum Hill. In 1976 it changed its name to Basingstoke Community Church. In 1981 Basingstoke Community Church divided into a number of regional congregations, with local leadership teams, the result of growth in and around the town and The King's School for children of the church was started. Tadley Community Church is a regional church within Basingstoke Community Church that meets in the Main Hall at The **Hurst Community School** on three Sundays in the month. In 1976 when the Basingstoke Baptist Church changed its name there was one house group in Tadley, in 1999 there are four; two in Tadley, one in Baughurst and one for Pamber and Silchester. The church overall is led by a team of elders, some who are employed full time; two work with the Tadley leadership team.

Congregational (Independent) Church See **United Reformed Church**.

Old Community Centre, Newchurch Road during the early-1960s.

Photo: Burnham Copse WI Scrapbook

Congreve Arms (590 653) An old name for The **Hinds Head** public house in Aldermaston village. See **Aldermaston Estate.**

Cons Cottage (606 609) Formerly two cottages, Cons Cottage is a Grade II listed building in **Malthouse Lane,** within the **Tadley Conservation Area.** It is believed to have been built in 1628.

Conservation Area See **Tadley Conservation Area.**

Cook (née Smallwood), Kathryn Kathy was born in Winchester on 3 May 1960 and lived most of her childhood in Tadley, attending **Burnham Copse Infant** and **Junior Schools,** and The **Hurst Community School** before going on to Queen Mary's College, Basingstoke and Loughborough University. Starting her athletics career as a high jumper she joined Reading Athletics Club and became a member of Jim Spooner's sprint group. She went on to win Olympic, European and Commonwealth medals and at one time held more major event medals than any other British athlete. She also held United Kingdom records at 100 m (11.0 seconds), 200 m (22.1 seconds) and 400 m (49.43 seconds). These records still stand today. Kathy was also a member of the UK women's 4 x 100 m and 4 x 400 m relay teams. At the end of her career she was honoured with an MBE and now lives with her husband, Gary, and their three children in Walsall. Locally, Smallwood Drive is named after her.

Coombe House Windmill (590 590) See **Windmills.**

Co-op (591 623) Initially the Basingstoke Co-operative Society started as a travelling shop and delivery service, taking orders for anything from coal to clothes and delivering them from Basingstoke two days later. This operated until they opened their first shop in Tadley, on Mulfords Hill, where Toucan Travel is today. It sold haberdashery and clothes as well as food. They purchased the present site in Franklin Avenue (previously **Black's Cafe**) in November 1956 and began trading from there soon afterwards. In October 1966 the Basingstoke Co-operative Society became part of the Portsea Island Co-operative Society. The modern store was opened in August 1988 and was refurbished in 1999.

Cooper See **Hoops.**

Coppicing Coppicing is essentially a system of tree farming aimed at producing a regular crop of young wood. The wood is cut periodically, replacing itself naturally by shoots growing from the base of the tree. It is a type of woodland management or farming which in the past supplied local industry and trade with its raw materials for, e.g. **besoms** and **rakes.** Most of the coppice was hazel, chestnut, ash or oak underwood interspersed with standard timber trees. In the Kennet Valley coppiced woodlands of hazel and ash were grown as underwood beneath a canopy of oak, with birch grown on the sandy soils and alder in the gullies. The coppice was cut on a rotation, the length of which was dependent on the species and size of material required. Hazel was cut every 7-11 years while oak and chestnut were cut every 15-20 years.

Crafts and industries making use of coppice-wood as their raw materials go back to medieval times. Prior to the late eighteenth century the main demand for coppice-wood was as fuel. This market declined as coal became more popular. Instead of declining, overall demand for coppice-wood increased because the agricultural and industrial revolutions opened up new markets for coppice products. From the late-eighteenth century the wood trades increased in number and in volume of output, until they reached their peak in the period from 1850-1870.

Situated in the centre of the woodland district of north Hampshire, Tadley was ideally positioned to benefit from the development of woodland industries. Hazel coppice was used for bavins (bundles of firewood), hoopsticks for barrel making, hurdles and crate rods; oak coppice was used for corner posts to support hurdles and the bark was used in the leather tanning industry; chestnut coppice was used as fencing posts and birch coppice for making besoms. The product which formed the bulk of the underwood was the trimmings. These were bundled up, according to thickness, for firewood. The woodland industries however went into slow decline from about 1870 onwards because of various factors, two of the most important being the growth of more modern methods of packaging including the substitution of metal for wood and the increasing importation of cheap woodland products from abroad. Locally, coppices which had been sold for £10 an acre in 1850, fetched barely £3 in 1914 and were virtually unsaleable in 1939.

The parish of Tadley had very little woodland of its own, only about 200 acres (87 ha). Large agricultural estates (e.g. Englefield and Wasing) controlled the majority of it. The wood was sold standing by auction or by tender to wood dealers in November each year. In 1862 over 1000 acres (405 ha) of coppice was offered for sale across the district, 400 acres (162 ha) of this within a five-mile (8 km) radius of Tadley. Locals remember Englefield agents holding auctions in public houses for 2, 3 or 4 acre areas of the forest to be coppiced; areas having the most birch fetched the highest bids. The wood-dealers employed woodmen to do the cutting. The woodmen usually slept rough in lean-to shelters, moving from wood to wood, felling and sorting. Cutting took place from 25 November to 25 March for which the woodmen were paid by the piece. For a six-day week a man could earn from 10s (50p) to £2 10s 0d (£2.50). The coppice-dealers usually worked 20-30 acres (8–12 ha) a season, employing 4-6 woodmen. They arranged the disposal of the produce to local tradesmen and for dispatch to distant markets like London, Bristol and South Wales. The residue was sold as firewood to local bakers, brickmakers and householders.

As well as working locally woodmen also went away to work. One local recalled: 'They mostly rode their bicycles as far away as Wiltshire and Dorset, going off very early on a Monday morning, taking with them a huge lump of home cured bacon and bread and cheese, on which they lived until Friday evening, when they returned home for the weekend. They would have slept rough, when the weather was fine, otherwise get a bed just for the night. They earned a lot of money and most bought their own cottages paid for in £1 notes.'

It is difficult to calculate how many were employed in the coppicing trade. Many of the activities were seasonal – carried out mainly in the winter months – and woodmen were often returned as 'labourers' or 'agricultural labourers' in the census which took place in April. Today only a few local woodmen still do traditional coppicing, supplying besom makers like Arthur **Nash**. There have been several attempts to revive traditional coppicing, mainly through the agency of conservation volunteers. Some has been done recently in Pamber Forest, attempting to recreate the conditions that made the forest such a haven for butterflies.

Corner Cottage, Baughurst A timber framed thatched cottage opposite The **Badgers Wood** public house on the corner of Wolverton Road. Rod stripping was carried out here in the early 1900s for Browns of Woolhampton. The work was mainly done by local women who were paid either 1d per hour or 3d (1p) a bolt. See **Brown's Rod Yard**; **Willow osiers**.

Cottage pig See **Pig butchers**.

Council houses Houses or flats built by the council, or local authority, and let to tenants at a subsidised rent. Born of an awareness of the need to clear the slums from industrial cities and build better working-class housing, several Acts were passed leading to a rise in council house building after World War I. Minutes of local parish council meetings give details of various developments of local council housing through the years.

Tadley Parish Council minutes for 1919 record a proposal for six 'council cottages', and in 1926 twenty council houses were requested. In 1927 the village still had only four council houses, with six more built in 1931 followed three years later by a further four. More followed later in the decade. After the end of World War II the council continued their building programme. Late in the 1940s some Swedish timber-type housing was built in Tadley and elsewhere, for letting at rents of 12s a week. From the end of the war until 1974 they built 170 council houses, with a further 70 built in Hangar Lane.

The Housing Act of 1980 introduced the right of council house tenants to buy their houses. See **Baughurst Parish Council**; **Frog Lane Farmhouse**; **Pamber Parish Council**; **Tadley Parish Council**.

Countess of Huntingdon See **Mortimer West End Chapel**.

Courage See H & G **Simonds Ltd**.

Court Corner (608 591) The meeting place of Pamber Court in the seventeenth century; it is located near Wakeford Farm, north of The **Queen's College Arms** at **Pamber End**. As far as can be ascertained no Court was held in Pamber until the seventeenth century. 'The Court was thereafter held yearly on 20 July in an orchard under an apple tree within The Parish of Pamber but outside The Liberty of the Forest… where the Tythingman for the time sits in his Elbow Chair. With his hat on he is as the Lord of The Manor.' It is believed the court was re-established to strengthen the hand of commoners over the Marquis of Winchester. He and his descendants made successive bids to enclose lands which had, over the years, been granted to local families. These 'Pamber Lords' (common) contrived to hold their court and elect a Tithingman as late as 1817 despite a ruling by the Winchester assizes in 1793 that their land was part of 'The manor of Powlett Wright' (later **Englefield Estate**). See **Hundred**; **Tithing**.

Coxwell, Henry See **Tadley God Help Us.**

Coy Pond See **Aldermaston Decoy.**

Cricket Tadley Cricket Club was formed in June 1880; the Hants & Berks Gazette records the formation of the club with W.W. Beach MP and Revd **Saulez** amongst the members. Several fixtures were played that year, one against a team called the 'Whynots and Butterflies'! A year or so earlier, Pamber and Ramsdell both had cricket teams, but their formation dates are not known. In the early 1880's, Silchester and Baughurst also had teams; they played fixtures against Brimpton, Hannington, Bramley and Worting. In 1906 Tadley Cricket Club asked the Council for exclusive use of the Recreational Ground (The **Green**), as it was impossible to make a fence around their cricket pitch secure enough to keep out the cattle. Eventually the Council agreed to a compromise that the cattle should be kept off the ground for three clear days prior to a match. In 1920 a deputation from the football and cricket clubs made an application for the Recreational Ground to be used solely for recreational purposes. This was agreed providing the public were not debarred from using the ground and no games would be played on a Sunday. The clubs were asked to pay £2 per annum rent each. Records regarding Tadley Cricket Club are in existence from 1946, with minute books, fixture cards, score books and even balance sheets. Matches were played on The Green on a matting wicket, and in 1964 a new mat was purchased at a cost of £32 4s 11d (£32 24p). Most fixtures were against fairly local villages and clubs, but an annual event was played against a team from Widley, near Portsmouth. In 1973 Tadley Cricket Club amalgamated with Tadley Sporting Cricket Club. Unfortunately the club folded in 1979.

Ramsdell Cricket Club did not have their own ground until 1947. Until then all fixtures were played away. Practice venues were at Grass Meadow, Povey's Farm and even the allotments at West Heath. Mr William Stanley joined the club in 1936 and has held every position in the club. He is currently their Secretary and Honorary Life Vice President.

Silchester Cricket Club is still in existence, playing their fixtures on Silchester Common. They play league cricket and friendlies. In the 1930s Alec Waugh, brother of Evelyn Waugh, uncle of Auberon Waugh of literary fame, who lived in 'The Old Manor' (in Auberon Waugh's autobiography he refers to a house called 'Edfington') on the Bramley Road, was a member of the MCC and would hold net practices with cricketers from major County teams, including international players. Local lads acted as ball-boys and had opportunities to bat and bowl. Alec Waugh also opened the batting for the village side.

Baughurst Cricket Club played on Kent's field to the south of Smiths Garage. For many years after World War II they used an old military Nissen hut as a pavilion and played friendly weekend fixtures with local teams. When the field was sold for development in the early 1960s the club transferred to a Parish Council ground near The **Pineapple** where they played until the club disbanded in the late 1960s.

Cricketers, The (582 622) Public house in Heath End Road, known to have been in use in 1871 when Ellen Hedges was listed as a beer seller.

Cricketers, The, Latchmore Green A public house; deeds for the site date back to 1789. It was originally a thatched cottage which was converted into a public house. At one time it was owned by John **May & Co**, who merged with H. & G. **Simonds**. It closed in 1953 and reverted to a private house. For a time it was known locally as The Pig and Whistle.

Crooked Cottage (606 609) A thatched cottage in **Malthouse Lane**. It is a Grade II listed building, within the **Tadley Conservation Area**. Similar to **Cons Cottage**, it was built in the early 1600s. At one time it was a general stores and bakery – during Ernie **Kimber**'s childhood Henry Pearce was the owner. It was known as 'The Shop' throughout its later trading time, the dates of which are unclear. By 1891 Henry Pearce had sold the property to Mr and Mrs E. West, both **Salvation Army** officers. Mrs West continued to run the shop until 1937-38. There is disc on the outside wall showing the head of a lady wearing a bonnet. One explanation for the disk is that it indicates the owner's grazing rights, another is that it is an insurance company's mark showing the property was insured, possibly against fire.

Crown, The See The **Calleva Arms.**

Crowther, Derek A cross in **Great St Mary's Church** was donated by Derek in March 1964. Taking two years to make in his spare time, the base and frame are of oak with the cross highlighted in silver. Derek, a member of **Tadley and District Society** (TADS), died in 1999.

D

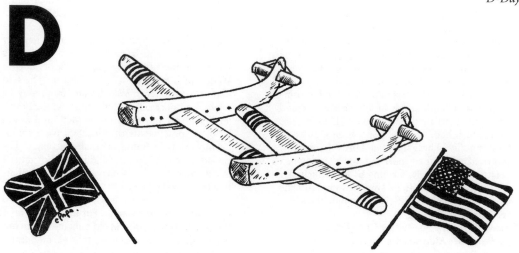

D-Day During World War II, D-Day (6 June 1944) was the beginning of the invasion of France by allied troops. Prior to the start of the invasion, troops were billeted throughout the south of England and in Tadley American troops were camped in the triangular area now bounded by Franklin Avenue, Newchurch and Bishopswood Roads. At 00.10 on D-Day, the first wave of 52 Dakota aircraft tugs and troop-carrying gliders (Operation Chicago), part of the spearhead of the invasion forces, carrying the 81st anti-aircraft (AA) battalion from the 101st Airborne, took off from **Aldermaston Airfield** and joined similar flights from Greenham, Welford, Membury and Ramsbury Airfields, heading for a landing zone (LZ) behind the Omaha beachhead near St Mere Eglise in Normandy. They landed at about 04.00. A second wave of 32 tug aircraft and gliders (Operation Keokuk) left Aldermaston at 18.30 and a third wave at 04.30 on 7 June, all with troops and equipment. Subsequent flights in the days immediately after D-Day were principally to deliver stores and bring casualties back to England.

Daly, Dr Nolan Medical practitioner who originally practised in Bramley, and then in **Little London** between 1935 and 1954. He also had a room in Tadley where he saw patients. He was later helped by his son-in-law Dr Davis. When Dr Daly retired in 1954 he was succeeded by Dr **Mullen**. He supported St Dunstan's Charity, which cared for people blinded in the two wars. See **Health care and medical services; Hospitals; Appendix ii.**

Dame School Prior to the Education Act of 1870, the only teaching many children received was in the home of single or elderly woman. The usual fee would be between 2d and 4d (1-2p) per week for teaching the alphabet, probably using only the family Bible. It is known that such schools existed in the local area. In a sale document for a cottage in West Heath it states that 'the said property is let for use as a school'. Florence **Davidson**'s *The History of Tadley* quotes '…the only education they got was by going to a cottage where an old woman lived…'. In 1909, in her booklet, *Monk Sherborne. A History of the Parish and Priory,* she makes reference to a dame school in the village and two small schools in existence in 1820, one where The Red House was. A villager had also told her that his grandparent reported that children were '…so ill taught that when they left at the age of eight they could neither read or write.' See **Education.**

Dancing In 1923 Tadley's Morris dancers won first prize in the Reading competition of the English Folk Dance Society. There was almost certainly a Maypole on The **Green** at the annual **Tadley Revel.** More recently, it is still a popular pastime today amongst adults and children, with many different types of dancing supported. Some groups still give displays at fetes and charity events throughout the year. See **May Day.**

Davidson, Florence A.G. An author whose full name was Florence Agnes Gregory. Her historical research and writings have been significant in piecing together the history of the area. She was a contributor to the Hampshire Field Club's quarterly journal during the first part of the twentieth century and also wrote for the Monk Sherborne and Pamber parish magazine. In 1913 she published *The History of Tadley,* which is still one of the most comprehensive accounts of the history of the village.

de Port Charity, Adam Adam de Port was Lord of Mapledurwell in the early twelfth century. In Henry II's reign he gave to **Pamber Priory** 'all tithes of all my mills in Sireburn' (Sherborne). White's Directory for 1878 says £1 3s 4d (£1.16p) was left by an unknown donor through **Queen's College, Oxford**, although Kelly's Directory for 1903 names the donor as Adam de Port. See **Charities**.

de Port family Hugh de Port was a great lay (non church or crown) landlord during Norman times. William the Conqueror appointed him Sub-Constable of Dover Castle. In Hampshire Hugh held about 56 manors direct from the Crown, 13 as a tenant of the Bishop of Bayeux. The de Port family were Lords of the Manor of Basing, building a castle which lies beneath the ruins of Basing House. The family was undoubtedly devout; Hugh spent his final years as a monk in St Swithuns Priory in Winchester. His son, Henry, built **Pamber Priory**, then called Sherborne Priory, which was consecrated in 1110 by William Gifford, Bishop of Winchester.

Decoy Heath (609 633) A former **gravel extraction** site naturally returning to heathland in Aldermaston Parish. It is one of the richest sites in Berkshire for dragonflies and damselflies – more than 20 species have been identified. See **SSSI**; **Wildlife**.

Decoy Pond See **Aldermaston Decoy**.

Den, The (596 624) The building was originally the Aldermaston Airfield gunnery and crew procedure block (Building 205). During the war Bob Hope and the Glen Miller Orchestra are alleged to have performed there but the only confirmed appearances were by Edward G. Robinson and the Eisenhower Band who, before **D-Day**, did entertain servicemen at the airfield and **Aldermaston Court** and therefore possibly at The Den. There was an RAF Astra cinema there, using 16 mm projectors. After the war part of the building became Tadley's cinema, The **Royal**. Other parts of the building have been used primarily by local scout and guide groups The **Royal** closed in 1995 and the site is due to be redeveloped. See **Guiding**; **Scouting**.

Dentists The first dental practice in Tadley was opened in October 1957 by Dennis Parker. The surgery was a former Ministry of Defence building behind the **Bishopswood shops**, close to where the **Ambassador Club** is today. Prior to this dental treatment was only available in the nearby towns. In 1961 John Sambrook-Smith, a former RAF colleague, joined Mr Parker and they moved to purpose-built premises in Newchurch Road. This building has been extended to accommodate more dentists as the population has increased. Mr Parker retired at the end of 1990 after 33 years in the area. There are now two dental practices, Mr Jones in Millers Road and the original one in Newchurch Road, which has been further extended to accommodate an optician.

Devil's Highway (645 625) The name given to the route from Londinium (London) across Bagshot Heath to **Calleva Atrebatum** (Silchester) which formed part of an ancient, possibly neolithic, trackway to the south-west. It enters Calleva at the East Gate, close to the **Amphitheatre** in Church Lane. Marked on most current Ordnance Survey maps, it forms part of the Hampshire /Berkshire boundary midway between Mortimer and Bramley. See **Portway**.

Directories, Trade and Commercial See Kelly's Directory.

Dissenters Protestant Dissenters, wishing to follow their own forms of worship and not that of the Church of England, were allowed to register their meeting houses with the Bishop of the Diocese. From those listed between 1702 and 1844 in *A Hampshire Miscellany* it is possible to link these 'certificates' with a number of chapels and private houses in and around Tadley. In Baughurst a 1791 certificate granted to a Thomas Mayers was for a Baptist Church by the roadside at Lovedays Farm, near Brown's Farm. For other denominations, see **Chapel House, Baughurst**; **Mortimer West End Chapel**; **Primitive Methodists**; **United Reformed Church**.

Dix Hill (608 605) The small stretch of the **A340** road between Main Road and Aldermaston Road is known as Dix Hill. The name is possibly a corruption of 'Dick's Hill', after Richard (Dick) Cottrell of The **Star** beer house. Whether by accident or intent the spelling is the same as that of Herbert Dix-Pegg, publican of The **Fighting Cocks** in the 1940s, and previously, The **Fox & Hounds** in 1935.

Doctors See **Health care and medical services**; **Hospitals**; **Appendix ii**.

Doe's Lane Now called **Malthouse Lane**.

Domesday Survey A comprehensive survey of England ordered by William the Conqueror in 1086 to record the economic wealth of the country he had conquered in 1066. Several local places were recorded: **Aldermaston** (Heldremanestone), **Ewhurst** (Werste), **Monk Sherborne** (Sireborne), Sherborne St John, **Silchester** (Silcestre) and **Wolverton** (Ulvretune).

Donkey Tree A large and ancient tree in **Pamber Forest**. The legend is that many years ago a Tadley man's donkey had outlived its useful life as a beast of burden. Not knowing how to dispose of it, he went into the forest and hung it from a tree. The tree's exact location is difficult to confirm; possibly near Beggars' Bridge, just within the forest from its entrance on Impstone Road, **Pamber Heath**. Pat Minter and Roger Searing suggest a location in their book, *Tadley Tracks, Tadley Facts*.

E

Eagle Aviation An air transport company founded by Harold Bamberg after the end of World War II. It began flying converted Halifax bombers. The company was involved in the Berlin Airlift (27 July 1948-16 August 1949), after which it established its headquarters at **Aldermaston Airfield**. It had left by April 1950 when the airfield was relinquished by the Ministry of Civil Aviation for **AWRE**.

Eagle Gates (591 651) Large wrought iron gates standing between two well-preserved seventeenth century lodges at the head of Aldermaston village main street. The gates are topped with a golden eagle, the crest of William Congreve, then owner of **Aldermaston Estate**, who won them in a game of cards from the owner of Midgham Manor. Before the gates were erected, a fine house – very like a Dower House – stood there. When it was demolished, two buildings were left standing which were converted into the Tudor Lodges. The gates are not the main entrance to the estate; that is some few hundred yards further along the road, before the church.

East Street (593 623) The former name for Franklin Avenue, pre-1950s. Prior to World War II only common existed to the east of **Newtown**. During the war the area was part of **Aldermaston Airfield** and a concrete road was laid between Mulfords Hill and **Hangar 5**, the Ministry of Aircraft Production (MAP) building which was near where the **Bishopswood shops** are today.

Ebenezer Cottage, Silchester (623 625) Built on **Silchester Common** in 1864. It was the Manse for the **Silchester Primitive Methodist Circuit** from 1866 until 1932 when the Deed of Union was agreed and the Methodist Church was formed. The name changed to The Manse in 1932, only recently reverting back to Ebenezer Cottage. In 1996 the new minister responsible for the Silchester Church went to live in Burghfield Common and the cottage was let to tenants. See **Silchester Methodist Chapel**.

Education The earliest reference in books about Tadley with regard to education is in Daniel **Benham**'s book *Some Account…*: 'John Hannington, a native of Tadley, was admitted BA of New College, Oxford, 23rd February 1556…having been a pupil of John Martial'. This would suggest that for those families who could afford private tutors schooling has not ever been a problem. All the surrounding towns had their grammar schools, founded mainly to help the poor. In Reading, as early as 1125 with the foundation of Reading Abbey, in Newbury, with St Bartholomew's founded in either 1446 or 1547: in Basingstoke with the Holy Ghost Grammar School from at least 1538 or 1524 when Henry VIII granted letters patent to the Guild, and with Kingsclere Free from 1618. All were schools for boys, all were funded by private benefactors and all supposed to be teaching Latin. By the late nineteenth century there was controversy over the way the wealthy were sending their children to these foundation schools to the exclusion of the poor.

By 1840, according to Daniel Benham's book, a Day School and a Sabbath School were operating, and another school 'connected with the Established Church' (i.e. The Church of England) in a cottage in Tadley. The Day School at Old Meeting may well have been the **British School** where Esther Allen, age 25, recorded in the 1871 census as living in Malthouse and, as a British School Teacher, would have taught. Further to this it is noted on page 19 of C.R. Davey's *A Guide to the Records*: 'Nonconformists generally did not share the Anglican hostility to state intervention (so) …about half… British Schools in Hampshire were handed over to

School Boards in the 1870s.' As the day school connected with the Established Church could well have been only a small affair and not a recognised **National School**, both schools would have closed when the Tadley Board School opened in 1876.

Until 1832 the administration of education on a national scale remained in the hands of voluntary bodies, mainly connected with the churches. In that year the government voted £20,000 towards the building of schools, with the Treasury allocating the money through the two societies, the National Society, with its links to the Established Church, founded by Andrew Bell in 1811, and the British Society, founded by Joseph Lancaster in 1808 and linked with the nonconformist churches.

At its establishment in 1889 the County Council had no statutory responsibility for general education; today the Education Department accounts for more than half the County Council's budget. In 1870 Foster's Education Act established Board Schools to make up deficiencies, and from 1876 elementary education became compulsory up to the age of 12. In 1880 school attendance up to the age of 10 was made compulsory. At 10 a child could obtain a certificate and leave, but if they had registered too few attendances they would have to stay on until 13. The Education Act of 1902 appointed County Councils as the local education authority, replacing the School Boards. In 1889 County Councils were allowed to charge a 1d rate for technical education; in 1891 elementary education was made free. In 1902 secondary education began; in the main there were grammar schools for boys and high schools for girls. In 1918 the leaving age was raised to 14 and in 1944 fees and the title Elementary Education were removed. The 1944 Education Act set up a three tier educational structure: Primary (up to the age of 11), Secondary (divided into Grammar, Secondary Technical and Secondary Modern for different aptitudes), and Further (for those above the compulsory school-leaving age). Comprehensive Education plans began to be put in place in the 1960s and in 1972 the School leaving age was raised to 16. Changes in examinations had taken place since 1917 when School Certificate and Matriculation were introduced. In 1951 GCE (General Certificate of Education) 'O' and 'A' levels were introduced as single subject exams. In 1965 the Certificate of Secondary Education (CSE) was introduced and merged with 'O' levels by 1988 into GCSE (General Certificate of Secondary Education). The 1988 Education Reform Act brought further changes. For an overview of individual schools associated with the area see **Appendix i**.

82nd and 101st Airborne Divisions The 82nd and 101st Airborne Divisions were, during World War II, parachute and glider-borne assault troops of the United States Army. In 1943 and 1944 units were dispersed around airfields in the South of England for training and on **D-Day**, 6 June 1944, they formed the spearhead of the American assault on the Cherbourg Peninsula. The shoulder flash badge of the 82nd bore the letters 'AA', this standing for 'All American', the soldiers having been recruited from every American state. The flash of the 101st showed an eagle and the Division was called 'The Screaming Eagles'. The 82nd and the 101st Divisions still exist and have been involved in recent actions such as 'Desert Fox' in Iraq. See **Operation Market Garden**.

Electricity Electricity for domestic use did not become widely available locally until the early 1950s although the Air Ministry had their own generator/transformer on the airfield from when it opened. **Tadley Parish Council** minutes for 1940 mention planning permission for electricity poles over the common for a supply to a property in Pamber Heath (possibly The **Red House**). In 1947 the owners of **Tadley Court** applied for permission for a private underground cable from the airfield to their property. By 1949 electricity lines were reported to be going up all around the area, although in 1951 it was recorded that there was still no definite date of completion. Shyshack Lane residents did not receive their supply until 1954. Nowadays Southern Electric plc extract power from the National Grid near Bramley at 132,000 volts and after transforming it to 33,000 volts at their Thatcham substation it is fed to the Tadley substation, near Lakeside Garden Centre, where it is reduced to 11,000 volts for supply to the 50 or more individual distribution substations around the area. Should the supply from Bramley/Thatcham fail, the Tadley substation can also be fed from the National Grid at Fleet through the Basingstoke substation. See **Street lighting**.

Elliott family Guy Elliott was born in Tadley, but has spent all his life at **Frog Lane Farmhouse, Little London** where he has farmed continuously. He is able to trace his ancestry back to Kingsclere in 1625. Within the recent past, three generations of the Elliott family have worked Frog Lane Farm, bought in 1921 by Guy's grandfather Charles. Guy's great grandfather, David Elliott, also worked College Farm, Stacey's (now Martingales) Farm and later Pamber Farm, which was rented from the Beaurepaire Estate for 25 years. Guy's father, David, was born at The **Rifleman** public house which was kept by Guy's grandmother Elizabeth: his grandfather, a timber haulier, being absent from Sunday to Saturday. Guy has served on **Pamber Parish Council** for 18 years but is probably best known for his use of traditional methods of growing and harvesting corn and straw for thatching. His father being renowned for his rick building. In the late 1980s, Guy and his brother Gordon could be seen in the summer months working in the fields along the Bramley Road, **Silchester** and around Little London. They now only exhibit these traditional skills and methods at local shows. See **Ricks**.

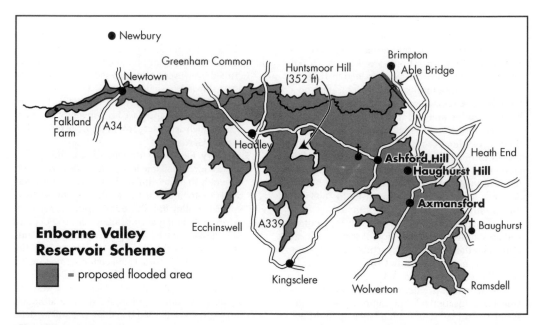

Newbury

Greenham Common

Huntsmoor Hill
(352 ft)

Brimpton
Able Bridge

Newtown

Falkland
Farm   A34

Headley

Ashford Hill
Haughurst Hill

Heath End

Axmansford

Baughurst

**Enborne Valley
Reservoir Scheme**

Ecchinswell   A339

= proposed flooded area

Kingsclere

Wolverton

Ramsdell

Ellis, Ruth Ruth Ellis (née Neilson) was the last
woman to be hanged in this country. This was for
the murder of David Blakely, aged 25, who she shot
outside the Magdala public house, Hampstead,
London on 10 April 1955. She was executed on 13
July 1955 at Holloway Prison. Ruth was born in
Rhyl, North Wales on 9 October 1926, the fourth
child of Arthur and Bertha Neilson. During Ruth's
early childhood, these being the depression years,
the family moved to Basingstoke where her father,
an out of work musician, secured a job as a cinema
pianist for the last few years of the silent movies.
Between 1930 and 1935 it is thought that Arthur
and Bertha took varied domestic employment in
this area. Records show that the family lived at various times in Baughurst, Brimpton Common (near
Abel Bridge) and Tadley (Newtown) before her father secured a more permanent position at **Park
Prewett Hospital** as telephonist and hall porter.
This latter position had the advantage of a 'hospital' house in Sherborne St John. Ruth's primary
school days were spent between Tadley and Baughurst schools before she moved to Fairfields Girls
Senior School in Basingstoke, which she left when
she was 14 to start work as a waitress at the
Gaumont cinema cafe in Reading. Several elderly
local residents have recollections of spending some
of their childhood days with Ruth.

Elm Park Farm and Garden Centre (612 586)
The original part of the farmhouse is said to be 200–
300 years old. The name Elm Farm is not specifically mentioned in the census until 1881 when a
William Follett, one of many from Monk Sherborne, was listed. By 1891 a James Harding from
Portsmouth was farming there. Previously, in 1861,
another William Follett whose blacksmith's shop
on the corner of Bramley Road adjoined the farm,

was listed as also farming 80 acres. It is possibly all
or part of Elm Farm. In 1871 his son James was
farming the 80 acres (32 ha). William moved to
Pamber Farm (240 acres/91 ha), where he remained
until his death. At some point the name of the farm
changed from Elm Farm to Elm Park Farm.

In April 1969 the farm was sold to John (Jack)
Philp by the Wellington Trust. The previous resident was the grandson of the Duke of Wellington. Jack Philp's family originated from
Heathrow, where they can be traced back to
1695. Part of their family nursery business was
compulsorily purchased by the British Airports
Authority for an extension runway at Heathrow
Airport. They searched for several years for a
property with soil suitable for rose growing before finding Elm Park. The farm was stocked
with a Hereford herd, to which Jack introduced
Hereford Cross with a Hereford bull for beef
production. This ceased on Jack's death in 1995.
Elm Park Garden Centre opened in 1975, spe-
cialising in growing roses. In 1976 Jack created
a new apricot rose which he named after his
youngest granddaughter, Elizabeth Philp. After
the death of Princess Grace a memorial garden
was created in Monaco with 40 Grace de Monaco roses, grown and supplied by Elm Park.

Elmhurst (602 614) A large house and farm which
stood to the west of the roundabout at the junction of Tadley Hill and New Road. Over the years it
had several names including Bishopswood House,
Elmhurst Farm, The Beams and Old Beams. It is
not certain when the house was built, but the original Bishopswood House dates back to the 1560s.
Kelly's Directory lists the Chetwynd-Christy family, 'Liberal supporters of all institutions for the
social welfare of the village', as living there between

1911-1939. In the 1960s Fox's Riding School operated from the farm. The foundations of the house or farm are believed to have been uncovered in 1997 during the excavations for **Tadley Swimming Pool**. Names associated with the site have been perpetuated in modern street names (Elmhurst, off New Road) and in the nearby flats (Christy Court).

Enborne Valley Reservoir Scheme By the end of the nineteenth century, London's thirst for water was insatiable and many schemes for improving the capital's supply were considered. Amongst these was a scheme proposed by The Lambeth Water Company in 1899 to create a massive impounding reservoir in the valley of the River Enborne. The reservoir would be filled from the river Enborne by gravity and by pumping from the Kennet. In times of drought, water would be taken by conduits back into the Enborne and Kennet and thence to the Thames, where it would be abstracted lower down. Nothing was done, but the scheme was revived by the Metropolitan Water board in 1907; it was to be implemented in three stages between 1916 and 1933 at a total cost of £8,397,000. Eventually the scheme was shelved in favour of a less costly one.

In the years immediately following World War II, water consumption increased dramatically and the Enborne Valley scheme was once more considered. The vulnerability of the existing supplies had been highlighted by unusually dry summers. Once more the Enborne Valley reservoir seemed to offer a viable option. The plan was to connect the reservoir by conduit to Pangbourne; when water was plentiful it would be pumped up from the Thames for storage in the reservoir; in times of drought it would be allowed to flow back under gravity to supplement the flow in the Thames.

The reservoir was to have a surface area of nine square miles (23 sq km); this vast lake would have stretched from Falkland Farm, just south of Newbury, to Heath End and Baughurst in the east, and Brimpton in the north, with watery fingers stretching as far south as Ecchinswell and Kingsclere. It would have been a massive undertaking; 55,000 million gallons (250,000 million litres) would be impounded behind a 100 foot (30 m) high, four thousand foot (1219 m) long dam at Brimpton; three further dams were proposed which would carry the principal roads and divide the lake into four sections. At their meeting in April 1948 the Metropolitan Water Board concluded that a reservoir in the Enborne Valley would be 'the most economical and practical proposal to meet the anticipated future requirements'.

But the scheme had one fatal flaw; biological experts reported that in the summer months the lower level of water would become foul. In certain conditions, this layer would 'turn over' and mix with the rest of the water, so making it unsuitable. Once again, the scheme was shelved, no doubt to the relief of the residents of Ashford Hill, Headley and Newtown, major parts of which would have been flooded. Dry summers led to the revival of the reservoir proposals in 1966 and 1976, but each time they came to nothing. As recently as 1990, the hot summer and inevitable hosepipe bans led to Thames Water further reviewing their long term solutions to water shortages; but they stoutly denied any suggestion that, once more, their thoughts were turning towards the Enborne Valley.

Enclosure Acts Formerly also known as inclosure. The substitution of enclosed fields for the open field system began in the fourteenth century with informal inclosures and culminated in the Act of 1845 which authorised commissioners to consider applications for inclosure and report them to Parliament. Historically, in law, all land was owned by the monarch who granted parts to individuals in return for the provision of fighting services. These 'Lords of the Manor' in turn tenanted land, some of which held rights to use manorial 'waste' or **Common Land**. As a result of Enclosure Acts these common lands became protected and could only be enclosed if thought to be beneficial to the community. As a result of Tadley's Enclosure Act of 1850 (1852), the parish was awarded land now overseen by the Turbary Allotment Charity. Out of the Act also came the allocation of land for exercise and recreation: i.e. The **Green**.

While a commissioner did his best to allocate the private land how the proprietors desired, the process could only be achieved by agreed exchanges of plots of land between parties. The quantities of land exchanged were not always equal but the convenience of having plots together would compensate for any lower quality land acquired. As might be expected, the largest land owners were the most likely to obtain their chosen plots. Under Tadley's Enclosure Act of 1850 (1852) the largest allocations of private land were to William Beach, Thomas Prior and the Duke of Wellington, with over 50 other listed freeholders: Noah Allen to Jonathan West, including six women.

As a direct result of enclosing land, many public and private roads were laid out and alterations to water courses planned. Existing lines were generally followed but some footpaths were blocked up or re-routed and many carriageways were widened and gravelled. This, together with instructions regarding 'fencing' and who took responsibility formed a considerable part of an enclosure document. In the document, it stated that, in the main, Tadley boundaries were to be bank and ditch with some quickthorn. It is not surprising that it took Thomas Hasker three years to survey and document Tadley's enclosure. See **Allotments; School Allotment Charity; Vestry meetings; Appendix iii.**

Englefield Estate Englefield Estate comprises land not only north and south of the Bath Road but also land in Scotland and on the outskirts of London. Throughout the centuries it has been a significant employer and land owner in the area. As owners of much local woodland, many Tadley and Pamber people were dependent upon the **Coppicing** and felling of Englefield woodland for their livelihoods. The Englefield Estate still owns **Pamber Forest** and three pockets of land along its perimeter in the parish of **Pamber**. See **Benyon family**; Richard **Benyon**.

Entertainment for village halls Since February 1996 the **Pamber Heath Memorial Hall** Committee has taken advantage of a facility, provided by Hampshire County Council and sponsored by the Royal Mail, to provide professional entertainments at the Hall. The first was 'Bella – the story of Mrs Beeton' the famous cookbook writer, acted by actress Alison Neil. There have been nine productions since, all with small casts and minimal technical support and including musical and comedy productions, as well as dramas and plays about well known individuals.

Evacuees During World War II many people were evacuated from high-risk areas and billeted with local families. They included children from London who were evacuated to the safety of the countryside, and adults, often with families, who had been bombed out of their homes in the towns. A lot of Tadley's evacuees came from Portsmouth. Many were from the same school and came with their teachers who joined the staff at **Tadley School**.

Evans, Florence 'Florrie' See Tadley **Post Offices**.

Evans, William William Harry Brereton Evans was listed as resident at **Fairlawn House** at the time of his death on 7 August 1913. Aged 30, he was killed in a flying accident at Farnborough with the famous aviator Col. Samuel Franklin Cody. Together they were testing an aircraft when it crashed. A member of the Civil Service in Sudan he was home on leave and staying with his sister Mrs Gerald Strange at Fairlawn House. His body was cremated, unusual for the time, and the ashes buried alongside the body of his grandmother in the chancel of **St Peter's Church**. William made a name for himself in Public School cricket, being the outstanding all-rounder for Malvern in 1901. He was awarded blues at Oxford in 1902, 1903, 1904 and 1905, before going on to play for Hampshire County Cricket Club. He was followed by his brother D.M. Evans in 1911 and another brother, Commander A.E. Evans made his Hampshire debut in 1919.

Ewhurst Park (570 568) Ewhurst Park estate lies to the south of the route of the **Portway**. Remains of a Roman villa have been discovered on the estate, and, nearby, countless coins of the Emperor Constantine unearthed. Ewhurst is mentioned in the **Domesday Survey** when it was held by Hugh de **Port** and had '2 villagers, 2 smallholders a Woodland & 5 pigs'. The spelling at that time was Werste meaning 'yew wood', probably on a hill. A wood called Ewhurst Wood still exists in the parish. The medieval village was deserted by the time Ewhurst House was built in the eighteenth century. The house is at the centre of the estate and comprises a U-shaped group of brick Georgian buildings, including the house, chapel and stables. More recently Ewhurst House was the home of the 4th Duke of Wellington. He came to the house in 1900 as heir to the title and much preferred Ewhurst to Stratfield Saye. He lived there until his death in 1934. The firm Radio Frequency Investigation (RFI) occupy purpose-built laboratories on the estate, some of which are within converted outbuildings of the farm adjacent to Ewhurst House.

Exchange Cottage, Heath End (582 622) See **Telephones**.

F

Fairground Prior to World War II the land upon which 'Gorselands', on Mulfords Hill, is built (Pope's Meadow) was used by the **Williams family** and other showmen to open and close their Fair Season. In April or May the rides and equipment would be set-up, checked and repaired. Local people welcomed this opportunity to ride the gallopers (carousel) and it has long remained in people's memories. Due to blackout restrictions Sammy Williams' fairground ride ceased to operate in 1939. See **Black's Cafe.**

Fairlawn House (605 609) A large house, situated at the corner of Fairlawn Road and Main Road, within the **Tadley Conservation Area.** The house and its grounds have had a variety of uses since its construction; dating of roof timbers has given this as about 1750. It was then two dwellings, in front of which was a farmhouse, later demolished, and a blacksmith's shop which remained until the 1920s. At some point the Georgian style frontage was added and the two dwellings became one substantially sized house. This gentrification probably coincided with its use as a rectory between 1882 and 1888 by Revd **Saulez** and Revd **Oliver.** The name Fairlawn first appears in the 1871 census when it was listed as unoccupied. In 1881 it had 11 occupants including a governess and boarding scholars. This reinforces the fact that Fanny Monger, mother of Effie Saunders (see **Honeysuckle Cottage**) is known to have attended a school at, or above, the stables of Fairlawn House. Dr Evans held his surgery at the house between 1895 and 1898. His widow sold the house to Colonel and Mrs Lynden-Bell in 1912 but they did not occupy it until sometime later, allowing Mrs Evans to remain. The Lynden-Bells were in residence until 1950 and Colonel Lynden-Bell is remembered still as a sprightly man of military bearing. The next owners, the Cobbolds, members of a Suffolk brewing family sold the northern end of the grounds for the development of Cedar Close. Other pockets of land along Malthouse Lane were also sold at this time. The current owners purchased the house in 1998 and have made structural repairs and improvements to the property. See **Blacksmiths.**

Fairlawn Road On the 1936 Ordnance Survey maps this appears as Pamber Lane.

Falcon Gate (596 629) This was the main entrance to **Aldermaston Airfield** and, today, one of the entrances to **AWE.**

Falcon, The (594 627) Public house (known locally as 'The Fuzzbush') situated on the southern edge of the old **Aldermaston Estate**, between the Falcon Garage and an entrance to **AWE.** The falcon emblem is from the crest of the Congreve family, owners of Aldermaston Estate in the early 1800s. In 1950, a time of severe rationing of building materials, permission was given by the Ministry of Supply for extensive improvements to be made. The reason for this was to provide facilities for the expanding workforce brought in to construct the nearby AWRE site. The public house has at varying times been the focus for anti-nuclear demonstrators – during the CND marches of the 1960s and, more recently, the **Greenham Peace Women** demonstrations of the 1980s. See Maria **Hale.**

Festival of Britain A nation-wide exhibition held in 1951, the centenary of the Great Exhibition of 1851. Locally, the **Calleva Museum** was established as a part of the celebrations.

Fighting Cocks, The (607 606) Public house on Dix Hill, at the southern end of Tadley. The name comes from the old sport of cock or bantam fighting. In 1841 Jesse Pink was publican. In 1871 the then innkeeper, Joseph Hunt, was also a bricklayer. At one time the pub was well known for Saturday night fighting. This included the distinctive shin, or leg, kicking that the local lads used against outsiders. In some areas shin kicking was an organised, competitive and very bruising game using specially studded boots and not just a casual fight.

Part or all of the original thatched building was burnt down in about 1900 and was rebuilt in the present style. A 1924 photograph shows it little different from what it looks like today. For 15 years,1924-39, Frederick James Martin was the publican. The public house was owned for a period by Basingstoke brewers John **May & Co**, then in 1947 ownership passed to H. & G. **Simonds**, eventually becoming part of Courage Ltd. The area where Mariner's Close now lies (previously known as Martin's Field) was at one time owned by the public house.

Fire services Prior to World War II the provision of fire services in Hampshire was piecemeal; county boroughs had major services and some small local authorities and parishes had efficient fire brigades. There was no county-wide network. The Hants and Berks Gazette for 10 August 1878 records the Basingstoke Fire Brigade and engine attending a barn fire at **Wyeford**. Depending as they did on a horse-drawn engine, the response time must have been long and a far better fire service must have been provided by local people with buckets of water. Reports in the local papers of the earlier fire at **Aldermaston Court** in January 1843 also refer to horse-drawn engines and long delays. During World War II the Americans had their own fire crews at **Aldermaston Airfield**. Fire cover continued after the war whilst the airfield was used by other agencies. When the site became **AWRE** the decision was made that it needed its own fire service which continues to this day. Civilian protection for Tadley continued to be the responsibility of Basingstoke Fire Station. A National Fire Service (NFS) was created in 1941 to cope with the wartime emergency. The Fire Services Act 1947 transferred responsibility for the Fire Brigade to the County Councils and County Borough Councils. This situation continued until 1997 when responsibility was transferred to a Joint Fire Services Authority following the creation of Southampton and Portsmouth as unitary authorities.

During the 1950s and 1960s as Tadley grew, the distance from Basingstoke to Tadley meant that response times continued to be long. The anomaly was that engines from AWRE would be able to turn out faster than those from Basingstoke. It was eventually decided that Tadley should have its own fire station and building work started in the early 1970s on a site opposite the Holmwood Health Centre in Franklin Avenue. Crews began training in 1973 and the station was operational by 1974. The first incident it attended was a barn fire in Silchester. Classed

as a 'Retained Station', Tadley has a current strength of about 14 fire-fighters who work a rota system to provide 24 hour call-out cover. The station answers between 200 and 250 calls a year, seeking to meet efficient response times for all emergency calls.

Firewood A by-product of **coppicing**, the product which formed the bulk of the underwood was the trimmings. These were bundled up, according to thickness, for firewood. The brushwood was made up into bavins and puffs; the small loppings into bunts and pims; and the larger loppings into faggots. There were kiln bavins and larger faggots which were used for firing brick-kilns and baker's ovens; chip bavins (from the hoop shavings), bush bavins and small faggots were for domestic fires. Bavins and faggots varied in size from 91 cm to 1.37 m in length and 61 cm across. See J. **Stacey & Sons**.

Fishponds Fish were an important element of people's diet in medieval times. However, owing to the high cost of building and maintaining them, it was usually only the rich who could afford to have their own fishponds. Several local fishponds are recorded in documents and on maps: **Baughurst House**; **Pamber Priory**; **Ufton Court**; **Wyeford house**. Those at Ufton Court, which have recently been restored, are among the best flights of medieval fishponds in existence today outside of a monastic establishment.

Five Mile Act (1665) The Five Mile Act of 1665 restricted the movement of nonconformist ministers. They could not preach within a five mile radius of a corporate town or place where they had previously preached. Instead of reducing their numbers it merely spread them over a wider area. The **Quakers** at Baughurst probably evolved as a direct result of this act, being remote yet within easy reach of the ejected Quaker communities in neighbouring boroughs. The Five Mile Act was not repealed until 1812, even though religious toleration was granted in 1689. See **Act of Uniformity**.

Flitter, Hylton Born near **Tadley School**, which he attended. After leaving school he worked on his grandfather's farm. During World War II he served with the 2nd/4th Royal Hampshire Regiment in North Africa, where he was hit by shell fragments and left for dead. Fortunately he survived but was permanently disabled. He lived in Fairlawn Cottage on the site now occupied by Ash Tree Cottage, Fairlawn Road, where he was self-employed as a shoe repairer and leather worker. He devoted much of his time to serving as Welfare Officer for the Tadley Branch of the Royal British Legion. In recognition of his work the Royal British Legion flats in Bowmonts Road (**Hylton Court**) were named after him. He died in 1990, aged 69.

Flower picking In the late 1800s and early 1900s women would pick flowers from copses in **Pamber Forest** to sell in Basingstoke. William Rawlings, speaking on a 'Country Ways' television programme, said: 'Our wives and daughters used to

Photo: Gazette Newspapers

Tadley Fire Brigade fighting the fire at Heather House in 1995

collect lilies of the valley, bluebells, wild daffodils, heather and violets out of the forest and we would take 'em to Basingstoke and sell 'em. Practically everyone hereabouts used to get a pick out of Pamber Forest'. Mrs Daly, wife of Dr **Daly** in **Little London**, cultivated the roadside outside their home, growing flowers which she sold to raise funds for St Dunstans Home for the Blind.

Flying circus During the 1920s Sir Alan Cobham was active in stimulating popular interest in aviation. He made long distance flights and later organised 'flying circuses' around the country, coming to Basingstoke in September 1929. In Tadley, at a similar time, many locals recall the arrival of an aeroplane in the fields along New Road. Prior to World War II this was undoubtedly a major event attracting many sightseers, some of whom were brave enough to pay the 5 shillings (25p) for a flight. Ernie **Kimber**, writing in *Tadley During My Time and Before*, recalls his flight in the open-topped aircraft when his companion's cap blew off and floated gently down to earth.

Footpaths Although the majority of footpaths and bridleways have their origins in the everyday needs and requirements of the local community, nowadays they are used more for recreational purposes. The National Parks and Countryside Act (1949) required each parish to undertake a survey of Public Rights of Way, following which definitive maps were prepared showing the route of all public rights of way and their status. Under the law all such paths are now public rights of way for all time. Details of paths are held by local councils; rambling groups

are another source of information. A good introduction to some of the local footpaths is contained in Pat Minter and Roger Searing's book, *Tadley Tracks, Tadley Facts*. See **Enclosure Act**.

Fords of Silchester See **Bus and coach services**.

Forensic Science Laboratories (588 629) In 1966 the Home Office set up a Forensic Science Laboratory (FSL) together with a Central Research Establishment (HOCRE) within the AWRE site. The FSL served the Home Counties and soon became involved with two local murder cases ('Minicab' and 'Beenham'). When drug problems increased nationally the FSL assisted the police at pop festivals, notably at Reading. An intelligence unit was set up to provide drug-abuse intelligence to national police forces. This provided valuable assistance in a major case involving illicit drugs, known as 'Operation Julie'.

HOCRE was one of the foremost forensic science research establishments in the world, developing many new scientific techniques which are still widely used today. It attracted international respect and scientific collaboration. Its role was to develop new techniques for examining traces of material found at crime scenes. This included fragments of glass, paint, hair, clothing fibres, blood and so forth. Improvements were also made in techniques for detecting drugs and poisons in human bodies. Close collaboration with AWE scientists enabled the detection of minute elemental traces of material, e.g. arsenic in human hair using neutron activation analysis in the Herald Reactor. Other early, fundamental work included the detection of characteristic blood groups in biological stains (e.g. murders and sexual assaults) and the measurement of blood alcohol levels (traffic cases). Comprehensive collections of clothing fibres, fibre dyestuffs and shoe print patterns etc were made to help identify evidence recovered from crime scenes. For solving 'hit and run' cases use was made of collections of tyre prints, vehicle paint colours and headlamp glasses to help identify and trace the vehicle involved. In 1976 the 'Blennerhassett Group' was set up to develop methods to be used in roadside breath testing of alcohol levels. HOCRE also maintained a comprehensive library of scientific books and papers to support the regional FSLs in England and Wales. Rigorous quality assurance trials were set to check on the accuracy of casework methods. Fingerprint technology was improved.

A major success story at HOCRE was the development of extremely sensitive DNA methods for 'fingerprinting' blood stains and other body fluids. It assisted in setting up a National DNA database to link biological stains with known criminals. Other high profile scientific work included tests in 1992 on bone samples believed to be those of the murdered Russian royal family, the Romanovs. The remains were recovered from Ekaterinburg, Russia, in 1991. DNA established almost certainly that these remains included those of the Tsar, Tsarina and three of their five children. Comparison of DNA material was made with living descendants including HRH Prince Philip, Duke of Edinburgh.

HOCRE changed its name to the Home Office Forensic Science Service in 1985 and in 1993 the research activity was amalgamated with administrative departments in Birmingham. The casework FSL closed in 1998, its workload being taken over by the London Forensic Science Service.

Fort Halstead An outstation of Woolwich Arsenal, in Kent, where early research on Britain's atomic bomb was started after World War II under the title High Explosive Research (HER). The work was transferred to AWRE in the early 1950s. The name is perpetuated in the **Bishopswood shops'** building.

Fox and Hounds, The (598 622) Public house on the corner of Mount Pleasant and Mulfords Hill, possibly dating back to 1824. In 1871 Charles Mudge is recorded as the 'licensed victualler'. It was used during **World War I** as a muster centre where locals assembled prior to joining the armed forces. During the inter-war years it was also on the route of the **Hospital Sunday** parades.

Friendly Societies During their heyday – the Victorian and Edwardian era – the basic purpose of Friendly Societies was to provide a form of social security through mutual self-help from the devastating consequences to families of accident, ill-health or death of the principal bread-winner. In addition to providing financial benefits, they formed a focus for social life with their regular fortnightly or monthly meetings and annual celebrations. Some societies also built halls to provide social and educational facilities, and some lent money for mortgages. There are several references to local societies in the Hants & Berks Gazette. For example, in December 1879 the Pamber and Tadley National Deposit Friendly Society was formed and in July 1880 a meeting was held in The **Old Malthouse** to establish a branch of the Hampshire Friendly Society. Other references mention societies in Baughurst in 1893 and Silchester in 1888. See **Health care and medical services; Hospitals**.

Frog Lane Farmhouse (628 601) A stone plaque set within the brickwork states the farmhouse was built by the Corporation of Basingstoke in 1852 and was probably the first council house built in Pamber parish. It was listed by name in the 1881 census, when it was occupied by Charles Hannington and his family. For most of the twentieth century it has been occupied by the **Elliott family**. See **Ricks**.

Fuzzbush, The (595 627) Another name for The **Falcon** public house. The correct spelling is Furzebush; furze (from the Old English fyrs) is another name for gorse. It is not clear if The Fuzzbush is just a nickname for The Falcon or an old name which has changed. One explanation is that an earlier inn sign showed a falcon sat on a furze bush. The area was also sometimes called Furzebush Corner.

G

Gabardine Horse owned by Major **Roller**, a gift from Mr **Burberry**. The major did not admire Gabardine at first, describing her as, 'painfully small and nondescript and looking like a brown bear'. However, time showed that although 'funny tempered and having no nice feelings for anyone' Gabardine was a tough, speedy, brave mare 'who could bound over obstacles like an india rubber ball'. Gabardine carried Major Roller through the Boer War and he was convinced that the mare's qualities saved his life on more than one occasion during the campaign. In peacetime, Gabardine was a star on the race course, especially when steeple chasing. The partnership of Gabardine and the major prompted this verse in a 1900 newspaper:

There's a smart yeoman called Roller,
Whose mount it will pay you to foller,
At the name 'Gabardine',
The bookies turn green,
As they pay out the dime and the dollar.

Gabardine spent her last days in retirement, literally in clover and died at the age of 25. There is some confusion as to where she is buried. One account says she lies in the garden of Major Roller's house (The Wilderness) under the tombstone bearing the tribute – 'Gabardine, a gallant little horse'. Another story says that when she died the Major wanted her buried in the graveyard at **St Peter's Church**. The vicar refused so he bought land by the graveyard fence and buried the horse there. When the major died he was buried close to the horse but inside the graveyard. In time the graveyard was extended to include the horse's grave, so Roller got his wish. See **Tadley Court**.

Gardiners The house, on the west side of the road from St Peter's Church to Bishopswood, where early religious meetings of the Independents, later Congregationalists, were held. See **United Reformed Church**.

Gas Although gas was used for street lamps in London in 1819, it was a century and a half before it came to Tadley. Apart from Daniel **Benham** being secretary of a London Gas Company there is little documentary evidence of gas even being mentioned in the area before natural gas came in the 1970s. However some large houses e.g. The **Red House,** Pamber Heath, boasted of being lit by 'acetylene gas' in the 1920s. This gas was generated by dripping water on to (calcium) carbide and then piping it to lamps in the house. Our present day natural gas originates from the southern North Sea Gas Field, coming ashore near Cromer, Norfolk. It is then 'pushed' through pipes at 25 mph to Aylesbury and Reading, where, if necessary, it is stored before reaching Tadley in the now familiar yellow plastic pipes.

Geology The geological structure of the Tadley area is essentially composed of Lower Bagshot Sands overlaying London Clay with occasional drifts of Plateau Gravel. The resultant landform is a fairly level plateau to the north above the 300 feet (91 m) contour, with the land falling to the south-west and south-east to form a more undulating terrain. The northern part of **Tadley** is underlain with a deposit of plateau gravel which also emerges at Tadley Hill. Extensive areas of land immediately to the north of Tadley have been worked for the extraction of this gravel in recent years. See **Gravel extraction**.

George and Dragon, The (566 587) A public house in **Wolverton**, built in 1760. It was formerly a smallholding on The Duke of Wellington's estate where cottage rents were collected. The keeper in 1841 was named as a William Carssell. An earlier inn of the same name, near Brazen Head Lane,

Wolverton, is reputed to have been used during the Crusades.

Ghergesti In March 1990, only three months after the downfall of the oppressive Ceausescu regime in Romania, a group of people from Tadley set off with medicines, food, clothing, soaps, nappies, blankets, and sweets, for the town of Ghergesti, population 7000, and 1600 miles (2575 km) away. The supplies were provided by schoolchildren, companies, shops, and individuals from a wide area around Tadley. A second visit in September 1990 concentrated on taking medicines, food and educational supplies. An orphanage in a neighbouring village was found to be in very poor condition and blankets, sweets and toys were left for the children. At the end of this visit it was decided, in conjunction with the local doctor, that the most urgent need was improvements to the infrastructure at the health clinic and the schools. During the third visit, the health clinic was completely redecorated, a new electrical system was installed with lighting and power points, running water was connected, and the dentistry was re-equipped. This work improved the morale of the staff and encouraged them to start on similar improvements themselves. Further visits continued with work of this nature, the most recent, the ninth, being in June 1999 to refurbish the community centre and check on the health centre, the orphanage and a psychiatric hospital.

Ghosts Like many other villages Tadley and the surrounding area has its share of ghosts. Perhaps the oldest and most bizarre story concerns the Padworth ghosts which date back to the **Civil War** and the 1st Battle of Newbury in 1643. They appear in great number, especially at Christmas time. It transpires that they are both Cavaliers and Parliamentarians who fell in the skirmish at Padworth Gully. The Royalists, it is said, in this short and murderous affair lost something like 300 men and Padworth Church has a memorial to the 'nameless dead who lie near'. Such stories stop many people from going near this lonely spot at night especially at Christmas.

The Brimpton ghosts originate from a cold January evening in the mid sixteenth century when a carriage taking revellers to the local hunt ball in Thatcham or Newbury, skidded while descending a steep hill and plunged into the then fast flowing Enborne river at Able Bridge. Travellers at this spot at night 'may still hear psychic echoes of the tragedy – the screams of the passengers and the snorts and whinnies of the horses. They may even catch a glimpse of the doomed carriage and pair'. A similar story, involving a coach and horses in January time is also associated with **Lane End Cottage, Brimpton**.

Thomas Chandler is said to be the resident ghost at the Queen's College Arms, Pamber End. He died in July 1880, after working at the public house as a woodsman and handyman for nearly 50 years and is buried in the grounds of Pamber Priory.

Tadley can boast of two ghosts. The first manifests itself at **Tadley Place** and is said to be the apparition of Henry **Ludlow**. The peasantry in the seventeenth century say he made his appearance at intervals 'to favoured eyes' through an underground passage connecting Ludlow's Hole with Tadley Place. (Ludlow's Hole is a pool of water in an obscure and overshadowed dell or gully on the borders of a large wood called Washer's Coppice about 140 metres from Tadley Place.) Since the spirit of this restless being, who is said to have led a very wicked life, was laid to rest by 'twelve parsons for a thousand years' in the waters of Ludlow's Hole, it has not been seen. Tadley's second ghost is that of a lady, clad in a lovely silk gown with hands outstretched in front of her but with no head. No indication of where in Tadley she appears has been handed down with the legend, but it is believed to be linked with a duel between two gentlemen admirers. By firing simultaneously, both were killed and she haunts the house searching for her lovers, though why she is headless is still a mystery – perhaps she lost her heart and head to love.

Most of these ghosts have not been seen for many years, although there have been more recent 'sightings' of the **Pamber Heath** ghost. It 'lives' in Church Road and has appeared to a succession of residents. Nicknamed 'Uncle Arthur' by previous owners of the house, he mostly appears just sitting and waiting in a favourite armchair, his presence felt by a long cold icy blast at low level and the disappearance of small things like ear-rings. Through a medium, the current owners have discovered that 'Uncle Arthur' was actually Bernard, one of a large family who lived there in the past. It seems that one of Bernard's brothers, who remains nameless, was a thief; having stolen some jewellery, he threw it down the well. This brother was eventually caught, tried and hanged for his crimes. Bernard hunts for his brother and is averse to leaving. The couple living in this house, and those who tell of these happenings, have become resigned to the fact that they will have to continue to share their home with 'Uncle Arthur'.

Gibbs, Anstice Commonwealth Chief Commissioner for the Girl Guides between 1956-66; she was later made a Dame and awarded the CBE. She lived for a time at Blacknest Lodge, Brimpton Common. See **Blacknest**; **Guiding**.

Guiding Nationally, Girl Guides were formed in 1910, Brownies in 1914 and Rangers in 1916. Locally, Silchester definitely had a Brownie Pack in the 1930s and possibly Tadley as well. They were in the Kingsclere and Silchester District – part of the Basingstoke Division. There may have been guides in the area earlier than this but no records have been found. By the 1940s Tadley had a Guide Company and a Brownie Pack. Their Brown Owl for many years was Miss Leah Stacey (known affectionately as Aunt Leah). In 1947 Miss Sarah Branson started a Guide Company in Pamber (later to become 1st Tadley). She was later to be the Commissioner for all England and the Guide Advisor for Commonwealth Headquarters. She wrote books and many articles for *The Guide* and *The Guider*. Guiding had become very popular in the area in the 1950s due to the population expansion generated by AWRE; Guide Companies were formed in Baughurst and Aldermaston, as well as two Brownie Packs and a Ranger Unit. Many of these units met in a hut where Boundary Hall was later built. The 1960s saw even more growth in local guiding with the formation of Pamber Forest District with Miss Sarah Branson as District Commissioner. Another change at this time, due to the adverse publicity AWRE was getting, was to drop the name Aldermaston from units and substitute Tadley. By the 1970s the District had become so large that it was decided to split it into two and Burnham Copse District was formed. New units of Guides and Brownies started at Little London and Ramsdell and by then Tadley had five Guide Companies and Brownie Packs. Mrs Valerie Hyde, Pamber Forest District Commissioner went on to become Division Commissioner and is now County President. The 1980s saw the formation of the Rainbows, for girls aged five to seven years, then in 1993 a combined Scout and Guide group was started for teenagers. In 1999 there are currently 16 Guide Units in the area with a membership of about 300 girls. See Anstice **Gibbs**.

Goddard's Builders A family business begun by James Goddard at the turn of the century. First listed in the 1903 **Kelly's Directory** for Silchester, the business was described as 'builders, carpenters, joiners, wheelwrights and undertakers, private hearse for hire, price on application'. James was also listed as church sexton. The business later moved to a cottage with adjoining stable block in Silchester Road, belonging to The Wilderness, where Major **Roller** had kept his horses. James's granddaughter Louisa Benham (née Goddard) remembers seeing him make coffins there during the 1910s and 1920s. By 1923 Kelly's Directory lists his son, Robert, as having continued the business and his grandson, Albert 'Jack', was later also involved. Goddard's built the **Tadley Main Road Methodist Church** in 1931, but in 1939 when the men went to war the business ceased trading. Goddard's Builders worked amicably alongside **Blake's Builders**, each making major building contributions to the area.

Goodenough's Stores, Baughurst (575 623) General stores that was in Baughurst, opposite where the **Hurst Community School** is today. There was a shop there for over 100 years. The Goodenoughs ran it for over half a century and in the late 1950s and early 1960s it was run by Norah and George Smith. It closed in the 1960s, becoming a private dwelling called London House. Locals have fond memories of the stores – which sold everything from a packet of pins to a besom broom;

corn and meal for chickens and pigs; making its own lemonade and stocking father's hob nails and mother's fleecy lined knickers!

Gospel Hall, Pamber Heath (609 619) In the summer of 1911 an evangelist, George Titcombe, erected a gospel tent at the eastern end of Burney Bit and preached the Gospel, living beside the tent in a caravan. Villagers who were converted to Christ were baptised and a small company of Christians began to meet together. By the end of that summer a wooden building, known as the Wooden Tent had been erected at the western end of Burney Bit. It was clad with iron in about 1936 and remained as the Pamber Heath Gospel Hall until the present one was built in 1973, on land that had at one time been a **broomyard** operated by William West. See **Bethany**.

Governess Private tutoring for those who could afford it was still preferred even after the establishment of village schools in the 1870s. The occupation of Governess appears quite frequently throughout the local census: in 1851 Ann Wickens, age 14, of Browning Hill and in 1861 Ellen Hobbs, age 19, of **Heath End House**. Some of the larger houses in the vicinity also took boarding scholars; in 1861 Pamber Place had ten such and in 1881 **Fairlawn House** had four boarders in addition to the three children of the occupants. See **Dame School**.

Grant's Farm See **Burrell's Farm**.

Gravel extraction Geologically the local area is rich in gravel, a great deal of which has been extracted e.g. Soke Road, Barlow's Plantation and, recently, Larkwhistle Farm beside the Hurst School. Part of the 1850 (1852) Enclosure Act granted inhabitants the right to remove gravel from designated areas, in particular a five acre (2 ha) site north and south of Franklin Avenue, just west of the traffic lights. However, locals were known to extract gravel from other parts of the common. A letter from Major George **Roller** to **Tadley Parish Council**, dated March 1903, makes reference to this: '… many inhabitants of Tadley are in the habit of taking gravel from **all** parts of this common. About 100 cartloads having been taken during the past few months from a place about 20 yards from my studio. Now I believe there is already a rule prohibiting anyone from taking gravel from anywhere except from the one pit in the neighbourhood of the Basingstoke and Aldermaston road.' Parish council minutes frequently record concern about the depth of some gravel pits and there is at least one instance of a child drowning in a flooded pit. See **Geology; Pamber Parish Council; Appendix iii**.

Great St Mary's Church, North Tadley (590 621) With the large growth of the population of north Tadley, around AWRE, the Conventional District of Tadley St Mary was formed in 1957 from parts of the parishes of Aldermaston, Baughurst and Tadley, with **Little St Mary's Church** and Huts 600 and 601 in Bishopswood Road as places of worship. The

Great Western Railway offices at Aldermaston during World War II

huts closed on 28 March 1960 in preparation for a permanent church being built on the site. Building work commenced on 2 May 1960 and was completed in time for the consecration service on 5 June 1961, attended by 350 people; the collection of £48 10s 0d (£48.50p) went to the Church Building Fund. The first vicar, Revd Michael Pennington-Simcock, started on 25 May 1957. He was nicknamed the 'Atom(ic) Parson' by the national press. See Derek **Crowther**.

Great Western Railway The Great Western Railway which had a significant influence on local history, was responsible for the Reading to Newbury line through **Aldermaston** and the Reading to Basingstoke line. The line from London to Bristol and later to Penzance was constructed under the engineer Isambard Kingdom Brunel. The first line had a gauge of 7 ft (2.13 m) but this was later reduced to a common standard of 4 ft 8½ ins (1.44 m). Lengths of the original broad gauge rails can still be seen used as fencing in front of the cottages close to the canal bridge at Aldermaston.

During World War II the company evacuated their office staff from Paddington to Aldermaston. Plans for the evacuation had been drawn-up prior to the outbreak of war with six steel framed brick panelled buildings being constructed near **Aldermaston Station**. However, these buildings were not ready for occupation until December 1939 and as an interim measure the staff were evacuated to various country properties in the Thames Valley area. The largest of these was Beenham Grange. Another

was **Wasing Place** where the accounts section was for most of the war. Other staff were evacuated to sidings at Newbury Race Course where restaurant cars were used as offices. The purpose-built offices ('The Huts') at Aldermaston were opened on 18 December 1939 and staff were brought out daily from London by two trains to Aldermaston Station from where they walked to the offices. As an indication of the size of the complex, it included a 400 seat staff canteen. See **Railways**.

Great Windmill Meadow See **Windmills**.

Green, The (603 609) The Green is just off Main Road, opposite **Allen's Garage**. An 1851 **Enclosure Act** granted six acres of land there as a recreational ground. Several nineteenth century maps mark it as the 'Bowling Green' or 'Cricket Ground' and **cricket** was played there until the 1970s. Football is still played there, as it has been for most of the twentieth century. Daniel **Benham**, in his book *Some Account...*, records that the **Tadley Revel** was held annually on The Green prior to 1822.

Greenham Peace Women In the late 1980s a group of women started a campaign against cruise missile bases in Britain; in particular they established a camp outside Greenham Common Airbase. Some campaigners also camped outside **AWE Aldermaston** and **AWE Burghfield**.

Grim's Bank (635 665) A line of earthwork fortifications, between 1.5 and 2.5 metres high, dating from ancient British times, if not earlier. It begins in Ufton parish, near the church, running westward through Padworth to near **Decoy Pond**. The bank, consisting of a fosse (ditch) and bank, is still visible in places. Several theories have been proposed to explain its purpose. One is that the word 'grim' comes from an old Saxon word meaning giant and was used by superstitious folk in medieval times who attributed the earthworks to a supernatural agency. A more commonly accepted theory today is that it was part of the boundary dykes erected in the fifth century by Britons at **Calleva Atrebatum** as a bulwark against the growing threat of Saxon incursions. Other earthworks of the same name are to be found elsewhere.

Grocers The village shop was an important part of local life, both for goods and as a meeting place. Nationally, they were first recorded in the late sixteenth century. Initially they drew their custom almost exclusively from the gentry, wealthy farmers and clergy – the poor making their purchases at markets and from travelling pedlars. The arrival of the railway in the 1840s brought the mass market to rural areas like Tadley and the surrounding villages. They brought a wide range of processed goods, at prices low enough that local people could afford; e.g. Huntley & Palmer's biscuits, Cadbury's chocolate and Pears soap. Increasingly, village shops sold tea and sugar rather than spices and silks and by the 1860s they had largely replaced the travelling pedlar. Evidence from census returns and trade directories shows the number of village shops increasing during the mid-1800s. There were three main types of shop generally listed in the census: grocer, grocer and baker and shopkeeper, the latter selling a wide range of articles. An invoice from **Goodenough's Stores** lists groceries and provisions, drapery and boots, brooms and brushes, china, glass, iron, tin and enamel goods, oils, paints, stationery, hay, straw, corn, flour and offal! Most shops were family-run, sometimes passing down through the generations. In the nineteenth century, in the days before refrigeration, housewives did their shopping on a daily basis, picking up what they needed when they needed it. From 1900 village shops faced increased competition from shops in towns like Basingstoke, Reading and Newbury. Town shops were likely to be cheaper, and have greater choice; many even offered a delivery service to local villages. Further improvements in communication, e.g. the growth of **carriers**, **bus and coach services,** and the motor car, and the decline in village population all contributed to the decline of the village shop. See Albert **Blake; Kimber's Shop; Lowe family; Oakdene Newstore; Pamber Heath Stores; Pamber Heath Post Office and Stores; Pearce's Stores; Thick's Bakery.**

Gypsies The name is a corruption of Egyptian to 'Gyptian' and hence 'Gypsy'. Gypsies had arrived in Western Europe by the early fifteenth century and presented themselves as pilgrims from 'Little Egypt'. The leader of a group would call themselves a Duke or Count of Little Egypt. At first they were popular with royalty and nobility, but by 1554 the death penalty was introduced for those refusing to leave the country. Its use later declined and by the early seventeenth century, gypsies were dealt with under the vagrancy laws. In 1543 Heckfield (Hampshire) parish register records the arrival of Egyptians in the village. In the nineteenth century they were more likely to be regarded as Romanies, vagrants, travellers, hawkers or pedlars.

It is not conjecture to say that some Tadley families may find their origins within such groups. Proof lies within local church and civil documents and in the framework of Tadley life in the nineteenth century. Although most gypsies were baptised in the Anglican Church many appear in the Congregational Church records. From the early nineteenth century, missionary work was undertaken among the hop fields and the 'Alton Hop Pickers Mission' was founded primarily to visit the gypsy camps there. It resulted, no doubt, in the conversion of many families. In 1841-61 the census enumerators were only required to group those people not living in houses together and so are often easily found at the end of the census records listed as living in tents, carts or wagons and with occupations commonly associated with gypsies: basket maker, tinman, hawker. From 1871 everyone was recorded within a street or lane and so such families became less easily traced. Tadley census returns also reveal names favoured by gypsy families, the unusual (Silvanus, Neptune and Nelson), the biblical (Elijah, Elisha and Noah), and the names ending in an 'a' often used for girls (Tryphena, Priscilla).

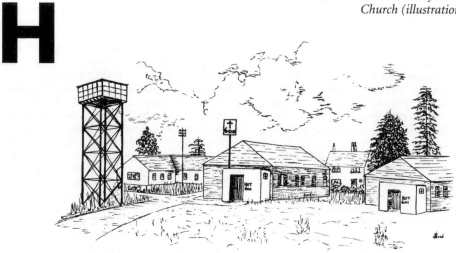

Huts 600 and 601, site of Great St Mary's Church (illustration by J Beck)

Hale, Maria (Martha) Purported to be the **Aldermaston Witch**. Whether a Hale by birth or marriage is unclear but she is reputed to have had a son and daughter who 'withered away', although there is no mention of a husband. A Hale family certainly exists in records of Aldermaston village. Maria, so the story goes, was buried in 1873. William Hale, (born 1779 died 1844), and a Mary Hale, died 1837 aged seven. When **Aldermaston Estate** was sold to Higford Burr in 1849 the sale catalogue showed Maria Hale and James Arlott as tenants of lots 596 and 597: two cottages and gardens. In 1842 the tenants of the same lots were James Arlott and Will Hale (the husband). The annotated map accompanying the 1849 sale document shows that the Hale lot was on the southern boundary of the estate near The **Falcon** public house. The remainder of the witch story remains pure hearsay.

Halstead House See **Bishopswood shops; Fort Halstead**.

Hampshire County Council Constituted in 1889, Hampshire County Council is responsible for a range of **local government** services to **Tadley** and **Basingstoke and Deane Borough Council** has responsibiliity for a further set of services. Services provided by the county include **education**, social services, **library**, highways (**roads**) and waste management (not collection).

At its inception in 1889 it was formally known as the County Council for the County of Southampton. Only in November 1958 did the county council agree that the name of the administrative county should be changed from the County of Southampton to Hampshire, the change taking place on 1 April 1959. See **Kingsclere and Whitchurch Rural District Council**.

Hampshire Record Office The main task of the Hampshire Record Office is to collect, and make available generally, records 'about the past' relating to Hampshire. There are well over 300 entries in their catalogue covering Tadley, Baughurst and the Pambers. These records include vestry, parish and town council minutes and records of the various churches and chapels including their original baptism, marriage and burial registers dating from 1659 to the 1980s. For example, the records for **Tadley School** include log-books and admission registers dating back to the school's foundation in 1876, together with 'a large portfolio containing mounted examples of childrens' work displayed at the centenary celebrations held in 1977'. Also at the Record Office are sale catalogues of some of the larger houses and estates in the area.

Records for Berkshire are kept at the Berkshire Record Office, currently at Shire Hall, Reading, but soon to be moved to new purpose-built premises in the town.

Hangar 5 Hangar 5, the Ministry of Aircraft Production (MAP) assembly building at **Aldermaston Airfield**, was built in 1942 and demolished in the early 1970s. The building was located at the southwest corner of the airfield, on the opposite side of the A340 road; near where the **Bishopswood shops** are today, hence the street name: Hangar Road. Production at Hangar 5 started in July 1943 and during the war approximately 500 Spitfires, mainly the photo-reconnaissance (PR) Marks IX and XIX and some fighter Marks IX and XIV, were assembled and tested at Aldermaston. Production finished in spring 1945 and the site closed in July 1946.

The Spitfire was designed by R.F. Mitchell and developed during the 1930s by the Southampton aircraft manufacturer Supermarine (later to become Vickers Supermarine). During World War II it was initially produced at Supermarine's factory in Southampton. After heavy bombing of the works by the Germans, Lord Beaverbrook, Minister of Aircraft Production, ordered production to be dispersed among a number of smaller units in southern England, one of which was Reading. Fuselages, details and sub-assemblies were manufactured at Vincent's Garage in Station Square; wings at Great Western Garage in Vastern Road and fuselages and engine assemblies at the Caversham factory. Final assembly, checking and testing took place at Aldermaston Airfield and Henley Aerodrome. Planes assembled in Hangar 5 were taxied out onto the testing bays immediately outside, then across the road onto the main runway where they would take-off for testing and then their destination. Parts were also stored at Baughurst Bus Garage (**Lattice House**), and parts for distribution were packed at the Boy's Club, Baughurst, later to become the Scout Hut (now replaced). See **Scout Hut, Baughurst.**

Hants & Berks Gazette See Local **Newspapers.**

Hare and Hounds, The (557 590) A public house in Wolverton built in the late sixteenth century and owned for generations by the Davis family. The last Mr Davis also ran a carrier service to Basingstoke and Newbury, using a 14-seater bus during the 1920s. It ceased to be a public house in the 1990s, becoming a private dwelling.

Harry's Cottage (606 611) Cottage in Winston Avenue, within the **Tadley Conservation Area**. In 1745 there was one cottage; by the early part of the nineteenth century there were two semi-detached cottages and at the beginning of the 1900s there were three terraced cottages. 'Will' Rampton owned all three, occupying the one nearest the forest. Will, one of Tadley's besom broom makers, lived to be over a hundred years old.

Hatchet, The (612 626) A beer (ale) house situated on what is now the western corner of Springfield and Silchester Roads, **Pamber Heath**. In 1881 the publican was George Bowman, aged 75 years. Two years previous, on 31 May 1879, an inquest into the death of his son was held at The Hatchet. Frederick Bowman age 36, who lived with his father, had left home with a pony and cart to fetch wood. He was found dead on the Ufton Road, probably as the result of a fit. Reference to The Hatchet is made in the **Pamber Parish Council** minutes as late as 1920. The house was demolished when the land behind was developed in 1975.

Hatch Cottage A Grade II listed cruck framed cottage in Church Road. One definition of 'hatch' is 'a fenced piece of land'. Built in the 1550s, making it one of the oldest buildings in Tadley, it was originally an open-hall type structure with a roof vent for fire smoke; the upper floor and internal walls were added later. The cottage was owned by Revd **Saulez** from 25 March 1882, later transferring it to his sons Alfred (23 years old) and Edmund (21 years old) in 1883. They owned it until July 1891.

Haughurst Hill A hamlet north-west of Inhurst. In 1256 the spelling is Hauekehurst 'Hawk wooded-hill' and this is reflected in the sometimes used, Hawkhurst. It is also suggested that Haughurst influenced the name/spelling of **Baughurst**. Haughurst was part of the manor of Kingsclere and in 1331 was the centre of a land dispute. Four years after the war with France the dean and chapter of Rouen regained possession of the manor of Kingsclere and claimed that King Edward III's foresters at Pamber had taken 300 acres of pasture and 100 acres of adjacent wood at Hauekehurst as part of the royal forest. The matter seems finally to have been resolved in 1335 when the parish connexion with Rouen was severed. In the nineteenth and early twentieth century Haughurst (Hill) was almost a self sufficient community. In 1880 reference is made to an infants school there and in 1888 the **Haughurst Hill Drum and Fife Band** was formed. On 3 October 1903 an independent mission hall opened. It has remained part of the Methodist circuit, but will close in Autumn 1999. During the 1930s and 1940s there was a shop in the hamlet.

Haughurst Hill Drum and Fife Band Sometimes known as The Baughurst Drum and Fife Band, it was formed in 1888. There were seven members of the Hutchins family amongst those in the original band. Like other local bands, it was a popular attraction at local fetes and public houses. It also took part in the annual **Hospital Sunday** parades. In the beginning the band had its headquarters at The **Pineapple**. It changed its name to The Kingsclere Drum & Fife Band when a majority of its members came from the Kingsclere area rather than Haughurst Hill; at the same time it also moved its headquarters from The Pineapple to The George and Horn in Kingsclere. The band closed, due to diminishing numbers, sometime during the 1960s and 1970s.

Hawley, Sir Joseph Owner of Derby winner **Blue Gown**. Born in 1814, Sir Joseph was a major Victorian racehorse owner, winning the Derby on four occasions. In the latter part of his life he founded the Kingsclere stables originally built on Cannon Heath but now at Park House. He installed the young John Porter as trainer. On Sir Joseph's death in 1875 John Porter acquired the property. Hawley House was named after Sir Joseph. See **Hawley Farm**.

Hawley Farm (595 610) A large Grade II listed, detached house in its own grounds on the corner of Church and New Roads. A stone in the brickwork states: 'JP 1823', possibly the initials of the builder and year of construction. It was previously known as Hawley House and in the mid 1800s was owned by Sir Joseph **Hawley**. In the late 1800s he gave it to his jockey, John **Wells**, who is listed as the occupant in the 1871 census. A portrait of Wells on the Derby winner, **Blue Gown**, is believed to have hung in the dining room at that time. **Kelly's Directory** lists Captain **Peat** as living there in the late 1880s, and Lieutenant-Colonel Lynden-Bell between 1903-07. By 1915 it is recorded as Hawley Farm, not Hawley House, by Kelly's Directory and was occupied by dairy farmer, George James. It is mentioned as being where the local **Hospital Sunday** parades finished. An annual carnival and fete were held in the grounds during the mid 1920s to raise funds for the new **Tadley Main Road Methodist Church**; See **Fairlawn House**; **Tadley Bands**.

Health care and medical services In the past, health care was very different from what it is today. In the eighteenth century only the upper classes and very rich could afford to pay for the medical services of those who were members of the Royal College of Physicians. Medical treatment for the majority was via an apothecary who had received his training by apprenticeship. From the late eighteenth century onwards provincial medical schools were established and in 1858 medical education came under the authority of the General Medical Council, making General Practice the rule. This is supported by the census records which show no evidence of doctoring in any of the local villages until 1861 when a practising physician Charles Mogg is listed as living in the Bishopswood area (Church Road). Isolated references from other sources help build up a sketchy picture. For example, in March 1879, the **Tadley School** headmaster's report notes: 'Medical certificates from Dr Fox, Aldermaston, respecting the large amount of general sickness in the parish during 1878, of a kind calculated to keep children from school.' Other than occasional references to midwives and monthly nurses, no other doctor is recorded until 1891: Henry Linden living at **Fairlawn House**. Whether he practised there or merely occupied the house is unknown, although the Hants and Berks Gazette for 24 November 1894 did report that he attended a Major Dunn who was injured as a result of his horse bolting. Dr Evans and his family followed Henry Linden at Fairlawn House in 1895 and is believed to have practised there until his death in 1898.

An established general practice for the area appears to have begun in 1902 with the arrival of Dr William **Langley** at Kiln House, Silchester Road. In those pre-National Health days, medical practices were bought and sold, rather like shops and businesses are today. Dr Langley purchased the practice on 25 March 1902 and continued working until his retirement in the early 1930s. There then followed a period from the 1930s to 1951 when local health care was provided from premises in Aldermaston, first by Dr **Beale** and then Dr Lionel **Holmwood** and Dr Geoffrey Wynne **Thomas**. During World War II Dr Holmwood also held a surgery in the front room of 46 Mulfords Hill and in the 1940s and 1950s Dr Wynne-Thomas ran a surgery in The **Iron Room** beside **St Saviour's Church**. There was also a surgery in South Tadley at 29 Main Road where Dr **Mullen** (a Little London doctor) saw his local patients on three nights a week.

With the advent of the National Health Service in 1948, medical practices could no longer be bought and sold. Dr Holmwood was the last doctor locally to have to buy his practice. In the early 1950s Dr Joe **Morland**, initially Dr Holmwood's assistant and then his partner, began to run surgeries from his home at Kiln House. He practised from there until 1956 when Wessex House, Tadley's first purpose built surgery, was built in the garden. At that time a great deal of home visiting was done and many women had their babies at home. Most of the accident and minor surgery was performed by the general practitioners. With the development of AWRE and consequent increase in population, the number of doctors has increased significantly, Dr Morland joined in 1951, Dr Geoffrey Bennett joined Dr Morland in 1956 and Dr Michael Speight came as an assistant in 1957, becoming a partner in 1958. Dr Bennett left in 1958 to go into Aviation Medicine. Dr Hudson joined the practice in 1958, having been both at school in York and medical school at St Mary's Hospital, London with Dr Speight. In 1960 Dr Hawken, also from St Mary's Hospital joined the practice. There are no accurate records of the patient population during the 1950s but when Dr Speight joined in 1957 the Tadley branch looked after about 7,000 patients. The present patient list is 19,650.

When Dr Speight joined in 1957, in addition to surgeries at Silchester Road he did sessions in Aldermaston Village and in the bakery at Woolhampton and later in the Gill Campbell Hall, Woolhampton. Home visits were done not only around Tadley but at Bucklebury, Frilsham, Tilehurst, Calcot, Kingsclere, Sherborne St John, Bramley and Ewhurst, and Brimpton and Crookham Common. He also attended The **Shrubbery** maternity home in Basingstoke for the delivery of patients of the practice. In the first full year of work after Dr Holmwood's retirement he did 22,000 miles visiting patients and the maternity home. The average annual visiting mileage for Tadley doctors now is about 6–8000 miles.

With the pace of expansion in and around Tadley, Wessex House became too small. It continued to be used until the **Holmwood Health Centre** in Franklin Avenue was built, by which time there were six partners in the practice. Land for the centre was purchased in 1972, plans drawn-up and building work started. The centre opened the following year and was enlarged and refurbished in 1984. In the early 1990s, the land, house and butcher's shop in New Road were bought from Brian Gooch, and redeveloped as the **Morland Surgery**. The Holmwood Centre and the Morland Surgery are now known as the Woodland Practice, which also includes a newly constructed Health Centre at Bucklebury.

The baker's shop and the Gill Campbell Hall, Woolhampton, which were both used for seeing patients, are no longer used. If a doctor wished to examine a patient in the baker's shop, the upstairs front bedroom had to be used. Another old practice which has had to be discontinued was that of leaving patients' medicines in the porches of various public houses such as The **Pineapple** or The **Falcon** to be more easily collected by patients. This was still done in the 1960s! See **Friendly Societies**; **Hospitals**; **North Hampshire Hospital**; **Royal Berkshire Hospital**; **Appendix ii**.

Hearth Tax Introduced in 1662 in an attempt to alleviate Charles II's financial difficulties. In the aftermath of the **Civil War** Parliament calculated that the King needed £1,200,000 a year to run the royal household and country during peacetime. A hearth tax had been used abroad with some success and so this supplementary taxation law was passed rapidly through parliament. The annual levy of 2s (10p) was charged to the occupant, not the landlord, on every firehearth or stove within a dwelling. There were exemptions in respect of those not paying the Poor Rate, on low value dwellings and in the case of ovens and furnaces used as a form of income i.e. brick kilns and hearths in alms houses, hospitals etc. The levy was paid twice yearly on Lady Day (25 March) and Michaelmas (29 September). The tax ceased in 1689 but records of each parish's assessment survive to give some indication of the number of dwellings, their value and occupants at this time.

Hearth Tax assessment (1665)		
	Number of dwellings	**Non taxable dwellings**
Tadley	115	43
John Hedges paid tax on 11 hearths		
Thomas Appleton paid tax on 11 hearths		
Baughurst	60	10
Richard Dicker paid tax on 4 hearths		
Pamber	82	27
William Omedee paid tax on 8 hearths		
Wolverton	42	5
Mister Sutton paid tax on 6 hearths		
Bramley	110	0
Inhurst	31	11
Ewhurst	17	3

Heath End One of several small settlements or hamlets which grew up on **Tadley Common** after 1750. It is situated in the north-west corner of Tadley parish. Heath End is a descriptive name that originates from the time when the terrain in the north of Hampshire was mainly heathland. It also defines the western end of the Parish of Tadley. Prior to the 1950s it was more closely allied to Baughurst. From the mid nineteenth century a self-sufficient community existed, having its own church (**Little St Mary's Church**), public house (The **Cricketers**) and industry. A large majority of Brown's bark stripping was carried out at Heath End rod yards. Besom broom making by the Wigley and Appleton families is recorded in the 1861 census and continued for over a century. By the beginning of the twentieth century a shop (Hodders), a blacksmith (Richard 'Dick' Kernutt) and a post office run by Mr and Mrs George Appleton completed the village picture all centred around Heath End Road. After World War II much of the area had radically changed. The smithy and shops had been demolished, together with eight other dwellings at the northern end of Heath End Road; two pairs of cottages on Baughurst Road, Aldermaston were also demolished. All were considered a danger to low flying aircraft as they were in line with the main runway of **Aldermaston Airfield**. Initially the occupants were evacuated and the houses left empty until a plane clipped a chimney whereupon they were demolished. Since the extensive **AWRE housing** programme in the 1950s and 1960s Heath End now sits on the fringe of Tadley town. See **Brown's Rod Yard**; **Heath End House**; **Heath End Village Hall**; **Mount Pleasant**; **Newtown**; **Telephones**.

Heath End House (582 622) A large house similar in style and appearance to **Inhurst House**. It was situated to the south-east of The **Cricketers** public house. Its architectural features would indicate that it was built in the early part of the twentieth century but reference to a Heath End House is made in the census returns. In 1861 it was occupied by John Hobbs, farmer, and in 1871 George Bishop, retired banker. In 1903 Major T.J. Bockett Dunne was resident just prior to the **McConnel family**. William Houldsworth McConnel remained at the house until his death in 1943. Following this, for a short while, the house was used by the Auxiliary Fire Service, followed by the WRNS (WRENS) and the Royal Navy. It was later converted to flats, but in the 1970s it was demolished to make way for Sheridan Crescent housing development.

Heath End Village Hall (581 620) The village hall for Heath End and Baughurst. The land it was built on was donated in 1921 by the **McConnel family** of **Heath End House**. They also donated the land for the scout hut and green. The original hall was a wooden structure, heated by hot water pipes and lit by acetylene gas produced in a shed at the rear of the building. Mrs Margaret Wigley was the caretaker for a number of years. The building of the original hall was financed by the Heath End Village Rooms Trust; many of the shares were held by villagers. The present brick-built hall was opened on 29 October 1988 by Her Grace The Duchess of Wellington, grand-daughter of the McConnel fam-

Photo: J.W. & C.A. Stevens

The Hollies, Silchester, home of Lt-Col. Karslake during the 1930s

ily. The fund raising committee for the new hall was led by Terry Hoyles.

Heather House (587 624) Standing at the heart of the AWRE housing estate at Heath End, Tadley. Heather House was built in 1951 to accommodate Dr and Mrs William **Penney**, the first Director of **AWRE**. During the eight years they lived there it was a centre of community life; few facilities existed in Tadley at the time and it served to provide a social and educational nucleus; e.g. sewing classes for wives of AWRE employees were held in the dining room. It was auctioned on 7 October 1965 and bought by Joseph **Michnik**. In later years mature trees screened its presence amid the housing estate. Fire severely damaged the empty house in 1995. The site was subsequently sold for the building of a centre for people with **Juvenile Batten's disease**. The centre retains the original name, thereby perpetuating its link with AWE and the past. See **Charcoal burning**; *see*ABILITY; **Penney Appeal**.

Hicks, Reuben Member of a well known local family, Reuben Hicks owned land along the banks of the **Bishopswood Stream** (New Road) where he grew strawberries and withies. When his widow, Ada, died in April 1997 she bequeathed £250,000 specifically to **St Peter's Church** They are remembered by Reuben's Crescent and Hick's Close.

Highbury Cottage (607 606) A Grade II listed timber-framed cottage in Knapp Lane within the **Tadley Conservation Area**, built in the seventeenth century. A thatched single storey building with attic and irregular fenestration, it has an exposed frame with rendered (upper) and painted brick-

work (lower) filling and modern leaded casements. Ship's timbers were used in the construction; it is believed to have been built by a ship's captain. On the east side there is a taller modern extension in the same style with an open porch. It was formerly known as 'Yew Tree Cottage'; a recent owner was a keen fan of Arsenal Football Club and renamed the cottage after their ground. Attached to the cottage was a 1.5 acre (0.61 ha) meadow which was Martin's Field (see The **Fighting Cocks**) and is now Mariner's Close.

Hind's Head, The (590 653) A public house in Aldermaston village. The present building was predated by an inn dating from the fifteenth century, owned by the De la Mere family who were later, in the time of Henry VII, joined by marriage to the Forster family. Most of the present building dates from the seventeenth century, with alterations taking place in 1650. For a time it was a posting inn with the main Bath to London road close-by. In 1800 it was in the possession of the Congreve family, then owners of **Aldermaston Estate**, and it became known as The Congreve Arms. The Hind's Head takes its present name from the Forster family arms. The village 'lock-up', at the back of the public house, was last used in 1865 when an unfortunate drunk was left in there overnight and was found burnt to death the following morning. After World War I, until his death in 1921, the brew made on the premises by John Wright was well known locally, the price of a glass of good ale being 2d (1p)! In a room adjoining the bar there is still part of the brewing equipment that was used until 1900.

Hollies, Silchester (628 624) A large house that stood on the corner of the junction of Kings and Bramley Roads and was occupied by Lt-Col **Karslake** in the early 1900s. Originally a two-storey brick house on which Lt-Col Karslake superimposed a rendered third storey, larger in area and supported on cast-iron pillars. It had a flat roof accessible by an outside staircase. A modern property, Acre House, now occupies part of the site.

Holmwood, Dr Lionel S (Bobby) Medical practitioner who practised from his home in The Street, Aldermaston. He purchased the practice from Dr Stanley **Beale** in 1933 for the sum of £4915 10s 0d (£4915 50p). Initially he was a junior partner with Dr Stanley Beale and then senior partner with Dr Geoffrey Wynne **Thomas**. He had assistance from other doctors during World War II, while Dr Geoffrey Wynne Thomas was in the army, but there are no written records of this time. After his retirement in 1959, he and his wife lived in Baughurst. See **Health care and medical services; Appendix ii**.

Holmwood Health Centre (595 624) Part of the **Woodland Practice**, the purpose-built Holmwood Health Centre in Franklin Avenue was opened in 1973. The land was purchased from the parish in 1972 and plans were drawn up by the practice partners. The land was transferred to the Hampshire County Council at the purchase price and the premises are now leased to the practice partners by the current owners, Basingstoke and North Hants Health Authority. The centre was enlarged and refurbished in 1984. See **Health care and medical services; Appendix ii.**

Home Guard Sometimes known as 'Dad's Army', the Home Guard's original title was Local Defence Volunteers (LDV). It was formed in 1940 to counter the perceived threat of invasion, particularly by German parachutists. Secretary of State for War, Anthony Eden, called for volunteers on the radio on 14 May 1940 and within 24 hours there were 250,000 recruits. Disbanded on 31 December 1945 after the war was over, it was re-established in the early 1950s to face the threat of the 'Cold War', finally being disbanded on 31 July 1957.

Locally, B Company of the 3rd (Basingstoke) Battalion Hampshire Home Guard was formed in May 1940 and disbanded on 14 December 1944. It covered the parishes of Monk Sherborne, Wootton St Lawrence, Church Oakley and Deane, with Silchester, Pamber and Sherborne St John being added on 3 June the same year. (Silchester, Pamber and Sherborne St John were transferred from the Aldershot Battalion and the Company was renamed The Park Prewett Company.) There is no mention of either Tadley or Baughurst amongst the records for the 3rd Battalion. The Silchester Platoon was under Lt-Col. John Lumsden Lunham and the Pamber Platoon was under Lt John Herbert Midgeley. The platoons were renamed on 8 October 1940 (No 1 Platoon: Silchester and Pamber Heath and No 2 Platoon: Pamber). On their disbandment these two platoons had a strength of 127 men.

Several posts were manned nightly by the Home Guard: Silchester, Little London, Woodgarton and Park Prewett tower (until 23 August 1940). There was also a Home Guard unit at Charter Alley/Ramsdell. Their main headquarters was based at Fir Tree Farm, which were owned by Frederick Stanley the principal organiser. Every Sunday, all members of the unit would assemble in the farmyard and carry out their drill. They also had a mess room situated in a building at **Ramsdell Brickworks** where every night two men would do guard duty, taking it in turns to sleep. The units used to hold their rifle practice in a claypit at the brickworks. See **Black's Cafe**.

Honey Mill Bridge (608 604) A bridge at the southern end of Tadley, below The **Fighting Cocks**, which carries the main A340 road over Honeymill Brook.

Honeymill Farm (609 606) Farm on the edge of **Pamber Forest** in Honeymill Lane. Possibly nineteenth century; refurbished in the late 1970s and early 1980s. It was also known as Keeper's Cottage.

Honeysuckle Cottage (606 611) A one and a half storey brick cottage in Fairlawn Road, within the **Tadley Conservation Area**. Built in the 1700s, it has a thatched roof and casement windows. It is thought that the cottage was built in two or three sections; the first was the chimney, the other being the one up and one down rooms, both built before 1750. Around 1800 the second downstairs room and upstairs bedroom were added, the latter being on a different floor level from the first phase. The cottage was purchased from the estate of Effie Saunders in 1992; Effie was born in the cottage in 1890 and died just a few months short of her 101st birthday.

Hoops At one time hoop-making was a significant local woodland industry. Until the early twentieth century most dry goods, from groceries and fruit to fish and gunpowder, were stored and transported in wooden barrels. The staves were held in place by wooden hoops fashioned mainly from hazel rods. The wood was split and shaved so that each hoop retained bark on one side. The experienced hoop shaver could produce 300-400 hoops in a twelve hour day. In Tadley, hoop-making was second only to besom-making in importance, but across the south of England during the last century it was probably the foremost woodland craft. In Sussex alone there were 368 coopers in 1871, and each barrel needed many times its own number in hoops during its lifetime because replacement was usually necessary each time the barrel was used. Apart from the increasing population and the concomitant increase in food consumption there was one commodity which influenced the hoop market more than all the others, namely sugar. From the end of the eighteenth century hoops were exported to the West Indies in increasing quantities for the sugar trade. Entries in a Tadley wood-dealer's ac-

Photo: J.W. & C.A. Stevens

Hospital Sunday parade (1922) outside The Fox and Hounds, Mulfords Hill

count book for the summer of 1864 show that 27,100 hoops sold for £20 0s 0d. Most of these hoops were sold to London merchants, an outlet that would have been uneconomic before 1800 because of high transport charges and poor roads.

All this changed in the late eighteenth century with the opening of the Kennet and Avon canal and the Basingstoke canal, each within easy reach of Tadley. The canals were favoured even after the railways opened in the 1840s, probably because of the higher transportation charges by rail. The industry died out in the early 1900s when iron hoops replaced the wooden type.

Hop-picking From Victorian times until the 1940s hop-picking for the brewing industry was a common seasonal occupation for local people. Tadley families would spend usually between three to four weeks in September hop-picking in the **Alton** area. They were employed at about eight farms around the villages of Bentley, Binsted and Isington. One of the employers in the 1930s was the father of Tony Holmes from Glade Farm who featured in the television series 'The Village'. School summer holidays were adjusted to allow children to go with their parents; in 1897 **Pamber Heath School** closed from 13 August to 4 October. Between the wars hop-picking was such a popular way of providing extra income that Tadley in September was described as 'a ghost town'.

However, hop-picking was not popular with everyone. Albert **West**, who went every year for most of his life, would do it all again 'twice over'. Mabel Fell on the other hand, who went as a small child

and later in the 1930s with her husband 'hated it'.

It was something of an adventure for those who enjoyed it. In the early years Tadley families made their own way into Basingstoke, usually by pony cart, to be picked-up by farm wagons from Bentley. These wagons had come up the day before to The Self-defence Inn in Church Street, where the carters stayed and the horses were stabled. In the morning the hop-pickers and their luggage were loaded-up in the inn yard. A stop was made on the way to Bentley at The Golden Pot, where the horses had a rest and many of the people a drink. Mabel Fell recalls the stop being more entertaining one year when a fight broke out between some Tadley men. From about 1930 lorries came directly to Tadley picking-up people outside The **New Inn**.

Once at the farms conditions were rather basic. Huts were provided for sleeping, each family having a partitioned section (the partitions did not reach the ceiling) with access from an outside door. A rough blanket spread on straw made up the bed. Cooking was usually done outside on an open fire with benches to sit on, and water was fetched in buckets from a nearby spring or tap outside the farmhouse. Mabel Fell remembers the sanitary arrangements, a screened hole in the ground, with anything but fondness. However, as time went by the facilities were modernised.

Everyone worked in the hop gardens for five and a half days a week, finishing at Saturday lunchtime. Payment was per bushel and based on the type of hop being picked. People from London and gypsy families also worked in the hop gardens, and for many years a gypsy horse fair was held in Bentley during the season.

Mechanisation and competition from foreign hops finally killed-off the need for seasonal labour from Tadley. By the middle of the 1950s only a very few people continued to go hop-picking. Nevertheless, while it lasted it was for many an enjoyable time and for all who went it provided a valuable additional income. See **Brewing and licensing**.

Hospital Sunday Prior to the formation of the National Health Service in 1948 hospitals were maintained by voluntary means. Many villages held an annual 'Hospital Sunday' parade to raise funds. Locally the event was a highly organised affair and considered a social highlight in the year. Held on the second Sunday in May, it comprised processions of local bands (as many as five) and church organisations. Villagers joined the processions as they passed through the parishes, walking as much as ten miles, collecting as they went. Despite the great clouds of dust this raised from the gravel roads, 'Sunday Best' was always worn. The day usually began and ended with a service and many earnest addresses were given. A fair and tea would also form part of the day's activities. Photographic records show gatherings at Silchester Common and Hawley Park where crowds were addressed by representatives from the local hospitals. See **Bands, Hawley Farm**; **Health care and medical services**; **Hospitals**; **Idenden family**.

Hospitals The provision of hospitals and places for the treatment of the sick is quite a recent development. At one time only the rich could afford medical advice; for the majority, until well into the nineteenth century, treatment was administered at home, with only the very severe cases being admitted to the workhouse infirmary where treatment was free. Few families did not lose at least one child from illness or accident due to the lack of efficient medicines. As late as 1900, 150 of 1000 babies born would die before their first birthday from common childhood diseases like measles. Medicines and medical advice was obtained from an apothecary or the local herbalist. At the beginning of the nineteenth century, medical science was still very primitive and the range of treatment that was administered in hospital was quite limited. For example, during the 1840s the only diagnostic aids available to doctors were stethoscopes and thermometers, while prior to the introduction of chloroform as an anaesthetic at the **Royal Berkshire Hospital** in January 1848, surgeons had only opiates and alcohol available to deaden a patient's pain. Infection after an operation was also a problem and it was not until 1866, with the advent of Joseph Lister's antiseptic treatment, that surgery could be attempted with any degree of safety. It is hardly surprising then that only 51 operations were carried out in the first three years the Royal Berkshire Hospital was open.

Matters improved during the century. Alongside the workhouse infirmary, voluntary hospitals funded by subscriptions from the wealthy were established in the early nineteenth century (The Royal Berkshire Hospital was opened in May 1839). Although in Reading, the Royal Berkshire Hospital was the nearest large hospital to Tadley, prior to the building of the North Hampshire Hospital in the 1970s and many local people went to it for treatment. The nearest comparable hospital in Hampshire was The Royal Hampshire County Hospital in Winchester. As a result of the Crimean War and Florence Nightingale's work more infirmaries and fever hospitals were built. The **Basingstoke Cottage Hospital** opened in 1879 and by the late 1800s there is evidence of locals being sent to these hospitals. Prior to the formation of the National Health Service in 1948 they were maintained by voluntary means: e.g. subscriptions and charity fund raising. Locally this took the form of **Hospital Sunday** parades and **Friendly Society** subscriptions. At one such fund-raising event, reported in The Basingstoke Gazette of 14 October 1882, Revd E. **Saulez** is reported preaching about the Royal Berkshire Hospital, '…never a week passed but some one or other was received from the village within its walls'. He went on to add, 'to Tadley it was more easy of access than the County Hospital… At Basingstoke they had started a Cottage hospital, and though it was an excellent institution it could not be expected to do half or quarter the good as this Hospital'. Also built in Basingstoke at the end of the 1800s, Cowdery Down Hospital in Basing Road was where the chronically sick were admitted. It was used until the North Hampshire Hospital was opened in 1974. See **Health care and medical services**; **Kingsclere Workshouse**.

Hudson, W.H. Nationally renowned naturalist who had local connections. See James **Lawes**.

Hundred The subdivisions of counties and especially important in Saxon and Norman times. The hundreds were probably established in the tenth century and lasted until some time during the Medieval period (eleventh-sixteenth centuries) when the manor and the church became stronger administrators. As a unit of government it formally existed until late in the nineteenth century. In 1894 the Local Government Act established District Councils which were the successors to the **hundred courts**. Well into the nineteenth century tithingmen continued to carry a stave of office in official processions. The origin and definition of a hundred is unclear and has several explanations: a) that each consisted of a hundred families or ten tithings; b) that it was an amount of land which contained 100 geld hides (a hide being the amount of land which could be ploughed in a year, 24-32 ha). The *Victorian County History* for Hampshire gives details of Hundreds and Tithings.

Hundred Court Each hundred had a Reeve who acted on behalf of the King and presided over the hundred court. Held monthly, court meetings were usually in the open at a place distinguished by some feature, i.e. boundary stone, tree or cross roads. Locally there was one at **Court Corner, Pamber End**. The court levied taxes, considered criminal offences, private pleas and grievances.

Hunting-BRAE Current managers of **AWE**, since April 1993. A 'GOCO' (Government Owned, Contractor Operated – arrangement), it is a joint venture company formed as a consortium by Hunting Engineering Ltd, Brown and Root Ltd and AEA Technology plc.

Huntingdon Connexion, Countess of Selina Hastings, Countess of Huntingdon (1707-91), financed the Calvinist branch of the Methodist movement led by George Whitefield, whom she appointed her chaplain in 1751. Services were conducted in conformity with the Church of England, even after the Methodist break with the Anglican Church in 1779. At the time of the **religious census** of 1851 the Connexion had over 100 chapels, including **Mortimer West End Chapel**.

Hurst Community Centre (576 623) See **Hurst Community School**.

Hurst Community School (575 624) In September 1957, amid building rubble and debris, 381 pupils were welcomed by the Headmaster Maurice Bound; 121 were first year pupils from local catchment schools, the remainder were second, third and fourth year pupils from Kingsclere Secondary Modern, Shrubbery Girls' School and Fairfields Boys' School (both in Basingstoke). The school was not officially opened until 16 September 1958. His Grace The Duke of Wellington, the then Lord Lieutenant of the county, commented in his opening speech that part of the land on which the school was built had at one time belonged to his family's estate. Since then the school has been extended considerably and in 1998 had 900 pupils. The second headmaster John Evans retired in 1982 and was succeeded by Ronald Bower, who retired in August 1999. Initially a secondary modern school, it probably changed to a comprehensive about September 1971, when the Basingstoke area of North West Hampshire went comprehensive. It became a Community School in 1979. Over the years the buildings and facilities, which are shared between school and community users, have been widely extended and modernised and are used regularly by thousands of people of all ages. The school and community centre employ over 200 staff. See **Education**.

Hurst Singers The Hurst Singers choral group was founded in 1976 by David 'Dai' Ogborn who was at the time a teacher at the **Hurst Community School**. After an initial meeting of interested singers the numbers rapidly grew and the choir was established as the Hurst Centre Choir. In 1983, David

left to take over conducting the Basingstoke Male Voice Choir and the baton was passed to Stephen Oliver, who still leads the choir. The Singers have a wide repertoire, ranging from such major works as The Messiah and St John's Passion, to Beatles songs. Over the years the Singers have performed at many charity fund-raising concerts, including annual participation in the Mayor's Christmas Carol Concert together with the Basingstoke Male Voice and Ladies Choirs.

Hussey, Fredrick See **Butchers**.

Hut 227 One of the **Aldermaston Airfield** buildings. In the late 1950s and early 1960s it was used as a temporary church prior to the completion of **Tadley Common Methodist Church**.

Hut 283 (596 625) The first Hampshire County Council branch **library** in Tadley was located in Hut 283, off Bishopswood Road. It was rented by the council from its owners, UK Atomic Energy Authority.

Hut 600 & 601 (590 621) Ex **Aldermaston Airfield** buildings in Bishopswood Road used for church services in the late 1950s prior to the building of **Great St Mary's Church, North Tadley**.

Hutchins, Monty Author of a series of five articles in the 'AWRE News', the first of which appeared in October 1984, describing his childhood memories of life in Baughurst and Ashford Hill. Born in Haughurst Hill, he worked at **AWRE**, retiring in 1974 and moving to Wales. See **AWE News-Link**.

Hutchins, Ted Ted ran a cycle shop in the 1930s, on the western side of Mulfords Hill, where he repaired bicycles, sold small amounts of groceries and also ran a taxi service. The shop, run by his son, Fred, continued as a bicycle shop after World War II until the 1960s and is now the music shop, Tadley Instruments.

Hyde's Charity, Silchester In memory of Richard Hyde. A deed of bequest was made in 1671 to 12 poor inhabitants of the parish, to be distributed on St Mathias Day (24 February) and Good Friday. Payment was derived from the rent and profits of a house and land known as Flex ditch. This endowment was revised to allow a wider range of grants to be made. The yeoman's house was demolished and replaced with a small housing complex, Hyde's Platt, off Little London Road. See **Charities**.

Hylton Court Block of flats in Bowmonts Road, built by the Royal British legion in 1976 and officially opened on 13 May 1978 by The Rt Hon The Earl of Malmesbury, Lord Lieutenant of Hampshire. Phillip Wallis (of **Wallis & Steevens**) was Chairman of the British Legion committee which inaugurated the building project. The flats were occupied by members of The British Legion, ex servicemen and/or their dependants. Since 1992 the flats have been managed by a housing association, 'Housing 21', and tenants are no longer necessarily connected with the British Legion. See Hylton **Flitter**.

I, J

Ice-houses Most ice-houses were built in the grounds of country mansions and were underground masonry chambers with a drain at their base and a door at their side. Ice was carted from a local source (e.g. a nearby lake or pond), rammed into a solid block in the ice-house and surrounded by insulating layers of straw which, with the masonry walls and the earth, provided sufficient protection from the changing climate to preserve the ice all year. The ice-house would be sealed until the summer months, when the ice was removed and used as required. In the following autumn or winter the ice-house would be emptied, cleaned and refilled. Many examples date back to the seventeenth century. By the nineteenth century, when many ice-houses were stocked with ice imported from America or Norway, even middle class houses had one. Many were abandoned during World War I when sources of supply ceased and there was no longer the staff to stock them. By the 1930s most people had forgotten that ice-houses had ever existed. There were several in the local area, some of which survive: **Aldermaston Estate; Baughurst House; Ewhurst Park; Ufton Court; Wolverton Manor; Wyeford house.**

Idenden family Kelly's Directory for 1907 and 1915 indicate that there was a John Idenden living at Heath End and later Baughurst, who was a skilled wood turner. His skills appear to have been passed on to Arthur Idenden, presumably his son, who was also listed as a wood turner in Baughurst in the 1923 to 1935 directories. Norman Goodland, local broadcaster and writer on country matters, said of the Idendens, that they made the long wooden collecting boxes for **Hospital Sunday**. Arthur had two sons, Frank and Cyril. Frank was born in 1907 and also became known in his adult years for his skills as a woodcarver, making small wooden pill boxes for pharmaceutical companies, and carved decorated boxes. He was also known for his skill as an artist, mostly paintings of the local countryside. Some of his paintings are still treasured by local people. Frank's wife, Lucy Ellen, who came from Birmingham, was well known as a piano teacher, teaching many local children. They lived at **Sarnia** in Winston Avenue and had no children. Frank died in 1963, aged 63, Lucy in 1987, and both are buried in St Peter's churchyard. Part of the stained glass window (on the south side) in **St Paul's Church** was donated by Lucy to the memory of Frank. The remainder of the window was donated by Mrs Eliza Ann Eden, Lucy's sister, to the memory of her husband, Percy Eden, and only son, John Eden, and of their parents.

Immanuel Centre, The (606 608) The **United Reformed Church**'s new Meeting Place, The Immanuel Centre was built at the southern edge of the graveyard. Intended for use by local church-based groups, it was opened in September 1995.

Impstone or Imp Stone (610 625) A stone on the north-side of the road at the junction of Silchester Road (Pamber Heath) and Pamber Road (Silchester), opposite Impstone Road. It measures 46 cm wide by 28 cm deep, with 30.5 cm above ground. It is not made of greensand as was once thought. It does have a bench mark and forms the corner boundary of four parishes. In 1280 it was called the (a) hyneston or hyrneston and marked a corner of the boundary of **Pamber Forest**. Several theories and legends exist to explain its origin. The commonly told legend claims that a giant called Onion, who dwelt within the walls of **Calleva Atrebatum** hurled the Imp stone to its present site. Another theory, based on some fact and from which it gets its name, is that it was a Roman milestone.

Photo: J.W. & C.A. Stevens

Inhurst House, Brimpton Road during the early-1900s

As such it would have been inscribed 'Imp (eratori)…' with the name of the then emperor. However, the nearest known Roman road from Calleva Atrebatum to Bath is a half mile away, which would indicate that at some time it was moved. It was first recorded in its present site in 1776. During excavations at Silchester between 1890 and 1909 the stone was dug up but reputedly no lettering was found.

On a map of 1817 it is marked as 'Nymph' stone presenting us with another explanation, which says it commemorates a visit to Silchester by Queen Elizabeth I in September 1601. While on her way to Basing House, she was greeted by a brilliant cavalcade of people who held a grand pageant and fete on the common in her honour. Elizabeth, by then an old lady, still possessed great vanity and the accomplished courtiers, Lords and Ladies, proclaimed with great flattery that it should be called the 'Nymph's Stone'. It is however an easy transition to 'Imp stone' or vice versa.

Inclosure Act See Enclosure Acts.

Inhurst Anglo Saxon Isenhurst or Ineshurst – possible meanings being Ines copse or wood or iron copse which may be a reference to a place where iron was smelted. Together with nearby Ham it was a tithing within the parish of **Baughurst**. Being in the north of the parish, they were not only geographically detached from the early village of Baughurst but had a separate identity being mainly woodland and common wasteland. They are referred to as a 'Manor' in their own right in 1298,

and given by the King to the Coudray family who continued to hold them until the sixteenth century. In the fifteenth century it is recorded there were less than ten houses at Inhurst. The two tithings passed to a number of families until eventually becoming part of the Wellington estate in the early 1800s. The gradual extension northward of Baughurst village has resulted in Inhurst being absorbed into its numbers.

Inhurst Brickyard (575 620) Clay pits are marked at Heath Row on the 1877 Ordnance Survey map and reference to Kiln House (now Unicorn House) and brick burners appear throughout the census returns for 1841–91. Thomas Clark and one son are recorded in 1851 but by 1861 he had five men in his employment, including two sons, one of whom was a tile maker. In 1871 Thomas Painton was employing six men and one boy. The kiln ceased operating in 1894, possibly as a result of Thomas Painton's death in 1892. see **Brick and tile making; Tadley Brickyard**.

Inhurst Farmhouse See The **Badgers Wood**.

Inhurst House (574 623) A Regency style house probably built in the late eighteenth or early nineteenth century. It is set in ten acres of ground and has a walled kitchen garden. A map of 1759 shows a large property in the vicinity but it is not known if it is an earlier building or the origins of the existing house. There is also a reference to an 'Academy' at Inhurst House in the 1740s. The only known occupants of the house have been the Kirbys from 1840 to 1905 followed by the Stokes who remained until 1946. They were responsible for the first extension to the house. Mr & Mrs Weiselberg occupied it as a family home initially in 1946 but, following the death of her husband, Anna Weiselberg began The Inhurst House Preparatory School in 1968. The coach house, stables and other outbuildings were converted for use as classrooms. It became an annexe of Cheam Hawtrey Preparatory School for a while but finally closed its doors to pupils at Easter 1999. See **Inhurst**.

Inhurst School (574 623) See **Inhurst House**.

International Football Club Started by Frank Harris (local barber) in 1955. The team played in the Basingstoke leagues and had some very successful seasons. In 1956-67 they won every competition they entered. They played in Bishopswood Lane initially, then had to disband when their ground was no longer available. They reformed for a short period in the early 1960s, playing at Ashford Hill until finally disbanding in 1964. See **Bishopswood shops**.

Iona (608 608) Originally two cottages existed on the site, which is in the **Tadley Conservation Area**. They are referred to as the 'parish houses' in the **vestry** minutes for 27 January 1853. The occupants at the time were Daniel Hunt and William Chandler and each were to be charged 5 shillings (25p) rent per annum. The said William Chandler was married to Maria who was purported to be the **Tadley Witch**.

Iron Room (603 609) A recreation room built of galvanised iron, next to **St Saviour's Church** (where Rectory Close is today). At one time it was the only place in the village where entertainments could be held. It was pulled down when Rectory Close was built in 1966.

Jackdaw, The (659 624) See The **Silchester Arms**.

James family Johnny James a blacksmith whose forge was on the Tadley side of Pamber Heath Road. The site is now occupied by Des Helyar's motorcycle showroom. A John James (born 1858), whose father David was a carrier to Reading, is first recorded as a blacksmith in the 1871 census. The location is not specified. By 1891 he is at the Pamber Heath Road site together with Drucilla and their eight children living in the cottage which still exists adjacent to the showroom. His son John (born 1880) and later his grandsons Stan and Louis continued to work the forge until its closure. In between shoeing Stan would carry out a hair cut or two while locals gossiped under the holly tree at the front of the forge. Latterly Stan had a cycle shop on the premises and also ran a taxi service. See **Blacksmiths**.

Jennings, George, Revd The minister of the Old Meeting (**United Reformed Church**) in 1828. George Jennings (1800-79) raised funds for the Chapel and started the first day school to be opened in Tadley. He was the pastor at the Old Meeting (United Reformed Church) until 1862, completing 35 years of ministry in Tadley. He died in January 1879 and is buried in the chapel burial ground. See **Education**.

Jones, Susan Susan Jones was a hawker who became a captain in the **Salvation Army**. She was said to be a native of Baughurst, but was in fact born at North Waltham as her family were travellers. She trained in Leicester and travelled far to preach, at one time in her career travelling to America. In 1891 she was the principal leader of revival meetings held at **Baughurst Primitive Methodist Chapel** but died the following year, aged 34. She was buried at Baughurst. See **Baughurst Methodists**.

Jubilee Centre (604 623) Community Hall on Tadley Common Road, on the edge of **Tadley Common** (near **Tadley Court**). Built at the time of Queen Elizabeth II's Jubilee, it was officially opened on 25 June 1977. It is owned by the **Turbary Allotment Charity** which also oversees the common.

Juvenile Batten's disease A genetic disease that strikes apparently healthy children between the ages of eight and twelve. It deprives them first of their sight, then all their physical abilities. Most sufferers die in their mid-twenties. Research on this tragic disease is currently being undertaken in The Netherlands. See *see*ABILITY; **Heather House**.

K

Karslake MA FBA, Lt-Col. J.B.P. Keen amateur archaeologist who lived at The **Hollies**, Silchester. Born in 1868, John Burgess Preston Karslake was educated at Eton and Trinity College Oxford before being called to the Bar in 1892. A member of London County Council for Paddington between 1910-31, he was Mayor of Paddington 1937-8 and 1940. He was also a member of the Metropolitan Water Board from 1903 and Chairman 1920-22. He joined the Berkshire Yeomanry in 1895, was a Lieutenant-Colonel in 1914, and served in France during World War I. Between 1930-38, he was President of the Hampshire Field Club. He lived in Silchester for 40 years and his personal collection of archaeological artefacts formed the nucleus of the **Calleva Museum**. He is believed to have had a series of interesting aerial photographs of the Silchester area taken by 58 Squadron RAF on 16 July 1928. See **Little London Brickworks**.

Kelly's Directory Trade and commercial directories are a major source of information about aspects of Victorian and Edwardian Britain, particularly when used in conjunction with census material. The major directories were Kelly's, Pigot (taken over by Kelly's in 1853) and Whites. They had a common style. Entries of local villages began with brief notes on the history and topography, followed by a listing of all the important local inhabitants and tradespeople. The earliest directory covering the local area is 1852.

Kennet & Avon Canal A canal linking the Thames at Reading to Bristol, via the rivers Kennet and Avon. It passes to the north of Tadley with locks and moorings at **Aldermaston Wharf**. The task of making the Kennet navigable for boats began in 1718 and was completed in 1723. Wharfs were built at either end (Newbury and Reading) and in the middle at Aldermaston. The man-made canal link between the **River Kennet Navigation** and the River Avon was established in 1810 (engineer: John Rennie) and the Kennet & Avon Canal Company formed. The company became prosperous carrying coal, iron, stone, agricultural and other products from Bristol through to London. In the early years, before the arrival of the railways the canal was busy, but its success was short-lived. The arrival of the **Great Western Railway** (GWR) at Aldermaston in 1847 offered a cheaper and more efficient service to London, Bristol and elsewhere. In 1852 the GWR bought the canal for £210,415; from then onwards trade was gradually lost to the railway and after years of neglect the largely derelict canal was closed to navigation in 1951. Restoration of the canal in Berkshire began in 1962 and in September 1986 **Aldermaston Lock** was officially reopened by the Queen. There is a small visitors' centre at Aldermaston Wharf. During its commercial existence local trades used the canal as a route for transporting their produce, besoms etc, to markets. See **Basingstoke Canal**; **Berkshire & Hampshire Junction Canal**.

Kent family Between 1911 and 1978 three generations of the Kent family were involved in providing public transport in the local area. At one time members of the family operated their services quite independently of each other and therefore it was not a 'family business' in the normal sense.

Edith Kent started her career at Ramsdell Post Office in 1888 and was subsequently a farmer's wife in Baughurst. She started her bus operations in 1923 when she purchased a small coach to run seaside excursions. Soon after, she began a bus service between Kingsclere and Newbury, later extending some of the services onto Basingstoke on Wednesdays (market day) and Fridays. Operations remained like this until 1936 when she acquired Vincent's Service (a carrier serving Ashford Hill). The fleet name adopted by Edith was 'Kingsclere Coaches' despite the vehicles being based in Baughurst. The colour of the livery was heather. At the age of 70, she sold out to Newbury & District Motor Services on 6 April 1937. Right up until that time she worked as a conductor on her buses. Edith had two sons, 'Fred' and William, both of whom started their own bus services.

'Fred' ran a service (Blue Bus) based at Charter Alley. The service, starting between 1924-6, ran between Baughurst and Basingstoke via Charter Alley and Ramsdell on Monday, Wednesday, Friday and Saturday. Unlike his mother and brother, Fred did not do private hire work or excursions and the business did not grow. During 1935 the service was taken over by his brother, William.

William 'Billy' Kent started a horse-drawn carrier service between Baughurst and Basingstoke (via Tadley, Pamber and Sherborne St John) in 1911. By the beginning of World War I the service, now mechanised, ran daily except on Thursdays and Sundays. Billy served in the army during World War I, resuming his carrier business on demobilisation and expanding into bus transport gradually during the 1920s. Like his mother, he experimented first with seaside excursions and private hire before turning to bus services. His initial service probably began in 1925 and consisted of daily services between Baughurst and Basingstoke. By 1929 routes covered Baughurst to Basingstoke (via Tadley) on a daily basis except for Sundays; Little London to Basingstoke on Wednesdays and Saturdays only; and Basingstoke to Newbury (via Baughurst) on Thursdays only. The service continued with various alterations during the 1930s, until Billy sold his interests to Venture of Basingstoke in October 1937. He retained a pair of vehicles and continued to operate private hire and contract work. World War II brought additional work and in 1946 with the return of son John from military service (eldest son Arthur was already working for the firm, having been exempt from military service) the firm reorganised and expanded to meet the post-war travel boom. Running under the name of Kents Coaches it continued until 1978 when it was taken over by Whites of Camberley. Their livery colours were grey and green. See 'Albie' **Blake; Bus and coach services; Wallis & Steevens.**

Kents Coaches See **Bus and coach services; Kent family.**

Kiln House (598 624) House in Silchester Road previously owned by Dr William **Langley** and later Dr Joe **Morland**. It is now used as offices by ACM Machinery Ltd.

Kiln Pond (627 633) Small pond situated in Benyon's Inclosure. At one time the nearby farm was known as Kiln Farm and had a lease giving permission to make bricks and tiles. A large four kiln complex was built to the north of Kiln Pond. The farm was known as Pound Farm before it was demolished.

Kilns See **Inhurst Brickyard; Kiln Pond; Little London Brickworks; Ramsdell Brickworks; Tadley Brickyard.**

Kimber, Ernie Born in Tadley in 1900 the son of Mr & Mrs Arthur Kimber who owned and occupied **Burrells Farm** prior to the Grants. Mrs Kimber lived to be 100 years old and as a young woman was a teacher at **Pamber Heath School**. Before his retirement Ernie was a civil servant at the Central Ammunition Depot, Bramley. In 1935 **Kelly's Directory** lists Ernie as an insurance agent. He made many contributions to the area: as clerk to the local Parish Councils, a post his father held before him, as governor of **Tadley School** and as a long time member of Tadley Silver Band and co-founder of Tadley Concert Brass. He was author of a book written in 1983, *Tadley During My Time and Before*, which recounts his memories of the parish and its people; proceeds from the sale of the book went to Tadley Concert Brass. He also wrote 'My Story of the Tadley Band and my 75 Years as a Bandsman'. Ernie died in 1988. See **Tadley Bands.**

Kimber's Shop (609 600) Records of a grocers shop at Pamber Green, run by Thomas and Mercy Kimber, first appear in the 1861 census. By 1871 it is listed as a bakers, and continued as a bakery until the 1930s. Thomas and two of his sons, Thomas and Frederick, are recorded as bakers in 1881, Frederick continuing to run the business until his death. The bakery closed, but it remained a shop until the 1970s, although by then it was no longer owned by the Kimber family. The nearby lane retains the family name. See **Bakers.**

King's Bakery (599 614) Bertram 'Bert' King established a bakery in New Road, in 1963, where he baked a variety of bread, rolls and cakes. Prior to this he had a mobile grocer's shop. The premises now form part of the Reading Warehouse complex. See **Bakers.**

Kingsclere and Whitchurch Rural District Council The local government body responsible for Tadley until it was replaced by **Basingstoke and Deane Borough Council** in 1974. The Kingsclere and Whitchurch Rural District Council grew out of the earlier Board of Guardians and began in 1898. Its area consisted of the parishes of Kingsclere, Baughurst, Tadley, Ecchinswell and Sydmonton, Burghclere, Newtown, Highclere, East Woodhay, Litchfield and Woodcott and Ashmansworth. Before 1914 the council was mainly concerned with public health problems, education and the expanding range of public services, Kingsclere being the first of the villages to be provided with piped water supplies by the council in 1904. The Housing Act of 1919 initiated the 'Addison Scheme' for grant aid to Rural District Councils prepared to erect hous-

Photo: J.W. & C.A. Stevens

Kimber's Shop making deliveries – Lizzy Kimber (born 1889)

ing estates. Thus Kingsclere saw its first row of council houses in about 1923. In 1929 a Parliamentary Act required a review by the County Council of local government boundaries, with a view to establishing more realistic units. Thus in 1932 Kingsclere was amalgamated with Whitchurch to form the new Rural District Council, with 31 members elected by the various parishes. The joint Council was committed to a variety of duties, the maintenance of highways, sewage collection, water supplies, housing, the operation of building by-laws, petrol and carbide storage licensing, milk and dairy orders and rating and valuation. This period in local government history was marked by a growth in the intervention into local affairs by **Hampshire County Council** and a decline in the powers and influence of the **Parish Councils**. The State had little say in local affairs.

However, after 1945 there was a marked extension of the government's powers, considerably reducing the scope of local government activities and responsibilities. The Local Government Act of 1948 transferred the responsibility for rating purposes from local councils to the Board of Inland Revenue. The foundation of the National Health Service and the passing of the National Assistance Act took away many functions from the Councils in the field of public health, which was their major concern early in the century. The Electricity Act of 1947 and the Gas Act of 1948 transferred the supply of these two services from local authorities to central statutory authorities and placed them under the ultimate control of the Ministry of Fuel and Power.

After **World War II** major housing schemes were undertaken and the Rural District acquired a national reputation for the success of these. From 1958, through the 1960s and 1970s, the relentless growth of Tadley increased the strain upon the sewage and rubbish disposal services. Large scale council house and private building was undertaken and the population was estimated at 7,000 people by 1974, outstripping every other parish in the entire rural district. By 1966 the government was preparing a wholesale reorganisation of local government. With the publication of the Maud Report it became apparent that the days of an independent Kingsclere and Whitchurch Rural District Council were numbered, as the total population of about 28,000 did not measure up to the 40,000 envisaged by the Government as the minimum feasible for a District. Discussions were long and complicated and the outcome was a decision to include the entire Rural District of Kingsclere and Whitchurch within the new Basingstoke District with effect from 1 April 1974.

Kingsclere Coaches Inter-war bus company serving the local area, operated by Edith Kent. See **Bus and coach services; Kent family**.

Kingsclere Poor Law Union A population of 2532 in 1834 was responsible for the choice of Kingsclere as the administrative centre of the Union (Tadley's population at the time was 603). The Board of Guardians, who were to manage the Union, first met in 1835 and their early concerns were the appointment of officials, establishing the new workhouse and taking over the responsibilities from the **Overseers of the Poor**. Relieving Officers under the new system had the job of deciding individual cases of hardship – usually admittance to the workhouse. The first one appointed by the Board was David Amey, at a salary of £80 per annum. His area included Tadley. He does not appear to have been universally popular as in September 1835 the Board of Guardians offered a £10 reward (payable on conviction) for any information about the tile thrown through his window. John Targett, a retired soldier 'equal to teaching children' was appointed temporary workhouse master in 1835. He was paid 15 shillings a week plus candles, fuel and supplies from the workhouse stores. Rates from Tadley were to help pay for the Union and the first demand, due by 22 August 1835 was for £37 7s 0d (£37 35p) from Tadley parish. See **Kingsclere Workhouse; Poor Law**.

Kingsclere Woodlands See Ashford Hill.

Kingsclere Workhouse In 1836 at a cost of £3500 the new workhouse was built on four acres of land in Kingsclere. After an extension was added in 1850 it provided accommodation for 300 people, but this estimate of poverty proved somewhat pessimistic: in 1851 there were 143 inmates and in 1931 only 42. The first permanent Master of the Workhouse, appointed in 1837, was George Githen on an annual salary of £60. His wife Isabella received £25 per annum for her duties as Matron. John Targett was employed as Porter and his wife Hannah as Laundress.

Once inside, people became paupers who were expected to work for their keep, in conditions meant to be worse than outside the workhouse. Without a welfare state people were often forced to seek help in the workhouse, and Tadley residents were no exception, as examples from the workhouse records testify. On 21 October 1875, William Saunders was admitted due to infirmity – as an 86 year old labourer, it was no wonder he was infirm. On 7 April 1875, Harriet Cripps entered the workhouse be-cause of a 'weak mind' (she was later admitted to a lunatic asylum).

Other Tadley people sought refuge in the workhouse because of illness or destitution. Desertion was also sometimes a reason for entry. In 1876 Thomas Richards, aged five and abandoned by his mother, spent two days in the workhouse until he was taken out by his grandmother. Ellen Dicker and her six children spent from January 1878 until February 1879 in the workhouse after desertion by her husband. The family of Charlotte Winkworth spent somewhat longer there: on 16 September 1874 Charlotte and her seven children entered the workhouse; on 13 June 1875 Charlotte and her baby discharged themselves; on 5 November 1876 the eldest daughter was taken out by her father; on 30 November 1876 all remaining children were taken out by both parents ('desertion' might well have been the only way a large family could survive in hard times).

A more enlightened attitude to poverty in the twentieth century eroded the role of the workhouse and in 1948 its function was taken over by the Welfare State. Finally in 1957 the Kingsclere Workhouse closed. See **Kingsclere Poor Law Union; Overseers of the Poor; Poor Law**.

Knight, Sidney A By the turn of the century the 'safety' bicycle was in general use and the sale and repair of them provided a good business for many local villagers. In 1907 Sidney Knight of Heath End was classified in Kelly's Directory as a 'Cycle Agent'. In the 1915 edition his business was listed as being located in Baughurst Road. These premises were bought by H C Smith in 1938 and from these modest beginnings **Smiths of Baughurst** grew. See **Brewer's cycle shop**.

Knight, Major Austen B Major Austen B. Knight of **Wigmore Farm**, Pamber End was the Head Air Raid Precautions (ARP) Warden for the Northern Group of the ARP in the Basingstoke Rural District during World War II. Mrs Austen Knight was the Red Cross Superintendent.

L

Labourers Revolt The name given to the widespread destruction of threshing machines and the burning of barns and ricks during the Labourers Revolt of 1830-31. Threatening letters sent to landowners and officials by militants were signed 'Captain Swing'. On 16, 17 and 18 November 1830, agricultural workers gathered at Thatcham and went out to destroy farm machinery which they felt was taking away their livelihood. They visited **Aldermaston** where, not content with destroying machines, they were reported as robbing cottages and small shops. At **Brimpton** a skirmish was broken up by 'a force of special constables, gentry, yeomen and faithful labourers under the command of a county magistrate, the Revd Cove'. On 23 November rioting and robbery took place in **Pamber**, **Monk Sherborne** and **Ewhurst**. A mob that had assembled at The White Lamb in Ewhurst was rounded-up, and 45 men and women were taken to Basingstoke by Sir Claudius Hunter and the 9th Lancers. Most were suitably admonished and discharged; among these was a Mark Baker of Pamber. The 1841 census records him as being one of twins born in 1806 and so a mere 14 years old at the time of the riots. Mark Wiggins, age 19 from Monk Sherborne was, however, sent to Winchester jail. Instead of improving working and living conditions, many families found themselves worse off as a result of the riots with the bread winner in prison or transported..

Laidlaws, Jack Jack ran a small haberdashery business, between the wars, from premises on Tadley Hill Road near **Allen's Garage**.

Lambden MBE, Joyce Joyce has seen generations of local children safely across the increasingly busy A340 at Tadley Hill on their way to and from **Tadley School**. She has operated the school patrol crossing twice daily since 1976. A fervent fundraiser, Joyce is the longest serving member of the **Tadley Memorial Hall** committee. She began in 1947 when she helped raise funds to build the hall. Recently she has been elected Chair of the Tadley branch of the women's section of the The Royal British Legion, having served as Vice-Chair for six years. In 1995 she was awarded the MBE in the Queen's Birthday Honours List and in 1997 Basingstoke & Deane Borough Council's 50 years of Community Service award.

Lane End Cottage, Brimpton Common (567 633) A four-bedroomed cottage in Brimpton Lane, with part-rendered and part-brick elevations under a Norfolk reed thatched roof. During the late 1930s Aneurin 'Nye' Bevan lived there. As Minister of Health in the post war Labour government he introduced the National Health Service in 1948. Later the cottage was owned for a long time by Baron Sieff of Brimpton (1889-1972), founder with Simon Marks of Marks and Spencer. See **Ghosts**.

Langley, Dr William Johnson A medical practitioner long remembered by locals. He lived and practised at **Kiln House**, Silchester Road, purchasing the practice on 25 March 1902. It is thought he retired sometime in the early 1930s, but did not sell the practice until 1 September 1937. See **Health care and medical services; Hospitals; Appendix ii**.

Lattice House, Baughurst (582 614) An office development in Baughurst Road. The original timber-framed building was built by the Venture bus company following their take-over of W.E. Kent's bus business in 1937. As well as a coach and bus garage, it was used for buses from Basingstoke that required garaging overnight. During World War II Spitfire fighter parts were stored there. The building is significant for its 'Belfast' roof. A Belfast truss is a technique for building a strong but lightweight wooden girder out of small sections of wood with a supporting lattice work and nailed joints. Very large spans can be bridged with this method of construction. The use of solid beams would be impossible because of the mass and lack of support. The beams of Lattice House, of which there are eight, are close to 90 feet (27 m) long. Lattice House continued to be used as a bus garage until the mid 1980s. It was then used for a while to store equipment by a hire company. In about 1987 a complete refurbishment of the building was carried out retaining the original roof as part of the new structure. The current occupiers are Wood and Douglas Ltd. See **Bus and coach services; Hangar 5; Kent family.**

Laundries In the past, before the introduction of domestic electricity and household washing machines most families did their own washing, traditionally on a Monday. There was also a demand for a commercial laundry service to serve the needs of local large houses. In 1851 Inhurst House had 12 occupants, and three local ladies record their occupations as laundress. They were undoubtedly occupied with the laundry, either at the house or in their homes. By 1871 there are five, of which four reside at the south of the parish, near Baughurst House and the Rectory. This occupation remains central to Baughurst; virtually no one in either Tadley or Pamber is recorded throughout the census, although by the late 1800s **Barn Close Laundry** was operational. By the early 1900s there were also two laundries at Heath End, operating side by side. Violet Englefield ran hers on a site near Ash Lane, while Hilda West (née Rampton) and her sister Ruth Westbrook ran the larger of the two, near **Little St Mary's Church**. Both were housed in wooden buildings next to their homes. The laundry near the church was still operating in the years following World War II. See **Tadley Court.**

Lawes, James The man on whom W.H. Hudson based the character of Caleb Bawcombe in the book *A Shepherd's Life.* James Lawes first met Hudson in Silchester in the spring of 1901. Probably as a result of lameness and infirmities, shepherd Lawes had left the village of Martin, Wiltshire in the late 1890s and moved to **Silchester** where his family are believed to have been local carriers for a time. He is known to have lived at Oakfields, Soke Road. He died on 26 March 1914, aged 84, and is buried in the churchyard at **St Saviour's Church, Mortimer West End** together with his wife Emma who died on 5 May 1921.

W.H. Hudson, the son of an American family who farmed in Argentina, emigrated to England in 1874 and earned considerable respect as a field naturalist. He wrote prolifically, but until the last decade of his life his work was little regarded. He received a Civil List pension in 1901. Many of his books are about the southern English countryside;

e.g. *Hampshire Days* and *A Shepherd's Life.* A lover of the New Forest, Hudson preferred southern Hampshire, but also visited Tadley, **Pamber Forest** and Silchester where he stayed at *The Pines.*

Library (598 623) Hampshire's Library Service began in 1924. The service to the Tadley area was provided by a mobile library until 1958 when the first branch library was opened. This was in Hut 283, off Bishopswood Road, and was open 10 hours a week (the hut was rented from its owners, the Ministry of Defence). A new prefabricated library costing £9,746 was opened on 27 September 1971 in Newchurch Road. It had a floor area of 1,500 sq feet (140 sq metres) and was open for 30 hours a week. A new permanent building (600 square metres), adjacent to the shopping development on Mulford's Hill, was officially opened by The Lord Lieutenant of Hampshire, Mrs Mary Fagan, on 12 October 1994. **Berkshire County Council** also provided a small library, called Aldermaston Library, to serve the AWRE housing estate in 1954. However in 1976 it was recommended by the Berkshire Library Service that it be replaced by a mobile library because of its low usage and it was closed soon afterwards. It was housed in a building behind the Franklin Avenue shops at the eastern end of Almswood Road.

Lighthouse Trust, The An ecumenical project that provided a mobile Christian drop-in centre operating in a double-decker bus, parked in **Budgens** car park. The volunteer staff sold refreshments and offered friendship to the customers while a play area was available for their children. The bus operations started in April 1991 under the chairmanship of Muriel Harrison. Granted charitable status in 1994, The Trust's purpose is 'to provide a point of contact and pastoral care for the community'. In 1992 it won a bronze award in the Queen's 40th Anniversary Awards. The bus operations ceased in July 1999, due to lack of volunteers, however, the Trust is to continue.

Link, The A monthly inter-denominational church magazine started in September 1993. It serves the parish of St Mary's, North Tadley, and the Methodist Church congregations at Tadley Common and Main Road. 'St Mary's Review' ceased publication at the same time as 'The Link' was started.

Lion, The, Ramsdell (588 575) Shown on the 1817 Ordnance Survey map, the cottage, which was previously the public house, or beer house, is situated opposite the recreational ground.

Lion, The, Stoney Heath (581 580) A large impressive red brick, eighteenth century, building with attractive arched windows and door. It was once a coaching inn, becoming a guest house, known as Hollybush Farm, in the early 1900s.

Lipscombe family The family lived in Back Lane, in a double fronted house similar to The **Manse**. The house had no name. There was also a fine brick-built barn and well on the land. They kept various

Photo: Burnham Copse WI Scrapbook

Tadley Library situated in Hut 283 between 1958 and 1971

animals including cows and horses. Alfred Lipscombe ran a local carrier business from the property. In **Kelly's Directory** he is listed between 1899 and 1915, running a service to Basingstoke on Wednesdays and Saturdays, carrying passengers and goods and also doing shopping for customers. The house and grounds were eventually sold to a builder and in 1973-4, after lying empty for several years, were developed as Churchill Close. See **Carriers**.

Lisney, James Concert pianist James Lisney was born in Reading in 1962 and lived at Heath End. He attended **Burnham Copse Infant** and **Junior Schools**, progressing to the **Hurst Community School** and Queen Mary's College. His Infant teacher, Miss Whittaker, noticed his musical talent and he started piano lessons in 1966 with Jean Murphy. While at the Primary School he received a County Exhibition grant to continue his studies. He started lessons with Phylis Sellick OBE in 1974, gaining his Diploma at the age of seventeen and winning a Scholarship to the Royal College of Music. There he won all the major prizes open to him and he subsequently made a successful formal debut at the Wigmore Hall, London. In 1988 he was selected for representation by the Young Concert Artist's Trust and from this point he has sustained an international career performing with major orchestras, producing several highly regarded CDs and collaborating with many leading artists.

Little London (623 594) Village about 3 miles (5 km) south-east of Tadley in the civil parish of Pamber, but which since 1976 has been in the ecclesiastical parish of Bramley. One suggestion for its name

is that it could have been originally occupied by Londoners escaping the plague – it would have been remote and wooded at a distance not too far from London to where they might return at a later date. However, it is more likely to be a corruption of the Little Loddon river, a name sometimes applied to Bow Brook. It was once only a small hamlet comprising a few farms, two public houses and farm workers' dwellings. It has changed little over the years except to have a greater concentration of houses along the Silchester Road. In Victorian times much of the land was owned by the Rt Hon William Wither Bramston Beach of Oakley Hall. Beach Crescent is now the only memory of this once important country family. See **Beach family**; **Little London Brickworks**; **Little London Primitive Methodist Chapel**; **Post Offices**; **St Stephen's Church**.

Little London Brickworks (621 591) As a result of deep ploughing in the autumn of 1926, a brick and tile kiln and brick field were discovered at Little London, north east of The **Plough**. Fragments of Roman bricks and tiles were brought to the surface, which prompted Lieutenant-Colonel J.B.P. **Karslake** to dig trenches on the site. They covered a wide area and the inscription on some indicated that there was considerable building activity at **Calleva Atrebatum** during the reign of Emperor Nero in 54-68 AD. Adjoining this site was evidence of a road by which the bricks made at Little London were delivered to Calleva. In the 1851 census it is recorded that the licensee of The Plough, Joseph Holloway, his son Daniel and others in the vicinity give their occupations as 'brick and tile makers', continuing a tradition that existed in the area for 1800 years. On the 1873 Ordnance Survey map two brick yards existed positioned either side of the road, incorporating clay pits and brick kilns. Very extensive clay pits remain near The **Plough** but no structure survives. See **Brick and tile making; Inhurst Brickyard; Ramsdell Brickworks; Tadley Brickyard.**

Little London Primitive Methodist Chapel (623 594) Built in 1867 this small red brick building with decorated barge boards, still stands, located on the west side of Silchester Road between the bridge and New Road. The land was originally part of the adjoining cottage garden and was purchased for £5.00 from Mrs Sarah Noyes. The last recorded meeting held there was on 10 October 1985. See **Primitive Methodists.**

Little St Mary's Church, Heath End (582 622) A 'mission church' of **St Peters Church**, situated on the south-west side of The **Cricketers** public house in Heath End Road. It was built at his own expense by Revd Dugald **Campbell Gill** in 1874 to seat a congregation of 120. Records tell us that in 1897 the church became the property of **Queen Anne's Bounty**. This would indicate that at that time the rector did not receive a very good living from this small parish and his income was supplemented by this fund. In later years it attracted good congregations until the building of **Great St Mary's Church** in Bishopswood Road which became the parish church of North Tadley. Latterly, it has been converted into a private dwelling called 'Church House'.

Little Windmill Close See **Windmills.**

Living Paintings Trust The Living Paintings Trust is a charity that produces tactile versions of well-known paintings, for the enjoyment of people with impaired vision. The 'paintings' are accompanied by detailed descriptions on audio tapes and coloured prints of the original works, so that the blind can enjoy discussions about the paintings with sighted friends. The inspiration for this work came from Alison Oldland, an Art History lecturer, who lived at Silchester House, Silchester. The Trust has now established offices and a production and distribution facility at Kingsclere and has given much benefit and pleasure to people with impaired vision.

Lloyds Bank See **Banks.**

Local Defence Volunteers See **Home Guard.**

Local government Before 1888 local government in Hampshire was undertaken by a wide variety of different, uncoordinated bodies. Outside the municipal boroughs (Winchester, Southampton and others) the basic unit of government was the parish, where vestries aided by parish overseers, churchwardens, highway surveyors and other unpaid officials managed local affairs under the overall supervision of the Justices of the Peace. Justices supervised the records of the parish **Overseers of the Poor** who had to collect local poor rates and apprentice poor children; they also ensured that each local parish surveyor kept his roads in fair repair. Meeting at Quarter Sessions, County Justices were responsible for suppressing poaching and administering the few national taxes (e.g. Land Tax and the better known **Window Tax**). In addition there was an assortment of 'ad hoc' boards and elected councils.

The Local Government Act of 1894 set up Urban and Rural District Councils and, in rural districts, parish councils. On 1 April 1889 the administrative duties of the Justices of the Peace were transferred to elected county councils, organised in a committee system. The Local Government Act 1972 altered the structure of county government in Hampshire. The former rural and urban district councils were replaced with 13 new district councils. Locally this meant the replacement of **Kingsclere and Whitchurch Rural District Council** by Basingstoke and Deane District Council. Following several years of consultation and negotiation local government in Hampshire changed on 1 April 1997 (Local Government Review). The major changes were the removal of Portsmouth and Southampton from county council responsibility – they became unitary authorities responsible for all local government services in their area. See **Basingstoke and Deane Borough Council; Baughurst Parish Council; Berkshire County Council; Pamber Parish Council; Tadley Parish Council; Tadley Town Council.**

Loddon Valley Lions The Loddon Valley Lions Club was chartered in 1975 as a member of Lions Club International, the largest voluntary service organisation in the world, there being over 44,000 clubs with over 1,400,000 members worldwide. The Loddon Valley club consists of about 30 men from all walks of life. They meet to plan a variety of humanitarian and community projects and, assisted by their partners, raise many thousands of pounds for charitable purposes, most of which is distributed locally in the villages within the triangle bounded by Newbury, Reading and Basingstoke. Organisations and activities, supported locally include the Tadley **Citizens' Advice Bureau, Hurst Community School**, fun days for people with disabilities, parties for children in care, clubs and outings for the elderly. The Lions also sponsor clean water wells and eye camps in Third World countries. Major fund-raising activities include Tadley **Treacle Fayre** (a revival of an earlier Tadley event, the **Tadley Revel**), the Father Christmas float, and the spectacular Wellington Country Park firework fiesta.

Lodge, John John Lodge, an international violin and bowmaker, came to **Ramsdell** in 1980 and aptly named his house (previously the village store), Fiddler's Folly. For the previous 16 years he had a shop in Twickenham where he restored and sold violins. He has been involved with music all his life. He was sixteen when he met his mentor Henry Hall, with whom he worked for some time as a copyist and arranger. He was trained in the army as a musician in the Blues Band Orchestra. He has been a professional musician for some years playing clarinet, saxophone, flute and oboe. He retired to the country to concentrate on making violins, violas, cellos and bows. In all he has made about 300 instruments and 100 bows but has never kept any. All his instruments are hand-crafted. Each tree is personally selected and stored. Spruce, which is used to make the top plate on the fiddles comes from Switzerland, Austria and Yugoslavia. Everything else is made from maple from the Balkans. His instruments have gone to China, Hong Kong, Australia and America. A number of gypsy fiddle players buy his instruments. His other achievements include lecturing regularly on his work, giving talks to the Italian Society of London and working for the Menuhin School. He has run classes at the Richard Aldworth School for the last 15 years, teaching instrument making and has a passion for helping young people to progress well in music and the making of instruments.

London House, Baughurst (576 623) House opposite the **Hurst Community School**; now a private dwelling but previously **Goodenough's Stores**.

Lowe family John Lowe ran a shop on the corner of Silchester Road and Broadhalfpenny Lane, in what is now The **Treacle Mine** public house. **Kelly's Directory** first lists him as a grocer in 1907. During the hop-picking season he would take a van of groceries to the hop fields around Alton, selling to Tadley folk working there for the season. By 1927 his son, Yorke, had taken over the general store. The business transferred to Mulfords Hill, to premises previously occupied by Albert 'Albie' **Blake**. This 'front parlour' shop was bought in 1945 by James Whatmore. See J.S. **Whatmore & Sons**.

Lowes Corner (602 614) The local name for the junction of Silchester Road with Broadhalfpenny Lane. It was here in the early 1900s that John Lowe ran a general store. The family name was perpetuated in Lowes Corner Hotel (now known as The **Treacle Mine**) which was owned and run by Mr and Mrs P.W. Monger between 1959-1982. See **Lowe family**.

Ludlow family A significant Wiltshire land-owning family, the Ludlow's links with the local area began when Joan More of **Wyeford** married William Ludlow bringing **Tadley Place** into the family. Sir Edmund Ludlow was knighted by Queen Elizabeth I at Basing House when she was making a Royal Tour of Hampshire in 1601. Henry Ludlow, born in Tadley in 1577 was the eldest son of Sir Edmund and inherited Tadley Place. His nephew was the Regicide Colonel Edmund Ludlow who put his name to the death warrant of Charles I in 1649. Henry was constantly reported in State Papers for failure to make payments, and failing to appear before the Council to answer charges for oppression. In 1607 he was fined £500 for perjury. On 14 November 1634 a Ralph Hillier together with 'a number of other poor inhabitants of Tadley' made formal complaint against him: that he had, over a long period, wrongfully detained wages, and had pulled down 10-12 houses, including the church house, in Tadley and had procured people to commit perjury against the villagers of Tadley who complained about him. This evidence forms a strong basis for the belief that the migration of the villagers of Tadley from a site near **St Peter's Church** to Back Lane was as a result of the oppression by Henry Ludlow. In the early 1900s it was said that his ghost haunted Tadley Place. See **Ghosts**.

M

Malthouse See **Old Malthouse**.

Malthouse Lane (607 609) Once part of the commercial centre of Tadley, it is now a narrow quiet lane. Ernie **Kimber** noted that it was formerly known as Doe's Lane. The only census entry for a person called Doe is in 1851 and 1861: George Doe, born at Padworth in 1784, was an agricultural worker and pauper lodging with an Ann Spencer. The only reference to 'Doe Lane' is in the 1891 census.

Manor House, Aldermaston (596 649) The modern name of **Aldermaston Court**. The estate was bought by Blue Circle Cement in 1981 who proceeded to build a new headquarters building (Portland House) beside the lake. The Manor House – the old 1849 country house – was converted into a conference centre with 34 bedrooms catering for conferences, corporate events, functions and weddings. Blue Circle sold it in 1998 to Richcliff Securities. See **Aldermaston Estate; Portland House**.

Manor of Manydown See **Baughurst**.

Manse, The (608 608) A private house in Manse Lane, within the **Tadley Conservation Area**. Until the late 1970-80s, it was the residence of the incumbent of the nearby **United Reformed Church**. Daniel **Benham**, writing in *Some Account…* says 'The Minister's dwelling-house having fallen to decay and become otherwise inconvenient, was, with the exception of a small part at the west end, pulled down and rebuilt in the year 1792'. In Victorian times it was clad in brick. At one time the single storey part on the west side was reputedly a butcher's shop.

Mariner's Copse (613 603) A copse in **Pamber Forest** reputed to have been named after Edward Marryner, a merchant living in Pamber in the seventeenth century. Mariner's Close is also reputed to have been named after him. See The **Fighting Cocks**.

Marks, Tommy See **Butchers**.

Marshall, Miss See **Barn Close Laundry; Scouting**.

Martin's Field (608 606) See The **Fighting Cocks**.

May and Co Ltd, John Brewers of Brook Street, Basingstoke. The company was registered in 1894. It was taken over, together with about 100 licensed houses, in 1947 by H & G **Simonds**. Locally, Mays ran The **Fighting Cocks** public house.

May Day May Day celebrations were held at **Tadley School** in the 1920s where pupils took part in the dances, often performed on the rectory lawn of **St Saviour's Church**. It also included the crowning of a May Queen. At a later date May Day was 'moved' to June and the name changed to 'Rose Day' in an effort to get better weather! See **Dancing**.

McConnel family The family occupied **Heath End House**, coming sometime between 1903 and 1907. William Houldsworth McConnel JP (born 1858) is believed to have made his fortune in the steel industry. Married twice, he is known to have had several children, at least two of whom died young. His 14 year old son George was tragically killed in an accident with an electric generator in 1908 and is buried at **St Peter's Church**. Another son, Merrick, was killed in **World War I**. A daughter was married to Major Knollys of **Pamber Heath**. William Houldsworth died in November 1943 and the contents of the house were sold at auction the following year. The family were strong supporters of the local community, donating land for the original Heath End Village Rooms, scout hut and green. In 1988 Diana, Duchess of Wellington and grand daughter of William, officially opened the new **Heath End Village Hall**.

Medway Hut See **Air Training Corps**.

Merlin See **AEI Research Laboratory, Aldermaston**.

Photo: J.W. & C.A. Stevens

The Mole (The New Inn) public house, Monk Sherborne about 1907.

Methodists Members of the Christian Church which derives from the eighteenth century evangelical movement led by John and Charles Wesley. Wesleyan preachers were very influential locally until the **Primitive Methodists** (1810) became active in the area in the mid 1830s. Primitive Methodist chapels were built at Silchester in 1839, Baughurst in 1845 and Tadley in 1859. A manse was built at Silchester in 1864 (**Ebenezer Cottage**) and by 1866 there was a **Silchester Primitive Methodist Circuit** stretching from Mortimer to Wootton St Lawrence. During the nineteenth century the Methodists split into several mutually disaffected groups, but the most important of these (including the Primitive Methodists and the Wesleyan Methodists) united again in 1932 to form the present Methodist Church. See **Baughurst Methodists; Baughurst Primitive Methodist Chapel; Little London Primitive Methodist Chapel; Ranters; Silchester Methodist Chapel; Silchester Primitive Methodist Chapel; Silchester Primitive Methodist Circuit**.

Michnik, Joseph A charcoal burner, well known locally for his business in Soke Road. Joseph was born in Poland but lived in Austria with his Austrian wife, Anna, where he had a timber burning and charcoal business. They came to England in 1936 and he initially worked at a site in the Savernake Forest, later moving to Tilehurst. He purchased **Heather House** in 1965, where he lived. It later passed to his son Henry. Joseph died in 1979. See **Charcoal burning**.

Mina Una Mai A village in Romania which since 1991 has received support from a village in Gloucestershire. The North Nibley Romania Team charity has two members from Baughurst, Vanessa and Peter Tolson, as treasurer and secretary respectively of the charity. In their spare time Peter and Vanessa organise clothing distribution and childrens' games.

Minter, Patrick 'Pat' A founder member of **Tadley and District Society**, he was also treasurer of the Society between 1990 and 1994. Born in 1929, he came from Southampton, as did his wife Hazel, whom he married in 1950; they had six sons. He was a chartered engineer and, during his career, manager of the drawing office at **AWRE**. Pat had been a Tadley Town Councillor, trustee of the Ambrose Allen Trust and of **Mothe's Charity**. He worked for REMAP, a voluntary group of engineers who design specialised equipment for disabled people, and was treasurer of the local group. He was joint 'rights of way' secretary with Roger **Searing** in the Basingstoke Ramblers Club between 1982 and 1988. This association lead to them publishing a local walks booklet, *Tadley Tracks, Tadley Facts* in 1982. He died in 1995. Minter Court, at the junction of Bishopswood and Hangar Roads is named after him.

Mission Churches In England, a mission church is a place of worship belonging to the established church, as opposed to the chapel of dissent, and put into an area at a distance from the parish or 'mother' church. It is a term that was common up until the 1930s and is still found in some organisations, e.g. London City Mission. In **Tadley**, as the centre of population moved north from around St Peter's Church, and the distances that had to be travelled to Sunday services increased, several mission churches were established (**Little St Mary's Church** and **St Saviour's Church**). See **St Luke's Church, Pamber Heath; St Stephen's Church, Little London**.

Mole, The (608 567) A public house in **Monk Sherborne**, previously called The New Inn.

Monk Sherborne (608 567) Small village between Tadley and Basingstoke. The name probably originated from a word meaning a bright and clear stream. In the twelfth century a Benedictine priory (**Pamber Priory**) was founded near a stream in the locality, hence Monk Sherborne. The village was mentioned in the **Domesday Survey**. All Saints' Church at Monk Sherborne is twelfth century, with **Queen's College, Oxford** as its patron. Locally, the College is still a significant owner of farmland, woodland and a number of cottages. The old marl-pit, commonly known as 'The Dell' is used by RAF helicopters for low flying manoeuvres.

Monk Sherborne School (606 581) See **Priory School**.

Monte Bello Islands Australian islands, the site of the first British atomic weapon device. See **Operation Hurricane**.

Morland, Dr Joe Medical doctor who came to Tadley in 1951, first as assistant and then, in 1952, as partner to Dr Lional **Holmwood** and Dr Geoffrey Wynne **Thomas**. Educated at Oundle School and Clare College Cambridge, he completed his medical studies at Middlesex Hospital, qualifying in 1947. He completed his house surgeon's job in obstetrics and gynaecology at the Royal Berkshire Hospital under Mr Peter Wheeler. Dr Morland lived first in Aldermaston, then with Mr and Mrs George H. Stacey in Hill House, The Green, before moving to **Kiln House**, Silchester Road where he practised from his home. Tadley's first purpose built surgery was built in the garden of Kiln House in 1956 and was used until the **Holmwood Health Centre** opened in 1973. Dr Morland retired in 1984 and moved with his wife, Nancy, to Dyke House, Padworth. He died in 1988. The **Morland Surgery** is named after him. See **Health care and medical services; Hospitals; Stacey family; Appendix ii**.

Morland Surgery (601 614) Part of the **Woodland Practice**, Morland Surgery, New Road, opened in 1989 to meet the medical needs of patients living in south Tadley, Pamber Green, Sherborne St John and Ramsdell. Owned and developed by the practice partners, the surgery is named after Dr Joe **Morland**. It occupies an old butcher's shop that had been run by Tommy Marks and then Brian Gooch. See **Butchers; Health care and medical services**.

Mortimer West End (641 639) In 1086 it was one of the two Silchester Manors but, unlike the main Silchester manor held by the Bluetts, it was held by Ralph de Mortimer who also held the Manor of Stratfield (Mortimer). By 1167 Mortimer West End had passed into the hands of the Bluetts. The manor passed via family connections to the Crown until 1564 when it was sold to the Marquis of Winchester. His descendent, John Paulet (Basing House) acquired Englefield and added it to the family land which then descended to the **Benyon family**.

One of the oldest buildings in Mortimer West End is at Coleshill, a sixteenth/seventeenth century cottage near the West End brook. It has a central chimney and the upper storey is part-timbered with herringbone brick infilling. West End Farm is of a similar age, the back of the house being Elizabethan with Queen Anne and Georgian additions. The farm drive can claim to be even older, following the route of the old Roman road. Most of the other older buildings in the village are eighteenth century. See **Englefield Estate**.

Mortimer West End Chapel (616 642) The congregational chapel at Mortimer West End was born out of the great evangelical revival in the late eighteeneth century. John Whitburn, a turf-cutter and convert who held services in his cottage, found it was too small to accommodate the people of Mortimer Heath, who were described by a writer at the time as 'profane and atrocious'. In 1798 John **Mulford** financed the building of the chapel on land provided by John Whitburn. The Bishop of Winchester licensed the premises for worship on 21 September of that year. By the 1820s, 300 people from as far as Thatcham, Bucklebury and Sherborne St John regularly attended services at the chapel. In 1826 the Reading Evangelical Society, which had been responsible for it, ceased to exist and the surviving trustees handed it over for a nominal sum to the trustees of the Countess of **Huntingdon's Connexion**, whose property it remains today. One hundred years later, the church's membership declined rapidly and, in 1964 the trustees of the Countess of Huntingdon's Connexion decided to close the unsafe building. An outstanding example of rural vernacular architecture, with its arch-braced tie-beams and queen-posts, it resembles a small barn more than a chapel. In 1980 the Department of the Environment gave it Grade II listing and in 1993 it was fully restored at a cost of £250,000. Following a rededication service in September 1993 services are now held there again. John Mulford is buried in the graveyard.

Mortimer West End School (634 636) A church school, with teacher's residence attached, opposite **St Saviour's Church, Mortimer West End**. Given to the village by Richard **Benyon** the school was open between 1860 and 1929, when it closed because of lack of numbers. In 1883 the buildings were enlarged to accommodate 70 children. After a period as a store-house during World War II the buildings were renovated in 1958 and it became a private residence.

Mota Housing Association A self-build project formed by 18 **AWRE** employees. The houses, begun in 1962, were all in Conifer Close, Baughurst.

Mothe, William William Mothe lived at Oakridge Farm, Basingstoke and was buried on Rooksdown in a tumulus, known as Mothe's Grave. See **Charities**; **Mothe's House**; **Mothe's Charity**.

Mothe's Charity It is stated in the returns made to Parliament in 1786 that William **Mothe** by deed in 1739 gave to the poor of the parish of Tadley: 'three tenements under one roof for the poor, rent free'. In 1881 the Board of Charity Commissioners appointed the rector and churchwardens as trustees but in 1922 the responsibility passed to the parish council. The trustees in 1949 were Frank Gray, Frank Herbert Lawrence and Ambrose **Allen**. The present scheme dates from 1967, when Connie Fairey, the parish clerk, her husband Jack, Jo M. Dixon, Pat West, Roger **Searing** and others negotiated a way to revive the charity. At that time the buildings were derelict, there was only one resident paying one shilling (5p) a week and the land supporting the charity (with its rent) had been conveyed to **Kingsclere and Whitchurch Rural District Council** in 1949. The scheme involved the formation of Tadley Green Housing Association that now manages the five flats built alongside the one owned by the charity, all on the charity's land. The three trustees appointed by the town council also look after the Ambrose **Allen** Charity. See **Charities**; William **Mothe**; **Mothe's House**.

Mothe's House (603 611) The eighteenth century building on the north side of The **Green** was demolished under a clearance order dated 21 September 1966. There are now six purpose-built flats for the elderly on the same site. The official opening was performed by Mrs Mason, Chair of the Kingsclere District Council's Housing Committee on the 2 October 1971, with a descendant of William Mothe present, together with the Tadley Green Management Committee. Residents all hold £1 shares and are part of that management committee. See **Mothe's Charity**.

Mount Pleasant (598 622) Mount Pleasant was one of several small settlements or hamlets which grew up on Tadley Common after 1750. They were eventually assimilated into Tadley. Others included: **Heath End**; **Newtown**.

Mulford, John Born on 1 October 1720, John provided the money to build two chapels. One, on the east side of Oat Street in Basingstoke, was registered on 27 February 1784 by John and Benjamin Loader with the remark 'the present meeting house is inconvenient'. The second chapel, which still survives, is the **Mortimer West End Chapel**. John died on 7 January 1814 and was buried in the graveyard of the Mortimer West End Chapel, where his tombstone carries his Christian testimony. His name is perpetuated in the local street name, Mulfords Hill. Ernie **Kimber**, writing in *Tadley During My Time and Before*, recounts how John Mulford claimed to be descended from one of William the Conqueror's mole-catchers. On the day he died he was reported to have looked out the window and said, 'this is a fine day for the gossips to go about and say "Old Mulford is dead"'. More details of his life and testimony can be found in Daniel **Benham**'s book *Some Account…*, where his obituary from the *Reading Mercury* for 13 January 1814 is quoted. See **Dissenters**.

Mulfords Bridge (601 616) No longer a commonly used name, but the metal bridge still exists where the A340 road crosses **Bishopswood Stream**. Nowadays painted a grey camouflage colour, the bridge's previously white-painted railings, similar to **Bowmont's Bridge**, were a landmark to locals. See **Bridge House**.

Mullen, Henry Dr A Little London medical practitioner who also held surgeries at 29 Main Road, Tadley during the 1950s and 1960s. See **Health care and medical services**; **Hospitals**; **Appendix ii**.

Munro-Ashman, Dr Donald Medical practitioner who joined Dr Lionel **Holmwood**'s medical practice in 1949 and established a surgery in Bucklebury, which is now part of the **Woodland Practice**. See **Health care and medical services**; **Hospitals**; **Appendix ii**.

N

Nash, Arthur Local **besom** broom maker who was awarded a Royal Warrant from 1 January 1999:
BY APPOINTMENT TO
HER MAJESTY THE QUEEN
MANUFACTURER OF
BESOM BROOMS AND PEA STICKS
A. NASH
TADLEY

Although now renowned nationally and internationally as a Tadley besom broom maker, Arthur was born at Pamber End but his family origins lie mainly in Tadley. He is descended from a Saunders family, one of many that dwelt alongside the Tadley Common in the nineteenth century or before. The Nash side of the family can originally be located in Aldermaston, probably moving to Tadley in the 1850s. None at that time are recorded as broom makers. It is from the Saunders' line that the long tradition of broom making comes. Arthur's grandfather John 'Twister' Saunders is known to have hawked the family brooms in the London area. Travelling with a pony and cart he would be away for several weeks. The story told is that he successfully sold the family's work but that he also successfully squandered the money on the way home! As a lad of ten or eleven (1949-50) Arthur cut birch for his father, Arthur, but did not make his first broom until he was 18. There followed a period of National Service and other jobs in the building trade before broom making. The demand for besom brooms had almost died out by the 1960s when Arthur captured the remaining market and rejuvenated the ancient Tadley craft. He is now one of only a few remaining commercial manufacturers of birch brooms in the country. It is a fitting culmination to the centuries of broom making in Tadley that he was awarded a Royal Warrant, taking the ancient craft of besom making into the next millennium.

Nash, Bill See **Pig butchers**.

National Schools Andrew Bell (1753-1832) was an Army Chaplain in India when he observed how the children were teaching each other, so that when he had charge of an orphanage school with not enough adult teachers he taught the older children in the morning, setting them to teach the same things to the younger children in the afternoon. In 1811 the Church of England set up the 'National Society for educating the poor in the principles of the established Church', run by Revd Bell using the same monitorial system of teaching as the **British Schools**. The National Schools were linked with the Church of England while the British Schools were linked with the Non-conformist Churches. See **Education; Appendix i.**

Nature Reserves See **Ashford Hill Meadows; Pamber Forest; Ron Ward's Meadow; SSSI; Wildlife.**

New Inn, Baughurst (579 619) See The **Badgers Wood.**

New Inn, Monk Sherborne (608 868)An old name for The **Mole** public house.

New Inn, Tadley (604 615) Public house at Tadley Bottom (Rowan Road). Evidence from the census shows that it was in use as a beer shop in 1851, run by James Woods whose occupation was given as 'Farmer of 2 acres (0.8 ha)'. From the 1850s onwards it was used as a meeting point for local people going hop-picking, when the outside of the building was decorated with bunting and floral displays. In 1891 George Nash, the licensee, resided there with his wife Ellen, their seven children and his parents. By 1915 George Wetherall is the beer retailer and subsequently Percy Saunders. For a time it was owned by Blatch's Theale Brewery until 1964.

The New Inn, Rowan Road, with George Wetherall, publican between 1915-31, standing on the left.

Photo: Albert Wset

During the 1950s and 1960s, there was an adjoining coalyard run by the publican, Bill Saunders.

Newbury District Council See Berkshire County Council.

Newbury Weekly News See Local **newspapers**.

Newspapers, Local Stamp-duty on newspapers in the pre-1855 period tended to restrict readership to the rich and educated. and newspapers generally contained little, if any, 'rural news'. The repealing of stamp-duty, coupled with improved public literacy, the development of printing machinery and railway distribution systems, opened up the way for mass 'local' newspapers. Coverage of Tadley and surrounding district events was split between three 'newspaper towns': Basingstoke, Newbury and Reading.

The *Basingstoke Gazette* began as the *Hants and Berks Gazette and Basingstoke Journal* on Saturday 5 January 1878. In the 700 word editorial of its first edition the editor asks why Basingstoke with a population of 6000 inhabitants, a large market and a good agricultural district should not have a local family newspaper. After some 91 years it was decided to change the title name and on Friday 3 October 1969 it appeared as The *Basingstoke Gazette incorporating the Hants and Berks Gazette and Basingstoke Journal*. This change of name was '…because we felt that a newspaper based in an expanding town like Basingstoke should have that name

prominently displayed'. (Basingstoke Library holds microfilm copies of the 'Gazette'). Since March 1992 the *Gazette* has also published the *Tadley Times*, a local monthly newspaper. It usually contains 12 pages, covering news and information particular to Tadley and the surrounding areas. The masthead lists: Tadley, Baughurst, Heath End, Silchester, Pamber, Bramley, Sherfield on Loddon, Kingsclere, Sherborne St John. Archives of the paper are kept by Tadley Library.

Through the years there have been several other local newspapers published in Basingstoke. The *Basingstoke Standard* was in production from 1882 to 1885; no copies are kept locally, although original copies can be seen at the British Library's Newspaper Library at Colindale, London. The *Basingstoke Observer and Basingstoke News*, boasting to be a county and local newspaper and general advertiser, first appeared on Saturday 28 February 1903, ceasing publication on Saturday 11 March 1916. A microfilm copy of the paper is available in Basingstoke Library.

Another *Basingstoke Standard*, later to be called *Basingstoke and Hart Standard*, was a mid-week 'freebie' which ran as an offshoot of the *Reading Standard* from 22 March 1984 until 2 July 1987. Basingstoke Library holds original copies of this newspaper.

The *Newbury Weekly News* covers news and events in west Berkshire and north Hampshire and has been in production since 1867. Many local events missed by the *Basingstoke Gazette* have been reported in the *Newbury Weekly News*. During the 1950s and 1960s it had a section titled 'Tadley Topics'. Microfilm copies of this newspaper are available for viewing at Newbury Library.

The *Reading Mercury*, first published in 1723 by two printers, William Parkes and David Skinner, is the earliest local newspaper. One of the oldest in the country (it predates *The Times*), its original subtitle was The *Weekly Entertainer*. There was, however, very little really local news about the villages, on the assumption that the literate and educated lived in or near to the main towns of Reading and Newbury. It was not until post-1860 that it carried more local news. The *Berkshire Chronicle* came onto the streets in 1825 and ran alongside its rival the *Reading Mercury* even after 1913 when both papers came under the same ownership. The *Reading Mercury* survived into the last quarter of the twentieth century. The *Berkshire Chronicle* is still in circulation today as the weekly *Reading Chronicle*. The *Reading Standard*, originating in 1887, was bought out by Lord Thompson in the 1960s who 'froze' the title of the 'Standard' and produced the daily *Reading Evening Post* in its place. He resurrected the *Reading Standard* in the 1980s as a weekly 'freebie'. The *Reading Express* was a short-lived paper and was only published between 1879 and 1884. The same publisher also produced a local *Newbury Express*. Copies of most of these Reading newspapers are available on microfilm in Reading Local Studies Library.

Newtown (594 621) Newtown was one of several small settlements or hamlets which grew-up on Tadley Common after 1750. They were eventually assimilated into Tadley. Others included: **Heath End**; **Mount Pleasant**.

Nicknames A word derived from an 'eke name' meaning an alternative. The limited range of Christian names in earlier times and the tradition of repeating names within the same family often led to people being 'characterised' by a nickname; e.g. Alfred 'Stumpy' West and Arthur 'Ticky' **Saunders**. While some nicknames are characteristic of certain regions, others probably began as a descriptive trade name but soon became the hereditary surname; e.g. Monger, Smith, Cooper, Thatcher, all of which were and are still to be found in Tadley and the surrounding villages. See **Broomyards**.

North Hampshire Hospital (612 538) Originally known as Basingstoke District Hospital, North Hampshire Hospital was built in the 1970s in the grounds of Park Prewett Hospital. Planning for it began in the 1960s, coinciding with the rapid growth of the town. The maternity wing was built in 1970, alongside the proposed site of the main hospital. It was known as a mini hospital until the main one was opened. The first patients were admitted to the main hospital in March 1974 and it was officially opened by HRH Princess Alexandra on 5 November 1975. See Ruth **Ellis**; **Health care and medical services**; **Hospitals**.

Nymph Stone (617 625) Another name for the **Impstone**.

O'Bee MBE, Bob Born in 1932, Bob was a member of **Baughurst Parish Council** for 40 years and a trades union representative at **AWE,** retiring in 1990. He served on various local organisations, including the **Citizens Advice Bureau** steering committee, of which he was the chairman, and, later, on the management committee. He was Mayor of Basingstoke twice, in 1979-80 and 1991-92. During his second term of office he initiated, and became chairman of, the fund to build the YMCA hostel at Riverdene in Basingstoke. In 1996 he was Chairman of Baughurst Parish Council and received an MBE from Prince Charles. He died in November 1997. A memorial clock on **Heath End Village Hall** was unveiled on 30 May 1999.

Oakdene Newstore (609 618) Situated on the eastern side of Pamber Heath Road. There has been a shop on the site for most of the twentieth century. Originally run by the Bowmans, prior to their emigration, it was subsequently run by Stan and Nellie James who remained throughout the post-war period selling sweets and simple daily needs. More recently known as Oakdene Newstore, it ceased trading in August 1998 and the site redeveloped as a private house in 1999. See **James family**.

Oaktree Cottage (621 616) An eighteenth century two storey cottage in **West Street** with brick walls, a tiled roof and casement windows. The room nearest the road is known to have been used as a shop at some time, probably during the late nineteenth and early twentieth centuries. A Thomas (born 1831) and Sarah (born 1837) West are listed in the 1881 census as shopkeepers and continued to be listed as bakers and grocers in **Kelly's Directory** until 1903. Thomas and Sarah were Albert **West**'s grandparents and his father, Job, was born in the cottage. The adjacent original veterinary surgery,

now demolished, was used for smoking bacon and fish. Previously called Perry Cottage, it was sold to Mr Ray in 1961 when the **veterinary practice** was established. See **Bakers**.

Ogborn, David (Dai) Born in Swansea, he studied at the University of Wales before becoming a teacher at the **Hurst Community School**. He founded The **Hurst Singers** and organised many concerts featuring international artistes, including the late Roy Castle. He joined the Basingstoke Male Voice Choir (BMVC) in 1981 and is the longest-serving musical director in the choir's history. Founded in 1961, the BMVC has an enviable reputation, nationally and internationally, touring both Europe and North America. It has also raised thousands of pounds for charity.

Oil pipeline See **Pluto**.

Old Beams See **Elmhurst**.

Old House at Home, The (609 600) A small two-up two-down thatched cottage in **Pamber Green**, built in about 1780 and occupied by John Lambden and his wife Elizabeth née Barlow. It was extended during the 1800s when it became an ale-house. The keeper in 1861 is recorded as David Lambden. In 1881 John Woodeson and his wife lived there and by 1891 William Smith, his family, and two 'live-in' servants were the incumbents. In 1956 it was de-licensed and became a market garden owned by Mr E. Fiddes until 1960. In the mid 1970s it was given another identity as a guest-house. It is now a private dwelling.

Old Malthouse (605 609) A brick built house in **Malthouse Lane** opposite the **United Reformed Church** in the **Tadley Conservation Area**. It is believed to have been owned by the same family for 200 years. Information from the census and local directories shows that in 1841 David Penfold, a carpenter, and his wife, Sarah, lived there. By 1851, Sarah was remarried, to Thomas Allen, a bricklayer's journeyman. In 1861, he is recorded as the maltster but by 1871 Sarah, now widowed, is the beer seller and remained so until 1891, at the age of 74 years. Her daughter Esther Allen, later Elliott, continued to live at The Malthouse, initially, as a **British School** teacher and later, when it was also the general stores, as shop-keeper and eventually in 1899 the beer retailer. Between 1903 and 1935 her daughter Sarah Ann Youen Stacey (Tom Stacey's mother) was the licensee and shopkeeper. Photographic records show that as a general store it operated deliveries by horse and wagonnettes. See **Brewing and licensing laws**; Tadley **Post Office**.

Old Meeting (604 608) See **United Reformed Church**.

Old Meeting Whit Monday Fete See The **Walk**.

Old Mill, Aldermaston (592 663) A four-storied flour mill, built about 150 years ago, and originally part of **Aldermaston Estate**. The mill house is older than the mill, probably dating from the eighteenth century. It ended its life as a flour mill in 1920 and the original milling machines were shipped to Canada. Nowadays it is a venue for wedding receptions and other social functions. The Arlott family have owned and run it for the past 60 years.

Old Moor Cottage (595 602) The last old dwelling in Church Road, possibly dating back to when Tadley was centred on **St Peter's Church**. Ernie **Kimber** speculated as to whether it was a survivor of Henry **Ludlow**'s destruction of the village.

Old Place, The (607 611) Formerly called Yew Tree Farm, in Fairlawn Road, within the **Tadley Conservation Area**. Built about 1700, until recently it was owned by descendants of the original family. At one time a pond was located near the road on the north side of the property.

Olde Vyne, Ye A beer house in West Heath. In 1851 Charles Allen, an agricultural labourer, is listed as the keeper and in 1871 Sarah Kew, probably his widow, carried on the business. It continued as a public house until the end of **World War II**. In 1935 William Roberts is publican and in 1939 Cecil Beard. On some old maps it is marked as The Vine. It is now a private dwelling. See **Brewing and licensing laws.**

Oliver, Revd Charles N. Rector of Tadley (1883-92) who is believed to have instigated the building of **St Saviour's Church** and a rectory, a large brick building with stables, where 8 Rectory Close is today. See **Iron Room**.

Onion See **Impstone**.

Operation Hurricane The code-name for Britain's first atomic test device which took place on 3 October 1952 in the Monte Bello Islands, off the north west coast of Australia. Much of the scientific work leading up to the test was carried out initially at **Fort Halstead** and then **AWRE**, in conjunction with many other research establishments, including Harwell and Windscale. The important radioactive parts were made at AWRE. The aircraft carrier, HMS Campania, was the flagship and base for the operation, accompanied by several other warships. One of these, HMS Plym, which carried the device under its foredeck, was largely destroyed in the explosion. The national press of the day dubbed the event 'Penney's Dreadful', after William **Penney**, Director of AWRE. The senior AWRE scientist, who did the countdown for the test, was Ieuan Maddock. He was nicknamed 'The Count of Monte Bello'.

Operation Market Garden The code-name for the unsuccessful World War II airborne attack in September 1944 to take and secure bridges at Eindhoven, Nijmegen and Arnhem (Holland) and facilitate an early entry into Germany. The USAAF 9th Troop Carrier Command 434th Troop Carrier Group (TCG) flew Dakota C47s to Nijmegen from **Aldermaston Airfield**. Troops of the American 82nd and 101st Airborne and 1st British Airborne formed the spearhead. The operation is described in the film 'A Bridge Too Far'. **See 82nd and 101st Airborne Divisions.**

Operation Neptune The code-name for the initial airborne and seaborne assault phase of Operation Overlord on **D-Day** (6 June 1944) during **World War II**. Aircraft from **Aldermaston Airfield** took part. See **82nd and 101st Airborne Divisions**.

Operation Overlord The code name for the allied invasion of France on D-Day in June 1944. See **82nd and 101st Airborne Divisions**.

Operation Torch The code-name for the World War II landings in North Africa, occupied by the Vichy French. 39 aircraft took off in November 1942 from **Aldermaston Airfield** for St Eval and Predannack in Cornwall, where they picked up paratroopers from the 503 Paratroop Infantry Division before making the longest ever paratroop flight (1,500 miles). In the days prior to take-off all personnel, both civilian and military, were confined to the airfield without warning, creating alarm amongst local families when relatives failed to return home without explanation. Similar restrictions occurred prior to subsequent operations from Aldermaston.

Oppé family Mrs Pauline Oppé (born 1849, died 1940) was the owner and occupant of The **Red House**, moving there sometime between 1903 & 1907. Her husband, Sigmund Armin, a silk merchant, had died prior to her move to **Pamber Heath** and for the entire time she lived there she remained in mourning black. Both are believed to have been of German Jewish origin, becoming naturalized British citizens. By the time she came to The Red House many of her family of eight children were already in a profession and/or married, but often visited, and were seen and known throughout the village.

The family were well liked being both friendly and generous. Of the eight children only two were daughters. One was tragically killed, the other was confined to the house and on the death of her mother, removed to a nursing home. Five of the six sons attended Charterhouse School and two, the twins Henry (Harry) and Thomas, were killed in action during **World War I**. Thomas wrote a brief account of the **Civil War** at Basing which was published in 1915. Paul Adolph (born 1878 and listed in Who Was Who) became Deputy Director of The Victoria & Albert Museum. He often visited his mother and was instantly recognised by his height and 'red' hair. Ernest returned to live with his mother after World War I, during which he had been a prisoner of war, and John emigrated to Canada. Albert's son Armand 'Freddie' lived much of his young life with his grandmother and played with the local children. The daughters of James Smith, gardener to Mrs Oppé, remember going fox hunting with him. Aged 91 when she died, Mrs Oppé was cremated following a funeral service at **St Luke's Church** and her ashes were scattered over the flower garden of The Red House.

Osier beds Late nineteenth century maps show many osier beds throughout Tadley, chiefly in the Church Road and Bishopswood Road area. An entry in the Burnham Copse WI scrapbook suggests that 1958 was the last year that osier beds were cultivated along the **Bishopswood Stream** as the area was being redeveloped for housing, and foundations were already in place. See Reuben **Hicks; Willow osiers**.

Overseers of the poor These were officials chosen about Easter time at a **vestry meeting** of a parish to administer the **Poor Law** for the following year. In 1761 Thomas West and John Spencer served as overseers for Tadley; they were probably middle-aged yeomen, husbandmen or craftsmen, able to read and write. They were empowered to raise local taxes or rates to pay for poor relief in the parish. The rates, like today, varied somewhat. For example in 1764 Tadley resident John Haus paid 7s 9d (39p) and 6d (2.5p) for his copse, whereas Richard Harmsworth only paid 1d.

Help for the poor was given in various ways, often being payment for food, rent, clothing or the vague 'at his or her need'. Records held at Winchester show this variety. In 1760 George Appleton was given half a gallon loaf by the Tadley overseers and in the same year Mary Dibley received shoes, while James West was paid for 'nursing and providing small beer for Elizabeth Tigwell in her illness'. Mary Merywether was given wood in 1761 and later in 1763 the parish paid for her burial. The overseers also met the cost of transporting John Smith to Winchester Jail in 1763.

In 1769 it appears a Poor House was built in Tadley, as the overseers authorised payment of the following sums for its construction: wood and rafters 16s (80p), thatching 6s 6d (32.5p), bricklaying and nails 6s (30p). However it has not been possible to identify the site of the Poor House. See **Kingsclere Poor Law Union; Kingsclere Workhouse**.

Overton Town about 10 miles (16 km) south-west of Tadley. Ecclesiastically, until the mid-nineteenth century, Tadley was grouped with Overton and the rector of Overton was in charge of Tadley. Because of the difficulties of distance and absence of a rector it was usual to appoint a vicar who in turn appointed a curate to take responsibility for the church's affairs in the parish. In excess of 38 curates were responsible for Tadley between 1322 and 1878 when the first rector, Revd **Saulez**, was appointed.

P

c. Pope.

Padworth (612 633) The manor of Padworth had its beginnings around 956 AD when 'five cassates of land in Peadenwurthe were granted by King Edwy to his man Eadric'. Later it is listed in the **Domesday Survey**. The estate passed through various families, Cowdray, Littlefield and Forster, before Christopher Griffith (MP and grandson of Samuel Brightwell) became owner in about 1750. Christopher and his wife Catherine decided the house was not grand enough so they commissioned an architect, J Hobcraft, to design them a building more in keeping with the fashion of the day. Much of the older Tudor manor house was encased in the east wing of a new Georgian mansion in about 1769. In 1801 it passed to Catherine's nephew General Matthew Chitty Darby and, in turn, down the family to his grandson Major Christopher William Darby-Griffith, who, until his death in 1932, was the last member of the family to live there. Padworth House is still owned by the Darby-Griffith family although it is now leased to Padworth College, a private international boarding school for girls. Adjacent to the house is the church of St John the Baptist. Constructed in the twelfth century, its design is unusual. It has a semi-circular apse typical of early Christian architecture and Roman basilicas. A plaque in the porch records the burial of 300 **Civil War** soldiers in 1643.

Paine, Miss See **Barn Close Laundry; Scouting**.

Pamber Spellings through the centuries have been Penberga (1166), Pembre, Panber (thirteenth century) becoming Pamber by the fifteenth century. The first part of the Anglo Saxon word means 'pen' or 'fold' and the 'baer' or 'ber' means woodland, in particular swine pasture. The fact that most of Pamber was forested with common rights of pannage may have encouraged this interpretation of the name. Originally within the Royal Forest of Windsor, the Pamber land passed from the Crown to Sir William Paulet (later Marquis of Winchester) in 1535 and subsequently to the **Benyon family**, who still own what remains of the forest and small parcels of land within the parish. Other land was held by the Brocas family of Bramley from the fourteenth century and the Mores of Wyeford, later passing to the Hicks Beachs of Oakley. Some land in the vicinity of **Monk Sherborne** and **Pamber Priory** is still owned by **Queen's College, Oxford**. Through various grants and inclosure, land was also given to families in the neighbourhood, and, as there was no Manor of Pamber, inhabitants would have been known as free franchisers or freeholders. However, this land was later held in dispute. The land immediately bordering the forest to the south and west was the earliest settled area of the modern parish, evidence of which exists within the documentation of the Manor of Tadley (Wyeford) and **Pamber Forest**. The area to the north of the forest was, until the nineteenth century, like the rest of this part of north Hampshire, heathland and common covered in gorse and berries. Pamber Common, unlike Tadley, was not retained as part of an **Enclosure Act**. See **Court Corner**.

Pamber End (612 583) Lying within the ecclesiastical parish of Monk Sherborne, Pamber End denotes the end of the parish of Pamber and is more a description of an area than a village. Its importance historically is not immediately apparent but it was from the eleventh century or before, central to the activity around and within the Royal Forest. There are, to the west of the A340 at this end of the parish, some of the oldest buildings in the area. See **Court Corner; Elm Park Farm and Garden Centre; Pamber Gate; Pamber Place; Pamber Priory;**

Priory Church; Priory School; Queen's College Arms; Sims family; Wigmore Farm; Wyeford house.

Pamber Forest (616 618) A 478 acre (193 ha) area of ancient semi-natural woodland, Pamber Forest was designated a Local Nature Reserve in 1980. The forest is managed by Hampshire Wildlife Trust on behalf of **Basingstoke and Deane Borough Council**, who have leased it from its owner, **Englefield Estate** (Benyon Trust). Designated a Site of Special Scientific Interest (SSSI) in the 1950s, the forest consists mainly of oak with an understorey of hazel coppice. The structure of the woodland varies from dry open heathland through dense hazel and chestnut stands, to rich stream valleys lined with alders and willows. This variety of structure is linked both with past woodland management and the local topography and soil types: Bagshot Sands, Reading Beds and Plateau Gravels.

The forest is a remnant of the once extensive Royal Forest of Windsor, dating back at least to Norman times. At that time it was a royal hunting ground with sport provided by wolves, wild boars, wild cats, foxes and hares. Although the Norman kings frequently enjoyed hunting in the forest, they soon began to give away pieces of land, including parts of Pamber Forest, and by the time of Henry VIII, it was no longer continuous from Silchester to Windsor and the King only hunted in it whilst a guest of Sir William Sandys at The **Vyne**. In 1535 Henry VIII granted the governorship of Pamber Forest to Sir William Paulet (afterwards the Marquis of Winchester), but by 1610 the forest was no longer part of a great royal hunting ground, James I having sold it to John Waller. It was sold again soon afterwards to The Lord Winchester. The ownership of Pamber Forest thereby became part of the Englefield Estate, which passed to the **Benyon family** in 1745 on the marriage of Richard Benyon to Mary, widow Powlett Wrigte, and descendant of The Lord Winchester.

Gradually a partnership developed between the forest's owners and those who sought a livelihood from it. Although still used by the Benyon family for sport, e.g. pheasant shooting, increasingly the forest became a major source of materials for local woodland crafts (e.g. **besoms** and **rakes**). As well as supplying local trades, wood from the forest was also used to make packing cases for shipping chinaware from the Staffordshire potteries. A cycle of woodland management (**coppicing**) developed, with the owners, Englefield Estate, auctioning off areas of woodland to wood-dealers. Cutting of the woodland would be carried out during the winter, finishing by late March to allow sufficient time for the stripping and carting of the wood before mid-May when pheasant rearing began and the woodland had to be left undisturbed till the autumn and winter, when the cycle would begin again. This pattern of woodland management survived until the first half of the twentieth century when the woodland trades began to decline and by the early 1960s no coppice was being cut in the forest at all.

The period of coppiced woodland management accidentally benefited wildlife in the forest and it has long been known to both entomologists and botanists as an area of exceptional wildlife interest, in particular so-called ancient woodland species. These include wild service tree, solomon's-seal, primrose, yellow archangel and wild daffodil. Forty species of butterfly have been recorded, including the white admiral and purple emperor. Both roe and fallow deer can be seen in the forest. Common lizard, slow worm, grass snake and adder are also found in good numbers. However, the decline of coppiced woodland management has had a dramatic effect on the wildlife of the forest which had adapted so successfully to the coppice cycle; six species of butterfly became extinct, many plants became dormant and nightingales stopped breeding. Current management policies, which include a reintroduction of rotation coppicing, are aimed at providing a range of habitats for a variety of wildlife. See **SSSI**; **Tadley Watch**.

Pamber Forest Football Club The club was 'born' in the sitting room of founder, Peter Monk, who, together with Mike Smith and Ian Kerr, started the club in 1980. The initial years were dominated by heavy defeats, hard work and painful fund-raising. From the initial season with only one team Pamber Forest grew to being able to field teams at all levels from Under 8 to Under 16. The teams distinguished themselves in both the South Chiltern Minor League and The Peter Houseman League as well as being regularly represented in the Hampshire Cup. The home games were played at a variety of pitches including Bishopswood School, The Pineapple Field, Tadley Common and latterly at AWE RecSoc. The club's future was secured in the early days by sponsorship from local firms and the patronage of Charles Byart (Chairman of **Pamber Parish Council** and Mayor of Basingstoke), who is remembered by the Charles Byart Trophies, presented annually to players in each age group who display outstanding achievement. See **Calleva Football Club**; **Tadley Football Club**.

Pamber Gate (612 583) See **Aldermaston and Basingstoke Turnpike Trust**.

Pamber Green (613 596) The 'village' between Pamber End and the parish of Tadley which lies primarily to the east of the A340. In this case the term 'green' does not denote the typical village green but refers to what was probably an area of grazing land within or adjacent to the forest. In the nineteenth century it had its own nucleus of village life, supporting a shop and bakery, a public house and the parish pound. See **Kimber's Shop**; The **Old House at Home**.

Pamber Heath (613 622) A village situated one mile (1.6 km) east of Tadley, which, in the nineteenth

Looking west along Silchester Road, Pamber Heath, with The Pelican public house on the left-hand side

century, was also referred to as Pamber Common or Benyons Heath. It is the most northerly of the four 'villages' in the parish of Pamber, originally just part of a continuous heathland that extended from Silchester to Heath End. Pamber, unlike Tadley and Silchester, does not have its own common allotted as part of an **enclosure** award and because of the lack of a manor it was possible to form a settlement there. No evidence of buildings or crafts prior to the nineteenth century exists. Its growth was probably due to the need to find additional land and employment outside the perimeters of the forest. Many of its residents were employed by the **Englefield Estate** over a wider area of their Berkshire lands. As a result, Richard **Benyon** built a church/school, parsonage and houses for his estate workers in the late 1880s. It is now a densely populated village of less than a quarter of a mile square (0.4 km) but which, unlike Pamber End and Pamber Green, still supports a public house, shops and village hall. See **Brewers Cycle Shop**; **Ghosts**; The **Hatchet**; **Oakdene Newstore**; **Pamber Heath Stores**; **Pamber Heath Post Office and stores**; The **Pelican**.

Pamber Heath House See The **Red House**.

Pamber Heath Memorial Hall (610 620) The original wooden hall was built in the 1920s as a memorial to the men of the village who died in **World War I**. Probably an ex-army hut, it was erected on parish land between February 1920 and January 1921. The land at that time was occupied by Mr G Monger who agreed to give up 50 feet (15 m) by 20 feet (6 m) of his land '…subject to a read-

justment in the rent'. The current brick building replaced the original hall in 1975. Charles Byart MBE, ex-Mayor of Basingstoke, is credited with helping to establish the new hall. The Pamber Parish Rolls of Honour for both World Wars are hung in the main hall. See **Entertainment for village halls**.

Pamber Heath Post Office and stores (610 623) The first of the three long-standing Pamber Heath shops to be established. In 1871 William Stroud (born 1840) is listed as a grocer running a shop from the roadside-room of his house, Cherry Tree Cottage on Pamber Heath Road. During the 1930s and 1940s groceries were delivered to families in **Little London** and Pamber Heath. A true village shop, selling something of everything, orders were collected on Mondays and groceries delivered on Thursdays. The shop outgrew its premises and 'Barry' (Barzillai), William's son (born 1899), erected a purpose-built shop on the north side of the cottage. In the 1980s it was The Ice Box, a freezer food shop. It reverted to being a grocery store in the early 1990s and became the village post office for the first time on 3 January 1995. See **Pamber Heath Stores; Pamber Parish Council**.

Pamber Heath School (613 623) Pamber Heath (C of E) Infants School opened on 12 February 1881 with space for 93 pupils. It occupied the St Luke's Mission Church on weekdays, with a service held there on Sundays. It is probable that the schoolmistress at that time was May Melrose, from Scotland, who is listed at Pamber Heath in the 1881 census. By October of the same year it was decided to open as a mixed school (all ages). In a letter sent to

the Clerk of the **Wootton and Tadley School Board**
by Revd H.L. Browne, of **Monk Sherborne**, it is
stated '…we have been obliged to make the school
at Pamber Heath a mixed school because we found
parents were reluctant to send their children to two
schools and thus pay double for them'. The change
had an immediate effect on **Tadley School**; their
log-book for 17 October 1881 states, '24 scholars
left to attend Pamber Church School'. The life of
the school was, however, short-lived. By October
1908 the Director of Education deemed it 'unnecessary' and made an order to close it. Prior to the
closure on 28 January 1909 a tea party for the pupils was organised by Mrs **Oppé** of the **Red House**.
The school log-book records a number of other interesting events: in 1900 a jumble sale was held, and
the school closed for four weeks in November of
the same year because of an outbreak of scarlet fever – three pupils died. Because of **hop-picking**,
the summer holiday closures were particularly long
and late, the school often not reopening until October. The building is now **St Luke's Church**. The
school-master's house (now called The Old School
Cottage) was used by the curate until the 1980s
when it was sold and a newer property, close-by,
was purchased. See **Oppé** family.

Pamber Heath Stores (612 624) Originally Benham's baker's and grocer's shop. It was established
between 1903 and 1910 becoming Pamber Heath
Post Office in 1910-11. It was at that time run by
William Benham with help from his wife Lucy and
brother Tom. The shop entrance then was on the
western side of the house and the bakery at the rear.
Later Hector, their son, ran the shop, retiring in the
late 1970s or early 1980s. The shop retained the Post
Office until December 1994. See **Bakers**.

Pamber Heath Village Plan See **Tadley Local
Plan**.

Pamber Parish Council The Council held its first
meeting on 13 December 1894 in the Mission
Room, Little London at which the first parish councillors were chosen. The first business meeting,
chaired by William Stroud, was on 8 January 1895
in the school room at Pamber Heath alternating
with **Little London**, as they still do today. Prior to
this date all parish business was carried out at **vestry meetings**, held in the south of the parish at The
Queen's College Arms. Initially, few major deci-
sions were made. Business consisted of instigating
the clearing ditches, cutting back hedges and trees,
erecting fencing, and, later, selling the parish pound.
Such matters continued to be the council's main
concerns into the 1950s. The first less mundane
matter was a request in March 1910 to the Post-
master General for a Sunday delivery to the parish.
Later that year another request was made for Pamber Heath to have its own Post Office due to '…its
very much increased population'. Questions regarding the amount and allocation of '…housing for
the working classes' were raised regularly and in

1954 the council estate at Burney Bit was extended.
The parish gravel pit(s) at **Pamber Heath** (now the
site of the tennis courts) were regularly full of water, up to 6 ft (1.8 m) deep at times. This showing
how often they were in use. The ownership of this
land was in dispute until 1953 when the parish
council was eventually officially recognised as the
owner. It was 1962 before the little thatched cottage on the north side was demolished, following
the death of Mr/Mrs Cripps. The land was levelled
and grassed as a playing field almost immediately.

In 1932 Charles Stroud became Chairman. From
1935 began the endless requests to Basingstoke
Corporation for the provision of electricity to the
parish. At that date it was deemed 'too expensive'
however, eventually, by 1951 most of the parish had
electricity. As early as 1936 air raid precaution meetings were being organised in anticipation of war.
In 1942 application was made for the adequate provision of air raid shelters in view of '…the close
proximity of the parish to the new aerodrome'. In
1955 the name Impstone Road was officially
adopted, in preference to the existing White House
Road. At the same meeting the proposed Valley
Lane name was not adopted, **Kingsclere and
Whitchurch Rural District Council** preferring The
Glen. The first application for a 30 mph speed limit
on Silchester Road was made in 1963 when the reply
was: 'not justified'. It was 30 years approximately before it was eventually imposed. In 1999 concerns still
exist regarding speeding and a new proposal to in-
stal traffic-calming measures is under consideration.

In 1964 Charles Byart was elected chairman. The
profile of the parish was improved with the replacement of the old **Pamber Heath Memorial Hall** and
in 1971, Little London was entered for the 'Best Kept
Village' competition. However, also in 1971, the
'Pamber Heath Café' (location unknown) drew the
attention of the local constabulary because of its
'rowdyism and nuisance'. Following Charles Byart's
election to Mayor of Basingstoke, Frank Mitchell
was elected chairman in May 1980. Frank has
overseen many **Parish Council** proposals including the celebration of its centenary in the **Priory
Church** on 26 November 1994. The council's most
recent project is the provision of Pamber Park, sited
on the edge of Pamber Forest to the south of Burney Bit on land leased from the Benyon Estate. Here
the millennium beacon will stand and be lit on 31
December 1999, and at other ceremonial and parish events in the future. See **Baughurst** and **Tadley
Parish Councils; Parish Councils**.

Pamber Place (593 597) Formerly known as
Wakeford Farm, which dates from the seventeenth
century, it was built on the site of an earlier cottage
erected in about 1100. It is believed that it belonged
to Pamber Priory, together with two other cottages
which were built at about the same time on the sites
of **Wyeford** and **Tadley Place**. The property comprises a two-storey house, together with a group of

barns and outbuildings. The house is partly timber-framed with brick infilling and weather boarding with a tiled roof. It had one gabled wing and a main hall with a large oak staircase when it was originally built in 1600. A second symmetrical gabled wing was added in 1665. No further major alterations were made until the turn of this century when it was enlarged by the addition of rooms at the back and a covered walk was added by Major General Sir Wyndham Knight between the wars. Known owners have included: in 1665, a London merchant wishing to escape from the Plague; in 1800, Jenny Wakeford; in 1911, Mrs Neagle (margarine heiress from the Van Den Bergh family) who was responsible for the Edwardian alterations; in 1923, Major General Sir Wyndham Knight who was related to Jane Austen; in 1982, Mrs Hungerford.

Pamber Priory (609 582) Originally called Sherborne or West Sherborne Priory, Pamber Priory was built by Henry de Port, son of Hugh de Port and consecrated in 1110 AD by William Gifford, Bishop of Winchester. It was a Benedictine Priory, a dependency or cell of the Abbey of St Vigor of Cérissy (Bayeux) near the home of the De Ports. Such foundations which linked their recent conquest of England with the Duchy of Normandy were encouraged by the Norman kings. It suffered a lot during the Black Death; in 1350 only the Prior and seven monks remained. Henry V closed the priory in 1415 and the farm became part of Wyford estate in the hands of the De la More family. In 1446, a century before the dissolution of the monasteries, Henry VI granted it to his new college at Eton. The Prior and monks were expelled, the relics carried off, and prayers for the founder were dropped. In 1461 Edward IV granted the Priory to St Julian Hospital, Southampton (and thus indirectly to **Queen's College, Oxford** who owned St Julian Hospital). Since the Priory had previously been granted by Henry VI to Eton College, strong influence was needed for Queen's College to retain it. They turned the fine Norman choir – all that is left of the chapel – into a parish church for the scattered forest people of Pamber. In 1475 an Act of Parliament ordered the College 'to find one honest priest' who should daily say matins and masses. In 1564 the inhabitants of Pamber brought a Bill in Chancery against the Provost of Queen's, it being decided that the Priory was not a Parish Church and that the College must maintain and repair the fabric. **Priory Church** is all that remains to remind us of the past. See **de Port charity; de Port family**.

Pamber Priory Church (609 582) See **Priory Church**.

Pangbourne Pipeline (PPL) An underground pipeline built by William Press Ltd in the early 1950s to carry liquid waste from **AWE** at Aldermaston to an outlet into the Thames at Purley near Pangbourne. The pipeline consists of two parallel pipes varying between three and five ins (76-127 mm) in diameter, interconnected by a series of valves which enables it to be sealed off at any point. Constructing it entailed trenching, concreting and laying the pipeline over a twelve and a half mile (20 km) route, laid to an exact gradient so as to fall only two hundred feet over the entire distance. The pipeline was temporarily blocked by CND in 1998. In 1999 storage ponds were constructed on site which reduced the use of the pipeline. See **Aldermaston Marches**.

Parish Councils Parish Councils were created following the Local Government Act 1894. See **Baughurst, Pamber** and **Tadley Parish Councils**.

Park House, Wolverton (555 585) A Georgian mansion; it is a two-storey building with grey cement rendered walls and a slate roof. Wings were added in about 1820 to form a symmetrical U-shaped block. In the 1940s the house was used by the army and towards the end of **World War II** a Canadian army hospital was built to the north of the house. Previous buildings are known to have existed at Wolverton in the twelfth and thirteenth centuries. In the reign of Henry III a convent was established in Wolverton. See **Wolverton Manor**.

Park Prewett Hospital (613 539) This vast site on the A340 near Basingstoke, much of which is now being developed for housing, began as a part of The **Vyne** estate. Park Prewett Farm, 300 acres (121 ha), was purchased from the Chute family in 1898 for the building of an asylum to relieve overcrowding at Knowle Hospital, Fareham. Building of the therapeutic centre did not begin until 1913. Before it was completed **World War I** broke out and it was commandeered as a military hospital (No 4 Canadian General Hospital) for Canadian soldiers wounded at Salonica (Thessaloniki) in 1917. It was vacated in June 1919 and finally opened as Park Prewett Mental Hospital in August 1921. By 1936 the patient population of the hospital was over 1300. At the beginning of **World War II** it again reverted to being a war hospital; parts of it became wards for London teaching hospitals, another part became an American hospital unit and in Rooksdown House a plastic surgery hospital was established under the control of Harold Gillies. 31,000 patients had been treated at the hospital by the end of 1943 and in the four and a half months following D-Day a further 12,000 casualties were admitted. After the war it gradually reverted to being a psychiatric hospital. During the late 1960s and early 1970s the new Basingstoke District Hospital (**North Hampshire Hospital**) was built in the grounds. On 3 April 1981 there was a major fire at Park Prewett and the main hall burnt down. It took two years to rebuild and was reopened by Lord Denning on 16 November 1983. Today the mental hospital occupies a new building known as Parklands on a much smaller part of the original Tudor farm. Many former patients are in community houses in the area. See **Health care and medical services; Hospitals; World War I**.

Pea picking Mentioned in the Report of His Majesty's Inspector of Schools in 1906 as one of many reasons for the wholesale absence of children from **Tadley School** at various seasonal times throughout the year.

Pear Tree Cottage (608 608) A cottage in Manse Lane, within the **Tadley Conservation Area**. It was formerly two cottages built in approximately 1640. It was the home of Mrs Eden who, in the 1960s gave the stained glass windows to **St Paul's Church**, in memory of her husband, Percy, and other family members. See **Idenden family**.

Pearce's Stores, Baughurst (581 616) A general store on the Baughurst Road. In the 1851, '61 and '71 census returns William Pearce was described only as a shoemaker, master shoemaker and cordwainer respectively. By 1881, aged 54 years, he is listed as a baker and grocer. He died in 1886 and was described in the Baughurst Parish Burial Register as a 'Primitive Methodist Local Preacher at the Chapel for many years, Shoemaker, Shopkeeper and Mealman'. He was succeeded in the bakery and grocery business by his son, Ezar, and later Ezar's son, Albert. The business continued to be known as 'E. Pearce' until the early years of **World War II** when it was sold to Henry Thornton of Basingstoke, who had other bakers' shops. The Post Office was transferred to these premises in November 1949 from Webb's Corner (Shaw Lane). In the 1950s a George Smith brought the business (not the George Smith of **Goodenough's Stores**) and renamed it General Supply Stores. The shop and Post Office at Bristol House, as it was known then, changed hands several times but was, at the end, only a Post Office. In the early 1990s it was for a while also an estate agents before being converted into a private house, Primrose Cottage, in 1995. See **Baughurst Post Office**.

Peat, Captain Frederick H. Born in Jamacia in 1826 and listed in the 1881 census as a retired officer, living in Hawley House. He was a Captain in the 97th Regiment and is purported to have been a great and enthusiastic fighter, serving with Garibaldi in Italy and, later, with the Confederate Army in the American Civil War where he became Inspector General of Cavalry. He died in 1893 and is buried at **St Peter's Church**. See **Hawley Farm**.

Peg's Cafe (595 626) Owned by Peg and John Wyles. Peg's Cafe was situated on the Aldermaston Road, where Falcon Fields is today. Built for £3,400 in 1956, it closed in 1984 when the site was redeveloped by Peg's brother Denis Brant. See **Brant family**.

Pelican, The (612 626) Public house on the Silchester Road, Pamber Heath. Originally known as The Pelican Inn, it was first mentioned by name in the 1881 census but was probably in existence much earlier. In 1891 the publican was a Hannah Newman, age 73, who resided with her three daughters, all mature ladies in their 40s! An item in the *Herts & Berks Gazette* in 1899 reports that another landlady, Mrs Thursa Beer, had occasion to call out the

Silchester Police to remove a drunk and disorderly customer. Mrs Beer remained at The Pelican until the 1920s. Jack Benham, brother of Hector, was also a publican in the 1930s. The Pelican's appearance has remained unaltered over the last 100 years. See Local **newspapers**; **Pamber Heath Stores**.

Penney Appeal A local appeal begun in 1997 with Lady **Penney** as patron. It was part of the national appeal to raise £2.3 million needed to build and equip a centre for young people with degenerative diseases. The Penney Appeal raised in excess of £62,000, far exceeding the original target of £35,000. The appeal is commemorated by The Tadley Room at Heather House Centre. See **Heather House**; **Juvenile Batten's Disease**; *see*ABILITY.

Penney OM, KBE, FRS, William 'Father' of the British atomic bomb and first director of **AWRE** (1953-9), William George Penney was born in 1909 and educated at Sheerness Technical School, Imperial College, University of Wisconsin and Trinity College, Cambridge. Shortly after the outbreak of **World War II** he was on loan to the Ministry of Home Security and Admiralty investigating problems connected with the nature and properties of blast waves. Through this work, in 1944 he was sent to Los Alamos to join the British team working on the atomic bomb; he was one of the two British observers to accompany the flight when the second atomic bomb was dropped on Nagasaki and was also one of the British party at the Bikini tests in 1946. In 1946 he was awarded an OBE and appointed chief superintendent of armament research in the Ministry of Supply at **Fort Halstead**.

When Britain decided to build nuclear weapons the responsibility for their design and development fell to Penney. With the loss of US co-operation, scientific and engineering teams had to be built up from scratch, new technologies developed, and highly specialised facilities constructed at **AWRE**, before the first atomic bomb could be ready for testing in October 1952. For his distinguished services in this achievement Penney was created KBE. There followed the rapid expansion of AWRE, of which Penney was director between 1953 and 1959.

In 1954, the responsibility for the development of atomic energy was transferred from the Ministry of Supply to a non-departmental body, the United Kingdom Atomic Energy Authority (UKAEA). Penney was appointed a member of the authority with responsibility for the research and development of nuclear weapons. Under his leadership a vigorous programme led, in May 1957, to the first British hydrogen bomb being exploded on Christmas Island in the Pacific Ocean, followed by further tests in 1958. In 1958 Penney played a leading part in the bilateral treaty between the United States and the United Kingdom for mutual assistance in nuclear defence and the consequential exchange of a range of nuclear information. He also played a leading part in the talks which led to the

1963 test ban treaty which forbade atmospheric nuclear tests. In 1959 he was made deputy chairman of UKAEA and was chairman between 1964 and 1967. During his later years with the UKAEA he presided over many important developments, among them the prototype fast reactor at Dounreay, the diversification of the authority's work into non-nuclear areas and the first nuclear power programme, as well as the drawing up of plans for a second.

In 1967 he left UKAEA to become rector of Imperial College. He was created a life peer in 1967 and appointed a member of the Order of Merit in 1969. He died on 3 March 1991. Penney's success owed much to his personality and character. Essentially a friendly, undevious, usually humorous man, he nevertheless was a shrewd administrator and a good judge of people. See **Blacknest**.

Pennington-Simcock, Revd Michael See **Great St Mary's Church, North Tadley**.

People of the Forest or People of the Woods See **Atrebates**.

Perry Cottage See **Oaktree Cottage**.

Petrol pump (607 678) The first mechanical, hand-operated, petrol pump in Britain was installed by the AA, reputedly at the site of the Half Way Garage on the Bath Road (A4), near The Hare and Hounds public house. The service started on 2 March 1920. A manager of the garage in 1946 remembers two early pumps on a scrap-heap at the garage, but believes the original pump and associated AA shed were near the A4/A340 junction at Aldermaston. Prior to the installation of the pump, petrol was served from cans.

Another interesting feature is the petrol pump that was installed behind a wall in Aldermaston village. Edward Keyser, owner of **Aldermaston Estate**, tried to keep the village 'untouched' and would not allow the pump to be displayed. The pipe from the pump had to be passed through a square hole in the wall, which still exists, near **Aldermaston Pottery**.

Phillips family The Phillips family lived in The Wilderness during the early part of the 1900s; Kelly's Directory records them as living there between 1903 and 1915. Sir John Phillips MD FRCP was born July 1855 and died December 1928. He specialised in midwifery, was a consulting obstetrical physician to King's College Hospital and also Emeritius Professor of Obstetric Medicine at King's College. Author of a book 'Outlines of Diseases of Women', he was knighted in 1917 and appointed Hon Physician to the Queen in 1918. The stained glass window at the east end of **St Peter's Church** is a memorial to his wife, Rachel Rattray Phillips, who died on 16 June 1917. Sir John is buried in the graveyard. See **Tadley Court**.

Photography With the development of photography in Victorian times, we start to get a clearer picture of what life was like in Tadley. Prior to this we are dependent on written accounts, and paintings and drawings of which very few have survived. There are two types of photographic record: the amateur family pictures, often showing people in informal situations, and professional photographs usually taken of local scenes or events and sold as postcards. A great number of these postcards have survived and a thriving hobby exists collecting them. Using photographs it is possible to build up a fascinating picture of local life from the late 1900s through to the 1950s. Several professional photographers were active in the local area: P.O. Collier who worked from Reading, Terry Hunt from Basingstoke and 'Jimmy' **Thatcher** who lived in New Road, Tadley.

Picket posts Following the opening of **Aldermaston Airfield** in July 1942 the area around the base was secured by a number of picket posts (an American term for sentry posts). All access roads to the base were guarded 24 hours a day and local civilian residents were issued with passes to be produced each time they went in and out of the north end of the village. It is reputed that Dr Lionel **Holmwood**, whose surgery and home was in Aldermaston village, failed to stop at a check point one night following an emergency call out. As a consequence his Vauxhall car was fired at. Fortunately he was unhurt. Local people remember that not long after the erection of these posts the one at the Lloyds Bank site was moved southwards to Blakes Lane, thereby extending the secure zone. This may have coincided with the increased security and complete confinement of movement at the base, that is known to have occurred in November 1942, prior to **Operation Torch**. The locations of the picket posts were: at **Brimpton Common**, near Lakeside Garden Centre; Lloyds Bank site, later Blakes Lane; Padworth Road, near **Decoy Pond**; Silchester Road, near Stacey's Yard.

Pig butchers Before World War II many local families kept a pig at home which they fattened during the year and had slaughtered in December. The meat was used at Christmas and preserved for use during the next year. Travelling butchers or slaughterers (often known as 'pig butchers') would do this. Ernie **Kimber**, writing in *Tadley During My Time and Before*, recalls in some detail the annual pig killing by butcher Barnet Barlow and how it held a morbid fascination for boys of his day. Another 'pig-butcher' remembered by many locals was Bill Nash who lived in a cottage opposite **Vine Tree Farm**, close to where Churchill Close is today. When Churchill Close was developed in 1973–4 he was rehoused in one of the new properties, living there until his death in 1979.

The keeping of pigs was not without its difficulties. Parish records from the 1890s frequently refer to drainage problems associated with sewage from domestic piggeries contaminating local drains and ditches. During **World War II** rationing the regulations covering the keeping of pigs became restrictive: families required a permit which allowed them to keep one pig per family per year for their own consumption. The restrictions became no easier after the war ended and the tradition of keeping a pig at home eventually died out. See **Acorn picking**.

Pightle A small piece of land in the open fields, or a small enclosed plot (alterative spellings include pightle, piddle, pigtail and pingle). There are several local examples: Waterman's Pightle (inside AWE, close to the perimeter fence near The **Falcon** public house), Beale's Pightle and Black's Pightle.

Pilgrim's Cottage (599 622) A cottage on Mulford's Hill, it was demolished in the 1960s to allow Whatmore's Garage (now Wheelgame) to be built.

Pineapple, The (567 628) A public house on the B3051 road at **Brimpton Common**. It got its name not from the fruit but from the pine trees which were in the area; although known as The Pineapple, its correct spelling should be The Pine Apple. It is a timber-framed thatched building with brick infill on the exterior and wattle and daub on the interior. One of its many features is a salt cupboard in the back of the chimney, once used to store bacon. It is believed to have originally been a fifteenth century farmhouse. It is thought it may have been used as an overnight stop for Welsh drovers en route to London. See **Aldermaston and Basingstoke Turnpike Trust**; **Welshman's Mile**.

Pines, Silchester See James **Lawes**.

PL965 A Spitfire fighter, built at **Hangar 5** beside **Aldermaston Airfield** in 1944, which is still flying today. As a photo reconnaissance variant it saw active service with No 16 Squadron during the war, flying more than 40 sorties over Germany. After the war it was used by the Royal Netherlands Air Force before spending 27 years at Holland's National War and Resistance Museum. In 1987 the aircraft was sent to the Medway Aircraft Preservation Society where it was restored to full airworthiness, taking to the air in December 1992, 45 years after its last flight. Nowadays, limited to 50 flying hours a year, it is much in demand by film and television producers. See **Hangar 5**.

Plague See Black Death.

Plane crashes A small number of plane crashes occurred locally during **World War II** when **Aldermaston Airfield** was operational, but an earlier one which generated a great deal of local interest at the time occurred on 7 April 1916 in **Charter Alley**. A Royal Flying Corps biplane developed engine trouble and made a forced landing in a field. Unfortunately, the field was too short and the plane ran into a hedge, somersaulting into the road, narrowly missing Mr A. Beasley of Basingstoke who was driving a pony and trap.

Plough, The (622 548) Public house in **Little London**. In the 1841 census the publican was Joseph Holloway (born 1776) and in 1851 his son, Daniel, was listed as 'publican and brickburner'. It was often used by locals working in **Pamber Forest**. One landlord kept pigs for a time in one part of the bar and another ran a shop from the premises. See **Little London Brickworks**.

Pluto Pluto (Pipe Line Under The Ocean) was originally a **World War II** pipeline designed to carry fuel across the Channel to the Normandy beaches, supplying the troops following the **D-Day** invasions. The landward extension of this pipeline continued from Fawley near Southampton to Padworth. Locally, the pipeline ran from **Padworth** alongside Red Lane, then followed the Tadley-Burghfield Road, across **Tadley Common**, crossing the A340 at its junction with Rowan Road then passing close to **St Peter's Church**, leaving our area just northwest of Christ Church, **Ramsdell**. A present-day high pressure, 725 psi (50 bar), pipeline follows the same route, carrying fuel for redistribution from Padworth. It is not known when the original stainless steel pipe was replaced but the Government Pipeline and Storage System Agency state that the pipeline is now protected 'cathodically' and is monitored weekly from the air. Pipeline markers are installed each side of all relevant road crossings and **Tadley Town Council** hold detailed guidelines for potential developments within its easements.

Plymouth Brethren A non-conformist religious sect founded in Ireland in the late 1820s by Revd J.N. Darby and established in Plymouth in 1830. It had no formal creed or ministers; each local church is autonomous. See The **Room**.

Poaching In the past there was a strong tradition of poorer people supplementing their meagre incomes with a little poaching. Birds and rabbits were the main items caught and then taken by carriers to local towns like Newbury and Basingstoke where no questions would be asked about their source. Naturally there is very little factual, but a lot of anecdotal, evidence. The main source of factual evidence is from court cases where poachers who had been caught were tried and punished. In 1343, John Cooper and Richard Twyhere of Tadley were fortunate to be sentenced to nothing more than a long imprisonment for killing a young deer in **Pamber Forest**. More recently, Monty **Hutchins** recounts two incidents in *A Country Childhood*. In the first, 'Dad had an old muzzle-loading gun, and many a moonlight night saw him going off with it. He liked to go alone, and he never failed to come back with one or two birds. These the carrier took to Newbury where he knew no questions would be asked'. In the second, Monty remembers a less successful incident in 1853 when his grandfather (14 at the time) had gone with a gang of poachers to the woods in Bucklebury. There, they got involved in a running fight with the gamekeepers and police; although they won the fight they were all found out, arrested and tried for the offence. Some of the men were transported to Tasmania, but Monty's grandfather got away with it and was released.

Polaris Britain's first submarine-based nuclear missile system. The missiles were purchased complete from the United States, but the nuclear warheads were designed at **AWRE**. The submarines that carried the missiles were also British designed. The system was in service from 1967 to 1994.

Policing The police system up until the early nineteenth century was still based on that used in the middle ages, each parish being responsible for appointing a constable for one year. The duties of the parish constable did not just entail peacekeeping but often included some of the responsibilities later attributed to the church warden or **Overseers of the poor,** such as managing the parish economy or seeing to the welfare of the poor. Public disorder on a large scale was passed to the militia. The office was unpaid and considered to be part-time although it often took up so much time it prevented the constable carrying out his normal job. Vestry minutes for all local parishes record the election of constables. By the late eighteenth century usually more than one was elected and were men of social standing: land owners, farmers, shopkeepers. The socially-disruptive effects of the Industrial Revolution resulted in the formation of the Metropolitan Police Force in 1829 and there gradually followed the policing of the provinces. Hampshire complied promptly with the County Police Act of 1839 and is, with Essex, the oldest constabulary in the country.

Hampshire constabulary archives do not detail names or dates of policing in this area but census returns show that a constable, George Francis (age 40) and his family from Quarley, Hampshire, were resident in the vicinity of the present police house on the Baughurst Road by 1849. No other constables are recorded for the area until 1861 when George Abbott (age 28), from Christchurch, was assigned to Silchester. The earliest reference to policing in Tadley is made by Ernie **Kimber** in *Tadley During my Time and Before,* '...as to Law and Order – in my young days (1920s) we had our very own police force in the person of Constable Mead'. He was, however, stationed at Baughurst and not Tadley as the statement might lead one to think. PC Bulbeck was, in fact, the first policeman to be appointed to Tadley in 1950, undoubtedly because of the rapid expansion of the population at the time. In 1955 PC Donald Wells took over, also living in the police house at 83 Mulfords Hill. He remained PC until 1965 and was followed by PC Bennett. In 1967 the present police house was built. As both AWRE and a large percentage of its new housing lay within the county of Berkshire, there arose a need for additional policing, resulting in three police houses in less than 50 yards. Officially Aldermaston village police station, the two Berkshire police houses on Aldermaston Road, adjacent to Lloyds Bank, were built in 1953 and later given the address 1 and 2 Tadley Row. Until 1986-87 two policemen manned this station. Their number was later reduced to one, and the station closed in April 1991. At the present time the police houses in Burney Bit and Baughurst Road are occupied as 'Beat Houses', the resident constable being on call 24 hours a day. The Mulfords Hill station house is classed as an 'Enquiry Office' and is only open at set times, but operates a 24 hour telephone enquiry line. See **Vestry meetings.**

Poliomyelitis A contagious disease originally known as Infantile Paralysis but recently described by Tony Gould in his book as 'The Summer Plague'. Statistics from the Public Health Laboratory Service show that for 1912-45 there was an average of 1000 cases per year. However, from 1947 the number rose, peaking in 1950 with 7760 cases. 1957 was the last big epidemic and by 1962 only 271 cases were reported. By the end of the seventies the figure was down to single figures. Fatalities were approximately 9-10%. Locally, the 1955 epidemic resulted in many cases and at least one death. Statistics for Tadley are difficult to calculate as many polio sufferers were treated outside the area: Peppard Fever Hospital and The Nuffield Orthopædic in Oxfordshire, Prospect Park in Reading and The Lord Mayor Treloar at Alton.

In 1947, Jonas Salk began research in the USA for a vaccine; he discovered there are 125 different strains. By 1952 he had a vaccine which he successfully tried out on himself, his wife and his children. By 1955 it was approved and later exported. In 1957 Albert Sabin developed a new vaccine using live virus. Their research ended a great scourge and must rank alongside penicillin. In the UK there are branches and groups of the British Polio Fellowship who support polio survivors. Locally the Basingstoke Circle is part of the Berkshire branch.

Pond Farm, Mortimer West End (629 633) Demolished about 1970, but still marked on recent Ordnance Survey maps, Pond Farm was situated in Benyon's Inclosure. A 1675 lease records that the farm consisted of a mill, mill house, malting house, mill pond, a coppice, cottage and two acres of land. By 1772 the farm was known as Kiln Farm with a lease giving permission to make bricks and tiles. A large four-kiln complex was built to the north of the pond which is still known as **Kiln Pond.**

Poor Law Prior to 1834 the parish was the unit of administration for poor relief. Acts of 1597 and 1601 ordered the annual election of **Overseers of the poor,** answerable to each parish vestry, who were empowered to raise revenue from local rates. Later, the Act of Settlement of 1662 detailed the ways in which a parish was responsible for poor relief.

As the national population rose, so too did the expenditure on poor relief during the late eighteenth and early nineteenth centuries. Concern led to the Poor Law Amendment Act of 1834. This abolished the old system and sought to centralise control, putting poor relief on a wider basis than the parish and preventing able-bodied persons from

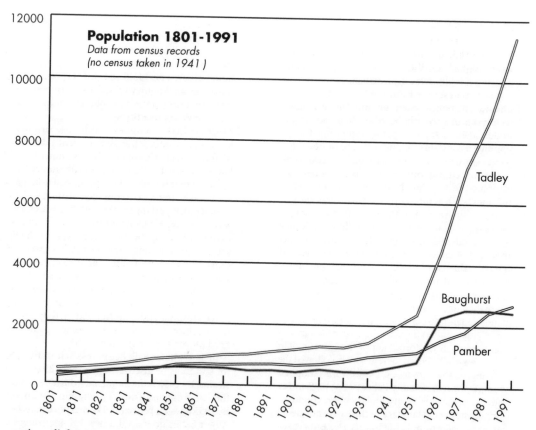

Population 1801-1991
Data from census records
(no census taken in 1941)

Tadley

Baughurst

Pamber

getting relief. A new system was introduced based on unions of parishes, run by boards of elected governors. Hampshire was divided into 23 unions, with each union building a workhouse. Locally, villages were served by several unions: Basingstoke Union covered Bramley, Pamber and Silchester while Kingsclere Union covered Tadley, Baughurst and Burghclere.

County and District Councils took over responsibility for poor relief in 1894 and the system was replaced in 1948 with the passing of the National Assistance Act and the creation of the National Health Service. See **Kingsclere Poor Law Union**; **Kingsclere Workhouse**.

Poplar tree (579 618) Prior to the 1920s the tree stood at the junction of Heath End and Brimpton Roads and gave its name to Poplar House opposite. This very tall tree was blown down during a storm and so no longer serves as the landmark it once did. The area is now cultivated for the enjoyment of local residents. See **Baughurst Gospel Temperance Band**.

Population (See chart above.) Population figures before the 1801 **census** are very unreliable. Even the census data has to be treated with caution, e.g. parish boundaries have changed over time, and the seasonal nature of work during Victorian times meant many inhabitants might have been away. However, some broad conclusions can be reached

from the census data. In 1801 the population of the three villages was: Tadley (497 – 45%), Baughurst (358 – 32%) and Pamber (238 – 23%). By 1931, the figures had increased to (1431 – 50%), (479 – 16%) and (969 – 34%), and by 1991 they were (11,407 – 69%), (2449 – 15%) and (2692 – 16%). Until World War II the population of the three villages increased gradually, the percentage difference remaining fairly constant. After World War II the population figures for all three villages increased dramatically and the percentage difference between Tadley and the other two widened considerably as it grew with the development of **AWRE**.

Portland House (594 649) A modern office complex built in 1982 by Blue Circle Industries, as their new Group Headquarters, beside the lake on the **Aldermaston Estate**. Changes in the economic climate during the late 1980s and early 1990s saw most of the company offices move back into London. Portland House is currently only partially occupied by Blue Circle's Pensions Unit and other commercial organisations. During the late 1990s the estate, including Portland House, was sold to Richcliff Securities.

Portway (636 623) The Roman road between **Calleva Atrebatum** (Silchester) and Old Sarum passes through **Pamber Forest**. It does not follow the line of any major path in the forest and therefore is not easily located – it crosses the long north-south path through the middle of the forest and the A340 road just north of **Honey Mill Bridge** and passes to the south of **St Peter's Church**. See **Devil's Highway**.

Post Offices The earliest recorded 'offices' in the area were at **Baughurst** and **Silchester**, first listed in the 1851 Census. Silchester had a succession of different postal administrators/officers beginning with Edwin McTier, at Dial Corner, who was also a baker and grocer. After 1903, when Henry Whistler was postmaster, they would have all overseen affairs at the same location: the corner of Whistlers Lane, opposite the **Calleva Arms** where the Post Office is photographically located on a card posted in 1905. It remained there until its closure. The most interesting Silchester post-master was in 1871-78 when John Plummer combined it with the job of school-master, probably from the school house on **Silchester Common**. Post Offices at Wolverton (William Soper, post-master), **Monk Sherborne** (Joseph Wickens, post-master) and **Ramsdell** (John Froome post-master) had been established by 1878 and at **Charter Alley** (Joseph Bryant, post-master) by 1903. The latter was located in a cottage, The Old Store, on Pamber Road, and that at Monk Sherborne, during **World War II**, was adjacent to The **Mole** public house. The post master was Riley Bleazard.

Little London Post Office, the next to open, in 1907, was at the home of Ada and William Long (now Old Post Cottage), until 1945. It was then relocated to Brook Cottage, previously The **Rifleman** public house. See **Post Offices, Baughurst** ; **Pamber Heath Stores; Post Offices, Tadley**.

Post Offices, Baughurst Elizabeth Carter, a widow, is recorded as post mistress in 1851, probably at the toll house next to the **Wellington Arms**. By 1861 this location is certain. The Baughurst Post Office remained there, and was in the hands of Elizabeth and subsequently her daughters, Caroline and Martha (Annie), until 1920-21. Its second location was at Webb's Corner, the junction of Shaw Lane and Baughurst Road. Florence Goodenough continued to run the Post Office there until 1955. It was then relocated to **Pearce's Stores** until 1995 when it moved to its present site on Heath End Road.

Post Offices, Tadley The Royal Mail, created by James I in 1609, is responsible for the conveyance of letters. In the early years mail was carried by 'poor boys'. Improvements in roads and the introduction of the mail coaches in 1784 accelerated the speed of the service. The cost of letters was charged by weight and distance and payable by either the recipient or the sender. In 1840 Rowland Hill introduced the 'Penny Post', a penny for half an ounce weight travelling any distance in Britain. This created an immediate 12% increase in the service. Pillar boxes were introduced in London in 1854 and Tadley is known to have had one at a site near or on Tadley Hill in 1871. This is critical to locating the first Post Office in 1877 which was run by Jane Harmsworth.

Known to live by the 'Post Letter Box', Jane was still post mistress in 1881 at the age of 75 years. Her brother-in-law William was the first recorded postman for Tadley in 1871. This occupation necessitated his bringing letters from **Monk Sherborne** in a donkey cart and also clearing the letter box at Tadley Hill. Before 1897, there was no free delivery of post to people's homes. This was granted by Queen Victoria as one of her Diamond Jubilee concessions. The purpose of the Post Office prior to that date was as a depository for incoming mail, which was later collected by the recipient, and for the weighing and issuing of postage. Some offices could also issue money orders. At later dates other services were introduced. In 1880 Tadley also operated a savings bank and in 1894 a telegraph (pretelephone) service. By then Caroline Fisher, also at Tadley Hill, was post mistress and her son Ernest a rural postman. In 1907 Mrs Alice Whitehorne was appointed sub-postmistress at, what is now, Hawthorns, Main Road. In the 1920s and 1930s she moved with the post office business to the bungalow adjacent to the Old Meeting ground and opposite **Main Road Methodist Church**. By 1935 the Post Office was established at its well remembered location opposite **Fairlawn House**. The postmaster was 'Tom' Stacey although it was run by his sister 'Florrie' Evans. Tom kept the adjoining fish & chip shop and mobile van service. It is no surprise that geographically Main Road was referred to as Post Office Road in the early part of the century. The Tadley Hill shop remained a Post Office for 60 years, finally closing on Wednesday 25 January 1995, transferring to the supermarket at Giles Court. The rapid expansion of Tadley in the 1950s necessitated the opening a second Post Office at north Tadley. Originally in the temporary accommodation of Simon's Stores at Bishopswood Road, it eventually moved to its present site in **Halstead House**. Tadley's third office, on Mulfords Hill, opened on 1 December 1979. The postmaster being Ray Anderson, the office run by his daughter Erica James.

Heath End, part of the parish of Tadley, also had its own Post Office. No office is recorded there in the 1911 **Kelly's Directory** but a postcard datestamped 'Heath End' in 1912 gives us a clue. In 1915 it was run by George Appleton and probably located, as later, at his home to the north of what is now Heath Court. The Post Office occupied a single-storey room built onto one end of the house. This was typical of many local offices located at non business premises e.g. Hawthorns, Old Post Cottage, Webb's Corner, Brook Cottage. It is known to have still been a Post Office in 1933-34 but the house was demolished in 1941-42. See **Post Offices; Post Offices, Baughurst**.

Potter, James A Quaker, who was imprisoned in Winchester for five years in 1657, for reading a Quaker pamphlet during a service in Baughurst

PRIORY SCHOOL, MONK SHERBORNE, HANTS.

Photo: J.W. & C.A. Stevens

Priory School, early-1900s

Church. Potter was imprisoned no less than five times between 1657 and his death in 1703. He became a major force amongst the persecuted nonconformists of Hampshire and Berkshire. Amongst the offices he held were Joint Treasurer of the County Stock, Clerk of the Hampshire Quarterly Meeting and leading advocate for the **Quakers** at the Assizes in Winchester during the period of greatest persecution against nonconformists. Potter founded one of the largest dissenting meetings in Hampshire and maintained its survival against all odds, ensuring the survival of Quakerism in northern Hampshire and southern Berkshire. He was buried in the second Quaker burial ground at Town's End Meadow, Wolverton. See **Baughurst House; Baughurst Quakers.**

Pound, The Also known as Pinfold. An enclosure in which stray cattle were impounded and released on payment of a fine. The Pound was originally kept by the manor or **vestry** and later the parish. The location of pounds can usually be found from the names of farms and cottages on maps, e.g. Pound Farm at Three Ashes in Silchester and Pound Cottage near the corner of Rowan Road). The pound keeper, also known as pinder, pinfold, punder, was a manorial or parish official in charge of the pound. Often forming the basis of a family surname, e.g. Pinfold = Penfold. See **Pamber Parish Council**; The **Wellington Arms.**

Primitive Methodists The Society of Primitive Methodists was formed by Hugh Bourne (1772-1852) and William Clowes (1780-1851) in 1810 when they were expelled from membership of the

Methodist Church. They felt that Methodism had lost it's early 'fire' and sought to introduce the 'Camp Meetings' that had become a feature of churches in North America, with their 'revival addresses' interspersed with prayer meetings amongst large numbers of people assembled at a camp in an out-of-way place. The Wesleyan Church meanwhile, was trying to conform to the requirements of the English government, and be accepted as Dissenters alongside Congregationalists and Baptists. Primitive Methodism was more radical and became associated with the emergent agricultural trade unionism in the south and miners in the north. See **Baughurst Methodists; Baughurst Primitive Methodist Chapel; Little London Primitive Methodist Chapel; Ranters; Silchester Methodist Chapel; Silchester Primitive Methodist Chapel; Silchester Primitive Methodist Circuit.**

Prior's Copse (594 627) Now part of the AWE complex, between The **Falcon** public house and Heath End roundabout, Prior's Copse was probably named after the prior of the Cathedral Monastery of St Swithin at Winchester.

Priory Church (609 582) Priory Church, formerly known as Sherborne Priory Church, is almost all that remains of **Pamber Priory**, one of the county's largest Benedictine priories during the twelfth and thirteenth centuries. The church, dedicated to St Mary and St John the Baptist, was consecrated by William Gifford, Bishop of Winchester from 1107 to 1129. Of the twelfth century church, which was cruciform shape without aisles, the only parts now standing are the arches of the crossing or central tower and a portion of the south wall or nave. The nave and basic foundations date from around 1100 and are the work of Henry **de Port**. The eastern arm was rebuilt and lengthened in about 1220, but much of the tower is of a later date. The church possesses two fonts, one Norman (probably a mortar) and one Tudor. There is an interesting wooden effigy of a knight, cross-legged, late twelfth century, and a very early bier. Most of the fine old church benches and the panelled font with flowers are the work of fifteenth century craftsmen. In 1986 an eighteenth century organ provided by **Queen's College, Oxford** was installed. The whole fabric of the building was restored in 1842 and again in 1936. Today the church is in the parish of the Sherbornes with Pamber and the current Rector is Revd John Hamilton.

Priory School, The (606 580) Priory School opened on its present site as the Monk Sherborne and Pamber (C of E) School in 1850, and was built from knap flint and local Ramsdell red brick. It had two classrooms and could accommodate 100 pupils. In 1916 a fire badly damaged the school when the roof and some beautiful stained-glass windows were destroyed and it had to be rebuilt. During the rebuilding, classes were held in Priory Church. In the 1980s the school roll was falling and in 1987, with only 28 on roll, it merged with **Ramsdell School**

which had only 19 on roll. The merged school opened as The Priory County Primary School in September 1987, with just two classrooms and one temporary classroom. In January 1993 it became grant-maintained and adopted the name The Priory School. Additional funding has enabled the school to build new classrooms and facilities; it now has seven classrooms and a large gymnasium, and the school roll has risen to 153.

Public Utilities See **Electricity**; **Gas**; **Post Office**; **Telephones** and **Water**.

Puritan Ejection 1662 Clergymen of the Church of England were deprived of their living by Oliver Cromwell. After the Restoration in 1660 the deprived clergy were reinstated. The clergy who had been given a living by Oliver Cromwell thought it improper that they should now be asked to retire to allow the rightful rectors to return. In Tadley, as in many other places, those who had been worshipping under Oliver Cromwell's appointed vicar, Thomas Kentish (1650-1662), wished to continue with him and so worshipped at prayer meetings held in private houses. Ministers who happened to be in the neighbourhood were also asked to preach, so began the independent nonconformist chapels. See **Gardiners**; **St Peter's Church**; **United Reformed Church**.

Q

Quakers The popular name for members of a non-conformist sect, The Society of Friends, was founded by George Fox in 1647. The description 'Quakers' was applied to Fox and his followers after he told an examining magistrate to tremble at the Word of God. Quakerism rejected formal church services, paid ministries, the sacraments, baptisms and the authority of the scriptures. It proclaimed that every human being was divine, thus contravening the Blasphemy Act of 1650 which resulted in Quakers being persecuted more than other sectarian groups. In the seventeenth century the Society of Friends was the largest nonconformist sect in the country. Membership in England possibly reached 35,000–40,000 by 1660. Early records of local meetings, births, deaths and marriages were not kept to a standardised form until 1776. Only recently, in 1992, have the local Baughurst meeting houses and burial grounds been accurately documented by Ken Smallbone. See **Baughurst House**; **Baughurst Quakers**; **Brown's Farm**.

Queen Anne's Bounty Due to his divorce disputes with the church, Henry VIII suspended the payment of annates to the Pope in 1532, and kept them for the crown. Annates were the first year's revenues from an ecclesiastical benefice. In 1703 Queen Anne established a fund (Queen Anne's Bounty) to receive and use this 'confiscated' money for the relief of poorer clergy, thereby supplementing their income. See **Little St Mary's Church, Heath End**.

Queen's College Arms (612 583) An eighteenth century public house (for a period called The College Arms) situated on Aldermaston Road (A340) at **Pamber End**, so called because it was, and still is, at the centre of the land held locally by **Queen's College, Oxford**. Census returns show that in 1841 the publican was John Chesterman, followed in

1851 by William, his son, who remained for at least ten years. During his time as landlord he was also listed as a grocer but it is not known if at the Queens College Arms. However, in the 1960s, there was a small general store at the rear. As with many old public houses it was often used for inquests, public sales and auctions, e.g. the sale of Ravenscot Farm in 1887 and 1888. In the main, Pamber vestry meetings were held there from 1880. The sign in its original position on the roadside of the front wall, and which formerly had a circular seat around it, is a protected monument. See Thomas **Chandler**; **Ghosts**; **Pamber Priory**.

Queen's College, Oxford Queen's College, Oxford was, and still is, a substantial local landowner. The College dates from a charter granted by Edward III in 1341, in which licence was given to Robert of Eglesfield to construct a collegiate hall 'under the name of the Hall of the Queen's scholars of Oxford'. Early in its life Robert gained Wardenship of St Julian's Hospital (commonly called God's House) in Southampton. In 1461 Edward IV granted **Pamber Priory** to the Hospital of St Julian in Southampton, which belonged to Queen's College, Oxford. The College still owns Redhouse, Manor and Priory Farms, which incorporate many small farms once held separately, e.g. Hanningtons on the A340. It owns the land on which the Priory stands and much of Monk Sherborne; small enclaves having been sold from time to time, notably the site of **Priory School**. The college also owned land in other parts of the Parish of Pamber. Their links with the area are remembered in the name of the public house: The **Queen's College Arms** .

R

Raghill (608 645) A pleasant rural area east of Aldermaston village. Raghill Lane, off Red Lane, has two farm properties and several residences along its length. It formed a division between two country estates (Keyser at **Aldermaston Court** and Darby-Griffiths at **Padworth**), but it was not the boundary line between Aldermaston and Padworth parishes. That lies along the course of Padworth Gully going south/north from the Reading Road. It is said the name 'Raghill' comes either from the habit of travelling families hanging their wet washing over the bushes to dry, or alternatively, from the presence of the ragwort, a weed which grew in abundance in the area.

Railways Railways started to be built in England during early Victorian times. In the days before motorised road transport, they were very important, in particular for the transport of goods. Tadley was never part of a railway network – the nearest local stations were (and still are): Aldermaston (Reading to Newbury line), Mortimer and Bramley (Reading to Basingstoke line). Aldermaston station was important for transporting the produce of local industries; Arthur **Nash** in the television programme 'Arthur Nash – Broom Maker of Tadley' recalls how local broom makers dispatched their brooms from there.

The **Great Western Railway** reached Reading on 30 March 1840 with the opening of the line between Reading and Twyford. The next section, the Berks and Hants Railway, was sanctioned by Parliament in 1845. The first 25.5 miles (41 km) of broad gauge section of track (between Reading and Hungerford) was opened for passenger traffic on 21 December 1847; the line included stations at Reading West, Theale, Aldermaston, Woolhampton (renamed Midgham in 1873), Thatcham and Newbury. The

Berks and Hants Railway became the Berks and Hants Extension Railway and remained independent until 1882 when it was absorbed by the GWR. During the nineteenth century the Didcot, Newbury and Southampton Railway planned, and had authorisation to build, a link route from Aldermaston to Old Burghclere but the line was never built. This would have come just north of **Brimpton Common**, through **Wasing Park** and Headley.

The line between Reading and Basingstoke was delayed owing to hostility between the GWR and the London and South West Railway which had reached Basingstoke from Winchfield on 10 June 1839, and Winchester by 11 May 1840. The 15.5 mile (25 km) Reading-Basingstoke broad gauge line was opened on 1 November 1848; I.K. Brunel was the line engineer. His Italianate building at Mortimer station was due to a clause in the Berks and Hants Railway Act requiring the Duke of Wellington's consent on any station within five miles (8 km) of his seat at Stratfield Saye. It is now a Grade II listed building. The line terminated at the GWR station in Basingstoke; this station survived until 1 January 1932 when it closed and services were transferred to the LSWR station. The station at Bramley was originally only a goods siding; it opened for passenger traffic on 1 May 1895. Primarily intended for local traffic, the line was opened for through traffic, i.e. Newcastle to Bournemouth, on 1 July 1902. The route became part of the Western Region of British Railways upon nationalisation in 1948, but most of it was transferred to the Southern Region in 1950. It became part of Network Southeast in 1986 and is now part of Thames Trains.

Rakes In the days before mechanisation the rake was the common method of collecting hay in the fields. A combination of lightness and strength were necessary to produce a hay-rake. The lightness would avoid fatigue in the user during the long hours of hay-making, and the strength would avoid any unnecessary stoppages because of breakages. Rake-making was one of the few full-time woodland occupations. Pamber was a centre for making rakes and scythe handles during the nineteenth and early twentieth centuries. Like most of the woodland industries, it was a family concern – large families providing a cheaper labour force than hired labour. The **Sims family** were synonymous with rakemaking in Pamber for over two hundred years, a tradition that ended with the death of Ernie Sims in the early 1980s. The increasing use of machinery for hay-making, from the early 1900s onwards, saw the decline of the rake and scythe industry. Like the broom industry, rake-making outlasted many other woodland crafts, enabling Ernie Sims to continue in his trade until well past his normal retirement age.

As well as being a very skilled occupation, rakemaking was also labour-intensive, needing some 50-60 operations to produce each rake. Nationally the design of rakes varied from area to area. The Pamber tradition dictated a simple construction. The rakes were reckoned to be disposable after a single season – virtually mass-produced and sold at low prices. The material for making the finished product was bought from local wood-dealers: ash, supple, light and strong, was used for the handles, and willow or ash, for the same reasons, were used for the head. Ideally, willow or oak was best for the teeth (tines). In the 1860s rake handles, usually of ash, cost 1d (less than 1p)each and sneads (as scythe-handles were more commonly known) 1½d. After cutting, the sticks and branches were seasoned in the open for about a year until ready for shaping. Rake and scythe handles were both steamed as the first process in their making. With rake-handles this was necessary to strengthen and straighten them, but with sneads it was done to bend them to the required shape. Once straightened the handle was smoothed with a 'stail engine'. The rake head was shaped with an axe, draw-knife and spokeshave. Holes for the tines were drilled with a brace and bit, together with larger holes for the handle and stays. The tines were produced on a driving stool where the craftsman drove wooden pegs through a tube-shaped knife. The tines were then hammered into the head and the handle attached before being smoothed with sandpaper. Generally the output was about ten finished rakes per day per man. See J. **Stacey & Sons**.

Rampton, Sidney 'Sid' A member of an old local family of woodcutters. Ramptons Meadow, off Fairlawn Road, is named after them; the estate is built on his meadow. Sid, born in **Newtown** in 1890, was still working in his 90s.

Ramsdell (589 575) A small village about 3.5 miles south of Tadley. Previous spellings of the name appear as Ramesdela (1170), Ramesdella (1248) and Ramsdale. None are too dissimilar from the modern spelling. The origins of the name are far less obvious than 'rams in a dell'. The book *Hampshire Place Names* tells us that the old English word 'Hramse' dell, 'dell where wild garlic is grown' is the most likely explanation for the name. It became an ecclesiastical parish in 1869 when it was formed from the surrounding parishes of Monk Sherborne, Tadley and Wootton St Lawrence. The village church of **Christ Church** was built in 1867; in addition there was a flourishing congregational chapel in the village a hundred years ago. The village had a **carrier**, David Monger, who travelled to Basingstoke on Wednesdays. See **Charter Alley Methodist Chapel**; **Priory School**; **Ramsdell Brickworks**; **Wyeford**.

Ramsdell Brickworks (593 576) The works were operational from 1839, or before, until 1979 when production ceased through clay exhaustion. In 1855 and 1857 T. Kimber is listed as the 'brick and tile maker'. Work was seasonal; during spring and summer the clay was dug and bricks made, while during autumn and winter the bricks were fired in the kiln. The works closed during **World War II**, reopening in 1946 with help from German prisoners of war. In 1975 the works produced 900,000 bricks, mainly red and multicoloured facing ones, from two down-draught rectangular kilns. Bill Stanley, the last manager, worked at the works for 37 years until he retired in May 1979. The site of the brick works is now occupied by a group of light industrial units – 'Old Brick Kiln'. See **Brick and tile making**; **Brown's Farm**; **Little London Brickworks**; **Tadley Brickyard**.

Ramsdell Cricket Club See **Cricket**.

Ramsdell Recreational Ground (589 575) Until 1947 Ramsdell did not have a cricket ground. Previous local teams practised at Brass Meadow and the allotments at West Heath, whilst the present team, which was formed in 1936, played on ground at Povey's Farm. All matches were played on their opponents' grounds. In 1947 locals decided to commemorate the war-dead with a recreation ground. The site chosen was church glebe land and the money needed to purchase it was raised by personal donations, whist drives and jumble sales. The cricket club took over the ground and with local support a clubhouse was built. Bill Stanley, who joined the club in 1936, held every position in the club and is an Hon Life Vice-President. See **Ramsdell Brickworks**.

Ramsdell School (588 574) Established as part of the **Wootton and Tadley School Board**, Ramsdale School, as it was known, opened in 1877. There was room for 120 pupils, including ones from Ewhurst. By 1987, when it was a County Primary School, the number of pupils on roll had dropped to 19 and so

Tadley Rest Shelter, showing adjacent blacksmith's forge/postal sorting office

Photo: Tadley WI Scrapbook

it was closed, becoming a private residence called The Old School. In September 1987 the 19 pupils joined those at Monk Sherborne under the new title of The Priory County Primary School. See The **Priory School**.

Ramsdell Village Hall (590 573) The present one is built on land owned by the Manydown Estate. The original village hall was burnt down. A wooden building, near **Ramsdell Brickworks**, it was used as a 'cinema' showing magic lantern shows.

Ranch House (605 609) See The **Rest shelter**.

Ranters A term used to describe the congregation of the breakaway **Methodist** sect known as Primitive **Methodists** (1810). There were many such in Tadley and the surrounding villages, as in the main, its appeal was to the humble people: farm labourers, urban poor and pit workers. See **Religious Census (1851)**.

Reading Hawks A local BMX racing club, started in 1988 by enthusiastic parents and children. In the beginning their local track was on Brant's Field. The club was active for a number of years with teams competing successfully in both local and national events. As interest grew a new track was built in Basingstoke in 1985 and the local racers moved their activities there. See **Brant family**.

Reading Evening Post, Reading Standard, Reading Mercury and Mercury Chronicle See Local **newspapers**.

Rec Soc (587 628) Short for the Aldermaston Recreational Society, the social club at **AWE**. The first meeting of the Society was held in May 1951 with Eric Cross as Chairman and Jack Hinsley as Secretary. By the end of the month there were 240 mem-

bers and a club room – a building behind **Boundary Hall**. The Society's aim is to provide a base for communal recreational and sports facilities for AWE staff and their families. It is managed by an elected voluntary committee of AWE employees who employ staff to run it. From a recorded income of £500 in 1950 it is now a business with assets of over £220,000. Over the years provision has been made for a wide variety of field and racquet sports, indoor pursuits and social functions and the Society now offers 'one of the broadest mixes of sports, recreation and social events in the area'. Most of these are controlled by individual sections within the Society. Since its foundation in 1951, membership has been extended to include local residents and their families; within the 10% rule, non-AWE membership being restricted to 10% of the total.

Red House (610 622) A large house in Pamber Heath also known as Pamber Heath House. It was built just prior to the turn of the century on land owned by **Queen's College, Oxford**. Set in 12.75 acres (5 ha) of land that included pine woods and tennis courts it was bordered by The Glen, Church Road and Pamber Heath Road. The house, designed by Mervyn Macartney of Woolhampton, the architect responsible for **Tadley Court**, comprised four reception rooms, nine bedrooms on the first floor and four in the attic. The gardener's cottage, the stables and garage, now converted into a dwelling, still stand on the corner of Heath Road. Its only known owners were the **Oppé family**. After the death of Mrs Oppé in 1940 the house was said to have been used by the Russian Embassy following their removal from London during the blitz. It is also believed that the house was used as accommodation for Home Office employees working at the wireless transmitting station at Hannington. The house and grounds were sold at auction on 10 November 1949. Following the auction, the house was demolished and the land redeveloped for housing. Heath, Westlyn and Eastlyn Roads now occupy the site. See **Gas**.

Red Lion, The (624 634) A public house in Church Road, **Mortimer West End**. It was originally a small farmhouse, known since 1700 as 'Kinchins', which can be dated back to 1552. It became a public house in 1794, and between 1862 and 1929 was run by the same family.

Religious Census (1851) In the course of preparations for the 1851 **census**, the idea of including a question about religious affiliation was mooted, only to be met with strong opposition. In the face of this objection the authorities fell back to a more acceptable line and proposed to seek their religious information not from individual households but at congregational level. This became known as The Religious Census of 1851. Incumbents of all places of worship were asked to complete a form giving various details of their accommodation and actual attendances for Sunday 30 March 1851. Questions included details about the building's consecration date, the accommodation available for worship, separated between 'free sittings and other sittings' with **Quakers** having to include their floor area. The numbers attending were recorded for each service and split for 'General Congregation and Sunday School Scholars'. Although there was a space for any remarks, this was generally left blank. However, in the return for Baughurst Parish Church, the incumbent (D Williams, Rector) wrote over 100 words, mostly about how popular the various Methodist Chapels in his area were becoming viz; '…in an adjoining parish, formerly proverbial for its heathen state, the beer houses on Sundays are no longer full; the people are gone to the ranters' chapels'. See **Ranters**.

Rest Shelter, The (605 609) Jokingly referred to at the time as 'The Ranch House', this equivalent of a modern bus shelter was erected at the edge of Fairlawn Road (beside Ted Ford's Smithy) in March 1938 to commemorate the coronation of King George VI. The *Hants & Berks Gazette* reported that the shelter was the first public building to be erected in Tadley and that the unveiling ceremony was a very grand and well-attended affair. Representatives from local churches, bus companies, **Womens' Institute** and **parish councils** were in attendance. It was officially opened by the local MP of the time, Mr Patrick Donner. An evergreen oak was also planted, a gift from Mr I.G. Symes of **Bridge House**. In 1965 it was decided to rebuild the shelter in brick. Sadly, the oak tree blew down in 1987.

Ricks Traditionally, ricks are made from corn or hay to allow it to dry prior to use. Straw for thatching requires corn to be cut and stored by traditional methods. Ricks are made-up of sheaves of corn built as an oblong or round; square ones are known but not locally. Each sheaf is produced by a binder which ties the corn into bundles and cuts the base diagonally, the longest point of which is called the peck. This shape is important as it facilitates the successful construction of the rick. The sheaves, with the ears pointing to the centre and the pecks to the outside, are built up in layers upon a base made from bavins. The base has straight sides while the top two-thirds, the stem, gradually gets wider extending over the base to prevent water running in. The roof is constructed with a gap, a pitch hole, to enable a man to stand and pass each sheaf to the rick-builder, this being the last piece to be in-filled. Finally, the roof is constructed to a point creating a conical shape. Often excess material was used to make a miniature rick, always known locally as a 'Tadley Rick'. It is jokingly said that this was because the fields in and around Tadley were smaller and had a lower yield. See **Elliott family**.

Rifleman, The (623 593) A public house in **Little London**. A contemporary engraving suggests the property existed prior to 1787 and that it was probably a beer shop before becoming a public house. In 1871 the census lists Albert Froome as the publican, in 1881 John Barker, and in 1891 Charles Elliott. It was de-licensed in 1912 and became a private house now called Brook Cottage. See **Elliott family**.

River Kennet Navigation The River Kennet Navigation between Reading and Newbury was a busy inland waterway long before it became part of the **Kennet & Avon Canal** in 1810. First proposed in 1714 to help provide good regular transport for local trade in agricultural products and timber, an Act of Parliament was passed in 1715 authorising its construction. Work on the 18.5 miles (30 km) of navigation began in 1718 and was completed by 1723 at a cost of around £50,000. 20 locks and 11 miles of artificial 'cuts' to bypass the meanders of the river, had to be constructed to overcome a rise of 134ft (41 m). Wharfs were built at either end (Newbury and Reading) and in the middle at **Aldermaston Lock**. Because of the latter's central position, the main carpentry depot for the canal was also established at Aldermaston, in 1740. The Master Carpenter was Thomas Omer. See **Berkshire & Hampshire Junction Canal**.

River Loddon A river which rises in West Ham, Basingstoke, runs close to Tadley and joins the Kennet near Reading. Tributaries of the Loddon run through **Pamber Forest**. See **Little London**.

Roads Many roads are prehistoric in origin but the first true ones were made by the Romans. With **Calleva Atrebatum** near, the local area was probably well served. From Calleva's gates, roads led to all points of the compass. The only one which can be traced with any certainty today, the **Devil's High-**

way, ran east. One of the others, the **Portway** passes through Pamber and Tadley, near **St Peter's Church**. Medieval and early modern roads were partly ancient ones that continued in use and partly new ones that connected medieval planned towns.

In Saxon and medieval times supervision of roads lay first with the Sheriff and, as their powers declined, with the **hundred** or manor courts. Tudor legislation (1555 Statute for Amending of Highways) placed the main responsibility for roads on the parish. Each parish had to elect a surveyor from its inhabitants, who served for a year, keeping accounts and being answerable to the Justices in Quarter Sessions. Parishioners had to provide repair materials, and do 'statute labour' in person or by deputy, for four, later six, days on the roads, the wealthier inhabitants also providing teams of horses, carts and men ('team duty'). Later, statute labour and team labour could be commuted to a cash payment. The Tudor system remained the basis of highway maintenance until 1835. Thereafter, a series of Acts of Parliament saw responsibility gradually transfer from parish to county councils. In 1888 responsibility for main roads was taken away from Highway Boards and given to the newly-created County Councils. In 1894 responsibility for local roads was transferred from the Highway Boards to the new Rural District Councils, who continued to maintain district roads until 1930 when the Local Government Act of 1929 transferred their powers to County Councils.

By the eighteenth century, traffic on the roads had increased so much that the statutory labour system could no longer cope. The answer was to form turnpike trusts which were empowered to levy tolls for the upkeep and improvement of named stretches of highway. It was hoped they would make a profit. The first turnpike trust was established by private Act of Parliament in 1663; by 1750 most of the major through routes in England had been turnpiked. The early turnpike trusts took over existing highways and improved them, sometimes with new diversions from the old route but entirely new roads were not constructed by such bodies until the end of the eighteenth century. Local Trusts included the **Aldermaston and Basingstoke Turnpike Trust**, founded in 1771-72 and the Reading and Basingstoke Trust, founded in 1801. Turnpike roads are largely associated with the stage-coach era. They ceased to be profitable with the coming of the railways, to which much long distance trade was transferred. The money generated from tolls declined relentlessly. During the 1850s and 1860s the condition of many turnpike roads deteriorated and trusts tried to pay off their debts. Most trusts were dissolved in the 1870s and 1880s and in 1888 responsibility for main roads passed to the newly created County Councils.

From the medieval period until the early nineteenth century there was virtually no change in the method of road maintenance. Hedges were chopped back, ditches cleaned, and the surface ploughed and harrowed. Sometimes loads of gravel, sand or soil might be spread over. As a result, particularly with the growth of the droving trade and of wheeled traffic in the late seventeenth and eighteenth centuries, roads were often a sea of mud impassable at certain times of the year. Major roads began to improve in the eighteenth century with the development of turnpike trusts, but it was not until about 1810-35 that civil engineering techniques began to be applied to road construction. For the first time, proper foundations were laid, and a drained and level surface provided. The principle was soon adopted on major routes and eventually applied to other roads in the course of the century. Tarred surfaces were introduced after the advent of the motor car whose rubber tyres tended to produce clouds of dust.

After World War II Tadley found itself with many robust concrete roads left over from its military airfield days. **Tadley Parish Council** minutes from 1948 to 1951 record many complaints from residents about the poor state of some roads in the area which was being caused by the installation of the various domestic services pipelines. Soon after the establishment of AWRE in the early 1950s the main concern regarding roads was the increasing traffic on the A340 through Tadley. In 1951 the County Council refused a parish council request for a 30 mph speed limit through the village on the grounds that there had been no recent serious accidents. It was not until the narrow bends around 'Chapel Corner' on Tadley Hill were straightened in 1955, producing a faster flow of traffic, that the current 30 mph speed limit followed in the autumn of 1956. Halt signs at the end of Silchester Road were approved in 1957. A traffic mirror was suggested for traffic negotiating the school road entrance to The **Green**; this however was made a one way entry instead. The **Co-op** arranged for lay-bys outside its shop in Franklin Avenue in 1960 while, in the same year, the 'cats eyes' were removed from the A340 in the village and replaced by a reflective white line. (At a later date the 'cats eyes' were replaced.) October 1966 saw the first 'no waiting' restrictions on Mulfords Hill from Silchester Road to Millers Road, this being followed by more 'double yellow lines' in 1972 along part of Franklin Avenue. In March 1970 it is recorded that a safety barrier was needed outside J.S.**Whatmore & Sons**. The original pedestrian crossing on Mulfords Hill was introduced in 1976 and was relocated near **Budgens** at a later date. The roundabout at **Tadley Bottom** was constructed in the early 1980s while, more recently in 1989, traffic lights were introduced at the Silchester Road/Franklin Avenue junction and single yellow lines appeared in Newchurch Road, in 1998. See **Enclosure Acts; Gravel extraction**.

Photo: Tadley WI Scrapbook

Major George C Roller (1856-1941)

Rod merchant A person who owned and cultivated an osier bed; see **Brown's Rod Yard**; **Willow osiers**.

Rod Strippers See **Willow osiers**.

ROF Burghfield See AWE **Burghfield**.

Roller DCM, TD, George C Major George Roller (1856-1941) was a multi-talented local resident – an artist, a writer, a soldier serving in both the Boer War and World War I, a steeplechase rider, a London magistrate, and a governor of London hospitals and the **Royal Berkshire Hospital**.

Born in 1856 to a Welsh mother and German father who became a naturalised British subject, he was educated at Westminster School and served with the Imperial Yeomanry in the Boer War, 1899-1902. He was mentioned in dispatches; commissioned after Senekal Kopje, 25 May 1900 and awarded the DCM. He was a Major with the Middlesex Yeomanry, 1903-11 and commanded the 3/3 County of London Yeomanry, 1914-16. Seconded to the Field Artillery, France, he was invalided out in 1918 and made an Hon Major. He travelled widely, in Australia, California, Peru and Argentina. The Major was a gentleman rider under National Hunt Rules all through the 1880s and 1890s. Although he excelled as a rider, it is as a skilled painter/artist, in particular as a restorer of pictures, that his world-wide reputation is based. He restored pictures at the Royal Academy which had been damaged by Suffragettes and illustrated **Burberry**'s (the

rain-coat manufacturer) advertisements for nearly 40 years, becoming a great friend of Thomas Burberry. He died on 4 January 1941.

Stories concerning his activities and exploits abound. His horse, **Gabardine**, featured in one. Major Roller was the officer in command of the 34th Company Imperial Yeomanry when it was engaged in a hopeless attack against the Boers who were positioned safely at the top of a steep slope. The yeomanry were forced to dismount under withering fire and lie down. Every horse was shot, except Gabardine. Only six men survived but the Major crawled to a safe spot, dragging a wounded colleague. He managed to recall Gabardine and pull the unconscious soldier across the mare's back and ride to safety. Major Roller was recommended for the VC by General Rundle but, unfortunately, there were no officers alive to confirm this brave action. In the 1890s he and his family lived at *The Wilderness* (now known as **Tadley Court**) near Tadley Common. He later moved to the nearby property now known as *Rollers*.

Rolls of Honour See **War memorials**.

Roman Well, Aldermaston See **Triangle, Aldermaston**.

Romania Since the revolution in Romania at the end of 1989, and the fall of President Ceausescu's regime, people from Tadley and adjacent areas have visited places in Romania to provide material, physical and moral support to the very poor and deprived people of that country, who have suffered extreme privations from the financial and collectivisation policies of the Romanian government. Two areas have been visited by people from the locality. They are **Ghergesti**, 50 kilometres west of the capital Bucharest, and **Mina Una Mai**, 20 kilometres west of the city of Brasov.

Ron Ward's Meadow (601 608) Ron **Ward** owned a 25 acre (10 ha) ancient south-facing hay meadow near The **Green**. He kept it in its natural state for over 35 years: no pesticides, insecticides, weedkillers or fertilisers were used in it. He resisted the temptation to sell the land for development during the building boom of the 1970s and 1980s. At least 5 species of orchid, 24 grasses, 15 forms of sedge, 10 types of rushes and 180 species of flowering plants have been identified in the meadow. Before he died he bequeathed the meadow to the Hampshire and Isle of Wight Wildlife Trust. Ron was granted permission to be buried in a corner of the meadow.

Room, The (610 623) Church meeting room in Pamber Heath, at the junction of Pamber Heath Road and Church Road, to the rear of **Treacle Cottage**. It was also sometimes referred to as either Mr Stroud's Room or the Plymouth Brethren Room. A small brick built building with a green galvanised roof, it could hold about 60 worshippers. At its peak three services and a Sunday school were held there to meet the needs of people who walked considerable distances to attend. It was also used for parish council meetings in the early 1900s. It was demolished in 1984 to make room for an extension to Treacle Cottage. See **Plymouth Brethren**.

Rose Cottage (606 610) A semi-detached cottage (with **Chine Cottage**) in **Malthouse Lane** within the **Tadley Conservation Area**. It has a thatched roof with two 'eyebrow' dormers, painted brick walling, three cambered-opening and casement windows. It has a modern brick porch. Both Rose Cottage and Chine Cottage are Grade II listed buildings.

Rowan Road Named after **Rowan Farm**. However, as late as 1936 the Ordnance Survey map shows the road as a continuation of Mulfords Hill.

Rowan Farm A dairy farm situated north of the junction of Rowan and Giles Roads. It was demolished in August 1966 to make way for the housing development in that area. In 1891, it was known as Bottom Farm, taking its name from **Tadley Bottom**, and was farmed by Joseph Diddams. By the 1930s, it was Rowan Farm when Frank Gray and, subsequently, George Bennett farmed there.

Royal Berkshire Hospital (723 727) Officially opened on 27 May 1839, King William IV was the patron and Richard **Benyon** one of the main subscribers. Although in Reading, the Royal Berkshire Hospital was the nearest large hospital to Tadley prior to the building of the **North Hampshire Hospital** in the 1970s and many local people went there for treatment. Local **carriers** would have transported them. øne collection-point for the Reading carrier was at the north end of **Winkworth Lane**. See **Friendly Societies**; **Health care and medical services**; **Hospitals**; Major George **Roller**.

Royal Ordnance Factory, Burghfield See AWE **Burghfield**.

Royal, The (596 624) Tadley's cinema, The Royal, was located along with The **Den** in the wartime gunnery-and-crew-procedure building (Building 205). It doubled as a concert hall and an RAF Astra cinema, using 16 mm projectors. In 1953 part of the building was converted into a 270 seat cinema with a 35 mm projector. Owned by the Ministry of Defence, a cinema lease was first taken up by Mr Thomas from Oxford. Alan Stiff, a cinema enthusiast who had a collection of over 100 projectors, took over the lease in 1964 and ran it until it closed in 1991 when competition from the multi-screen complex in Basingstoke made it uneconomic. The last film to be shown was 'Three Men and a Little Lady', parts of which had been filmed at Douai Abbey. During Mr Thomas's time the film which took the most money was 'Summer Holiday'; during Alan Stiff's time it was 'Abba – The Movie'. Gladys Yarwood was the cashier for many years before she died. As well as showing films, Bingo and Country and Western evenings were also held there.

S

c.Pope.

St Catherine's Church, Wolverton (552 585) It is thought that there has been a church on the site since 1286. Reconstructed in 1717 by a pupil of Sir Christopher Wren, it is considered by some to be one of the best early Georgian churches in Hampshire. It has a high, broad tower of light-red brick with alternating raised quoins (corner stones), a doorway in which there is much rustication on alternating-sized bricks, and a parapet. The nave roof is fifteenth century and has been preserved from an older building. The church was much damaged in 1908, by a fire under the tower. The gallery was burnt down, after which a new floor for the bellringers was installed halfway up the tower making ringing far easier. It still retains its boxed pews (lowered in 1872) and an unusual Dutch candelabra thought to have been a gift from Charles Van Notten who purchased the manor in 1782. The story that it is connected to **Park House** by an underground passage is false, however, on the south side of the church a small family vault, dating from 1770, is accessible. See **Wolverton Manor**.

St Luke's Church, Pamber Heath (612 625) A small church in Church Road which came into the parish of **St Peter's**, Tadley, from Monk Sherborne in 1976, following the redrawing of ecclesiastical parish boundaries. Built as a result of the concerns of the vicar of Monk Sherborne, appointed 1876, that the '…few scattered cottages at Pamber Heath had greatly increased but the cottagers were too far from either church (The **Priory** or All Saints, Monk Sherborne) to attend regularly' and so with the kind assistance of Richard **Benyon**, St Luke's Mission Church was built. It was used as a mission room on Sundays and an infants' school during the week. The official opening service was held on Tuesday 30 November 1880 when, it was reported, '…every available spot was taken up, and many were unable to gain admission.' Several changes have been made to the church since 1880. Most noticeable was the replacement of the plain school style windows with leaded lights and a stained glass window with a porch below.

The Revd Cecil Beadon Young, from Middlesex, was the first curate. He occupied the house now called 'The Old Parsonage' on the corner of Church and Silchester Roads. At that time it was called 'The Hermitage'. It is interesting to note how much larger The Parsonage seems small, in comparison with the size of the church. The adjoining cottage was later used as the curate's residence until the early 1980s, when it was sold and a new house, directly behind St Luke's in Oakfield Road, occupied instead. David Ashton, appointed in 1985, was the last resident curate. See **Pamber Heath School**.

St Mary the Virgin Church, Aldermaston (596 649) The **Domesday Survey** of 1086 recorded a church at Aldermaston. The present church dates from about 1150 and has some features from the Norman period, e.g. the fine western doorway, that could well have originally been in the south wall of the nave. Soon after 1250 the church appears to have been partly rebuilt and extended eastward. Dating from the mid fifteenth century, the tower, with its west window, had its upper part added as late as 1500. The vestry was added in about the mid seventeenth century. Early nineteenth century alterations to the interior have since been removed; a gallery and squire's pew, and battens covered with whitewashed lath and plaster which reduced the width of the church by three feet (1 m). In 1952 the tower was found to be in need of repair and brick piers and a steel support for the spire were put in place. There are numerous items of interest: original wall paintings, some from the early fourteenth century; monuments commemorating members of families who owned the Manor of Aldermaston and flags carried by the Aldermaston Troop of the Berkshire Yeomanry Cavalry in 1803. The church is also rich in plate, with the earliest chalice being dated 1576; other pieces are from every century between the seventeenth and twentieth. Two of the eight bells date from 1681, and there is a list of incumbents from 1297 in the nave and a list of churchwardens dating from 1560 in the vestry. See The **York Nativity Play**.

St Mary the Virgin Church, Silchester (643 623) The predecessor of this church is the earliest known Christian church in Great Britain, its remains lying a quarter of a mile west, next to the Roman forum. This small building, 42 feet by 33 feet (13 m by 10 m), was discovered in 1892. The present church, originally called The Church of Our Lady, was probably built between 1125 and 1150 at the instigation of a John or Ralph Bluett, Lord of the Manor of Silchester. The Bluett family spent most of their time at their seat in Wiltshire and it was some time before it was decided to build a church at Silchester. St Mary's lies just within the walls of **Calleva Atrebatum**: Roman bricks, visible in the walls and buttresses, indicate how convenient it was for Norman builders to make use of the wealth of materials on the site. This early church was simply a nave without aisles. A series of enlargements were made by the Bluett family throughout the thirteenth century. The first of these being the north aisle, which was added to accommodate worshippers from Mortimer West End. The chancel was extended and wall paintings from about 1230 remain on its walls. The first recorded rector was a John of Knovill in 1294. There were six rectors in 1349; possibly a reminder of the terrible consequences of the **Black Death**. Rector Coles (1812-65) was responsible for replacing the chancel screen which, during the Commonwealth period, was hidden in a nearby barn. The screen, one of the finest in Hampshire, dates from the time of Henry VIII's marriage to Catherine of Aragon. See **St Saviour's Church, Mortimer West End**.

St Mary's Church, Ewhurst (570 567) Originally a plain Early-English style church recorded as existing in the reign of Edward I (1272-1306). It was rebuilt in 1872-3 at the expense of W.H.C. Plowden whose ancestors lie buried there. Deconsecrated after its closure in 1982, the furniture was removed to the Ewhurst Chapel at **St Catherine's Church, Wolverton**.

St Mary's Church, North Tadley (590 621) See **Great St Mary's Church, Tadley**.

St Michael's Church (588 623) Roman Catholic church in Bishopswood Road. Tadley is part of the parish of Tadley and Kingsclere in the diocese of Portsmouth. The two churches in the parish are Saint Michael's, Bishopswood Road, and Saint Pe-

ter and Paul's, Kingsclere. Before St Michael's was built there was no resident priest in the parish. After World War II, the spiritual needs of the many Irish buildings workers and, later, of the first workers at **AWRE** were looked after by the monks from Douai Abbey; a weekly service was held at 6.00 pm on Sundays in the old **Community Centre**. In 1954 a site was purchased and a chapel-cum-hall was opened in 1959. Until 1962 Fr Michael Young continued to serve the community from Douai Abbey. In that year, the Diocese took over the responsibility and Fr Desmond O'Ryan became the first parish priest. At the same time the Kingsclere area of the parish, which had previously been looked after by priests from Basingstoke, became part of the parish.

St Paul's Church (603 608) Tadley's 'new' Anglican church at The **Green**, with seating for 300. It replaced **St Saviour's Church** and was built in its grounds. Revd Kenneth Davis, rector at the time (1961-75), played a considerable part in the project. The foundation stone was laid on 22 May 1965 by Commander J.S. Baker and blessed by the Bishop of Southampton. The church was consecrated by the Bishop of Winchester on 2 April 1966. Costing £28,000, it was designed by Pinckney and Gott, FRIBA, and built by W.E. **Chivers and Sons Ltd** of Devizes. It is constructed of laminated timber portal frames, supporting a close-boarded roof, covered with hand-made Bambino tiles. The outside walls are faced with local hand-made bricks. The special features of the design are the great west window of plain glass, and the apsidal east end with its central shaped altar of Portland stone. The bell, given by John **Stacey**, weighs five cwt (254 kg) and was cast from the old four bells of Basingstoke Town Hall. Part of the stained glass window (on the south side) was donated by Lucy **Idenden** in memory of her husband Frank, 'a craftsman and an artist'. The remainder of the window was donated by Mrs Eliza Ann Eden, Lucy's sister, in memory of her husband, Percy Eden and only son John Eden, and of their parents John and Ann Burgoyne and Richard and Keziah Eden. The font was made at **Aldermaston Pottery**.

St Paul's Church Hall (603 608) The foundation stone for the church hall, situated in the grounds of **St Paul's Church** at The **Green**, was laid by Bishop N.E. Cornwall on 15 October 1966 and the building was dedicated by the Bishop of Winchester on 14 March 1967. It replaced the **Iron Room**, previously used as a social centre.

St Peter's Church (597 600) A Grade I listed building. The first reference to a church at Tadley is in 1286 when Andrew Hotot is recorded as owning The Manor and Church. It could be assumed that a settlement and therefore a church existed at an earlier date in view of the documented references to owners of land at Tadley from 909 AD.

Only the nave would appear to date from the thirteenth century, the walls of which are now rough cast outside covering a crude flint and mortar structure over 2 feet thick. The rest is of brick, the tower dated 1685 by the master bricklayers stone. The tower roof was originally boarded but replaced with tiles in 1879. The remainder of the church is also a mix of periods and styles, primarily seventeenth century but with late fifteenth century wood work in the outer opening of the porch and a tenor bell made between 1553 and 1558. This is the bell that carries the, as yet, undeciphered raised inscription. This mix of periods could indicate that the original chapel had fallen into disrepair or, more probably, that it was extended to accommodate the inhabitants of the known settlement near Tadley Manor Place during the time of Henry and Lucy Ludlow.

Inside the walls are plastered, as is the ceiling of the chancel, but the nave ceiling is boarded. Much of the wood used inside the tower for the stairs and musicians gallery is said to be old ships timbers; brought up from Southampton en route to **Pamber Forest** to collect new timbers. There was no organ at St Peter's until 1970. Prior to this choristers and/or musicians led the congregation from the seventeenth century gallery. The oak seating and pulpit are also seventeenth Century. The pulpit, dated 1650, is a reminder that the church was used by one of Cromwell's puritan ministers, Thomas Kentish, recorded as being 'an excellent and useful minister'. He remained until the **Act of Uniformity** in 1662 when he was ejected from the post.

As the village of Tadley grew and developed around **Back Lane** and The **Green**, in the eighteenth and nineteenth centuries, St Peter's became isolated from its congregation and as a result a new church, **St Paul's**, was built. An architectural survey of St Peter's in 1996 resulted in £10,000 worth of repairs being carried out to the floor in 1997. See Reuben **Hicks; Ludlow family; Tadley Place.**

St Saviour's Church, Mortimer West End (634 636) The correct title is the Church of the Holy Saviour. Built with a donation from Richard **Benyon** in 1856, this church is in the Diocese of Oxford, although in Hampshire. In 1870 the Hampshire part of Mortimer became a separate parish. Two vestries were added in 1902, increasing the size of the little church – one for the vicar and one for the choir. There was no church on the site before 1856. For many years local people went to St Mary's, Silchester, where they were allocated pews in the north aisle known as 'Mortimer's Hole'. James **Lawes**, on whom W.H. Hudson based the character of Caleb Bawcombe in *A Shepherd's Life* is buried in an unmarked grave in the churchyard. See **St Mary, The Virgin, Silchester; Mortimer West End**.

St Saviour's Church, Tadley (604 608) A **mission church**, designed to seat 130 people, built by Revd Charles N. Oliver at his own expense. It stood where 1 Rectory Close is now. The church and recreational room, built of pine and corrugated iron, were dedicated to St Saviour at Christmas 1888. The recreational room, known locally as the **Iron Room**, was beside the church. At one time the room was used by **Tadley School** for cookery lessons and carrying out medical examinations. The church was demolished in 1966 and part of the land was sold to pay for **St Paul's Church Hall**.

St Stephen's Church, Baughurst (582 599) St Stephen's Church, Baughurst has a long history. Legend has it that Roman soldiers from **Calleva Atrebatum** who had been converted to Christianity, worshipped on a nearby hill. The present building dates from 1847, when, due to the collapse of the earlier Saxon church, a flint and stone church was built. The high cost of rebuilding, mixed with the villagers' sense of loss at the collapse of their church, compelled them to go on foot to the hills of Hannington and Kingsclere to bring back flints and chalk with which to build the new church. Extra stone was brought from Bath by canal to Aldermaston.

The church is in a Gothic style with an unusual octagonal tower which was pinned in 1990 after the top part was blown down. Surviving from the twelfth-century church is a blocked doorway bearing mass-dials, while the font, with its octagonal bowl is fifteenth century. The remains of a Norman arch are also built into the west wall. A particular treasure is the fifteenth century chancel screen, now at the western end of the church, which is said to have been a gift of William Warham, Archbishop of Canterbury (1504-32). The tower contains six bells cast by Thomas Swaine in 1775 and the tenor bell is inscribed 'Mr Maberly had contrived to run three into 5 in 1775'. The old church contained a Jacobean oak pulpit which was removed from the ruins and put in Chapel House and, later, Baughurst Methodist Church. The church has an enormous pipe organ, installed in 1969, from a redundant Methodist Church. The rectory next door to the church was sold in 1982.

St Stephen's Church, Little London (623 594) Situated on the east side of the road opposite New Road, the church is built of red brick with blue headers. It has a porch, vestry and a single bell. Undoubtedly it is another of the Benyon Mission Churches, as the land on which it stands was owned by the **Englefield Estate** at the time of building. The date is uncertain, but thought to be 1897 when many such churches were built to celebrate the Diamond Jubilee of Queen Victoria. It is now in the ecclesiastical Parish of Bramley but was previously part of Monk Sherborne. Due to the considerable distance of Little London from All Saints Church, Monk Sherborne and **Priory Church**, and prior to the building of St Stephen's, regular services were previously held in one of the cottages. See Richard **Benyon. See St Luke's Church, Pamber Heath.**

Salvation Army Hall, Mulfords Hill, post 1909

Photo: J.W. & C.A. Stevens

Salvation Army An Evangelical Christian organisation which evolved from the missionary work in the East End of London by William Booth, who had previously been a Methodist preacher. The Tadley Corps was formed in January 1898 when two ladies, Captain Edith Griffith and Lieutenant Alice Irham, were sent out from London. Early meetings were held in the open air on Tadley Common. Eventually a kind donor provided the first meeting place, the site of which is where Lloyds Bank is today. During the early 1900s, William Booth preached there. The growth of the Corps meant that a larger hall was needed. In 1907, land was acquired on Mulfords Hill and a new hall built there in 1909 by Noah **Blake**. Over the years several extensions have been added to the original structure, one of which was opened in 1955 by Lady Mount of **Wasing Park**. For many years the Tadley Corps, in keeping with local tradition, has had a good band. See Susan **Jones**; **Tadley Bands**.

Sarnia (608 608) A cottage in Winston Avenue, within the **Tadley Conservation Area**, standing on the site of a cottage which existed in 1720 but was, subsequently, burnt down. The present cottage was built in two halves in about 1800, using bricks from the **Little London Brickworks**. The hall on the left of the cottage was originally used as a dairy. There is a well in the garden. Frank and Lucy Idenden were former owners of the cottage. See **Idenden family**.

Saulez, Revd Edmund C.P. (1821-1883) The first rector of Tadley from 1878 to 1883. Prior to this he had been assistant curate to Thomas Flood from 1856. Edmund, his wife, Jane, and son, Al-fred, were resident in Spiers Green in 1861 but, by 1871, he was a widower with two sons. In 1878, as rector, he was resident at The Vicarage, probably Barn Close Cottage and still living with his sons. See **Barn Close House; Cricket; Fairlawn House; Hatch Cottage; Overton; Tadley Roll**.

Saunders, Arthur 'Ticky' Born in 1857 and the eldest of eight children, 'Ticky' was a blacksmith by trade, but given his **nickname** because he also mended clocks. Ernie **Kimber** refers to him in *Tadley During my Time and Before* as being the self-appointed town crier: '…if there was a fete or other forthcoming event to announce he would don his frayed old tail coat and top hat and with a loud clanging of his bell broadcast the news'. On Armistice Day, 11 November 1918, he walked along the main road through Tadley in the cold, wet and damp ringing his bell, proclaiming the end of the war at 11.00 am that morning. He died in one of the almshouses on The **Green**, now replaced by **Mothe's House**.

School Allotment Charity The Tadley School Allotment Charity was established by the **enclosure award** of 1850 (1852) when two plots of land were awarded; one acre (0.4 ha) on the east side of Tadley Hill and nine acres (3.5 ha) behind The **Salvation Army** hall along Briar Way. The fences were to be maintained by the trustees out of the rents and proceeds of the land. The object of the foundation was the maintenance of a school for the education of the poor. The rector and churchwardens of Tadley were trustees of the charity. The only known Tadley school connected to the established church, in existence at that time, was operating 'in a cottage' from 1840. The charity was closed in 1995; the remaining money was distributed amongst the five Tadley schools, each receiving amounts according to the numbers on roll. See **Appendix iii**; Revd George **Jennings; National Schools**.

Scout Hut, Baughurst (582 621) Baughurst Scout Hut began as a club room for men of the village, and was provided by Mr W.H. McConnel shortly before World War II. It was also used by Heath End United Football Club, who played their home matches on the field adjoining The Hawthorns. During the war, it served as a YMCA hostel for servicemen stationed locally. Later, during the war, it was used as an outpost for packing and assembling Spitfire fighter parts. After the war, Miss Lily Brown and Mrs Crane ran a small cafe in the hut and later it was used by the Scouts. The original wooden building was replaced by a brick-built structure in 1994. See **Hangar 5; McConnel family; Scouting**.

Scouting Scouting was founded in 1908 by Robert Baden-Powell. The National Scout Association archives record scouting in **Tadley** in 1914; a troop under the leadership of church verger, L.G. Clack, had a strength of 12. At the end of **World War I** a group, complete with band, was being run by two ladies Miss Paine and Miss Marshall. The present group, the 26th Basingstoke, was opened in 1955, later Burnham Copse was added to the name. The group consisted of four Scouters, 20 Wolf Cubs and 15 Boy Scouts with John S. Eynon as first Group Scout Master and Peter F. Beaver as Cub Master. Early meetings were held in the old **Community Centre**, later moving to The **Den**. On 1 December 1966 the 26th Basingstoke (Burnham Copse) Group became the Tadley Scout Group in the newly formed Silchester Scout District. In the late 1980s a Beaver Colony (6-8 year olds) and then a Venture Scout Unit (15½ to 21) were added. In 1999 the group consists two beaver colonies, two cub packs, one scout troop and one venture unit. The group recognises scouting achievements with annual awards: Woodchip award for beavers, the David Anderson Award for cubs, the Alan Stark award for scouts and the Ian Newsome award for venture scouts. Plans are in hand to build a new purpose-built Tadley scout den in Southdown Road.

The earliest recorded scout group in Baughurst was started in January 1924 and seems to have been active until 1947 when it ceased. The current group was registered on 18 October 1962 as 10th Basingstoke (Baughurst) and transferred to the (then) new Silchester District on 1 December 1966. Venture Scouts, originally only for boys, were started in Baughurst by Les Eaton in the 1970s. The unit was one of the first to admit girls. Currently Baughurst group consists of only one beaver colony and one cub pack.

Pamber Scout Group, the 21st Basingstoke, was registered in February 1950. Formed by Howard and Pearl Stanley, the group met in the old **Pamber Heath Memorial Hall**. The group closed for a time but was re-established as 1st Pamber Group. The present Den in Pelican Road was built on land donated by Mr Lional Wakeford who, as the first president, officially opened it in May 1969. Currently there is one beaver colony, one cub pack and one scout troop. Nationally, scouting was opened to girls in the early 1990s. See **Barn Close Laundry**.

Searing, Roger Born 1916, Roger was the first headteacher of **Burnham Copse Junior School**, serving 24 years in the post before retiring in 1979. During this time he was President of the North Hampshire Branch of the National Association of Headteachers. He is commemorated by the road Searing Close, which is built on the original site of the school. When he retired he became chairman of **Mothe's Charity** and Tadley Green Housing Association, a parish councillor, a member of the Ramblers Association, chairman of the **Tadley Revel** in the 1970s and early 1980s, and chairman of **Tadley and District Society** from 1984 until his death in 1997. Roger, an appropriate person for the latter post, had written several historical articles about Reading and Tadley for the *Reading Chronicle*. He was also joint author with Pat **Minter** of the popular *Tadley Tracks, Tadley Facts*, a walker's guide to the local area. He and his wife Joan met while he was a pupil-teacher at the Bluecoat School, Reading. They married in 1939. Roger was called-up into the RAF Volunteer Reserve (RAFVR) in 1940 and Joan joined the Women's Land Army (WLA) serving at Pangbourne. Soon discharged from the RAFVR, because of defective eyesight, he again took up teaching in Reading, followed by post-war teacher training in Surrey and a post at Sutton Scotney which lead to his appointment to Burnham Copse Junior School.

seeABILITY The charity is registered as The Royal School For The Blind. It provides a wide range of services for people of 18 years and over who are visually impaired and have other disabilities. Its new centre, **Heather House**, will provide day and residential care for those suffering from juvenile Batten's disease and other similar degenerative diseases. Because those with **juvenile Batten's disease** retain their mental faculties for many years the centre aims to provide stimulation and challenges as well as long-term care. The centre is the first of its kind in Britain and will be officially opened by HRH The Duchess of Gloucester GCVO in November 1999. See **Penney Appeal**.

Sewage The days of the septic tank and soak-aways are not too far removed for many folk in Tadley. A sewage works, associated with **Aldermaston Airfield**, existed off Bishopswood Lane during and after World War II. It was shown as site 16 on the 1945 airfield map. Although there is little record of when mains sewerage came to the district it has been suggested by Thames Water Utilities that pipes were first laid in the late 1940s or early 1950s. This would coincide with the post-war expansion of the area associated with the building of **AWRE** and its living accommodation, e.g. Baughurst Common went on mains when the AWRE houses of the Wildwood Estate were built by Lovelock in 1965-67. Council minutes refer to a 'sewage extension scheme' for Tadley in April 1955 and the 'go ahead for a Baughurst sewage scheme' as late as November 1974. The main flow from the area is by a gravity sewer through **Pamber Forest** into the Silchester sewage treatment works. The clean effluent discharges directly into **Silchester Brook** which runs into the Loddon. See **Baughurst Parish Council; Pamber Parish Council; Tadley Parish Council; Water.**

Sherborne Priory The original name of **Pamber Priory.**

Shrubbery, The At one time a well known house in Cliddesden Road, Basingstoke, The Shrubbery was built in 1830. Between 1909-1946 it was the home of the Burberry family. It was sold to Basingstoke Council who used it as a maternity hospital until the maternity wing of the **North Hampshire Hospital** was built in the early 1970s. Many local families had their children delivered at The Shrubbery. Prior to its demolition in 1992 the Horseshoe Theatre Company used the house as a store. See **Basingstoke Cottage Hospital; Health care and medical services; Hospitals.**

Sieff, Baron Israel See **Lane End Cottage, Brimpton Common.**

Silchester (627 620) A village, two miles east of Tadley. Previous names have been: Kalcoua (second century); Calleva (fourth century); Silcestre (1086); Cilecestre (1236); Sylchestre (1322); Chilchester (1349). The parish of Silchester contains the site of the Roman town of **Calleva Atrebatum.** At the time of the **Domesday Survey** there were two manors at Silchester, one corresponding to the present parish, the other to **Mortimer West End.** These were combined into one while still in the possession of the Bluett family. The Manor of Silchester was held by descendants of the Bluetts through the female line after 1316 until 1540. The manor thereafter changed ownership several times, eventually being sold in 1828 to Arthur Wellesley, the first Duke of Wellington. See **Calleva Atrebatum; St Mary the Virgin Church, Silchester.**

Silchester Arms, The (657 625) A public house, popularly known as The Jackdaw, and situated along the metalled stretch of the **Devil's Highway**, not far from the railway bridge. In a 1552 survey it was mentioned as a 'mansion' with an orchard and garden and about 50 acres (20 ha). With the coming of the railway in the mid-nineteenth century, the then owners opened a bar to provide ale for the navvies. It ceased to be a public house in about 1950 and is once again a private dwelling.

Silchester Brook A tributary of the River Loddon. It rises near Bishopswood Farm and runs through Pamber Forest on its way to the Kennet and eventually the Thames. It changes its name from **Bishopswood Stream** to Silchester Brook near Silchester. See **Sewage.**

Silchester (C of E) Aided School (627 627) A National School, built in 1844, with an adjacent school house. It was partly supported financially by the Duke of Wellington, probably by the donation of land. The school site and building is now owned and maintained by the Diocese. At its inception the education costs would have been met by the Church and or voluntary means. Later, as now, the County Council met these costs. Built to accommodate 90 pupils it had, by 1894, become so cramped that it was deemed to be having an effect on the pupils' education. Following a strongly worded letter a new classroom was built in 1896 to accommodate the Infants. In 1999 the school now has 7 classrooms and 220 pupils. The log book for the first 50/60 years records it as being badly equipped and the pupils poorly taught. The governors' report in 1893 indicated a desperate need for desks and the arrival of one new desk is duly noted, as was at other dates, 2 dozen slates and a large slate board, a donation from the Duke of Wellington. Staff retention was poor. The Plummer family: John, master, his wife and later daughter(s) served the longest; 1871 (or before) – 1887. An improvement in standards only began following the appointment of Margaret Payne as head in 1896.

In addition to the usual seasonal absences for **hop picking** and **acorn picking** the school had a considerable number of additional closures and absences. Silchester, being an agrarian community, meant days off for haymaking and visits to Reading Agricultural Show. Severe snow storms closed the school most winters. In particular January 1881, when between 5 and 6 feet was recorded. Heavy rain also made roads impassible for pupils. Epidemics of childhood illnesses necessitated closure due to low attendance. In 1900, **Pamber Heath** suffered an epidemic of scarlet fever and those pupils from that village were prohibited from attending school for 10 weeks. On one day in February 1902 scarlet fever reduced the numbers to 25 out of a possible 101 pupils. In June 1879 the **Band of Hope** passed through the village. It detained pupils so long that school eventually closed for the day. One way of improving pupils' attendance was by the issuing of clothing tickets. In 1885, 8 pupils each registering over 400 attendances were given 5 shillings. 2 infants received 1s 6d for 300 attendances whereas 16 older pupils each received 3shillings for the same number.

The importance of children to the incomes of families in the nineteenth century and early twentieth century is shown by an entry for April 1919. It relates to a Frank Cripps, whose parents refused to send him to school to complete the term because he was now 14. See **Education; Appendix i, Tadley**

School; Priory School; Ramsdell School; Pamber Heath School; Post Offices.

Silchester Common Common land between **Pamber Heath** and **Silchester** running into **Pamber Forest** to the south. Originally being recorded as 205 acres (101 ha) in 1653, there was only an area of 175 acres (71 ha) available at the tithe commutation of 1841. A manoral survey of 1804 discussed the possibility of enclosing some waste land within the manor. Manorial Rolls relating to ownership are said to be lost. Grazing, Turbary and mineral rights were originally attached to tenements, however, over the years all parishioners have tried to claim rights. Today, larger than **Tadley Common**, the part south of Pamber Road has recently been fenced in to enable the re-introduction of grazing.

Silchester Cricket Club See **Cricket**.

Silchester Gallery (716 736) A permanent exhibition about **Calleva Atrebatum**, recreating daily life in Roman Britain, which opened in The Museum of Reading in 1995. Among the items on show are cooking, eating and drinking vessels, jewellery, money and tools found during excavations at the town. Pride of place is given to the bronze eagle, found during excavations, which is thought to have formed part of an imperial group statue adorning the basilica and situated alongside the forum.

Silchester Methodist Chapel (624 623) The first camp meeting recorded was on 31 May 1807 and the first 'class' formed in March 1810, in Silchester. The first house-meetings were held in 1834, under the auspices of The Reading Mission, and the following year a primitive structure of tree branches covered with furze was built for worship on the common near the present village hall. It is alleged that the vicar had the public house, now called The **Calleva Arms**, built to stop the Methodist chapel being built there. The first permanent chapel, located on the south side of Pamber Road opposite the junction with Kings Road, was built in 1839, at a cost of £335 12s 6p (£335.62p). Built for the **Primitive Methodists** it is now used as the schoolroom and hall. It was registered as a dissenters' meeting house in 1841. In 1927 the present chapel was built. See **Ebenezer Cottage**.

Silchester Players The Silchester Players is an amateur dramatics society that first performed in 1976 when a group of local people decided to raise funds for leukaemia research. The production, an 'Olde Tyme Music Hall', was initiated by Mrs Debbie Joseph and took place in Silchester Village Hall. This was followed by the pantomime 'Snow White and the Seven Dwarfs', staged in January 1976. Since that time the Players have continued to entertain, usually with three productions a year: a play in Spring, a revue or music hall in Autumn, and a pantomime early in the New Year. Apart from providing enjoyable entertainment, the Players donate some of their income to local charities or handicapped people who live in the area.

Silchester Primitive Methodist Circuit The Circuit was formed in 1866 and comprised the Societies at Silchester, Chatter (now Charter) Alley(1852), Baughurst (1845), Little London (1867), Hannington (1871), Mortimer (Drury Lane 1867) and Wootton St. Lawrence. By 1871 Tadley Main Road (opened in 1859), and Wolverton Common (1867) had joined, but Wootton St Lawrence had left. Haughurst Hill joined the Plan by 1905 and in 1929 the Charity Commissioners made this official. With Methodist Union in 1932, 'Primitive' was dropped from the title and in 1982 it joined with the Reading Circuit to form The Reading and Silchester Circuit. See **Ebenezer Cottage**.

Simonds Ltd, H. & G. Local brewery which ran several licensed houses in the area: The **Fighting Cocks** (originally John **May & Co Ltd**), The **Pelican**, The **Cricketers**, The **Old House at Home**, The **Rifleman** (Little London), The **Fox & Hounds**, Ye **Olde Vyne** (West Heath). William Simonds, a maltster, began brewing in Reading in 1768. By 1839 the company produced 15,000 barrels a year and operated 37 licensed houses. H. & G. Simonds Ltd was registered as a limited company in 1885. Over the years the company took over several local small brewing firms: Atlas Brewery, Newbury in 1920; Newbury Brewery Co Ltd, Castle Brewery, Northbrook Street, Newbury in 1931; John **May & Co Ltd**, Basingstoke in 1947. In 1959, Simonds entered into a trading agreement with Courage and Barclay Ltd and, after merging the following year, it became Courage, Barclay & Simonds Ltd. The Bridge Street brewery in Reading town centre ceased brewing in 1979 and work was transferred to new premises at Worton Grange beside the M4.

Sims family Born in **Pamber** in December 1894, Ernest ('Ernie') Sims was the last of a long line of rake-makers that spanned over 200 years. The first recorded at **Pamber End** was Jacob Sims, born in 1776, the great-grandfather of Ernie. Like most rural crafts, rake-making was taught by father to son and the census returns for 1841-91 show that it was not only a family trade but one locally exclusive to the Sims. No other rake makers were listed in either **Tadley** or **Baughurst** parishes throughout the 50 years. Jacob had two sons and, subsequently, grandsons to carry on the trade and by 1881 there was sufficient work to support four Sims men making rakes, although by then Jacob had, of course, died. The original thatched cottage and workshop were destroyed by fire in the last century but were subsequently rebuilt. Following the death of Ernie in 1983, the three workshops were demolished and the house extended. The property is now known as 'Rakemakers'. Ernie's son, John, did not continue the family trade and so the contents of the workshop are shared between Alton Museum and the Rural History Centre at The University of Reading. See **Rakes**.

Smith and Eyres See **Bakers**.

Smithies See **Blacksmiths**.

Smiths of Baughurst (580 618) H.C. Smith, a Hampshire farmer, sold his farm in 1938 and bought Sidney **Knight**'s bicycle shop in **Baughurst**. Soon after the beginning of **World War II** the firm was directed by the government to maintain and repair agricultural equipment, appropriate in view of the Smith family's original farming connections. The youngest son, M.T.A. Smith, served his apprenticeship as a motor mechanic with the Newbury firm of Stradlings and J. **Thorneycroft** in Basingstoke before rejoining the family firm. The business expanded rapidly after World War II and today, following the retirement of M.T.A. Smith, is run by his son, Paul, who joined the firm in 1964. The garage, which celebrated its 60th anniversary in 1998, was first appointed Ford dealers in 1963.

Smuggling It has been written that an innkeeper near the gate of Kempshott Park was a recipient of smuggled brandy. The said innkeeper also dealt in the sale of birch brooms in the north of the country, for use in furnaces. The arrival or threat of the Customs men necessitated the enlistment of **Tadley** men and their broom carts. By day, carts arrived at the inn laden with brooms; by night, they returned to Tadley filled with barrels of brandy. When the threat of the Customs men had passed, the barrels were returned to Basingstoke under subsequent loads of brooms. 10 shillings (50p) to £1 is said to have been the rate for running this terrible risk. If caught, a smuggler was either put to death or transported to a convict settlement.

Soke A term used for land, often scattered over many manors or villages, which was held by freemen who owed personal allegiance to a lord or a court. There are many recorded in the **Domesday Survey**. It was originally a Danelaw term, the Danelaw being those shires north and east of Watling Street which were ruled by the Danes from the ninth to eleventh centuries. Later the word became generally used to cover any private jurisdiction of land whether owned by barons, guilds or religious houses. Locally the name appears in Soke Road, part of which is in Hampshire and part in Berkshire. It also borders three parishes: Silchester, Aldermaston and Mortimer West End. During roadworks, an old wooden bridge, thought to date from when the road was a 'drover's way', was discovered at the lowest point on the Soke Road.

Some Account of the Village of Tadley in Hampshire, and the Independent Church There A book written by Daniel **Benham** and published in 1862, possibly to coincide with the two hundredth anniversary of the **Act of Uniformity** in 1662. Almost certainly the earliest of local histories, it concentrates mainly on the religious history of the area known at that time. It has proved, through detailed referencing, a significant source of information for local historians. Both the original, and a later, bound, photocopy version, have

long been out of print. However, in 1996 **Tadley and District Society** published a re-set version of the book complete with its original reference sources and a reproduction of the 'drawing on stone' of the Independent Church as it was in the 1860s. The copy of the original book held at the British Library was signed by the author. See **United Reformed Church**.

Sorting Office, Tadley (595 618) The first sorting office in Tadley was in Main Road, near the junction with Fairlawn Road, in the premises previously used by Ford's blacksmiths. The present sorting office, in Newchurch Road, was opened in 1997, replacing an earlier prefabricated structure on the same site, built in 1978. See **Blacksmiths; Post Office, Tadley**.

Southern Works Organisation (SWO) (592 622) This was a United Kingdom Atomic Energy Authority (UKAEA) design office situated in a group of temporary buildings in Newchurch Road, now the site of **Burnham Copse Infants School**. It was administratively separate from the AWRE, being an outpost of the Industrial Group of the UKAEA, based at Risley, near Warrington, Lancashire. It was responsible for the design and construction of the major building works throughout southern England for the UKAEA, notably the building of Culham Laboratory in Oxfordshire. It was formed in 1958-9 and employed up to 100 architects, engineers, quantity surveyors, contract officers and support staff who used the dining and social facilities of AWRE. It was wound up in about 1966 when the major building programmes of the UKAEA in the area had been completed.

Spitfire fighter See **Hangar 5; PL965**.

Squatters After **World War II** there was a shortage of housing locally. Although some of the buildings near **Aldermaston Airfield** were still being used, a lot were empty and these attracted squatters. There are several references to them in publications of the time. The problem only disappeared with the growth of **AWRE** in the early 1950s and the associated development of suitable local housing.

SSSI (Sites of Special Scientific Interest) Sites of Special Scientific Interest, often referred to as Triple SIs, is the term used to denote an area of land notified under the Wildlife and Countryside Act 1981 as being of special nature conservation interest. In England SSSIs are notified by English Nature, the statuary body for nature conservation. These sites are the best examples of our natural heritage of wildlife habitats, geological features and land forms. The criteria include measuring against the variety and diversity of habitat and species within a nominated 'Area of Search'. Notified SSSIs within our area are currently Aldermaston Gravel Pits (596 668), Decoy Pits, Pools and Woods (612 632), Wasing Wood Ponds (578 635), West's Meadow (597 626), Brimpton Pit (566 651), Woolhampton Reed Beds (575 667), **Ron Ward's**

Meadow, Ashford Hill Meadows, Pamber Forest and Silchester Common. A detailed description of each site is available from English Nature. See Wildlife; Decoy Heath; Wasing Place.

Stacey family The lineage of the present Stacey and Sons has, to date, been traced to George and Elizabeth, born in Tadley in 1787-78 respectively. Their grandson, John Stacey senior (born 1852, died 1928) lived at Hill House Farm, The Green, as did his son, George H. Stacey. The house was later demolished, and two mock-Georgian houses and two bungalows built on the site (the south west corner of The Green). By the 1930s, George's son, John junior, (born 1912, died 1970) and his wife Lilian 'Lily' were living in the cottage at Tadley Brickyard, where all but one of their children were born. 'Lily'. née Moss was born in Aldermaston in 1910 and prior to her marriage was in service to Dr Lionel Holmwood. See Dr Joe Morland; J. Stacey & Sons; St Paul's Church.

Stacey & Sons, J. The first recorded Stacey 'wood dealer' (in 1871) was William, father of John Stacey (senior). This was the basis of the first company called J. Stacey & Sons, wood dealers, farmers, brick and broom makers, established in 1927. By the early 1900s the Staceys were probably the largest wood dealers in the area. They annually bought the rights of up to 60 acres (24 ha) of Englefield woodland, putting in 6-8 men to cut the underwood and timber for barge and hop poles. This was then sold to local besom makers, farmers, woodworking firms and most importantly to the Tadley Brickyard. The purchase of the brickyard by John Stacey (senior) was an obvious 'marrying' of two trades, interdependent on each other. The modern J. Stacey & Sons was formed by John (junior) in 1964 as a contracting company dealing specifically in haulage, demolition and plant hire, covering, on average, a radius of 50 miles (80 km). It is based at the site of what was the brickyard and is now managed by three of his sons. See Coppicing; Stacey family.

Star, The (597 606) Originally a beer shop situated opposite The Fighting Cocks on the Aldermaston Road (A340) at Dix Hill. Possibly in use in 1851, with Richard Cottrell being the beer retailer. It is thought to have been trading until after World War II, when it was demolished, possibly to allow for road widening and improvement.

Station 467 During World War II, Station 467 was the American reference number for Aldermaston Airfield.

Stiff, Alan Owner of Tadley's cinema, The Royal, between 1964 and 1991.

Strange, W.J. & Son Ltd (602 672) Local brewing firm which at one time owned several public houses including: The Plough (Little London), The Badgers Wood (Baughurst), The Ship (Ashford Hill) and The Falcon (Tadley). Situated by Aldermaston Lock, the Aldermaston Brewery drew its water from a 160 feet (48 m) deep artesian well. The brewery was established in 1770 and purchased by Thomas Strange in 1833. It was operated by William Jeffrey Strange and Sons until 1902 after which it was run by John J. Strange. The company was taken over in 1945 by Strong & Co of Romsey and the brewery at Aldermaston ceased soon afterwards. The site was used by Stirling Cables prior to being redeveloped in 1995 as a housing estate called The Wharf. See Brewing and licensing laws; Kennet & Avon Canal.

Street lighting Street lighting came to Tadley in the 1950s. Tadley Parish Council minutes record the first lights being installed in 1958, paid for by AWRE in conjunction with the council.

Street names The best source of information on the history of local street names is *Street Names and their Origins* by Alan Albery and Marie-Claude Lelliott.

Swedish Houses (605 613) A shortage of bricks and other traditional construction materials after World War II led to the need to use alternative materials for housing construction. The local authority at the time (Kingsclere and Whitchurch Rural District Council) set up a sub-committee to investigate such materials and, as a result, Swedish timber-style houses were erected in September 1945. Almost wholly made of wood, they could be built quickly at an acceptable cost from easily obtained materials. The style of housing is remembered today by the street name Swedish Houses.

Swing Riots See Labourers Revolt.

Sympson's Charity In 1674 Thomas Sympson, of Monk Sherborne, gave in his will the sum of £15 a year to the poor of six parishes (Sherborne St John, Monk Sherborne, Lawrence Wootton, Baughurst, Pamber and Tadley) for 'as long as the world shall endure'. The money was to come from his land at Monk Sherborne, Hill House, and Baughurst, Bullers Farm. It was to be distributed on St Thomas's Day (21 December). The amount for each parish, £2 10s (£2 50p), was given in varying amounts; as little as 6d (2.5p) and as much as 3 shillings (30p) depending on the need. Brass plates in each respective parish church set out the details of the gift. The charity was formerly known as Sympson's Gift. See Charities.

T

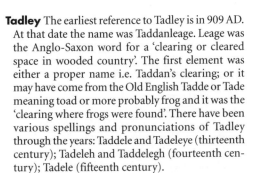

Tadley The earliest reference to Tadley is in 909 AD. At that date the name was Taddanleage. Leage was the Anglo-Saxon word for a 'clearing or cleared space in wooded country'. The first element was either a proper name i.e. Taddan's clearing; or it may have come from the Old English Tadde or Tade meaning toad or more probably frog and it was the 'clearing where frogs were found'. There have been various spellings and pronunciations of Tadley through the years: Taddele and Tadeleye (thirteenth century); Tadeleh and Taddelegh (fourteenth century); Tadele (fifteenth century).

As part of a grant of land made in a charter of 909 AD, a portion of the present parish of Tadley was given to Frithestan, the Bishop of Winchester, by King Edward. This land thus became part of the Bishop's manor of **Overton**. Although some distance away, the grant of land at Tadley was woodland and probably given because Overton did not grow sufficient timber for building or for pasturing swine. The original outline of this land was from 'Brunan Hylle' (Browning Hill) in the north to 'Wihie Forda' (Willow Ford – **Wyeford**) in the south. A later survey (1789) of Overton Hundred, which should show an identical piece of land at Tadley, does not match the original. It is suggested that in post-conquest times the land in the Saxon Charter was exchanged for that of the later survey. Alternatively, discrepancies could also be due to inaccuracies of surveying and mapping of the time.

The **Domesday Survey** makes no mention of Tadley. By the thirteenth century references are made to land held in Tadley by Robert Hotot who in 1205 granted 'half a knight's fee' (land granted to knights in return for arms, armour, and horse, i.e. military service) to Henry de Soberton, to be held by him and his heirs. Throughout the ensuing

centuries an independent Manor of Tadley, later called Withford or Wyeford is recorded. There are two centres of activity in this manor of Tadley: one associated to Wyeford house and the other to Tadley Place. The first reference to 'villagers' of Tadley, indicating a settlement, appears in a State Paper, dated 1634, referring to **Tadley Place**. This and the known existence of a church in 1286 and with it the possibility of a medieval settlement, establishes probably the first Tadley village near Tadley Manor Place/**St Peter's Church**. At sometime this village moved to what is now **Tadley Conservation Area**. Dating of properties within that area reveals at least four confirmed seventeenth century building dates with others dating from the early eighteenth century. This gives support to the opinion that migration may have been as a result of the oppression of villagers by Henry **Ludlow**. Other explanations do however exist: The **Black Death**; the strong support for non conformist religions in the seventeenth and eighteenth centuries and the subsequent building of the 'Old Meeting' (**United Reformed Church**), and the proximity to **Pamber Forest**, a source of materials for woodland crafts.

For approximately 250 years the present conservation area was the village of Tadley, with its general store and bakery at **Crooked Cottage**, The Malthouse, brewing and selling ale, and the **blacksmith's** forge at the end of **Malthouse Lane**. Gradually the village expanded northward but this was not significant until the development of **Aldermaston Airfield** in **World War II** and the subsequent building of **AWRE**. The conservation area is now primarily residential, but although division and subdivision of gardens and land has occurred to accommodate new properties, the original geography of the area remains largely unchanged since

1817 when the first Ordnance Survey map of north Hampshire was published. See **Ghosts; Tadley Place**.

Tadley and District Society (TADS) Tadley and District Society (TADS) held its inaugural meeting on the 21 November 1984 in **St Paul's Church Hall**. This meeting was arranged as a result of the considerable interest shown in old photographs of local people and places, and in illustrations borrowed from **AWRE**, showing the history of **Aldermaston** village and airfield, all of which were displayed at the St Paul's Church Summer Fete in June 1984. Twenty-eight people gave their names in support of the formation of a local history society. The first name on the list was Ernie **Kimber**. Roger **Searing**, who had produced a number of historical articles on Tadley and Reading for the *Reading Chronicle*, was appointed Chairman and other officers were elected. The first meeting of the Society was held on Wednesday 30 January 1985 and the subject was 'The History of Basingstoke' presented by Arthur **Attwood**.

Tadley and District Times See Local **newspapers**.

Tadley Bands The original band was founded in about 1875 by musicians who used to play at services at the Old Meeting (**United Reformed Church**) and the nearby **Tadley Primitive Methodist Chapel**. Their original name was the Tadley Gospel Temperance Band. For many years their activities were restricted to religious work. As Ernie **Kimber** recalls in *My Story of the Tadley Band and my 75 Years as a Bandsman,* 'the band used to play at open-air services and hospital charity parades and to help provide accompaniment for hymns at outdoor meetings held throughout the summers at local noncomformist meetings'. The Salvation Army later took on this role at open-air meetings. Membership of the band in 1886 contained family names still familiar today (cornets: Thomas Lambden, Bert Rampton and Albert Jones; horn: Ted Giles; euphonium: George Saunders; bass: Walter Saunders; side drum: George Appleton and bass drum: George Giles).

In 1914 at Shaw, Newbury, the band took part in its first competition, which was also Ernie Kimber's first, and were named as 'most promising band'. From then until 1973 Ernie was present at every competition the band took part in. In 1920, John Lambden was appointed bandmaster to succeed David Norris, and in 1922 Theodore Johnson, who for some years had toured the music halls with a family act known as the Bramusas, also offered to give the band lessons. It began to improve and take part in both regional and national competitions. An early success was in 1930 when, under the baton of John Lambden and the tuition of Joseph Dyson, they came second in a competition in Reading.

16 members of the band were called-up to fight during **World War II**. Sadly, not all returned home; two, Able-Seaman Stanley Bowman and Flight Sergeant Brian West, were killed. In 1945 the band be-

came active again, with Gideon West leading, they won the National Third Section Championships in London in 1962. Also in 1962, both Ernie Kimber and Gideon West were made honorary members of the National Brass Band Club in recognition of 50 years service to the band movement. The presentation of badge and certificate being made by the internationally known musician Harry Mortimer. Competing in *The Daily Herald* Band Festival in Brighton (1964) Tadley Silver Band (as they were now known) won the Third Division contest. Included in the band was the first female member, ten year old Ann Hutchins. On the retirement of Gideon West in 1964 Jack Clark became bandmaster and took the band on to other honours, winning three first prizes and a second during his time with the band.

The band practised in the Old Chapel Room from 1875 until the early 1950s when new accommodation was found in a converted barn in a field in Knapp Lane. When this was demolished to make way for houses at Mariner's Close rehearsals were at the United Reformed Church school-house. This was found to be too restrictive and the band returned to the Old Chapel Room until moving to Tadley **Jubilee Centre**. The band has gone on to further successes and still retains the name Tadley in its title. Going from Tadley Gospel Temperance to Tadley Silver Band and Tadley Silver Prize Band, it is now The Tadley Band (Martin Grant Homes). Gordon Saunders retired from the post of Musical Director of Tadley Band (MGH) in 1999 after completing 30 years with the band. They currently rehearse at the **Ambrose Allen Centre.** Tadley Concert Brass (previously Tadley Youth Band), and the training band, use **St Paul's Church Hall** where the Saturday learner classes have led some young musicians to study music at higher levels. Tadley Concert Brass will soon have their own purpose-built rehearsal rooms. Planning approval has been obtained to build on land provided by **Tadley Rugby Club** for this purpose, with completion in 2000.

The Tadley Youth Band was formed in 1975, with the help of Ernie Kimber. As Tadley Concert Brass, under the direction of Paul Chapman, they play at many social events in the community, continuing the local band tradition. Through the 1980s and 1990s both Tadley Band (MGH) and Tadley Concert Brass, with their training band, have continued performing often in concerts, competitions and outdoor band events. Over the many years that bands have existed in Tadley many of the local population have been members, and have continued the worthwhile tradition of music, reaching back to at least the mid-nineteenth century. See **Baughurst Gospel Temperance Band; Hospital Sunday; Haughurst Hill Drum and Fife Band.**

Tadley Board School See **Tadley School**.

Tadley Bottom (610 606) Current Ordnance Survey maps indicate Tadley Bottom as the plot of open land between Bowmonts Road and Brook Green. Old maps show that originally it was at the bottom of Tadley Common along the course of **Bowmont's Brook**, roughly where the Bowmonts Road housing development is today. See **Rowan Farm**.

Tadley Brickyard (599 623) At what date Tadley kiln first became operational is not known. The earliest census record of brickmakers in Tadley is 1861: James Prouten at Broadhalfpenny Lane and George Kent at Tadley Road (both close enough to assume they were probably working at the yard). Reference to Brick Kiln Gully, north of the Silchester Road, on maps in the 1870s and subsequent references in the census might indicate the gradual increase in output. In 1881 two men are recorded as brickmakers, William Nash and Joseph Stroud, with his father, William Stroud, as brick burner. In the same year, Thomas Painton (also spelt Panton) is listed as a brick and tile merchant. In 1890 Thomas sold his half share of the yard to John Stacey senior. By 1911 John had purchased the other half from Urban Rose. The brick yard at this time extended as far as Blakes Lane, with the main kiln workings approximately behind Wheelgame. John Stacey continues to be listed as wood dealer and farmer, and it is 1923 before George H. Stacey, his son, is recorded in **Kelly's Directory** as 'brick merchant'. Subsequently, John Stacey and Sons, Brickmakers, is formed. George H. continued to work the clay until **World War II** when blackout restrictions necessitated the yard's closure. Although the clay seam was not exhausted, the yard did not reopen after the war. See **Inhurst Brickyard; Little London Brickworks; Ramsdell Brickworks; Stacey family; J. Stacey & Sons; Tadley Memorial Hall; Pond Farm**.

Tadley Brook Small stream running through Tadley into **Pamber Forest**. It is known by various names along its course: within Pamber Forest it is marked on maps as **Silchester Brook**, while some locals know it as Tadley Brook. See **Bishopswood Stream; Bowmont's Brook**.

Tadley Common Prior to 1850, Tadley Common, in the strict sense of the name, extended along the north of the parish, from **Pamber Heath** to **Heath End**. As a result of the **Enclosure Act** of 1850 (1852) this area was allocated in three ways. Some previously settled plots of land were awarded to private individuals. Two other areas were awarded for the benefit of the parish. One, five acre (2 ha) plot, at the eastern end of Franklin Avenue, was originally awarded as a public gravel pit. At the present time, lands to the north of Franklin Avenue are rented to **Tadley Town Council**, the **Citizen's Advice Bureau** and **Ambrose Allen Centre**. Land to the south was sold for building (Turbary Gardens) and the money invested. The other, 100 acre (40 ha) plot, awarded for the digging of peat (turbary), subsequently became Tadley Common as we know it today, on which there are a number of recreational facilities:

tennis courts, football pitches and associated changing facilities in the **Jubilee Centre**. In addition, the land is managed for the safety of the public and there are a number of registered footpaths and fire breaks. Although its use has changed during the twentieth century, the common land is still administered for the benefit of the parish by the **Turbary Allotment Charity**.

Tadley Common Methodist Church (591 621) A group of local residents met at the home of Mr and Mrs John Foreman, 12 Deanswood Road on 2 July 1956 and decided to form a Methodist church on the new **AWRE housing** estate at Tadley Common. The site was the World War II hut 227. A temporary church was established in the hut until construction work started, after which services were held either in the open or in the old **Community Centre**. On 24 September 1960 the church moved into its new building in Newchurch Road. It cost £23,000 to build, the principal support coming from the J. Arthur Rank Trust which provided 80% of the basic building costs. Pastor Stanley Belcher had, from 1957, led the group in their efforts to establish the church, until the appointment of the first minister, Revd Alfred Olds, in 1962.

Although the church's official name was Aldermaston Methodist Church (no doubt because of its connection with the new populace associated with AWRE) it has always been known as Tadley Common Methodist Church by its congregation. In 1961 there was a move to change the name to Tadley Newchurch Road Methodist Church but this was rejected. Although the church received its Certificate of Registry for the Solemnisation of Marriages in 1960, the first marriage was not until 14 September 1963 when Aldermaston Methodist Church was entered in the register. The last date this was used for was for entry number 16 on 28 August 1970, with entry 17 on 24 July 1971 carrying the name Tadley Common Methodist Church.

The Superintendent of the Reading Circuit would have had overall responsibility for the church until the Reading and Silchester Circuits united in 1982 and the minister resident at Newchurch Road had pastoral responsibility for Tadley Common alone. From 1982 the Minister had responsibility for the churches at Tadley Common, Tadley Main Road, Hannington, Haughurst Hill, Baughurst (closed in 1987) and Charter Alley (closed in 1989). In 1998 Silchester was added to the list, but Haughurst Hill is due to close in autumn 1999 and members at Hannington now meet in a house in the village and come to share some services with Tadley Main Road.

Tadley Common Players Tadley Common Players have presented a Christmas Pantomime at Tadley Common Methodist Church every year since 1975. Initially, the company consisted principally of members of Tadley Common Church, but since 1992 members of the adjacent Anglican Church,

Photo: Albert West

Tadley Football Club, 1922. *Back row (left to right)*: Mr Drake (Old Meeting Minister), Charles Lambden, Len or Pete Saunders, Cyril Holly, Bill Emmens, Ambrose Allen, Revd Ward; *middle row*: Bill Savage, Tom Chapman, Tom Stacey; *bottom row*: Reuben Hicks, Frank Smith, Ernest Smith, Billy Broadhurst, Stan James.

St Mary's, have also participated. The original inspiration came from Jim Little, and the first mini pantomime was 'Mrs Gamp and her Wonderful Lamp'. Ray Chalk took over as producer/director in 1982 with the production 'Puss in Boots'. He has continued in this role since, as well as taking part in the subsequent pantomimes. The 21st anniversary of the first full length pantomime was celebrated in 1998 with performances of 'Beauty and the Beast'. David Dennis, as with previous productions, composed and arranged the original songs and also conducted the orchestra of ten players. The 1999 pantomine is to be 'The Pied Piper of the Millennium'.

Tadley Concert Brass See **Tadley Bands.**

Tadley Congregational Chapel (604 608) See **United Reformed Church.**

Tadley Conservation Area Conservation Areas were established by the Town and Country Planning Act of 1972. Tadley's Conservation Area was designated by Basingstoke and Deane Borough Council in February 1981. It consists of a roughly triangular 57 acre (23 ha) area bounded by Main Road, Fairlawn Road and Winston Avenue. There are seven listed buildings in the conservation area, including the **United Reformed Church.** In 1996 the Borough Council reviewed the area and several local groups, including **Tadley and District So-**

ciety, Burnham Copse **Womens' Institute** and **Tadley School**, assisted the Council in writing an appraisal, defining the special architectural and historical interest within the area.

Tadley Court (605 623) Originally called The Wilderness, Tadley Court is a large house and grounds off Tadley Common Road, near the **Jubilee Centre.** The site began as a charcoal burner's cottage. In 1841 William Benham (age 60), his wife and son, Thomas, are recorded as living there. William's age might indicate that the cottage had been built a lot earlier. Thomas (also a charcoal burner) continued to occupy the cottage at least until 1881. By 1891 however there is no reference to him, or his wife Jane, in the census and the location is referred to as 'The Wilderness'. The property, was by then, large enough to accommodate George **Roller**, his wife, two children and three servants. Over the years the site was considerably extended and by 1920 comprised four and a half acres. In 1903 John **Phillips**, gynaecologist to Queen Mary, was the occupant. He remained there until 1915 and probably later, until after the death of his first wife, Rachel Rattray, in 1917. Together with other land along Silchester Road (stabling) and at Mount Pleasant, the property, totalling 14 acres, was sold in 1920. A condition of the sale was that George Roller be allowed to remain in 'The Cottage' '…for the term of his natural life'. By 1927 the house had been renamed 'Tadley Court'. Over the next 40 years (1920-60) it had a succession of occupants, including a Col Menzies and his wife, an actress. They entertained such well-known people as John Profumo and Honor Blackman in the 1950s. Plans to convert it into a nursing home in the late 1960s failed because of financial problems and it was sold to the Water Supply Industry Training Board who remain there still. They amalgamated with the National Water Council in 1974 and transferred to the Water Industry Training Association (**WTI Training Group**) in 1983. Sympathetic modern additions have been made by the water industry but the attractive 'gentleman's country residence' still dominates the site. See **Charcoal burning**.

Tadley Cricket Club See **Cricket**.

Tadley Football Club Tadley Football Club has been running intermittently since the early 1900s. In 1920, at a Council meeting, a deputation from the football and cricket clubs made an application for the exclusive use of the recreation ground 'as the cattle who used it all week left such a mess'. The council stated they must not debar the public from using the ground and that no matches were to be played on a Sunday. The annual rent for each club was to be £2. In 1927 The football club was requested to remove a convenience they had built, as no permission had been given. In the late 1940s, and for many years after, two teams were regularly fielded. In the 1950s there was strong support for the team and in certain away tournaments double decker buses were hired to take their many supporters to these events. They were in the top Basingstoke league and supporters at home fixtures were three to four deep along the touchline. The present first team has achieved the highest league standing the club has ever had, playing in Hampshire County Division Two. The club run both Saturday and Sunday teams, catering for junior boys and adults. Their present home ground is The **Green** and their logo is crossed besom brooms. **Calleva Football Club** is affiliated to Tadley Football Club and it is hoped this will produce many future stars. See **International Football Club**; **Pamber Forest Football Club**.

Tadley God Help Us For many miles around, people often refer to Tadley as 'Tadley God Help Us'. How the phrase originated is unclear. There are several explanations, all involving a balloon flight. One, from the Tadley **WI scrapbook**, states that 'many years ago, at a time when they were first being flown, a balloon passed over Tadley near some men working in a field. It came down low and the balloonist shouted out "What's the name of this place?" Greatly alarmed by the appearance of something they had never seen before, one of the frightened men called out "This is Ta-a-dley. God help us", being evidently under the impression that the visitor was from another world'. How much truth

there is in this explanation is impossible to say. Pat **Minter** thought he might have found a possible source for the tale in a book of Alpine and balloon adventures by Frank Mundell, given to his uncle as a Sunday School prize in 1911. One adventure describes how Henry Coxwell, a nineteenth century balloonist, set out on 16 October 1853 but due to the sudden arrival of a strong wind and the sticking of a valve he drifted until dusk when the balloon descended in a field north of Basingstoke. He heard the sound of persons running, frightened by the sight of the balloon. Leaving it he found a local policeman and asked what county he was in whereupon he was threatened with the county jail. Searching further, he found the local inn locked and unresponsive to his knocks so returned to his balloon. The next day a farmer gave him breakfast and explained the churlish behaviour of the locals. A robbery had been committed and strangers were therefore regarded with suspicion. On departing, he was told 'You must not forget that you have come across the Hampshire hogs, and that a grunt or two is all in character'. Whether this is the source of the tale, no one can tell. Certainly there is no reference to 'Tadley God help us', but the mention of a balloon, which would have been a rarity in Tadley, is significant. Meantime the fable lives on and continues to amuse locals and others.

Tadley Gospel Temperance See **Tadley Bands**.

Tadley Green Housing Association See **Mothe's Charity**.

Tadley Local Plan A Tadley Township Plan was prepared in 1973, highlighting its economic dependence on **AWRE** and Basingstoke. The non-statutory Pamber Heath Village Plan was adopted in 1967 and the non-statutory Tadley Township Plan adopted in 1973. This was followed in 1978 by the Tadley District Plan which reviewed and updated the provisions of the Tadley Township Plan, the Pamber Heath Village Plan and the policies for the adjoining area. The existing plans covered built-up parts of the area.

In 1983 the provisions of these previous plans for the area, by then respectively 16 and 10 years out of date, needed reviewing. The main proposals of the draft local plan were the allocation of land for more houses, including small scale housing development, further redevelopment for light industry, more shopping and office floor space and allocation of land for open space and recreation. In addition, the draft plan contained proposals and policies covering a variety of other matters. It also indicated how development would be phased and the proposals implemented. It was drawn up by **Basingstoke and Deane Borough Council** and adopted by the council in November 1985.

By the 1990s a draft Basingstoke Area Local Plan had been produced which included the three wards in Tadley. The plan reviewed and updated existing local plans and set out an orderly phasing of development. Existing playing field facilities in the Tadley area were well below the structure plan's minimum requirement and a detailed study of existing and potential open spaces was undertaken. The need for a new **community centre** at Newchurch Road, Tadley, and a permanent branch library at Mulfords Hill was also highlighted. The land adjacent to **Budgens** supermarket was considered the area best suited for the provision of more shops to help confirm the area's 'town centre' status. This plan was amended and finally adopted in 1998.

Tadley Main Road Methodist Church (606 608) The new Methodist Church was built adjacent to the original **Tadley Primitive Methodist Chapel**. It opened on 21 November 1931 and continued as part of The Silchester Circuit until 1982 when the Reading and Silchester Circuit was formed. Until 1985 the minister attached to those circuits had responsibility for Main Road and not Tadley Common. In 1993, with a growth in numbers, particularly for the Sunday School and Youth Work, the Stewards began a programme of improvements that included a two-storey extension and car parking to the rear of the 1931 building. The internal changes saw the pews removed, the pulpit moved so that the congregation now faces the other way and entry made from the north side. The cost was met by their own fund-raising and the debt cleared by 1999. The alterations were completed by May 1996 and the building was opened by the Chairman of the District.

Tadley Manor Place (593 595) See **Tadley Place**.

Tadley Memorial Hall (602 608) It was built in 1952 to coincide with the coronation of Elizabeth II. The hall is situated at the western end of The **Green**, on land donated by George H. Stacey. The land had previously been Stacey's Broomyard – known locally as The Pompeys. Amongst the organising committee were George Stacey, Dr Joe **Morland**, Ron Carrington and Evelyn **Woodall**. See **J. Stacey & Sons**. See **Stacey family**.

Tadley Parish Council The first parish meeting was held in The **Iron Room** on 26 March 1895 and was attended by only one out of seven previously elected councillors. The chairman, Col J. Hart, closed the meeting after waiting 35 minutes. Meetings were held about twice yearly in The **Iron Room** until 1900 when they transferred to **Tadley School**. Early meetings dealt with the allocation of the allotments, letting of feed at the recreation ground, appointing a hay warden and the state of footpaths, hedges and what roads existed. In 1905 a letter was received from Sir John French, HQ Office, Aldershot, asking permission for the use of Tadley Common for troop manoeuvres from 7 to 12 August. Permission was granted, subject to stated conditions. In 1919 the building of six 'council cottages' was proposed, and in 1926 twenty council houses were requested. At the time an average weekly wage in the area was only £1 12s 6p (£1.62p). In 1927,

the village still had only four council houses, with six more built in 1931, followed, three years later, by a further four. More followed later in the decade. In 1932, in response to a letter from Basingstoke District Council, the council deemed a refuse collection unnecessary. Later in the year, telephone kiosks were installed on sites designated by the borough surveyor.

From 1940 to 1946 (the war years) council meetings were held in the home of Mr Gray at The Hawthorns, Main Road, where there was much discussion regarding electricity schemes and the supply of **water**. Later in 1946 council meetings were held once again in the school; in the following year the school's lavatories were changed to water closets. About this time parish councils were asked to recommend suitable names for various roads and streets in the village. Most of the names recommended are those used today, with a few exceptions: Cullom Lane was the suggestion for what is now Knapp Lane, Pamber Hill for Pamber Heath Road and High Road for Tadley Hill.

By the late 1940s and early 1950s most houses in the area had an electricity supply available, and also mains water. A street-lighting scheme was proposed for the A340 along with the straightening of some of the more dangerous bends on that road. Late in the 1940s some Swedish timber-type housing was built in Tadley and elsewhere, for letting at rents of 12s a week. The building of a **Memorial Hall** was proposed, to the west of the The **Green,** on land known as The Pompeys and donated by the **Stacey family**. At the end of the 1940s, the council opposed the Metropolitan Water Board's proposal to flood the Enborne Valley, and **Aldermaston Airfield** was now redundant.

In 1950 the airfield became an 'atom centre'; only in the following year was it referred to as an Atomic Research Station in the council minutes. The minutes at this stage were written up in biro! Coronation seats were placed on Tadley Hill and Mulfords Hill, and the go-ahead was given for 35 street lamps in Tadley and Aldermaston parishes, part funded by **AWRE**. In 1956 a 30 mph speed limited was finally agreed for the A340 through the village. In the same year a new electoral ward, covering the AWRE estate, was formed, with the composition of the council being three district and seven parish councillors. The Hurst School was built near the end of the decade and also the Mulfords Hill shops. In the 1960s the **war memorial** was moved to behind the Memorial Hall, the council offices occupied the prefabricated building in Franklin Avenue that had previously been the Midland Bank. The council continued their building programme and, from the end of **World War II** until 1974, had built 270 council houses, with a further 70 built in North Tadley in Hangar Lane.

Road safety was also a concern in the 1970s with the increase of traffic through the village. Double yellow lines were painted along part of Franklin Avenue, and a pedestrian crossing installed outside **Whatmore's** shop. The roundabout on the A340 at the bottom of Tadley Hill was installed in the early 1980s and traffic lights erected at the Silchester Road and Franklin Avenue junction, in 1989. See **Baughurst Parish Council; Enborne Valley Reservoir Scheme; Hurst Community School; Pamber Parish Council; Tadley Town Council**.

Tadley Place (593 595) A Grade II listed building in Church Road. What, if anything, existed on the site, prior to the building known as Tadley Manor Place, is not clearly documented. What is known is that it was regarded as the Hampshire seat of the **Ludlow** family (of Hill Deverell in Wiltshire) from before the time of the marriage of William Ludlow to Joan, daughter of Nicholas More of **Wyeford**, in 1496. This would lead us to think that over an ensuing period they had constructed a building suited to their status, foundations of which have been found in the gardens of Tadley Place. Only the east wing of this traditional 'E' shaped Tudor manor house remains: a two storey 'L' shaped building with a projecting eighteenth century wing. It has a tiled roof and typical Elizabethan stone-mullioned lattice windows. Inside, a large sixteenth century stone chimney place with doric pilasters and mouldings indicate the house's former splendour. In 1575, for purveyance, a Royal inventory of land was taken, when the yield and usage was recorded: George Ludlow's estate comprised 200 acres (81 ha) of pasture alone. How long ownership of Tadley Place remained with the Ludlow family after the death of the tyrannical Henry Ludlow is unknown. Records state only that it was bought by William Congreve of Aldermaston in 1822 from 'a Mr Searle in whose family it had been for some years'. The history of Tadley Place and its land is inextricably linked to that of Wyeford, as both were focal parts of the Manor of Tadley, or as it was later known, Wyeford. The land and its buildings only finally became independent of each other in the mid-twentieth century. See **Ghosts**.

Tadley Place Farm (593 595) See **Tadley Place**.

Tadley Police Station Tadley Police Station on Mulford's Hill was built in 1967. See **Citizens' Advice Bureau**.

Tadley Primitive Methodist Chapel (606 608) Situated in Main Road, it was built in 1859 on land which was bought from James Pearce, a shoemaker, for £1. The cost of building was £123 17s 3d (£123.86p). The congregation later moved to the adjacent new Methodist chapel in 1931. The original building remained in use by the Guides and as the headquarters and practice-room of the **Tadley Bands** until it was sold in 1986 and modernised. See **Tadley Main Road Methodist Church**.

Tadley Recreational Ground See **Tadley Common**.

Tadley Revel A day of festivity and merriment held annually when travelling merchants and entertainers visited the village. Daniel **Benham** in *Some Account…* states 'Tadley revel, held from time immemorial on the 22nd July, upon the Green near the house of the minister of the Independent chapel, was not much frequented in 1822, one tumbling show and three or four booths for the sale of crockery ware, gingerbread, etc being all that were exhibited. Since then it has been discontinued many years'. It has been revived twice, once soon after **World War II**, to raise money for the War **Memorial Hall** and, again, in 1965 when a 'Revel Committee' was formed, which organised various events and raised thousands of pounds to help local voluntary groups. It continued for several years until ceasing again, in 1985 because of a lack of interest and support. Much of the Revel's impetus and aims are carried on by the **Treacle Fayre**. See Samuel **Browne**.

Tadley Roll Unfortunately, despite considerable searching, the Tadley Roll has been missing for many years. Made in the mid-to-late 1870s, it consisted of a roll of paper three inches high showing coloured caricatures of about 600 figures. It is believed to have been produced by the Revd **Saulez**'s children, Alfred (11 in 1871), and Edward (9), on old scraps of paper joined together into one strip. The drawing was primitive, but full of life, and the caricatures were recognisable. It showed all the old village crafts and trades, various local families (Webbs, Saunders, Giles, Hicks, Ramptons etc), poachers, gypsies and even a party of Royal Engineers who were carrying out an Ordnance Survey at the time.

Tadley Rugby Club Tadley Rugby Union Football Club was formed in November 1985 when a meeting took place at the home of Frank and Paddy Jose. Founder members were Frank Jose, Roy Mears, Michael Jewel and John Thomas. The club started playing in the 1986-87 season, fielding a Sunday XV at the **Hurst Community School**. The first match was against the Chairman's XV on Sunday 28 September 1986, the Chairman's XV winning 26-16. During their first season, Tadley were the first winners of the Berkshire Sunday Cup, having registered as a Berkshire club. The second season (1987-88) saw the start of Saturday rugby with only the occasional Sunday fixture. For the 1998-89 season the club entered league rugby; it also saw the formation of a Second XV. For two seasons (1988-89 and 1989-90) as well as playing matches at The Hurst, some of the matches were played on The **Green**, which was something of a first, because rugby had never been played there before.

The big breakthrough for the club was the purchase of their own ground at Red Lane, Aldermaston in April 1992. A 13.5 acre (5.4 ha) site, club members loaned their own money to purchase it. Much hard work was required to produce pitches and convert a barn into a clubhouse. Playing commenced at the ground in September 1992, a bar was opened in January 1994, and the clubhouse was opened by Dennis Easby, President of the Rugby Football Union in September of the same year. The summer of 1996 saw the removal of the last of the temporary accommodation from the site.

The gradual growth of the club has seen the formation of both third and fourth teams and a rise from Berks, Dorset and Wilts Division 3 to the Southern Counties South, for the 1998-99 season.

Tadley School (603 608) Originally known as Tadley Board School, it was opened in 1876. Plans for a school in Tadley were drawn up for the **Wootton and Tadley School Board** by architect James H. Moore. The buildings, constructed during 1876 at a cost of £1340.00, consisted of the teacher's house and classrooms for 222 children. Plans of the original buildings are lodged in the Hampshire Record Office and they show an imposing brick building, much of which is still visible today. The first master of Tadley School was Robert Atkinson. He started work on 25 March 1877 and the school admitted its first pupils on 9 April 1877 – 151 children of whom 81 were boys and 70 were girls.

From the first the school was in trouble. Not only was the accommodation quickly inadequate, but the building, although handsome, was not built properly. The HM Inspector reported that the walls had settled out of true, and that 'the walls of the school seem hardly strong enough to support the roof'. The peat toilets were a continuous headache. The early teachers had to struggle with classes of 30 to 76 children, which would have been much worse if the school had not had a wretched record of absenteeism (any attendance over 50% was thought good). The inspector reported frequent absences for every excuse: **hop-picking**, pea picking, **acorn picking**, **Tadley Revel**, weather, street parties, illness and plain 'bunking off'. Nevertheless, the staff were frequently praised for their teaching efforts. In 1901 the Inspector records that the school is illegally overcrowded. However, it was soon 'commodiously enlarged' by the addition of the large classroom on the east side (still extant). In 1906 the inspector grudgingly reported 'good work done under depressing conditions', and 'more than a third of the children taught as Infants are between 7 and 9 years old'. In 1911 he recommended that the school be recognised as one of special difficulty. In 1914 he wrote 'The School is in a remote neighbourhood and serves a scattered population. It has long had the reputation of being a difficult school. Most of the population is of the gypsy class and are frequently absent. Pupils often have a long distance to travel. LEA considering hiring a conveyance to bring the children to school. Infants 88, Mixed 167'. The 88 Infants were taught in one room with two classes on the floor and one in a gallery. **World War I** did seem to make a change

in attendance and it is noticeable that the average rose sharply from about 60% up to over 90% and the school was congratulated over the decoration of the classrooms. In 1921 the School Board gave up trying to repair the bell turret, and declared that the large bell was too dangerous to be rung. A small hand bell was supplied, but the teacher reported it to be practically useless. By 1922 the Inspector was much more upbeat 'very good report – attendance now good, children neat and orderly and self-reliant. However Infants not so good – due to a considerable succession of Infant Head Teachers'. The school continued to be plagued by outbreaks of illness; June 1925 – 15 cases of scarlet fever, 8 of whooping cough, 4 of chicken pox and 7 of various other diseases.

In 1935, the school leaving age was raised to 15 (most children remained at Tadley till the end of their school careers). There were 217 seniors and 44 infants in 7 classes of which 5 were taught in separate rooms and the two infants classes in one room. The Headteacher had a class of 35, the Assistant Master one of 50, the others ranging from 35 to 48. The Inspector's report was generally good – 'classroom decoration good, behaviour good, maths poor'. The School Managers reported that a bathroom was to be installed in the school house. They were even considering installing a small oven over a classroom stove in the Infants' room to heat the pupils' own meals (no fish or greens were to be permitted). In 1939 five ARP shelters were provided, which immediately flooded to a depth of 18 inches and were unusable.

On 27 October 1940 the school served its first school meals from a kitchen specially constructed in the Orchard (now the car park). This kitchen was provided with mains water in 1943 although a well was still in use for the school-house. In 1947 the next phase of expansion occurred with the addition of a HORSA (**H**utted **O**pportunities for **R**evision of **S**tandard **A**ttainment) hut. This provided classrooms and a woodworking room for the senior boys. In 1950 the school was finally wired for electricity, and mains water was connected to the toilets. The kitchen, intended originally for 100 meals, now serves 270. The school-house was now to have an indoor lavatory. By 1951 crowding was so severe that the school acquired three rooms behind the cinema. This was referred to as the Aldermaston Annex. This outpost continued until 1955 when it was transferred, complete with pupils and teachers, to the Berkshire Authorities. In that year, also, the school had a new modern toilet block (but still no main drainage). In 1954, the school became a Primary school, all the senior pupils being sent to Secondary schools in Basingstoke. In 1955, Burnham Copse School opened and the numbers at Tadley fell to 205; there were four classes in rooms in the original building, two more in the HORSA block. The Inspector made derogatory comments about the lessons – unplanned and no school curriculum. By 1960 the school was up to 10 classes (four temporary classrooms and one class in the church hall) and the kitchen staff were 'at breaking point', serving over 300 meals. Thus began a series of major building alterations that continued for the next 40 years. A block consisting of 3 classrooms and work spaces was erected in 1964 and two more classrooms and an administrative wing, in 1967. In January 1965 a PTA was formed which by 1967 had raised enough cash to build a swimming pool. By 1970 the numbers had risen to 544 (16 classes) which were making use of all the HORSA block, plus four extra temporary double classrooms. The pupil situation was relieved by the opening of the Bishopswood Schools in 1975, but the school was still in need of modernisation, and in 1978 a major refit occurred with the construction of a new school hall and kitchens. In 1992 the temporary classrooms became too dilapidated for use, and were replaced by the four-classroom Allen wing. The current headteacher is Mr David Cottrell, and the school now has about 400 pupils in 14 classrooms. In 1999 the school's name officially changed from Tadley County Primary School to Tadley Community Primary School. See **Education; Appendix i.**

Tadley Sunday Market Begun in the early 1980s on land owned by Denis Brant to the north of Tadley Common. It was organised by Bob and Adrian from Birmingham. For a period of approximately four years it transferred to a site at Greenham Common reopening in Tadley in 1997. The market site is now owned by J. **Stacey and Sons** and run by Hugh Mark International. West Berkshire authority are responsible for the enforcement of Market Trading regulations.

Tadley Swimming Pool (603 614) Work started in March 1997 on the 6 lane, 25m pool at Herriard Way Open Space, on land provided by Hampshire County Council. The site had previously been **Elmhurst** and the foundations of some former buildings were uncovered when the site was cleared. The £3.3 million it cost to build came from **Basingstoke and Deane Borough Council** and The Sports Council Lottery Fund. Construction was completed in spring 1998 and it was officially opened by Olympic swimmer Nick Gillingham on 13 June 1998.

Tadley Town Council The council came into existence on 19 May 1987, using powers under the 1972 Local Government Act to make the change from being a parish council. Initially the council's offices were in a small building on the north side of Franklin Avenue, near the junction with Mulfords Hill, which had previously been occupied by Midland Bank. New offices were built near the site in 1994. See **Banks; Enclosure; Tadley Parish Council.**

Tadley Treacle Mines Tadley is probably as well known for its treacle mines, or lack of them, as it is for its besoms and bands. They featured on local television as an April Fools Day joke and the tale is kept alive in The **Treacle Mine** public house and **Treacle Fayre.** Where are the mines? There seem to be three common explanations for the term 'Treacle Mine', none of which has been confirmed. Honeybottom is where older Tadley residents believe the tale originates: a wet valley area where the soil is dark and sticky. It is rumoured that in earlier days, any young man from outside the area who came courting a Tadley girl would soon find himself thrown into the 'treacle'. Others will tell you it is where the American soldiers dumped their molasses cans during their time at **Aldermaston Airfield.** A similar version reports that whilst digging the foundations for a new building on the site of what had been a bakery, a pit was found filled with treacle tins; perhaps gingerbread had been made there. The site of this bakery is not known. Roger **Searing**, writing in the *Reading Chronicle*, gives another explanation: the discovery of a treacle tin containing 21 guineas and half guineas, from the reign of George III, in a garden in Winston Avenue, by four year old Christopher Forrest.

A more formal explanation is that the word 'treacle' may be a corruption of the Anglo-Saxon word 'Treag' which means flint. A great deal of flint was used in the construction of the Roman walls at **Calleva Atrebatum** giving this version some credence. Another possibility, although with no obvious connection, is that the word 'treacle' at one time meant 'an antidote for treatment of the bite of wild beasts'. In an old magazine there are references to 'treacle mines' at Tilehurst, Reading; Chobham, Surrey; Macclesfield, Cheshire; and Patcham, Brighton, all with no proven origin for the phrase.

Tadley Watch Tadley Watch, a junior environmentalist group, was the brainchild of the late Tadley naturalist, Ron **Ward.** An expert in identifying local flora and fauna, he cared greatly for the natural countryside. The Watch group was initiated by Ron in the Spring of 1988 and he recruited a Tadley teacher, Rosemary Bond, to assist. The group was intended primarily for children aged 6 to 16 years old, and in 1998 consisted of approximately 50 members including 20 adults. The purpose of the group is to encourage the children to learn about, and care for, the natural world of flowers, birds, plants, trees, insects and pond life. Ron, who died in December 1991, had his own Site of Special Scientific Interest (SSSI) at a hay meadow in South Tadley. It has many rare plants, and consequently rare insects, and rare birds; endangered animals thrive there because of the plentiful and unspoiled food supply, uncontaminated by herbicides, pesticides and artificial fertilisers. Ron, and the meadow, were shown on 'Countryfiles' and other television wildlife programmes several years ago. This meadow is a rare and precious asset to Tadley, Hampshire, and beyond. There are very few natural, or ancient meadows left in the country. Ron could have sold the land for house building for about £20,000,000, but instead he ensured that it remained 'unimproved' and in his will left it to the Hampshire Wildlife Trust. A local general practitioner and expert naturalist, Dr Peter Brough, showed great interest in Ron's work, and as a member of the Wildlife Trust Committee, advised Ron. The Watch group members, under their leader, Rosemary Bond, have night hikes (local police and gamekeepers having been informed), build survival shelters, and clear brambles, long grass and litter from local commons, to improve the habitat for wildlife. Local rivers, canals and gravel pits are visited, as are churchyards, places which are not cultivated and are valuable sites for the study of flora and fauna. The Watch group seeks to pursue Ron Ward's ideals. That it does so successfully, and creates much interest amongst the children, is shown by the high attendance at a spring 'Dawn Chorus' meeting in **Pamber Forest**, starting at 5.45 am! See **Ron Ward's Meadow**; Ron **Ward**.

Tadley Witch Most villages seem to have a traditional story about a local witch and Tadley is no exception. As recorded in the Tadley **WI scrapbook** she was 'one Maria Chandler, who lived in Back Lane'. Some older villagers who knew her, assert that she could – and did – assume the form of a hare at will and was often seen racing across the fields towards the forest. Eventually the hare was shot, but managed to escape and reached the cottage, badly wounded. Turning again into a woman, she struggled into bed and, sometime later, neighbours found her dying, exhausted from loss of blood.' On a more factual level, the census for Pamber does record a Maria Chandler. Born in 1813 at Wootton St Lawrence, in 1851, she was married to William and had 4 children. By 1861 she was a widow living on the forest side of Back Lane (Pamber). If fiction has any basis in fact, she should be the Pamber Witch, rather than the Tadley one. See **Aldermaston Witch**; **Iona**.

Tadley Youth Drama Tadley Youth Drama was born in 1985, the brainchild of Roger Jones, at the time a youth leader at Tadley's United Reformed Church. With leaders of other youth groups in the village, they agreed to work together to produce a Christian musical entertainment with a cast of teenagers. The first show, 'Daybreak', was performed in May 1986, and the response from the young people led the leaders to repeat the challenge and productions have followed every year since. Apart from 'Bibalive' in 1991 the songs and scripts have all been written by David Smith and Kevin England. The millennium production, in May 1999, was entitled 'Time Trial' – courtroom scenes with mankind on trial to determine if he was fit to live into the third millennium. Approximately 40 teenagers provide the cast for the productions, with adult help providing costumes, music, lighting and scenery. These annual May productions take place at the **Tadley Common Methodist Church**.

Telephones Invented by Alexander Graham Bell in 1876, the early development of the telephone in this country was led by private companies like the United Telephone Company and later the National Telephone Company. These private companies, operating under licence from the **Post Office**, concentrated on supplying the needs of the larger towns while the Post Office operated the trunk lines and telephones in the smaller towns and villages. In 1925 this two-tier service was replaced by the Post Office Telephone Service.

Tadley had to wait until the inter-war years before it was 'connected'. Heath End Telephone Exchange, serving the local area, opened on 26 March 1923. Known then as a 'Caretaker Operator Exchange', it provided only a daytime service to probably as few as 20 subscribers; night-time service would have been provided by a night switching apparatus to either Reading or Basingstoke Exchange. The exchange was located in the lane next to The **Cricketers** public house – the house still bears the name 'Exchange Cottage'. It was run by the caretaker operator, Mrs Warren, helped by her daughter, Dorothy. The first subscriber was a Mr Moss of Paices Hill; he occupied one of the cottages which were later demolished when **Aldermaston Airfield** was constructed. As demand for telephones increased, Heath End became a Rural Automatic Exchange with 3 figure telephone numbers replacing the old 2 figure ones, and the exchange was connected to Reading which had a fully automatic service. In 1964 the exchange in Reading was developed and small Rural Automatic Exchanges were phased out. A new exchange – Tadley Exchange – was built in Newchurch Road in 1964 and the prefix 4 added to the old numbers, creating the Tadley code. With the opening of this new exchange Heath End's link with telephones died. In the 1980s the code for Tadley changed from 0734 to 01734 and changed again on 1 January 1998 from 01734 to 0118.

The telephone exchange at Silchester opened on 29 March 1929. The exchange was originally located at Southern View, near the junction of Soke Road and Pamber Heath Road, and at one time Kate Ward was the operator. In August 1972 the VAX 13 exchange was replaced with a RND exchange and the '700' prefix added to the existing numbers. By that time the postal address for the exchange had moved around the corner into Soke Road.

Temperance movement Born out of the nineteenth century social problem of hard drinking, the anti-spirits movement originated in America. In the British Isles the movement started in Scotland and Ireland in the 1820s, spreading to the textile towns of Lancashire and Yorkshire in the 1830s, eventually broadening into the temperance movement. Its aim was to persuade politicians, both national and local, into a policy of prohibition. Local societies were an important feature of the movement; it was

Trunkpond Corner, looking north towards Mulfords Hill with Rowan Road and pond on the right

closely linked with liberal and non-conformist organisations which may account for its strong influence in and around Tadley. Local newspapers record details of meetings in most villages throughout the late 1800s. The movement lost much of its impetus and influence after **World War I**. See **Brewing and licensing laws; Band of Hope; A British Workman; Tadley Bands.**

Thames Valley Transport See **Bus and coach services.**

Thatcher, Jimmy A photographer who lived at 3 New Road. Born in Basingstoke, he came to Tadley in the early 1900s (prior to 1907). Assisted by his daughter Amelia he toured the lanes with his camera and tripod strapped to his bicycle. Via the photographs he took we have a valuable record of scenes and life in this area during the first half of the twentieth century. While in Basingstoke he ran A **British Workman.**

Thick's Bakery (604 610) Situated at the junction of The Green and Tadley Hill, probably the site of Frederick and Daniel Faulkners bakery (1861-91). It later became Roger's (1899) and subsequently Thick's. In 1923 James Thick is listed as baker by **Kelly's Directory** but from 1927 Frederick Thick has taken over the business. At a later date the shop became Smith and Eyre's and finally, in 1965, Pike's, by which time it had become a general store. The shop was demolished in the 1970s and the site redeveloped for residential housing. See **Bakeries.**

Thomas, Dr Geoffrey Wynne Medical doctor who joined Dr Lionel **Holmwood**'s practice in Aldermaston in the late 1930s. During World War II he served in the army, returning in 1945. He re-

tired in 1971 at which time the Aldermaston surgery closed. See **Health care and medical services; Hospitals; Appendix ii.**

Thornycrofts A heavy-vehicle manufacturer who started in Chiswick, moving to Basingstoke in 1898. In 1961 it ceased to be owned by Thornycrofts and was taken over by AEC who were subsequently taken over by Leyland (later British Leyland). It finally closed in the mid 1960s. Thornycrofts employed not only many people from Basingstoke but also some local people from Tadley. This was made possible when public transport improved enough to allow workers to travel easily into the town. Thornycroft vehicles will be displayed in the new 'Milestones' museum to be opened in Basingstoke in the year 2000.

Timber In the days when ships were made of wood, the south of England was an important source of timber. Initially, shipbuilders would have used timber close to the coast because it was easily transported, but as this was used up, they had to go further afield, eventually using timber from areas like Tadley. The local area was rich in timber in the past, e.g. **Pamber Forest**, and timber sales were significant. For example, between 1801 and 1838, William Congreve felled £41,233 worth of timber (oak, chestnut, hornbeam and ash), most of it for sale, from the **Aldermaston Estate**. There is evidence of It has been recorded that ship's timbers were used in the construction of several local cottages and the gallery and stairs of **St Peter's Church**. More recently, during **World War I**, an encampment of the Canadians Forestry Corps were felling trees, for the war effort, near Ufton Court. Today, the **Englefield Estate** has a large acreage of land given over to the raising of timber. See **Coppicing**; **Charcoal burning**.

Tithe Barn (593 595) An eighteenth century Grade II listed barn close to **Tadley Place**. It is a spacious building, which suggests that the tithes to be paid were heavy. The entrance would have enabled a large wagon to enter. The whole barn has a wooden floor and there must be some justification for thinking it is one of the largest thatched barns in the county, if not the country.

Tithing The subdivision of a **Hundred** consisting of about 10 families. They (the men) stood security for each other, ensuring good order amongst their number and bringing offenders to justice in the **hundred courts**. They organised a 'hue and cry' in pursuit of robbers and were responsible for the provision of labour towards the maintenance of **roads**, bridges and defences. Several tithings formed the basis of the later civil and ecclesiastical parishes. In historical documents a hamlet such as **Inhurst** is referred to as a tithing of **Baughurst**/Evingar Hundred. Tithings were often 'held' (owned) by families, perhaps given by the King. The Victoria County History gives details of tithings and hundreds. See **Policing**.

Toll House, Baughurst (584 605) Situated next to The **Wellington Arms** public house. It is to be assumed that this was a private toll levied by the Duke of Wellington for the upkeep of this road which crossed his land. It was no doubt well used by farming traffic, worshippers at nearby St **Stephen's Church** and as access to Wolverton and Kingsclere. By the 1861 census a toll keeper is no longer recorded and the premises has become the Post Office. In the 1990s it is known as Loveday Cottage.

Toll House, Pamber (612 583) See **Aldermaston and Basingstoke Turnpike Trust**.

Trains See **Railways**.

Treacle Cottage (610 623) Situated on the northwest corner of Church and Pamber Heath Roads. It was originally just a two-up two-down dwelling called Fir-Tree Cottage, part of The **Red House** estate. In the early 1900s it was occupied by the Yates family (8), until they moved to The **Falcon**, public house, and then the Martins who became tenants in 1928. The cottage was purchased at the auction of The Red House in 1949 by Armand 'Freddie' Oppé, grandson of Mrs Oppé. The Martins remained in the cottage, Mrs Martin eventually moving to Burney Bit in 1969 after 41 years. It was little altered until its subsequent sale to the Sewards (Mortimer). The present owners extended the rear of the property in 1984, after the demolition of The **Room**. See **Oppé family**.

Treacle Fayre Annual summer fair organised by the **Loddon Valley Lions**, held in Saunder's Field opposite Lloyds Bank. During the late 1980s and throughout the 1990s it was the main summer fair in Tadley, drawing large crowds. In 1976-77 it was organised by Tadley Scout Support Association. See **Tadley Revel**.

Treacle Mine, The (602 624) Hotel and public house at the corner of Silchester Road and Broadhalfpenny Lane. It was originally known as Lowes Corner Hotel, after John Lowe who ran a shop from the building in the early 1900s. See **Lowes family; Tadley Treacle Mines**.

Treacle Mines See **Tadley Treacle Mines**.

Triangle, Aldermaston (591 652) Triangle of grass at the southern end of the village, by the **Eagle Gates**, where the maypole stood. It is also known as 'The Loosely'. It contains a Roman well which is enclosed by a modern brick wall for safety and was found, in about 1940, when a cow from nearby Forster's Farm strayed onto the grass and partly disappeared into the earth. The triangle also contains a very weathered stone drinking fountain erected in memory of Queen Victoria's Jubilee 1837-97. See **Aldermaston, Aldermaston Court; Aldermaston Estate**.

Trident This submarine based missile system superseded **Polaris**. The missiles were purchased from the USA, but the nuclear warheads were designed at **AWE**. The submarines were also British designed. The system came into service in 1994.

Trunkpond Corner (603 625) A name used by locals in the early part of the century to describe the junction of Tadley Hill and **Rowan Road**. It was a reference to the pond near Pound Cottage and a nearby tree, or the remains of the trunk. It was also known as Station Corner because of the railway carriages there. Serving as temporary housing after **World War I** they were occupied by Mr May and Freddie Chapman. See **Pound**.

Tumuli See **Barrows**.

Turbary Also spelt Turberry, turbary is either, land or a piece of land, where turf may be dug for fuel, or the right to cut turf or peat for fuel on a common or another person's land. As a result of enclosure the residents of Tadley were also awarded the right to extract **gravel**. See **Appendix iii; Common Land; Tadley Common; Turbary Allotment Charity**.

Turbary Allotment Charity A registered charity (1898) that has in its ownership various parcels of land in Tadley which are used for a variety of purposes to the benefit of the parish. See **Jubilee Centre; Tadley Common; Turbary; Appendix ii**.

Turnpike roads See **Aldermaston and Basingstoke Turnpike Trust**.

Twincot (608 607) A two-storey cottage in Winston Avenue, within the **Tadley Conservation Area**. Consisting of rendered walls, a thatched roof and casement windows, it was formerly two cottages. It is believed to have been built about 1750.

2403 Aldermaston Squadron See **Air Training Corps**.

Ufton Court (626 667) Situated between Padworth and Ufton Nervet and owned by the **Benyon family** of **Englefield Estate**. It is currently leased to West Berkshire Council who use it as a short-stay residential centre for Berkshire schoolchildren. A Grade I listed building it gets its name from 'Uf' of 'Uffa' and 'ton', a clearing: Uffa's clearing. It was originally a cruck frame medieval hall, probably dating from about 1420. The cruck is now only visible in an upper bedroom. Today, what we see is a beautiful example of a Tudor manor house in the traditional 'E' shape which almost completely disguises the original medieval building. Many additions, made through the centuries, are visible only from the rear of the building. In the grounds there exists evidence of at least eight medieval **fish ponds**, an important food source for the house and, it is believed, a source of income. For most of its recorded history Ufton Court was owned by the Perkins family, Catholics, who, during the reign of Elizabeth I, did not swear allegiance to the Queen and paid heavy fines as a consequence. Evidence of their catholicism exists in the house: at least four known priest's holes, and painted panels in a bedroom depicting allegiance to the Catholic, Mary, Queen of Scots. In 1802 the property was sold to Mr Congreve of **Aldermaston Estate** who proceeded to strip much of the panelling to pay his debts. It was later purchased by Richard **Benyon**.

United Reformed Church (604 608) A Grade II listed building within the Tadley Conservation Area and known as The **Old Meeting**. The United Reformed Church (URC) was formed in 1972 with the merger of the Congregational Church in England and Wales with the Presbyterian Church of England, forming the third largest Free Church in Britain. The Congregational (Independent) Church in Tadley dates back to the **Puritan Ejection** of 1662. Churchgoers held their early meetings in a house known as **Gardiner's**. When the room there became too small to accommodate the congregation they decided to build a place of worship in what was then known as **Doe's Lane** (now **Malthouse Lane**). This was built in 1718-19. The first Dissenting Minister to live in Tadley was a Thomas Ovey who is known to have resided here prior to 1697. A dissenters Meeting House certificate, dated 4 October 1718, lists him as the pastor, but it was Joseph Tate who took pastoral responsibility during the building of the new church and up until about 1724. By 1828 during the ministry of Mr George **Jennings**, the Meeting House was enlarged to accommodate an additional 100 'hearers'. Also a new school room was built but which by 1862 was too small for the numbers attending. This is believed to have been a **British School**. Further restoration occurred in the early 1960s with a service of re-dedication on 2 June 1962. Today it is in the Guildford District of the Wessex Province. The current **Manse** is in Ramptons Meadow, the original in Manse Lane having been sold in the 1980s. When there is no resident minister in Tadley it comes under the care of the minister at URC, London Road, Basingstoke. See Samuel **Browne**.

United States Army Airborne troops of the United States Army, both paratroops and glider-borne troops, passed through Tadley and were flown from **Aldermaston Airfield** during **World War II**. The two principal units were the 82nd and the 101st Airborne Divisions. Both were heavily involved in Operation Overlord, the **D-Day** invasion of Europe.

United States Army Air Force (USAAF) Groups from the USAAF was stationed at several local airfields during **World War II**. These included units

Photo: Smithsonian Institute, Washington

US army paratroopers boarding C47 aircraft at Aldermaston Airfield, before D-Day, June 1944

of the 8th and 9th USAAF at **Aldermaston Airfield**. The 60th Troop Carrier Group (TCG), a unit of the 8th USAAF, with C47 Dakota aircraft was based at Aldermaston from August to November 1942. The first American paratroop practice-jumps in Britain were from their aircraft. The unit transported paratroops for **Operation Torch**. The 60th was replaced by the 315th TCG in December 1942. Sixteen aircraft from the 315th were sent to Algeria to support the invasion of Sicily in May 1943 and in November of that year the unit was transferred to Welford (9th USAAF). Another unit of the 9th, the 434th TCG, arrived at Aldermaston in March 1944 and began intensive training with American troops of the 82nd and 101st Airborne Divisions for the **D-Day** invasion of France. In September 1944 the 434th transported troops of the 101st Airborne on **Operation Market Garden**. In February and March 1945 the 434th left Aldermaston and moved to an airfield at Mourmelon le Grand in France later taking part in Operation Varsity, the Rhine river crossing. During their time at Aldermaston the aircraft of the 434th TCG were maintained and repaired by men of the 458th Air Service Squadron. This unit's accommodation was in Blakes Lane, and in 1997 a plaque was placed on the wall of a building there to commemorate this. One of the American veterans, Paul Gerbracht, was present at the ceremony. A total of approximately 3,000 Americans lived at Aldermaston Airfield and Tadley during this period. Other troops were brought in for exercises and operations when required.

V

Valuation records Records created as a result of the Finance Act (1901-10) which formed part of a national survey of land and property-ownership and its value. The actual records for each village give the names of the occupier and owner, the area of the land and its rateable value. As an example, the records note that **Mothe's Charity** trustees owned the almshouses in Almshouse Meadow and the occupant was a Mrs S.A.J. Stacey. Baughurst is recorded as having 172 entries (properties) and Tadley 350. Most of our villages are in alphabetical order of owner; e.g. Edward Allen to Duke of Wellington. There is also a cross-reference insert for places that may go under two names e.g. for **Tadley Court** see Wilderness etc. The Pamber list runs from George Auglis at Pamber Green to Edward Willies at Pamber Heath.

Venture Ltd See **Bus and coach services**.

Vestry Meetings Prior to the formation of urban and rural district and parish councils in 1894, local affairs were the responsibility of the parish vestry. The vestry's origin was the calling together of parishioners to discuss church business and was basically an ecclesiastical organisation. The growth of towns and villages meant the parish vestry had even more civil duties loaded upon it. The name came from the fact that the meetings were originally held in the church vestry. In partnership with the Justices of the Peace, the vestry system was a self-governing body subject to no control or audit and so in many places leadership fell to the mob or clique. Membership of the vestry comprised the minister, church-wardens, and leading parishioners, who were either co-opted (under a 'close' or 'select' vestry system) or elected ('open vestry'). Vestry meetings were the smallest unit of English **local government**. Minutes of vestry meetings help build up

a picture of local life. For example, the Tadley vestry minutes for April 1875 record that it had been decided to sell (subject to the approval of the Enclosure Commission) Tadley's Turbary Common in suitable lots; permission was granted on 5 June 1876, with the proceeds being invested and the dividends being used to buy coal and other fuel for the poor of the village. Between 1889 and the formation of parish councils in 1894 Tadley's vestry meetings were held in The **Iron Room**. See **Queen's College Arms**.

Veterinary practice Initially operating as a service run from Basingstoke, a weekly veterinary surgery was held on Tuesday evenings in the annexe of the church hall (The **Iron Room**) on The **Green**, in the 1950s. These weekly surgeries became so popular it became obvious a more comprehensive locally-based service was required and **Oaktree Cottage** in **West Street** was purchased, in 1961, by Mr Ray. The property consisted of the cottage and a separate small bungalow, once used for besom-making, and also, it was said, as a baker's. Although small, the bungalow was converted into a surgery with a waiting room, consulting room and store. Over the next twenty years Tadley grew and the surgery in the bungalow became too small. An application to build a custom-designed surgery was granted and the new building began operating in about 1983.

Victoria History of the Counties of England An invaluable reference guide for local historians. Unfortunately, the Hampshire volumes were written at the turn of the century. Almost one hundred years of history are unrecorded and, for some of the information, more recent research has re-interpreted events and conclusions.

Village Halls See **Aldermaston Parish Hall; Heath End Village Hall; Pamber Heath Memorial Hall; Ramsdell Village Hall; Tadley Memorial Hall**.

Vine Tree Farm (607 613) Located at the northern end of Winston Avenue and just within the **Tadley Conservation Area**. The original farmhouse was built of brick and timber in approximately 1720 and consisted of the usual two rooms up and down with a central door, now removed. The stairs to the upper floor were built external to the rear of the building and were probably protected from the elements by a wooden 'lean to' structure. They are now an integral part of the Victorian kitchen extension. A brick barn, abutted on the south end in the 1770s, now forms the modern entrance hall. Several interesting features exist, among which is a wooden lock, housed in an oak box and still in use on the back door. The use of brick in this building would indicate that at least one of the three local brickworks was operational in the early eighteenth century. The vine which covers the front, first gave its name to the farm in the 1860s. Before this it was probably known as Clift's Farm, certainly during the time Anna and son William Clift farmed there. Throughout the 20th century it has had in excess of 20 owners. Prior to this it formed part of the estate of William Wither Branston Beach. See **Beach family; Little London Brickworks**.

Vine Tree Farm granary (607 613) Built at a slightly later date than the farm to store its grain. It has recently (1997) been renovated by a Dutch craftsman previously employed in the building of the Globe Theatre. The original timbers were found to have been mechanically sawn, as opposed to pit sawn, and numbered. This would indicate that it was made 'off site'. Once constructed, it was dismantled, carted to its final site and rebuilt, using the numbering on the timbers. Raised on to nine staddle stones, to allow air to circulate and to hinder any depredation by rodents, it was then weatherboarded.

W

Wakeford Farm (593 597) An old name for **Pamber Place**. The present Wakeford Farm is situated nearby on the A340 (608 591).

Walk, The (616 609) A 20 feet-wide (6 m) green track running north for about 150 yards from near The **Manse**. The annual Old Meeting Whit Monday Fete was held there. When the land was redeveloped, the house in Malthouse Lane, next to the **United Reformed Church**, was named The Walk to retain the land's history.

Wallis & Steevens In the construction industry the name of Wallis & Steevens has been practically a byword for road rollers since the early 1900s. However, the firm also made important contributions to agriculture, in its early days through ploughs and implements and later, by threshing machines, portables and traction engines. R & J Kent of Baughurst owned, at the time of their closure in 1944, six steam road rollers and four steam threshing machines. At least one of their threshing machines, made by Wallis & Steevens (production model no 7667), had been purchased, as new, in November 1919.

Wallis & Steevens was a family firm which evolved from a wholesale and retail ironmongers, ironfounders and agricultural implement makers in Market Place, Basingstoke. Supplying the surrounding agricultural trade the firm moved to Station Hill, Basingstoke, and again to Daneshill Industrial Estate in 1967. In 1981 British Steel Piling bought the designs and goodwill for the roller business, and production moved to their modern plant at Claydon near Ipswich. The last roller made in Basingstoke was completed in July 1981 and the works closed at the end of that month.

Richard Wallis, grandson of the founder, was responsible for the agricultural side of the business and lived locally in the Baughurst Road. He worked with the company after leaving school, becoming a director in 1943. After his early death in 1952 the family moved to **Bridge House**. Wallis & Steevens vehicles will be displayed in the new 'Milestones' museum to be opened in Basingstoke in the year 2000. See **Kent Family**.

War memorials The first war memorials, listing the names of those who died, date back to the Crimean War. After **World War I** many memorials were erected by public subscription at focal points for memorial services, and on plaques and boards in churches, chapels and halls. The memorials list the deceased of the parish in alphabetical order, often giving their rank as well. The names of those who died in **World War II** have usually been added to the same memorial.

Tadley war memorial has, over the years, had three different locations. Built by public subscription, a traditional stone cross commemorating the men who died in World War I was originally placed on the western side of Mulfords Hill/Tadley Hill (opposite Rowan Road) in 1920. The names of those who died in World War II were added to the memorial. With the postwar increase in traffic and proposed road widening schemes it was decided to relocate the memorial. In 1963 it was transferred unceremoniously on the front of a JCB mechanical digger to the eastern side of **Tadley Memorial Hall** on The **Green**. In 1967 the memorial was moved again, to its present location at the front of **St Paul's Church**. A memorial garden, with a commemorative stone, has been created just north of New Road to mark its original location. See **Appendix iv; Pamber Heath Memorial Hall**.

Ward, Ron Tadley resident, keen cricketer and naturalist, who preserved an ancient (hay) meadow in

Staff of J.S. Whatmore & Sons Ltd during the 1960s.
Seated (left to right): Edna Old, Reg Hoare, Mrs Wood, Stewart Whatmore, Mrs Whatmore, Mr Whatmore, Ernie Awberry, Mary Hiscock, Ron Bartlett; middle row standing: Hannah Coyle, Gwen Bealing, Dot Pike, Rachel Gundry, Rosemary Gundry, Mary Prouten, Joyce Powell, Helen Rigby, Gran Burnell, Shirley Everson, Tommy Perry, unknown; back row standing: Margaret McGrath, Ken Branston, Mrs Hicks, unknown, Mrs Watson, unknown, unknown, unknown.

Tadley, despite lucrative offers to buy the land. Ron (1925–91) had lived at **Tadley Place** at one time and had been a building trade ganger. He served on **Tadley Parish Council** for 18 years and was a member of the management committee of the **Pamber Forest** Local Nature Reserve from its formation in 1980. Ron was also responsible for founding the **Tadley Watch** Group, one of the largest in the County. Ron died in December 1991 and was buried in his meadow, which he had bequeathed to the Hampshire and Isle of Wight Wildlife Trust. See **Ron Ward's Meadow**.

Wasing Place (577 643) Referred to in the eleventh century as Wasince and, at later times, Wavesing or Wasynge. From the time of Edward the Confessor the manor passed through various hands including the Forsters of Aldermaston, who held it from 1543 to 1620. It was then in the family Verney until 1730. John Mount of Tower Hill, London, bought the estate in 1760 and had the present mansion designed by John Hobcraft between 1770-3. There is now nothing above ground of the original manor house which was reputed to be a short distance away. Hobcraft's classic pedimented eighteenth century mansion was destroyed by fire on 2 February 1945 and reconstructed in 1955. During **World War II**, Wasing Place housed the accounts staff of the **Great Western Railway** (GWR) evacuated from

Paddington. It is not clear whether the GWR staff were still using the house at the time of the fire, but it is said that the alarm was raised by a charwoman early that morning. Fire tenders raced from Reading and five other stations, Maidenhead and Didcot being the furthest away. Water had to be pumped by relays of engines from lakes about a quarter of a mile away. Estate workers saved what they could of the family treasures. Sir William Mount was living at Wasing Farm at this time, having been invalided out of the Royal Armoured Corps. Wasing Place is still the seat of the Mount family. Ferdinand (William Robert), who does not use his title and is the grandson of Sir William, is listed in Debrett's as a journalist and author. His publications include: *Very Like a Whale*, 1967; *The Theatre of Politics*, 1972; *The Subversive Family*, 1982; *Umbrella*, 1994; *The Liquidator*, 1995. His heir is William Robert Horatio Mount, born in 1969. See **Aldermaston Parish Hall**; **Salvation Army Hall**; **SSSI**.

Water Locally, mains water only became common in the late 1940s. Before this, people would have got their water from a garden well. The district has been blessed with ample well-water throughout its history, with old maps showing an abundance of wells. This was made possible mainly because of the reasonably high water table situated above the impervious layer of London Clay. There is little documentary evidence as to when mains water came to the area, although **Kingsclere and Whitchurch Rural District Council** began a process of conveying piped water in 1933. It was probably **Aldermaston Airfield** and its associated living quarters in the northern part of Tadley that saw the first supply in the early 1940s. Mortimer Pumping Station, built about 1912, would have originally supplied water to the Tadley area, prior to the borehole source at Ufton Nervet being built in 1968. Ufton Nervet then supplied water directly to the water storage towers at Burghfield, Silchester and later Tadley. The Tadley tower (near **Calleva Park**) was built in 1975. It is 122 feet (37 m) in diameter, comprising 5,635 tons of concrete, and holds 756,000 gallons (3,437,000 litres) of water. Today there are four boreholes at Ufton Nervet (together with a chlorine gas injection disinfection system), each one being 450 feet (140 m) deep with diameters ranging from 24 to 35 inches (610 to 890 mm). Residents in parts of Baughurst, however, are supplied by Southern Water (a Scottish Power Company) from Bear Hill near Kingsclere. See **Sewage**.

Weather and climate The geographic position of Tadley (Lat 51 deg 22 min N; Long 1 deg 9 min W) gives a dual climatic benefit derived jointly from the distance from the seasonal position of the Icelandic depression and a fair amount of shelter from the moist prevailing west to southwest winds. Extreme temperatures over the region are influenced by proximity to the European land mass giving comparatively hot summers and cold winters. The average daily maximum for the summer months is 21 deg C while the average nightly winter minimum is just above 0 deg C. The average yearly rainfall is around 27 inches (700 mm).

Despite the apparent quiescence of the climate over our part of Hampshire, Tadley and its neighbours have experienced many extremes of weather over the years. Before local **newspapers** came into existence, all we have to gauge the coldest winters against are the archived reports of the years that the Thames at Reading froze over viz: 1363, 1595, 1649 and 1814. Closer to living memory, severe snowstorms and blizzards causing much disruption to daily life caught the newspaper headlines in January 1881, April 1908, December 1927 and December 1937, while January 1940 brought an unusual ice storm across most of Hampshire. The cruel bleak winter of January to March 1947 described at the time as the 'coldest of the century' felt much worse because of the accompanying post-war fuel crisis. However the winter of 1962-3 eventually took and still holds the title for the 'coldest of the century'. Locally, the coldest day of the century occurred on 14 January 1982 when a minimum of minus 18 deg C was recorded just east of Beech Hill.

'Glorious Summers' of the century are recorded by the local press as occurring in 1911 (maximum 36 deg C), 1921 (salad days), 1932 (heat wave), 1933 (drought), 1947 (following the cold bleak winter), 1959 (sunny and dry), 1976 (blazing early summer) and 1990 (maximum of 36.5 deg C at Mortimer) and more recently 1995 (global warming) During long dry spells, fires on the local gorse commons cause some concern for neighbouring residents.

Although most local storms (rain and wind combined) occur between October and January, the heaviest rainfall occurs in the summer thunderstorms of June and July. In one such storm in June 1910 it was reported that two horses were killed by lightning in Baughurst. On 6 July 1989 the afternoon's rainfall in Pamber Green was recorded as 82 mm while in Tadley hailstones of 35 mm were found. These events made the late night national Radio 4 weather summary for the day, the month and the year. The 'Great Storm' of October 1987 took its toll around Tadley with many trees being uprooted in **Pamber Forest**, on the **Aldermaston Estate** and at The **Vyne**. Tadley's small valley, cut by the Bishopswood stream, has seen several 'floods' in recent years; these mostly being caused by poor or blocked land drains around the area. It is thought that flooding would be more serious here if it were not for the 'holding power' of the porous gravel of the higher **Tadley Common; Silchester C of E School.**

Wellington Arms, The (514 605) A public house in **Baughurst**. Named after the first Duke of Wellington, whose family were principal landowners in the area from 1817 to 1943. There is a record of a land title of 1772–1848, with an abstract of The Wellington as a 'beer house' in 1846. In 1871 it was probably kept by Thomas Webb, though in keeping with common practice of the times, his occupation in the census is shown as being a wheelwright. Prior to being a public house the building had been a farm house beside the village pound and stocks. See **Toll House, Baughurst.**

Wells, John 'Tiny' The jockey who rode **Blue Gown**, the 1868 Derby winner, for Sir Joseph **Hawley**. Born in Sutton Coldfield in 1833, he was nicknamed 'Tiny' from an early age; in later years he was also referred to as 'Brusher'. He was careful with money and invested some in a flourishing pen-manufacturing factory in Birmingham and was comfortably off when he died. For winning the 1868 Derby, Sir Joseph gave him the prize money – £6,800. He was also reputed to have been given Hawley House (now known as **Hawley Farm**). The 1871 census certainly records him as being the occupant of the house together with his wife and four servants. He died in 1873, aged 39, and is buried in Kingsclere churchyard together with his wife Mary Ann (Jane) who died the previous year, aged 38 years.

Welshman's Mile (630 642) A road in Mortimer West End, between Chapel Road and Chapel Lane. It probably got its name from the Welsh and the West Country drovers who brought their cattle,

Albert West outside his cottage in West Street

Photo: Arthur Nash

horses and geese along the road into Mortimer for events like the Mortimer Horse and Cattle Fair. Welshman's Pool, a resting place along the road, is an area of grass in the midst of a well-wooded area, with a good supply of water at hand.

WE177 free-fall bomb The design for the WE177 dates back to the late 1950s. Intended as a multi-purpose nuclear weapon to be deployed by the TSR2 low level attack aircraft, development continued despite the cancellation of the TSR2 project. Non nuclear aspects of the weapon were designed by various firms with **AWRE** being responsible for the design of the warhead, which was tested on 1 March 1962 at Britain's first underground test (Pampas) in Nevada. The operational WE177 (Type B 950 lb bomb) was delivered to RAF Cottesmore in September 1966 with the Type A 600 lb bomb coming into service in 1969 and the Type C in 1973. During its long service life the WE177 was carried by a wide range of aircraft including the Vulcan, Jaguar, Tornado, Buccaneer and a range of Royal Navy anti-submarine helicopters. The weapon began to be taken out of service in 1992 with the last operational WE177 being withdrawn from RAF Marham on 31 March 1998. Weapon decommissioning began at **AWE Burghfield** in 1992 and was successfully completed on 21 August 1998.

West Heath (592 582) A village situated just north of **Ramsdell** in the parish of Wootton St. Lawrence. At the time of enclosure it was part of the parish of Tadley, but was given a separate identity: 'Tadley

and West Heath Commons'. In the enclosure report it was awarded a one acre quarry and six acres as **allotments for the labouring poor**. In 1841 it comprised of approximately 20 dwellings (130 inhabitants) but the hamlet was, by 1881, no longer identified by name. It was, at one time, thought that the Roman road between Winchester and Silchester was traceable over a part of West Heath (Witch Lane). See **Appendix iii**; **Enclosure Acts**.

Wesley, John An Anglican clergyman, son of an Anglican clergyman in Lincolnshire, born in 1703 and died in 1791. Together with his brother Charles (1707-1788) and George Whitefield (1714-1770) they were part of a devout group at Oxford University that were given a number of nicknames by their fellow students, one being 'Methodists'. After being ordained as a priest in the Church of England in 1728, he went to the USA as a missionary and on his return to this country in 1738 he experienced what he called 'a heart strangely warmed' and became a fervent evangelical. Whitefield had also experienced spiritual conversion and had been preaching in the open air to the colliers of Kingswood Chase near Bristol, a technique he had gained at the camp meetings in America, and when he wanted to return to America he invited John Wesley to take over the work. From this beginning in 1739 Wesley began to build up the structures that were to become the mainstay of Methodism. His brother Charles wrote many of the hymns used in The Evangelical Revival in the 1700s and that continue to be used to this day. Whitefield and John Wesley differed over predestination. John and Charles visited Baughurst regularly, staying with George Whitefield, in the seven years prior to their differences. Whitefield went on to be chaplain to The Countess of Huntingdon. See **Chapel House, Baughurst; Methodists.**

West, Albert Whether Albert is a descendant of the de Wests who are purported to have come to Tadley in 1116 we do not know, but his ancestry has been traced through eight generations to the seventeenth century. Albert and his twin sister Annie were born to Elizabeth and Job in August 1910. He was one of eleven children, all born in a simple wattle and daub dwelling that stood alongside the existing one room cottage, where he still lives. Devoid of hot water, central heating, a flush toilet or indeed most modern conveniences it reflects a lifestyle that was once common to all country people.

Although known for his broom-making, Albert's first job, at the age of 14, was stripping willow osiers. He did not make a broom until he was 25, first serving the customary apprenticeship under his father's guidance. **West Street**, home, in the nineteenth century, to innumerable broom-making Wests and Saunders, has always been home to Albert and his older brother Alfred, who died in 1996. Neither of the brothers ever married. At the tender age of one month Albert was initiated into the Tadley tradition of **hop-picking**, a pilgrimage he continued annually, even throughout the war years, until the age of 80.

Albert still speaks with the broad north Hampshire dialect of his youth, unique at the end of this millennium. He continues to visit the woods to coppice the birch and will still make a broom or two if asked. See **Oaktree Cottage**.

West Berkshire Council See **Berkshire County Council.**

West End Brick Yard (638 639) Marked on the 1873 Ordnance Survey map. See **Brick and tile making.**

West Heath An Inclosure Act of 1850 (1852) granted six acres of land there as allotments for the labouring poor.

West Sherbourne Priory (609 502) The original name of **Pamber Priory.**

West Street Not a location that appears by name in records or that was in common use in the nineteenth century, unlike the adjacent Broadhalfpenny Lane. Census records refer to it as just **Tadley Common** or Through Common. It is believed to have been named by the **Salvation Army** because of the large West population there. Analysis of the census records serve to support this belief: in 1841 70 out of Tadley's population of 817, and in 1881 105 out of 1017 bore the name West. In 1881 all but one of these lived between the brickyard and Back Lane i.e. Tadley Common. It was a conveniently-sited area with easy access to the forest for coppice ware,

heather for their brooms and land to store resources and graze animals. The gradual northward movement of Old Tadley was aided by this ever-increasing population of broom makers. However, West Street could just as easily have been named after the Saunders, who were interspersed along its length. Records show 77 Saunders living there, compared to the 104 Wests! It was not until 1998 that the name Saunders was acknowledged by the community in Saunders Gardens, off Swains/Millers Road. See **Besoms; Broomyards;** Albert **West.**

Whatmore & Sons, J.S. (598 623) Originally a front parlour shop on Mulfords Hill. James Whatmore bought it from Yorke **Lowe** in 1945. At that time the shop was inside the restricted area of **Aldermaston Airfield** with access via a **picket post**, operated by the Americans, at the top of Mulfords Hill. There was no mains electricity in the shop, power coming from a petrol generator. The business expanded during the 1950s as Tadley grew to meet the demands of AWRE. In about 1957 a chemist's section was started with Alan Hunter as the first chemist; later, Brian Fox took over and in 1965 he set up on his own. In 1961 Whatmores was converted into a self-service shop offering a very wide range of goods and services including groceries, hardware, toys, stationery and travel. A member of the Wavy Line group of stores, it eventually became part of the Bookers supermarket chain in 1977. See **Budgens.**

Wheat's Charity, Samuel A local charity established in 1700, whereby 30 shillings a year (£1.50p) was left for coats or jackets for three poor men of Pamber parish. White's Directory for 1878 says the money for it came 'out of Hall Estate at Silchester'. Vestry minutes from 1896 list the recipients for that year: John Simpson, William Stacey and G. Midford (Mulford). See **Charities.**

White Hart, The (594 577) A public house in Charter Alley. It began as a beer house in the 1850s. During **World War I** it was an assembly point for men wishing to join the army, on their way to Basingstoke. From here they marched to other public houses in the area, collecting more recruits as they went along.

White House, The (617 621) A large house in Pamber Heath with its entrance on Impstone Road. At one time it was part of The **Red House** estate. It was demolished during the 1970s to make way for housing development.

Whites of Camberley See **Kent family.**

WI See **Womens' Institute.**

WI scrapbooks Large albums of cuttings, poems, drawings and other local memorabilia collected by **Womens' Institute** (WI) groups. Probably a national scheme intended to reflect local life and events of the time, several scrapbooks from other branches in the county are kept at **Hampshire Record Office**. Arthur **Attwood** featured them in an article 'Scrapbook Memories of the Past' in the

Basingstoke Gazette in March 1989. Tadley WI produced two albums, one in the early 1950s and the other in 1965, and Burnham Copse WI produced one in 1965.

Wigmore Farm (609 593) A listed building in **Pamber End** thought to date from 1485 when it was built as a timber-framed halled dwelling with wattle and daub walls. Restoration work in the 1980s revealed many interesting oddities. An abundance of oyster shells (a cheap food in earlier times) were found buried in a pit outside the kitchen door. A mummified cat found in a bricked up fireplace was thought to have been a local tradition to bring good luck. The kitchen flagstones covered a sand-puddled floor (a mix of sand, lime, hair and manure), in which there were the impressions of many hand prints.

Wigwam School (596 624) See **Burnham Copse Infants School**.

Wilderness, The (605 623) See **Tadley Court**.

Wildlife In both regional and national terms, the area within and around Tadley has a rich wildlife interest, although it is now a much reduced representation of the remarkable countryside which existed here earlier than the twentieth century. As elsewhere, building development and agricultural improvement have taken a great toll over the past 50 years. However, few areas in Hampshire can boast seven designated Sites of Special Scientific Interest (**SSSI**) within a 4 mile radius, as can Tadley. The largest of these is the **Pamber Forest** complex, with almost 500 acres of Oak-Hazel-Ash woodland (a designated Local Nature Reserve), the herb-rich meadows on the west side, and Silchester and Tadley Commons to the north. The latter are important examples of Calluna Heathland lying on the Plateau Gravels, with both wet and dry heath. There are other remnants of heathland in Tadley, such as Wigmore Heath, reminders of the extensive areas of heathland which once dominated the landscape here before the development of **AWRE** and its associated housing. Calluna heather still lingers on many lawns and road verges in Tadley and Baughurst, occasionally with rarer plants such as Bee Orchid and Autumn Ladies Tresses, as in Burnham Road and Franklin Avenue. Outside Tadley itself, Padworth Common SSSI is a good area of acid heathland and grassland, and the neighbouring Burnt Common is planned to be a nature reserve following gravel extraction. Benyons Inclosure has remnants of dry heathland which become evident when the extensive plantations of conifers are felled, and is important for its wildlife. The nearby Decoy Pond and Pits SSSI is a former area of gravel extraction, with a rich dragonfly fauna and an important Alder gulley. Also important for its dragonfly interest is Wasing Ponds SSSI to the north west of Tadley.

Herb-rich grassland is now a nationally threatened habitat, with 98% of agriculturally unimproved lowland meadows having disappeared. The area has fine examples in **Ron Ward's Meadow**, the meadows to the west of Pamber Forest, and **Ashford Hill Meadows**. The late **Ron Ward** generously donated his 25 acre herb-rich hay meadow to the Hampshire Wildlife Trust as a nature reserve. Saunders Field SSSI to the north of Tadley is a small remnant of rich neutral grassland at the western end of the Decoy Ponds, Pits and Woods SSSI.

Some road verges in the area are protected for their wild flower species, one of the most notable being under the Beech woodland by the water tower to the north of Tadley, where good populations of three Helleborine species occur. Such verges are fragments of the former rich countryside which is being constantly destroyed. See **Aldermaston Decoy**.

William Penney Theatre (599 630) A 287-seat theatre at **AWE** where the **Boundary Players** perform their plays. It is named after William **Penney**. Work began on the conversion of part of a building at the end of the Players' 1963 season and in autumn 1965 the season opened in the new theatre with 'The Taming of the Shrew'. Offically known as the William Penney Lecture Theatre, it was formally opened by William Penney in February 1966. In 1996 it closed for repairs, reopening later the same year.

William the Conqueror It is believed that he passed through the Baughurst area after the Battle of Hastings, on his way to receive the surrender of the English armies at Wallingford, possibly stopping at **Aldermaston Estate**.

Williams family A family of showmen and steam circus proprietors who for four generations used Tadley as their winter home. Tadley census records show the Williams family only once in 1891, although it is known they wintered here in 1875 and probably before. Census records were taken in April, the time when such families were en route to local fairs; their records, therefore, appear more often in the census for surrounding villages and towns. Jimmy's great grandfather, Samuel and his family took up regular winter residence in Shyshack Lane where he stored his hoopla, swinging boats and later his pony-operated roundabout. The family later moved to 16 East Street (Franklin Avenue) and eventually to 48 Mulfords Hill where Jimmy and his gallopers now reside. In 1965, after a lapse of 26 years, Jimmy resurrected the family tradition and bought a succession of fairground rides which he restored and used to re-establish the Williams family's showman's rights. His first roundabout and a switchback ride were sold to Warner Brothers (USA) in the 1970s. The gallopers he still owns were built in 1896 and were last used in September 1990 at the Newbury Agricultural Show. Jimmy continues to execute the art of painting fairground rides, restoring museum pieces to their former glory. It is said that, like a painting, his style of artwork can easily be recognised throughout the showmans' guild. Jimmy has appeared in a number of television programmes.

Williams Pear The Willams Bon Chrétien pear originated in Aldermaston in the late eighteenth century. The pear was first described by William Hooker in the *Transactions of the Horticultural Society of London* (1817). The name came from Richard Williams, a nurseryman from Turnham Green, who had sent a specimen to William Hooker. William Hooker related that the pear had been grown from seed by a Mr Wheeler, a schoolmaster from Aldermaston, around 1797. George Lindley's *Guide to the Orchard and Kitchen Garden* (1831) puts the date earlier at 1770. However, in 1884 in Robert Hogg's *Fruit Manual* (5th ed) John Stair is named as the propagator; John Stair, who died in 1840, succeeded Mr Wheeler as the schoolmaster. The pear was taken to America in 1797 or 1799 to be grown in the grounds of Thomas Brewer of Roxbury, Massachusetts. This estate passed, in 1817, to Enoch Bartlett who, not identifying the tree, called it the Bartlett pear which has been a very prominent fruit in the American canning industry. In 1956 Mr Freeman of Berkshire Education Committee unveiled a plaque at the school commemorating the history of the pear. See **Aldermaston School; Bartlett's Corner**.

Willow osiers The stripping of willow osiers for weaving into baskets, fish traps, crinoline hoops, pack horse panniers and cradles was carried out locally. The osier beds need plenty of moisture and occasional flooding was considered desirable, while the soil needs to be rich and well cultivated. Locally, osiers were grown on the River Kennet, in particular near Woolhampton. They are also mentioned along Tadley Brook/Bowmonts Brook and New Road. Census returns show a flourishing osier industry in Woolhampton: in 1851 Daniel New, William Brown, William Chandler and George Langswell were listed as willow rod growers; in 1871 there were only two listed, William Brown and William Chandler, and in 1891 William Brown had a monopoly.

The rods were cut in winter with a reaping hook and tied into bundles sometimes called bolts. These bundles were tightened with two pieces of ash, then the ends of the bolts were levelled by beating with a paddle. The bundles were bound with a 'withe' or strip of split willow. The thicker and stronger rods were used for panniers and fish traps; thinner more flexible rods for baskets. Osiers were sold as green, brown, white or buff. The green were sold as cut, the brown (the ones Brown's sold mostly) were dried and stacked and often thatched or protected in some way. They were half the weight of the green rods due to loss of moisture. White rods were cut in the autumn and stood in several inches of stagnant water until spring. Buff rods were obtained by boiling green rods for 2-5 hours and leaving them to cool overnight. Rods were usually peeled or stripped by women thrusting them through the metal jaws of the stripping 'brake'. This work was mainly undertaken between the begining April and June. Many women went to work at **Brown's Rod Yard, Heath End**. They were paid either 1d (0.3p) an hour or 3d (1p) for a bolt of rods. Stripped rods would go by canal and rail to basket makers around the country.

The industry was particularly important in World War I as ammunition was carried in willow baskets, but declined in the 1930s when labour costs became too high compared with foreign imports e.g. from Belgium. There was also a disease affecting some of the willows. Brown's osier beds, marshland with old willow trees, is now designated a Site of Special Scientific Interest (**SSSI**). See Reuben **Hicks**.

Windmills Windmills, where corn was ground into flour, were usually located close to where the corn was grown and harvested. They were common prior to the Industrial Revolution and the growth of the railways. Mechanisation and cheap transport saw the growth of larger mills with better equipment and the decline of the small local windmill owner. Because of the abundance of timber in England, particularly near the woodlands around Tadley, it would probably have been a long time before windmills of brick and stone were adopted. Local windmills may have been either post or smock mills. The post mill was a wooden box shaped structure supported on a vertical post with, in some cases, a brick under building called a round house. The smock mill comprised eight vertical timbers tapering at the top and covered in weather boarding, its shape more octagonal. Their timber construction meant they had a relatively short life and so few, if any, remain today. A windmill stood near **Tadley Place** but it had ceased to exist long before Florence **Davidson** wrote about it in 1913. All that remains are the local field and place names: Great Windmill Meadow, Little Windmill Close, Coombe House Windmill. It is recorded that a miller, John Ward, resided at or near the site of the **Silchester Methodist Chapel** in 1786. The windmill fell into disuse and the then miller Joel Ward moved to a cottage opposite, the site of McCartneys.

Window Tax Replacing the **Hearth Tax**, Window Tax was imposed by Parliament in 1696 to help meet the cost of reminting damaged coinage. After 1792 houses with 7-9 windows were taxed at 2 shillings (10p) and 10-19 at 4 shillings (20p). From 1825 houses with less than eight windows were exempt. The tax was abolished in 1851. Many local houses of the time still bear witness to this tax – with blocked up windows still evident (e.g. Silchester Cottage, Silchester and Inhurst Farm, Baughurst). Window Tax was replaced by House Duty which was levied on inhabited houses, between 1852 and 1924; census records (1851-91) show uninhabited properties in each parish.

Winkworth Lane Known as 'Lovers' Lane' by locals well into the twentieth century. The name

Peace celebrations following World War I

Winkworth was usually applied to the byway running east-west through Ravenswing Caravan Park. As a surname Winkworth appears in the 1871 Silchester census and the 1881 Tadley census and a family of that name are known to have lived on the western byway in the early 1900s. See **Kingsclere Workhouse**.

Witches See **Aldermaston Witch; Tadley Witch**.

Withies See **Willow osiers**.

Wolverton Manor (555 585) Tun (later ton) is an Anglo Saxon word meaning hedge or fence, later, enclosure. Spellings have been; 1086 Ulvretune and later, Wulfertona giving the probable meaning of a settlement or homestead (within an enclosure) belonging to Wulfhere or Wulfred. Wolverton is mentioned in the **Domesday Survey** when it was held by Alvred (Alfred), the priest of William the Conqueror. Frequent references were made to a royal residence at Wolverton and the money spent in repairing the King's houses there. In 1165 Eleanor, Queen to Henry II, lived at Wolverton estate while her husband was absent in France and her expenses for her stay amounted to £18.0s.0d (£18.0p). Over the next 400 years it had a succession of owners. In about 1660 one George Browne bought the Manor which in turn passed to his son Sir George Browne. These Brownes were often mentioned by Pepys in his diary. In 1782 it was bought by Charles Von Notten who took his wife's maiden name, Pole. His son subsequently sold the estate to the first Duke of Wellington in the early 1800s. In 1880 the adjoining parish of **Ewhurst** was joined with Wolverton and in 1944 sold as one estate comprising 5000

acres. See **Browne's Charity; St Catherine's Church**.

Wolverton School (552 582) A **National School** built in 1844 to accommodate 50 pupils, the 1903 **Kelly's Directory** records the attendance as being down to only 25. The school was supported partly by the Duke of Wellington and partly by a voluntary rate. It closed around 1912, when the Management Board took account of the difficulties faced by the Master in running a school where most of the pupils failed to turn up in the summer months. The imposing and collecting of fines for non-attendance became a great burden. The children had at that time to walk to Kingsclere to attend school. The log-book recorded other problems for the vicar and the master, including the demands for sawdust to fill the pig-trough used as an urinal for the boys, all contributing perhaps to the decision to close. The old school is now a private residence. See **Education; Appendix i**.

Womens' Institute There have been several branches locally. Tadley and Silchester, the oldest, were both formed in 1918. Tadley was suspended after just six years but was reformed in 1933 and remained an active institute until it closed in 1982. Silchester, however, celebrated its 80th anniversary in 1998 and is still going strong. Baughurst branch was formed in 1927 and suspended nine years later, reopening again in 1948 before being suspended again in 1994. The Burnham Copse branch was founded in 1952 by Lady **Penney** for the wives of the first **AWRE** employees. It held its inaugural meeting in the Ministry of Supply canteen (old

Community Centre). 24 ladies attended, numbers rising to more than 100 members in the 1960s and 1970s. Calleva branch was formed in 1974 followed by Pamber Heath in 1977. The latter closed in 1999. Calleva WI is still very active and, along with Silchester and Burnham Copse, is part of the Berkshire Federation of Womens' Institutes, whose headquarters are at WI House, Mortimer. Tadley and Baughurst branches were part of the Hampshire Federation.

Woodall, Alf The radio officer on the – 'peace in our time' – flights made by Prime Minister Chamberlain to meet Hitler in 1938. During September of that year Chamberlain made three flights to Germany to discuss the Czech crisis with Hitler; it was on arriving back at Heston, London after the third visit that Chamberlain made his famous 'peace in our time' speech. Alf's widow, Evelyn, still has the signal-pads and hand-written notes he kept from the flights. In one of these, on the return flight, Alf was instructed to send a radio message calling the Cabinet together. It was reported in *Hampshire Life* magazine that this meeting was held at Hackwood House, near Basingstoke. During the war Alf helped with the evacuation of Poles from Lisbon and was awarded the British Empire Medal for his efforts. In the post-war period he was a radio instructor with **Airways Training Ltd**. He lived at Broadhalfpenny Cottage later retiring to Sussex where he died. Evelyn now lives at **Mothe's House**.

Wooden Tent, Pamber Heath See **Gospel Hall**.

Woodland Practice (597 627) Health practice serving Tadley and the surrounding area, centred on the **Holmwood Health Centre** and **Morland Surgery**. See **Health care and medical services**.

Wootton and Tadley School Board Founded on 29 September 1874 it took over responsibility for the existing schools in the area as well as building new schools. These included Wootton School (1836), **Tadley School** (built 1876) and those in the villages of Ewhurst, Pamber and West Sherborne. The Board exercised School Attendance powers under the Education Act of 1876 until the 1902 Act came into force in 1903, and the newly-created County Council took over responsibility. See **Board Schools; Education; Tadley School; Appendix i**.

Workhouses See **Kingsclere Workhouse; Overseers of the Poor; Poor Law**.

World War I (1914-1918) A large number of local men fought in this war. Charles Keyser, owner of **Aldermaston Estate**, gave five shillings (25p) each week to every Aldermaston man who enlisted and rent-free accommodation to any war-widows. A significantly higher proportion of those who served, died, in World War I, than in **World War II**. War memorials are evidence of this, e.g. Tadley war memorial lists 33 dead in World War I compared to 6 in World War II.

During the early part of the war the government relied on volunteers known as 'Kitchener's Army'.

Locally, volunteers gathered at public houses, e.g. The **Fox and Hounds** and The **White Hart**, Charter Alley, before proceeding on to Basingstoke, collecting others on the way. They assembled finally in the town, possibly in Hackwood Park. Both Monty Hutchins and Elsie Simpson remember contingents of troops marching through Tadley during the war. Monty, writing in *A Country Childhood*, recollected: 'Some time during the 1914-18 war, I can remember that one very hot day hundreds of soldiers came marching along the Baughurst Road'. Elsie remembered the same, or a very similar event, and recollected that children got a day off school because of this. One of these recollections may have been linked to the large troop gathering in Basingstoke on Sunday 29 April 1917 when Field Marshal Vicount French inspected the Hampshire Volunteer Regiment.

With the exception of Bramley Ammunition Depot, founded in 1917, there was little local military activity. As well as being a top-secret ammunition store, with ammunition being dispatched day and night, the site was also a prisoner of war camp, with 3500 Germans being held there by 1918.

Because of its good rail links to the south coast the wider area was more directly involved in the care of the war-wounded. In March 1915 the Reading Union Workhouse was handed over to the authorities, becoming Reading War Hospital, the centre of a network of linked hospitals throughout the county. Dr Alfred Alexander (Kiln House) was listed in the 1917 Medical Directory as the Civilian Surgeon at the hospital. The Tadley School log-book records that children sent vegetables, fruit and eggs to wounded soldiers at the hospital.

After the war, in 1919, many villages held 'peace celebrations', whilst in the 1920s those who died were commemorated by the erection of **war memorials**. See **Bramley Camp; Pamber Heath Memorial Hall**.

World War II (1939-1945) Although fewer lives were lost, World War II had a far greater impact on the locality than did **World War I**. The conscription act, re-introduced in April 1939, was when almost all local men aged 20 and 21 years left to serve their country. Essential 'trades', i.e. farming, continued to be carried out by those (crafts)men, but men too old or unable to serve replaced the serving men in the day-to-day jobs; Herbert Attwood, previously **blacksmith** at Baughurst became postman in 1941. Others worked alongside women volunteers at the ammunition depots at Bramley or Burghfield.

The fighter aircraft bases at Odiham and Lasham, and later Greenham and Aldermaston, added to the need for a local searchlight battery (Causeway Farm), but prior to July 1942, and the building of **Aldermaston Airfield**, there was little local air activity. The area suffered only minimal damage from wartime bombing: the small number known to have been dropped in Baughurst, Pamber Heath, Wasing and Monk Sherborne resulted in only a few (two/three) fatalities. Raids on Newbury, Reading and Basingstoke were no doubt worrying but not detrimental.

The introduction of a national volunteer defence system resulted in several home guard units being established. Fire watching became compulsory in 1940 and along the tops of the hills at Piccadilly (Ramsdell), a system of torches was set up whereby, should there be a raid on **Bramley Camp**, these would be set alight. There was a brick hut which was always manned and oil available to start the fire. The black-out restrictions resulted in the closure of the 2 local brick kilns and air raid shelters were erected in people's gardens, many of which still remain (Shyshack Lane, Franklin Avenue, Heath End Road).

In 1941 the people of Tadley, Aldermaston, and Heath End were suddenly 'thrown into' what had previously been a quiet war. This part of N. Hampshire was never to be the same again. An Air Ministry map of Tadley in 1943 shows a village saturated with wartime 'huts'. In less than a year buildings had 'sprung-up' on 17 sites from West Street to Bishopswood Lane and from Franklin Avenue to West Road. Many of which remained until the 1990s, some used as squatters' accommodation in the post-war years. The ensuing two to three years saw an influx of American servicemen, an increase in air activity due to **Operation Torch** and **D-Day** and with it the necessary restrictions to people's freedom of movement. Properties in the area, some requisitioned, others given up voluntarily (The **Red House**, **Aldermaston Court**, **Wasing Park**, **Heath End House**), were used to accommodate organisations evacuated from London during the blitz.

Men returning home in 1945 or later did not all go back to the rural, woodland crafts of the 30s but took up instead new and better paid jobs which were more reliable than the traditional, seasonal outdoor work of before the war. Life in Tadley after the war was probably no less hectic than it had been during those few intense years of 1941-44. The ongoing arrival of companies like **BOAC** and eventually **AWRE** contrived to change both the life style and the environment for ever.

Tadley **Memorial Hall** was erected in memory of those who lost their lives in World War II and the lectern at **St. Peter's Church** commemorates the end of the war. The village of Ramsdell created a new recreation ground as their memorial to those who died. See **Black's Cafe**; **Picket posts**; **AWE Burghfield**.

WTI Training Group Present owners of **Tadley Court**. The company was originally established by the Government in 1966 as the Water Supply Training Board. In 1974 it became the Training Division of the National Water Council (NWCTD). In 1983 NWCTD was abolished and a new organisation, The Water Industry Training Association, emerged. From April 1990 the company was re-named Water Training International and in 1997 its name was changed to WTI Training Group in order to encompass the expansion of services into the new business areas of gas, railways, mechanical and electrical, building and facilities management and street utilities. Tadley Court is one of the company's four UK centres and contains many support facilities such as main-laying and service-laying workshops and a hydraulic model for telemetry simulation.

Wyeford Situated at the south of the original manor of Tadley, the name is derived from the Anglo Saxon 'Withig Forda' meaning willow ford. It was used in early records as a definition of the southern boundary of the parish. The name was subsequently applied to a farm and buildings, one mile south west of the ford – Wyeford House and Farm.

Wyeford house (599 588) A Grade II listed house, with sympathetic early twentieth century additions, containing a finely-carved oak staircase, oak floors and some original fenestration. The main part of Wyeford dates from the early seventeenth century and is described as 'an interesting Jacobean manor of great charm and character'. The imposing house is set in a large rose garden, surrounded by a hedge, and a substantial rectangular moat of ancient origin. The property also includes a Grade II listed granary, a Grade II listed cottage (made from a seventeenth century barn) and an old **ice house**. There is also an outer moat and a number of very old listed **fishponds**. The land comprises 167 acres (68 ha) of pasture land, of which 52 acres (21 ha) are woodland. The property is an ancient site, said to have been a King John hunting lodge. Originally called the Manor of Tadley, the name changed to Withford and then Wyford. By 1305 it belonged to the de la More family, passing down that family for nearly two hundred years until, in 1496, Nicholas de la More died leaving two infant daughters, of whom the elder, Joan, married William Ludlow, of Hill Deverell in Wiltshire. It remained in the **Ludlow family** until Edmund Ludlow conveyed the manor to Joseph Blagrave in 1641. The later history of the house is somewhat uncertain, but by the end of the seventeenth century it belonged to the Oakley Hall estate where it remained until 1924. In the middle years of the twentieth century it was owned by a variety of people, including Mrs (Constance) Elspeth Fox-Pitt, eventually being purchased by the Vickers family in 1962. See **Tadley**.

Y

Yew Tree Cottage The old name for **Highbury Cottage**.

Yew Tree Farm The old name for The **Old Place**.

York Nativity Play, The This play has been held at **The Church of St Mary the Virgin, Aldermaston** every year since 1957. It is directed by Mrs Pat Eastop who was awarded the MBE for services to the community, particularly the Nativity Play in 1998. The play is based on the York Mystery Plays which date from medieval times with the text written in 1932 by E. Martin Browne, who came to see the play with his wife in 1960. Since the first production, music from the thirteen to sixteenth centuries has been performed, mainly chosen by Revd Stanley Young, the then vicar of the parish. It is sung, within the play, by an unaccompanied choir conducted by Peter Denny. Other hymns and psalms, contemporary both with the play and the church, as well as more modern compositions are also performed. Some of the players have been performing in the play for over thirty years and a huge team of parishioners has given time and expertise to stage manage, light the play, and provide secretarial and other administrative duties. The Lord Lieutenant of Berkshire attended the fortieth year production in 1996. The Bishops of Oxford, Reading and Basingstoke have also seen the play.

Appendix i: Schools serving Tadley and district (1810-1999)

An overview of the provision and use by Tadley and district residents of most, but not all, local schools in what is now termed Primary and Secondary Education. It covers those that are in 'state education' and what was known as 'elementary education' prior to the 1944 Education Act. It does not include research on the schools providing for pupils with special needs.

Information on the nineteenth and early twentieth century came from local history and reference books. Post-1940, information came from conversations with local residents. It is perhaps surprising that local children attended such a wide range of schools as listed in this appendix. Changes brought about by the Education Reform Act of 1988 and subsequent legislation dealing with the National Curriculum and school administration have not been dealt with in this overview, other than noting name changes for The Priory School and Tadley County Primary School.

Nineteenth century

Elementary education around Tadley
More information about most of the elementary schools around Tadley will be found in entries under their individual headings in the A to Z section of the encyclopaedia, as well as being listed in this appendix in date order with the minimum of information.

1810 Sabbath School attached to Old Meeting Church Tadley.

1819 Kingsclere Girls' National (C of E) School built.

1820 There is reference to an earlier Dame School in Monk Sherborne and another to two small schools in existence in 1820, one where The Red House was in 1909.

1825 It was reported that the Charity School in Monk Sherborne '…was carried on under great discouragement'.

1834 Wootton St Lawrence (National) School founded with space for 151 pupils.

1836 Aldermaston School, Church Road founded with buildings completed in 1838.

1840 A Day School and Sabbath School operating at Old Meeting Tadley, and another 'connected with the Established Church' in a cottage.

1843 Baughurst National School* opened with room for 105 pupils. Regulated by the Charity Commissioners from 1 November 1872.

1844 Silchester (C of E)/(National) School opened with a capacity for 90 pupils.

1844 Wolverton (C of E)/(National) School built. In 1862 52 pupils were on roll.

1850 Monk Sherborne and Pamber (C of E) school opened with space for 152 pupils.

1861 Kingsclere Free (C of E) School for boys rebuilt. It had been endowed by Sir James Lancaster in 1618.

1863 Ashford Hill School opened as Kingsclere Woodlands (C of E)/(National) School* with only 45 pupils present on the first day, but with space for 123.

1870 Education Act for England and Wales that led to the establishment of School Boards that were to fill in the gaps in the provision of schools.

1874 Wootton and Tadley School Board formed on 29 September.

1876 Tadley Board School built at The Green, with space for 222 children from Tadley and Pamber at a cost of £1340.

1876 Elementary Education was made compulsory to the age of 12.

1877 Ramsdale (Ramsdell) Board School opens with space for 121 pupils and took pupils from Ewhurst as well.

1881 Pamber Heath (C of E) Infants School, Church Road opened 12 February with space for 93 pupils. By October 1881 it had become an 'all age' school.

1891 Elementary education becomes free.

* Schools with Building Grant made by Treasury or the Committee of the Council for Education.

Grammar schools
By the nineteenth century the endowed grammar schools had lost a lot of their vigour and various Acts of Parliament between 1840 and 1899 allowed changes to be made to terms of endowment so as to substitute 'other useful subjects' where a 'classical education' could not be provided and the education of girls was to be encouraged. This area however had to wait to the early years of the twentieth century for girls' grammar schools to be founded.

Local grammar schools now include:

1849 St Bartholomew's Grammar School for Boys, Newbury. Founded in 1466 according to some sources, in others the date is given as 1547. The school closed between 1814 and 1849 when it opened with '20 free boys and 40 paying boys'.

1852 The Queen's School (Queen Mary's School), Basingstoke became the legal successor to The Holy Ghost School, in 1852. Reopened in 1855 on the present site of BCOT's (Basingstoke College of Technology) new buildings, North Block. By 1886 a new charity scheme was in place for the boarders and day boys.

1871   Reading School (Foundation Grammar School for Boys) reopened, founded probably in 1125 with Reading Abbey. In 1867 the Mayor of Reading, obtained an Act of Parliament to reconstitute the school, this Act made the council responsible if the trustees defaulted on the mortgage. By 1886 the council was picking up part of the costs without having direct influence. In 1908 it was resolved that the council take over and today (1998) it is still part of the state sector, as a direct grant school.

1877   Kendrick School for Girls, Reading. Its origins are in the Kendrick Charities of 1624 that led to the building of a workhouse called the Oracle. When demolished the money was used to establish a school for 100 boys and 100 girls in 1877. The boys were in a new building in the King's Road, and the girls in Watlington House. The boys amalgamated with Reading School in 1915 and the girls' school moved to its present site in London Road. in 1927.

Twentieth century – up until the implementation of the 1944 Act

Elementary education

In Hampshire the 'all age' elementary schools listed previously in the section on the nineteenth century continued to serve the villages with those pupils, over 11 or 13, who won scholarships or whose parents were prepared to pay, travelling mainly into Basingstoke but also to the grammar schools in Newbury and Reading. When, in 1902, the Counties and the Municipal Boroughs were given the responsibility for education, the Board Schools became Council Schools.

1909   Pamber (C of E) School closed on 28 January.

1912   Possible date for closure of Wolverton (C of E) school.

1918   The school leaving age was raised to 14. In 1914 it was recorded that some 40% were leaving before the age of 14.

1924   Kingsclere's two schools, Kingsclere Free (C of E) for boys, endowed in 1618 and the Girl's school, dating from 1819 were re-organised, with the under elevens taught at the school at the bottom of North Street and the over elevens attended the old boy's school that became the Secondary Modern school after the 1944 Education Act.

Grammar schools

It is reported that Hampshire County Council, around the turn of the century, had made 'arrangements with Reading and Newbury' as well as Wimborne, Salisbury, Farnham and Midhurst because of its own very limited resources. By this time the Grammar Schools had moved away from providing for the poor or providing only a 'classical education'. Latin, the basis of a 'classical education' continued to be taught, however, and the Grammar

Schools became the major means of entry to a university education. This was achieved through Matriculation or with Higher School Certificate and Scholarship Level exam papers from 1917 until 1951 when GCE (General Certificate of Education) O and GCE A levels were introduced as single subject exams. Matriculation meant six or seven credits at School Certificate at one session that had to include a language. French was the foreign language usually studied, though Latin was called for by Oxbridge Colleges or if you hoped for a medical or law career. In the 1930s, as public transport became readily available, fee paying and scholarship pupils travelled more and got into the grammar schools listed in all three towns, Basingstoke, Reading, and Newbury. (Reading School had a house for boarders at its Erleigh Road site).

During the early 1900s these grammar schools were added to the list:

1904   High School for Girls, Newbury. Founded by Newbury Borough Council.

1908   High School for Girls (Brook House), Basingstoke established by Hampshire County Council

Twentieth century – 1944 onwards

The 1944 Education Act removed the title Elementary Education and introduced the titles, Primary, Secondary, and Higher Education. This followed on from the Hadow Report of 1926 that had proposed; Infant (5 to 7 years), Junior (7 to 11 years) and Senior (11 to 14/15 years). As a result of the 1944 Act, Primary Education (Infant and Junior Schools) could exist and within Secondary Education there were to be Secondary Modern, Secondary Grammar and Secondary Technical Schools. Depending on the local education authority many different schemes came about. For example, Hampshire did not create secondary technical schools, though they did attempt to start 'bi-lateral' schools like Cranbourne School (1967) in Basingstoke that took all except the top grammar school pupils, who were 'creamed off' by the traditional grammar schools. The three types of school in the Secondary field were commonly referred to as the 'tripartite system'. The legislation did not get rid of the dual system of state and voluntary education. 'Council Schools' became known as 'county schools' whilst 'voluntary schools' became 'controlled' or 'aided'. Controlled schools were maintained by the local education authority, who nominated two thirds of the governors and aided schools were given 50% of their maintenance costs. Private schools or independent schools continue to exist but have to be registered centrally and are liable for inspection by HM Inspectorate. The school leaving age was raised to 15 in 1947. To accomodate the additional schoolchildren HORSA (Hutted Opportunities for Revision of Standard Attainment) basic accomodation blocks were built. This was the era of the 11 plus or 'scholarship' as some continued to call the exam used to select pupils for Secondary education.

Primary education

The implementation of the change to Primary and Secondary schools did not occur in this part of Hampshire until the early 1950s. Pupils over 11 travelled to Secondary schools in Basingstoke or Kingsclere. The neighbouring villages in Berkshire had to wait until the opening of the secondary modern school at Burghfield Common in January 1957.

All the village schools listed in the nineteenth and early twentieth century sections, that still continued to teach children under 11 years, used the title 'County Primary'. There were the following additions and changes:

1955   Burnham Copse Junior and Infant Schools were formed from the pupils attending the annexe to Tadley School next to the cinema, and within the Berkshire boundary at that time. The Junior School moved, under the headship of Roger Searing, into buildings in Newchurch Road that had been the canteen for the contractors building AWRE and the eleven hundred houses for its staff. The Infant School stayed in the annexe with Miss Smith as the Headteacher.

1956   Official opening of the two schools, Junior and Infant, by Prof. J.F. Wolfenden, Vice-Chancellor of Reading University at a ceremony in the cinema.

1960   Burnham Copse Junior school moved into its present buildings and the Infant School took over the old canteen area where Searing Drive (1997) houses now stands.

1962   Baughurst School closes and pupils move to Aldermaston and Burnham Copse Schools.

Secondary modern schools

All those listed below took some pupils from the Tadley area according to the catchment area allocated to the school and contract transport. In some cases scholar's season tickets on Venture buses would have been provided for Hampshire pupils to Basingstoke or Kingsclere and on Thames Valley to Newbury for Berkshire pupils. Movement of pupils between Grammar and Secondary Modern took place at 13+ in an effort to cope with 'late developers'.

1943   Shaw House School for Girls, Newbury. After a bomb destroyed the Council Schools on 10 February 1943 in Station Road, both the boys and the girls attended a school at Shaw House, an Elizabethan house of the late 1500s. Berkshire County Council bought the house and the site in 1946 and began to transfer the boys to Park House in the Andover Road leaving a girls' Secondary Modern with buildings in the grounds of the house. The House itself, ceased to be used in 1985 because of its poor state of repair.

1947   Park House Secondary Modern School for Boys, officially started in Newbury, and Fairfields Secondary Modern (Mixed) was established in Basingstoke at what had been Fairfields Elementary School.

1950-   Kingsclere Secondary Modern (Mixed),
54   Charles Chute Boys Secondary Modern School, next to Queen Mary's Boys Grammar, Basingstoke and The Shrubbery Girls School, Cliddesden Road, Basingstoke all opened, leaving Fairfields as a Secondary Modern Boys School until January 1960 when it became a Junior School.

Grammar schools

All those listed in earlier sections continued to serve this area, and Berkshire County Council added one new grammar school and provided Scholar's Season Tickets on Thames Valley buses and books of tickets for Reading Corporation Transport. Similar schemes would have been available in all areas after 1945 where there were not enough pupils travelling to justify contract buses. All school fees were abolished in schools administered by an LEA after the 1944 Act.

1945   Woodley Hill Grammar School for Boys, Earley, that later became The Forest School, Winnersh. This was for Berkshire pupils who passed the 11+, as Reading at that time was a separate education authority, and places at Reading or Kendrick Schools were for the most able, if there was space. Girls had to travel to The Holt School, Wokingham, so Newbury Schools were more likely to be used by all from the Tadley area who went to Aldermaston School or lived across the County boundary.

Twentieth century – 1957 onwards

Primary schools

These changes took place:

1972   Bishopswood Junior School opened in January and Infant School opened in April.

1985   Burnham Copse Infant School moved across Newchurch Road to the present site.

1987   The two schools, Monk Sherborne and Ramsdell closed. The Priory County Primary School opened on the Monk Sherborne site.

1988   Aldermaston School moved to its present site in Wasing Lane.

1993   The Priory County Primary School became a Grant Maintained Primary School and is called The Priory School.

1999   Tadley County Primary School became Tadley Community Primary School.

Secondary schools

By the mid 1990s, with more and more parental choice, changing patterns of travel and subject specialisation, particularly for 16+ students in regard to Sixth Form Colleges, Tertiary Colleges and Technical Education, students began travelling to places as far distant as Maidenhead, Farnborough,

Winchester and Andover at the age of 16. Prior to this travel had been restricted to the triangle formed by Reading, Newbury and Basingstoke. Examinations were also changing. The Certificate of Secondary Education (CSE) was introduced, starting in 1965 and by 1988 had developed into the GCSE (General Certificate of Secondary Education) when the GCE exam boards were merged with the CSE Exam Boards to provide examinations at 16 to replace O levels and CSEs. The syllabuses having been introduced to the schools in 1983.

1957   8 January, Willink Secondary Modern (Mixed) opened and the 'all-age' school in Aldermaston lost the 11+ pupils. By Easter, contract transport was carrying pupils that would have gone to 10 village schools from as far away as Upper Basildon to school at Burghfield Common. Those living in the roads of Tadley within the Berkshire borders filled most of the seats on two coaches run by Smith's Coaches of Reading.

1957   9 September, Tadley Secondary Modern (Mixed) opened and all the pupils who had been travelling by contract transport to Basingstoke and Kingsclere from local villages stayed in Tadley. The school log lists 212 boys and 169 girls present that day with 121 coming from the 'feeder' primary schools and those in the second, third and fourth years from Kingsclere Secondary Modern, Fairfields and The Shrubbery Schools in Basingstoke. During 1957/58 the Governors decided on the school being called The Hurst, before it was opened officially by the Duke of Wellington in 1958. Maurice Bound, the first Head jokes that to have called it The Duke of Wellington School would have caused some confusion between the pub and the school.

1966   Kingsclere Secondary Modern moved to Burghclere and became The Clere School.

1967   Theale Grammar School opened for all Berkshire pupils passing the 11+. Roger Searing has written about some of his pupils being able to take both Berkshire's and Hampshire's 11+ from Burnham Copse School, where he was the school's first Head.

1971   Comprehensive Education plans began in the Basingstoke area as a result of a decision made by Hampshire County Council in 1969. The Hurst would now take pupils of all abilities between the ages of 11 and 16 years. The grammar schools in Basingstoke wound down their Sixth Forms and combined to become The Vyne (becoming mixed). Harriet Costello also became a mixed school over the next two years after 63 years as the High School for Girls.

1972   Queen Mary's Sixth Form College (QMC) opened on the site of The Shrubbery School and pupils were offered the choice of going there or to The Technical College after leaving the Secondary school at 16. The school leaving age was raised in 1972 to 16, as had been suggested in the Spens Report of 1938. New buildings were added to Secondary Schools, known as HORSA (**H**utted **O**pportunities for **R**evision of **S**tandard **A**ttainment) and ROSLA (**R**aising **O**f the **S**chool **L**eaving **A**ge) buildings to accommodate the extra year.

1973   In Berkshire Theale Grammar School became Theale Green School and Willink Secondary Modern became The Willink School with both schools taking their first Comprehensive intake of pupils aged 11, and having their own Sixth Forms.

1975   The boys' and girls' grammar schools in Newbury combined as one Comprehensive School, St Bartholomew's, for 11 to 18 year olds and was the town's only Sixth Form. The other secondary schools in Newbury became Comprehensive Schools for 11 to 16 year olds. The same arrangements of choice between the Sixth Form and the Technical College in Newbury, that had started in 1948, applied, as with pupils in Tadley over BCOT and QMC.

1975   Bishop Challoner Roman Catholic (Aided) Secondary School opened in Basingstoke and provided Roman Catholic families with the opportunity to send their children to a state school where they previously had to make arrangements to go to such private schools as Presentation College in Reading and Douai Abbey. From 1999 known as Bishop Challoner Roman Catholic School. Children from other denominations are admitted if there is space.

1979   Shaw House, Newbury became co-educational.

1979   The Hurst School became a comprehensive Community School serving the educational, social and recreational needs of the locality.

Notes
In the debate over the provision of a Middle School in Tadley in 1978 the following details were given of schools in the catchment area of The Hurst: Ashford Hill, (Number On Roll = 130), Burnham Copse, (Juniors 358, Infants 203.), Bishopswood School, (Juniors 280, Infants 170), Tadley (414), Silchester, (234), Monk Sherborne, (90), Ramsdell, (46) and The Hurst (1 678) so giving a total of 3,603 pupils in all schools in the Tadley Area. Allowing for some flexibility of date and the extra numbers that came about through the raising of the school leaving age this compares with the 708 places provided some 100 years earlier, when school building began in earnest in the area.

Appendix ii: Overview of medical services

Doctors associated with Tadley and its district (pre Holmwood Healthcentre)

name	qualified	from	to	where	posts
Alfred Alexander	1890	1913	1920	Kiln House, Tadley	①
Stanley Beale	1909	1920	1935	The Street, Aldermaston	
Geoffrey Bennett	1953	1956	1958	Kiln House, Tadley	
Robert Cooper	1953	1971	1986	Aldermaston & Tadley	
Frances Cox	1824	1847	1850	Aldermaston	①
Nolan Daly	1896	1923 1935	1934 1954	Bramley Little London	
George Fox		1851	1897	Aldermaston	①②
Michael Hawken	1955	1960	1994	Tadley	
John Hollingshead		1971	–	Tadley & Brimpton	
Lionel Holmwood	1916	1929	1959	Aldermaston	
Charles (Keith) Hudson	1952	1958	1994	Tadley	
Frank Knowles		1965	1966	Little London, Bramley, Monk Sherborne, Sherborne St John, Tadley	
Mary Knowles		1866	1989	Bramley, Monk Sherborne, Tadley, Ramsdell, Sherborne, Little London	
William Langely	1892	1896	1920	Kiln House, Tadley	①
Henry Linden		1891	1895	Fairlawn House, Tadley	
R Maples		1897 1897	1899 1898	Tadley and Kingsclere Kingsclere	
Joseph Morland	1947	1951	1984	Kiln House, Tadley	
Doris Mullen (née Virgo)	1945	1953 1966	1965 1989	Little London Bramley, Monk Sherborne, Tadley, Ramsdell, Sherborne and Little London	
Henry Mullen	1940	1953	1964	Little London; surgeries in Bramley, Monk Sherborne, Tadley, Ramsdell, Sherborne and Little London	
Charles Sansom	1883	1886	1892	Aldermaston	
Frederick Simpson	1894	1897	1898	Tadley	
Michael Speight	1955	1957	1992	Tadley	
Geoffrey Wynne Thomas	1933	1935 1940 1945	1940 1945 1971	Aldermaston Midgham Croft, Woolhampton Aldermaston	
David Walker	1895	1896	?	Elmhurst, Tadley	
William Whitcombe	1891	1893	1912	Aldermaston	①②③

Key to table opposite
① Medical Officer, Baughurst & Tadley District, Kingsclere Union
② Medical Officer, Bradfield Union
③ Public Vaccination Officer

Information extracted from Medical Directories and Medical Registers.

Survey of home deliveries in Tadley, January 1960 to December 1966
Published by Dr C.K. Hudson in 'The Practitioner', November 1968

Dr Morland had obstetric training at Royal Berks Hospital, Reading with consultant Mr Peter Wheeler FRCOG. Dr Speight and Dr Hudson were obstetric house surgeons at St Marys' Hospital, Paddington under Mr J.P. Erskine FRCOG.

The nearest specialist obstetric unit was at the Royal Berkshire Hospital in Reading, 12 miles (19 km) away. 667 women were surveyed consisting of 60 in their first pregnancy and 607 in second or subsequent pregnancies. Of the 60 in first pregnancy, 24 had to be subsequently delivered in hospital and of the 607, 90 were delivered in hospital.

There was a very low perinatal mortality and low incidence of serious complications in home deliveries. There was a high rate of transfer to hospital in first pregnancy, both before and during labour, demonstrating clearly that all women in their first pregnancy should be booked into hospital. With conscientious antenatal care and careful initial selection of cases there was demonstrated a high degree of safety for both mothers and their babies born at home.

Medical Teams: early 1950s & 60s
District Nurses and Midwives
Patients were cared for at home by District Nurses and Midwives.

The Hampshire District Nurses and Midwives in the 1950s were Nurse Bailey and Nurse Oddie. Nurse Bailey left and was succeeded by Nurse Dorothy Coventry. Nurse Oddie died in the late 1950s and two new District Nurses and Midwives arrived, Nurse Evelyn Smith and Nurse Olive Jepps.

On the Berkshire side the District Nurses and Midwives were Nurse Cook and Nurse Rose. Nurse Evelyn Smith trained as a midwife and subsequently as a Queen's Nurse at Southsea. She started work as a midwife in 1941, working during the Blitz in London, and came to Tadley, with Nurse Jepps, in 1957. Nurse Smith retired in 1973 and Nurse Jepps in 1972. Nurse Smith delivered 1511 babies in her career in London and Tadley.

Nurse Midwives who followed Smith and Jepps were Ellen James, Wendy Little, Nurse Akosa, Gwen Hallam, Nurse Cross. Disrict nurses were Nurse Olive O'Dea, Jo Leverier, who married, becoming Childs,

Mary Heath, Nurse Hatch, Sister Ann Somerton (known as SAS).

In the late 1960s and 1970s pressure was put on general practitioners and their patients to stop home deliveries in favour of 100% hospital delivery. This has led to loss of skills in obstetrics in GPs and domiciliary midwives and it is difficult to see how the situation could be changed in the present or future.

The combined duties of midwife and district nurse declined, with the decrease in home deliveries, though ante natal and post natal care were still performed, as well as general nursing duties in the home and the surgery.

Health visitors were concerned in the early days with care of newly delivered mothers and their infants and extended into child care and preventative medicine and, to a certain extent, care in old age. In the 1950s health visitors were Joyce Zscherpel and Daphne Taylor followed by Wendy Copestake. The Health Centres have details of present nurses, midwives and Health Visitors.

Practice Nurses
From the 1960s practice nurses were employed by the doctors to work in the surgery. Gradually their work increased to the very comprehensive service they now perform. Before the employment of practice nurses, many of their functions were carried out by the doctors or not at all. Many patients who could not be seen at the surgery were visited at home by district nurses.

Practice Manager and Health Centre Team, Office, Reception, Secretarial, Dispensing
At Aldermaston surgery, in the time of Dr Holmwood and Dr Wynne Thomas there were no receptionists, or secretaries. Miss Ursula Clarke was the dispenser, manager, financial manager, wielding great power, even to paying the doctors' incomes!

At Tadley the first Practice Manager was Mrs Connie Burrows followed by Lily Ventom. Practice finances and business management was run by Mrs Margaret Shelton. The dispensing boss was Miss Paddy Nixon, who though not a qualified dispenser, ran the whole dispensing programme for many years. Since then professional dispensers have run the Health Centre pharmacies.

The preventive medicine and immunization service used to be run by County Medical Officers of

Health with attached Health Visitors. This programme is now run by the GPs and their staff. The principal diseases concerned were small pox, poliomyelitis, whooping cough, diphtheria, tetanus and measles and german measles (rubella). Small pox and polio are now non existant, and the others greatly reduced in the community. The last case of Polio occurred in Tadley in 1955.

Domiciliary Visits

GPs are able to invite consultants to see patients in their own homes. This was a relatively common practice until the last few years. This saved the patients either being admitted to hospital unnecessarily or having the discomfort of going to out-patient departments and having a long wait.

Cervical smear programme

The widespread development of preventive screening by cervical smears started in the mid 1960s and at first was a diagnostic test in suspected disease. The comprehensive service now established is run by the general practitioners and the practice nurses with the calling in and recall organised by the practice staff.

Investigative procedures of patients

The taking of samples including blood samples was started in the practice premises in the 1960s with the development of sterile disposable syringes and needles. An early ECG (Electrocardiograph machine) was bought and used by the partners in the late 1960s With the arrival of Dr Colley in 1983 endoscopic examination of the lower bowel and stomach became a part of the investigative procedures carried out at the surgery.

Contraceptive services

The first contraceptive services provided by general practitioners in the 1950s consisted of advice and barrier methods. The advent of the pill then enabled a more comprehensive service to be developed and the Tadley practice provided a service for most of the patients who wished it. Family planning clinics in Basingstoke and Reading were difficult to get to. Practice nurses play a valuable part in the provision of contraceptive services.

Appendix iii: Inclosure of Tadley & West Heath Commons

On 23 January 1847 Mr Thomas Hasker, a valuer from Basingstoke was appointed by the Inclosure Commissioners to report on the lands in the parish of Tadley & West Heath. His report was confirmed by the Inclosure Commission on 11 October 1850. Subsequently amendments were made and the document sealed on 23 January 1852. It gives details of all the land in the parish of Tadley, which at that time included West Heath.

His report comprised: A schedule of the land, detailing its owner, its size, and any other duty in respect thereof; map A setting out graphically the areas in question (each plot was numbered); map B, which was a copy of the tithe map setting out the lands referred to just prior to the inclosure. All three documents were produced in triplicate. The Turbary Allotment Charity holds the parish set of these documents.

From this Act of Inclosure there arose lands allotted for the benefit of the parish. All these parish lands, with the exception of the two public quarries listed below, were awarded under the jurisdiction of the Rector, Churchwardens and Overseers of the Poor of the Parish to manage and administer as required.

The Green
The land numbered 662 on the map (four acres). This was awarded for exercise and recreation.

The Allotments for the Labouring Poor
The land numbered 597 on the map (six acres), off Giles Road; 627 on the map (thirteen acres), Spiers Green south of Rowan Road; 858 on the map (six acres), at West Heath. These lands were awarded as allotments for the poor of the parish. Despite many changes over the years, the present areas occupied are still those of the original award and some of the plots are worked by descendants of the original allotment holders showing a continuous holding through the century. The charity also has the power to make special charitable donations from any surplus income after the upkeep of the allotment land has been paid for.

The Turbary Allotment
Prior to the Act of Inclosure, Tadley Common stretched along the north of the parish from Pamber Heath to Heath End. There were also a number of private allotments in this area. That which remained of Tadley Common as a result of the Inclosure, some 100 acres, were awarded as an Allotment for Turbary, that is the digging of peat for fuel, for the benefit of the poor of the parish.

One other parcel of land of five acres (725 on the map) was awarded. This is the land north and south of Franklin Avenue, just west of the traffic lights. It was awarded as a public quarry, the gravel to be used by the residents of the parish on their allotments [their properties] and not to be used outside the parish. There was also a right by the surveyors of the Highways of the Parish to enter onto and remove gravel for the upkeep of the roads in the parish.

In 1898 these lands passed to the Parish Council to act as trustee to administer. In 1963 the then Parish Council obtained a new scheme from the Charity Commissioners to use the land which formed Tadley Common as an open space and recreation ground for the benefit of the residents of the parish. This scheme removed the only common right recorded, i.e. Turbary. Today there are no common rights attached to this land, which is administered by the Turbary Allotment Charity of which the Tadley Town Council is the trustee.

The Surveyors of the Highways of the Parish
There are two other quarries 738 on the map, five acres in Heath End Woods and 859 on the map, one acre at West Heath. These two quarries were principally awarded to the Surveyors of the Parish. However, there is a right by the residents to remove gravel for use on their properties within the parish. The restriction for the use of the gravel to be used only within the parish resulted in a number of private quarries around the area, one being off Bishopswood Lane.

The maintenance of a school
The land numbered 596 (one acres) and 642 (nine acres) on the map. This was awarded for 'the education of the Poor...in such principles as by Law now established and recognised'.

A residence for a clergyman
The land numbered 641 (two acres) on the map. This was awarded 'as a site for a house of residence for a clergyman of the Established Church'.

Appendix iv: War Memorials

Aldermaston
Inside St Mary the Virgin Church.

1914-18
Michael McNeil Strange
Albert Lewis Buckland
Francis Charles George Buckland
Ernest Coleman
Walter Cripps
Maurice Galt
James Henry Gay
John William Gay
Herbert Greatrix
Shirley Harris
Hubert Roxby Iremonger
Fredrick James Jacobs
Sidney Ralph Jacobs
George Benjamin Jones
Gilbert Leonard Sanders
Arthur Scutter
Augustus James Smith
Herbert William Smith
Arthur Dick Tull
Roland Henry Walters
Harvey George Winkworth

1939-45
Bert Woodley
Flt Sgt John Brian Strange

Separate plaque
To the memory of
Major Gerald Strange DSO
1882-1953
and of his sons
Michael McNeil Strange
1912-1917
Flt Sgt John Brian Strange
1922-1944; killed in action.

Ashford Hill
Outside St Paul's Church, on Ashford Hill Road.

1914-18
Ernest Brown
James Christie
Daniel Dyer
Percy Eyres
David Ford
Edward Goodchild
Thomas Hussey
Arthur Leake
George Lovelock
William Kernutt
Harry Marshall
Henry Smith

Richard Smith
Harry Thatcher
William Thatcher
Reginald Vince
Albert Withers
William Withers
Herbert Englefield

1939-45
David Englefield

Baughurst & Heath End
On Baughurst Road, opposite The Badger's Wood.

1914-18
Baughurst
Francis R. Abbott
William S. Bennett
George E. Jacob
Robert Jacob
Alexander G. Kelly
Sidney M. Kelly
Frank Kernutt
William Kernutt
Harry Lawes
William Richardson
Charles Rowell
Frederick Smith

Heath End
William J. Monger
Leonard Rampton
Ernest Sandford
Tom Taylor
George Warren
Frederick C. Webb
Albert G. Appleton
Fred G. Appleton
Walter J. Cripps
John B. Greenup
Merrick H. McConnell

1939-45
Norman Addison Bramwell
Cyril Butler
Garfield Roy Hill
Jarvis Julian Kenrick
Brian Ferguson Leadbitter
Stanley Smith

Brimpton
In the village centre.

1914-18
William Armstrong
Norman C.H. Bartholomew
James R. Blake

Arthur T. Butcher
William Butler
Daniel Dyer
Sidney Edwards
Percy J. Elliott
Arthur Farquharson
Percy Frost
William Giles
Alfred Hemans
James S. Hutchins
Samuel Locke
Sidney J. Mildenhall MM
John T. Nightingale
Reginald P.A. Sexton
Edwin S. Smith
Basil A. Standley
Roger Standley
John Staniford
Harry Timberlake

1939-45
Dashwood Fowlermoir DSO
Reginald Wykes

Monk Sherborne
In the centre of the village, near the crossroads.

1914-18
Frank Bond
Seymour Cresswell
Arthur Duckett
Albert Englefield
Charlie Monger
Osmund J. Monger
William Nash
Harold Williams, died 1919

1939-45
Joseph Leslie Black
Reginald Arthur Monger
Kenneth Herbert Tate
Peter Gordon Tate

Mortimer West End
In St Saviour's Churchyard.

1914-18
John Collis
Thomas H Dicker
Percy Eatwell
Sidney Eatwell
James F Elford
Ernest Ford
Frank Goodchild
Philip Goodchild
Cecil Hall
George Hunt

Walter Hunt
Osborne Lampert
Frederick Penny
Harry White
Henry Giles

1939–45
Margaret Cannon,
Petty Officer WRNS

Pamber End
**In Pamber Priory Church,
on wall opposite the vestry.**

1914–18
Francis William Appleby
Charles Appleton
Frederic James Banbury
Albert Beechford
William Cottrell
William Dennis
Fred Freeman
William Hughes
Arthur Pearce
William Stanley Pullen
Charles Smith
Fred Smith
Bertie William Stamp

1939–45
Reginald Ballard
Bernard Hellier
Hubert Holmes
Peter Mott
Harold Murrell
Reginald Thomas
Robert Thomas
Brian West
Leslie West

**On the wall inside the church;
left-hand side of the entrance.**
Captain John Hobart Anketell-
Jones, 5th (Royal Irish)
Lancers. Attached Egyptian
Army who died of blackwater
fever at Talodi, Sudan Nov
16th 1919, aged 38.

Pamber Heath
In St Lukes Church.

1914–18
Frank Benham
Charlie Hunt
William Hunt
Everard Digges Latouche
Herbert Newman
Lt Harry Oppe, 11 Yorkshire
Regiment

2nd Lt Thomas Oppe, 4 Scottish
Rifles
Silvanus Pike
Fredrick Smith
Gilbert West

1939–45
Roy Benham
Nevil Brown
Frank Foard
Gordon Foard
Leonard Harris
James Meredith
Wilfred Rampton

Ramsdell
On walls inside the church.

1914–18
Edward Blake
Joseph Frankum
Cyril Froome
William Kimber
Beecham Lucock
Neville May
Thomas Mears
Edward Seward
James Vince

1939–45
Cyril Starr Allen
Charles Donald Allen
Francis Appleby

John Leonard Chapman died in
Australia, October 30 1901,
aged 20.
Ernest Walker Chapman, 1st Batt
South Wales Borderers. Died
Karachi India 1905 (Dec 18)
aged 22.
Herbert Knowles Fuller MBC
Camb MRCS. Surgeon HM
Forces Madras Army. Served
Burmah War 1885–1887;
invalided out, died 14 October
1889, aged 32 years.

Silchester
**On Little London Road, near the
Village Hall.**

1914–18
Reuben Knight
Walter G Aldridge
George Hunt
Robert W Neville
Francis E Stacey
Arthur W. Pearce

1939–45
Arthur C Bowman
Harry W Giles
John H Giles
Thomas F Hartley
Norman Hunt
Abraham Turner

Tadley
Outside St Paul's Church.

1914–18
Major M.H. McConnel
Capt T.E. Painton-Jones
Lt D.P. Lynden-Bell
2nd Lt J.B. Greenup
Sgt Maj C. Warren DCM
Sgt L. Rampton
Sgt H. Trusler MM
L Cpl F.B. Kelsey
Pte A.G. Appleton
Pte F.C. Appleton
Pte A.. Chapman
Pte W. Cottrell
Pte W. Cripps
Gnr F.T. Freeman
Pte G. Garrett
W. Giles RN
Pte H. Golding
Pte W.J. Monger MM
Pte A. Rampton
Pte W.P. Rampton
Pte T. Rawlins
Pte A.E. Sandford
Pte E. Saunders
Drv J. Saunders
Pte L. Stacey
Pte T. Taylor
Pte F.C. Webb
Pte A.G. West
Pte I. West
Gnr H. West

1939–45
S. Bowman
W.F. Barlow
F. Broadhurst
F. W Carter
H.S. Kite
G.H. Webb

Bibliography and further reading

Albery, Alan and Lelliott, Marie-Claude. *Street Names of Tadley, Pamber and Baughurst and Their Origins;* (1998)

'Aldermaston Fire'; *Illustrated London News* (14 January 1846)

'Aldermaston Manor'; *Country Life* (26 August 1899)

Aldington, Richard. *The Colonel's Daughter;* (1931)

———— *Death of a Hero;* (1931)

Armitage, Helen (ed). *ITN Fact Book;* Michael O'Mara Books Ltd (1990)

Ashworth, Chris. *Action Stations; Military Airfields of the Central, South and South East;* Patrick Stephens (?)

Attwood, Arthur. *Around Basingstoke – Arthur Attwood's Look into the Past;* Basingstoke Gazette (?)

———— *Basingstoke – Arthur Attwood's Look into the Past;* Basingstoke Gazette (?)

———— 'When £500 brought a village school'; *Basingstoke Gazette* (19 December 1980)

———— 'Town That Grew Out of the Nuclear Age'; *Basingstoke Gazette* (18 November 1988)

AWRE Recruitment Book; MoD Public Relations and Central Office of Information (1974)

Ayres, M and Saunders, K. *As Stupid as Oxen – A History of the Reading and Silchester Methodist Circuit;* (1988)

Badsey, Stephen. *D-Day – The Illustrated History;* Colour Library Books Ltd (1993)

Bailey, Albert. 'Tadley, God Help Us'; *Hampshire* (vol 16, no 11, p 41 October 1976)

Baldwin, Brenda. *200 Years of Rural Christian Witness;* (1999)

Baren, Maurice. *How it Began in the High Street;* Michael O'Mara Books Ltd (1996)

Barton, David A. *Discovering Chapels and Meeting Houses;* Shire Publications (2nd edition 1990)

Beamon, S.P. and Roaf, Sylvia Susan. *The Ice-houses of Britain;* Routeledge (1991)

'Beauty in North Hants'; *Hants & Berks Gazette* (18 October 1946)

Beddington, Winifred G. and Christy, Elisa B. *It Happened in Hampshire;* (5th ed 1977)

Benham, Daniel. *Some Account of the Village of Tadley in Hampshire and the Independant Church There;* (1862)

Bennett, Ralph. *Guide to St Peter's Church, Tadley;* St Peter's Church (1977)

Betjeman, John and Piper, John. *Murray's Berkshire;* John Murray (1949)

Birmingham, Peter and Pearce, John. *Venture Limited; The Story of Basingstoke's Own Bus Company*

Bond, Rosemary. Tadley Watch; *Hampshire* (February 1999, Vol 39, No 4, pp 32-34)

Boon, George C. *The Roman Town Calleva Atrebatum at Silchester Hampshire;* Reading Museum (1967)

Boon, George C. *St Mary the Virgin, Silchester;* St Mary the Virgin, Silchester (1989)

Boon, George C. *Roman Silchester;* Parrish (1957)

Bound, Maurice. *Methodist Chapel, Silchester 1839-1989*

Brewis, Anne. *Flora of Hampshire;* Harley Books (1996)

Brode, Anthony. *The Hampshire Village Book;* Countryside Books (1980)

Brough, Peter, Gibbons, Bob and Pope, Colin. *The Nature of Hampshire & the Isle of Wight;* Barracuda (1986)

Brown, Bob (ed). *A Taste of TADS;* Tadley & District Society (1990)

Brown, Bob (ed). *A Taste of TADS 2;* Tadley & District Society (1993)

Brown, Jonathan and Ward, Sadie. *The Village Shop;* Rural Development Commission (1990)

Browne, Samuel. *The Travels of a Seektruth – an Allegory;* Private (1805)

Bryan, Tim. *The Great Western at War 1939-1945;* Patrick Stephens (1995)

Bull, G.B.G. *History of the Kingsclere & Whitchurch Rural District Council;* Kingsclere & Whitchurch Rural District Council (1974)

Burghfield Parochial Church Council. *A Living History of Burghfield and its Church;* Burghfield Parochial Church Council (1993)

Burnham Copse Womens' Institute. *Burnham Copse WI Scrapbook;* Burnham Copse Womens' Institute (1965)

Burrows, Capt Montagu. *The Family of Brocas of Beaurepaire and Roche Court;* (1886)

Caiger-Smith, Alan. *Aldermaston Pottery;* Aldermaston Pottery (1972)

Cathcart, Brian. *Test of Greatness;* John Murray (1994)

Chapman, John and Seeliger, Sylvia. *Formal and Informal Enclosures in Hampshire 1700-1900;* Hampshire County Council (1997)

Citizens Advice Bureau – *The Inside Story;* National Association of Citizens Advice Bureaux (C1996)

Civilian War Dead; Imperial War Museum (c1948)

Class 3/4, Burnham Copse Junior School. *Tadley – A Town Guide*; Burnham Copse Junior School (1987)

Clew, Kenneth R. *The Kennet & Avon Canal*; David & Charles (1968; 2nd ed 1973)

Clift, William. *The Reminiscences of William Clift of Bramley*; (1908)

Clinton, W.O. (ed) *A Record of the Parish of Padworth*; W.O. Clinton (MCMXI)

Clough, J.Ruth. 'Return to Tadley'; *Hampshire* (October 1985, vol 25, no 12, , p16-17)

Clough, J.Ruth. 'Swings and Roundabouts – Franklin Avenue Between the Wars'; *Hampshire* (April 1992, vol 32, no 6, p10)

Coad, F. *History of the Brethren Movement*

Coates, Richard. *The Place-names of Hampshire*; B.T. Batsford (1989)

Collier, Phillip. *Besom Brooms*; Tadley & District Society (1997 History Project)

Collier RN, Capt T.A. HMS Plym; *AWRE News* (April 1971)

Currie, Ian, Davidson, Mark and Ogley, Bob. *The Berkshire Weather Book*; Froglets Publications (1994)

Davidson, Florence A.G. *The History of Monk Sherborne Parish*; Monk Sherborne and Pamber Parish (1909)

——————— The History of the Benedictine Priory of Monk Sherborne; *Papers and Proceedings of the Hampshire Field Club and Archaeological Club* (Vol. VII pt 1, pp 101-109)

——————— *The History of Silchester, Hampshire, its Manor and Church*

——————— *The History of the Quakers in Baughurst*; (Part I 1911, Part II 1915)

——————— *The History of Tadley*; C E Symonds, Basingstoke (1913)

Davidson, Mark & others. *The Hampshire & Isle of Wight Weather Book*; Froglets Publications (1993)

Davies, Ellis Roger. A History of the First Berkshire County Council, 1889-1974; Berkshire County Secretariat (1979)

Davies, Louise. *The History of Inhurst School*; Tadley & District Society (1997 History Project)

Davies, Rupert E. *Methodism*; Pelican (1965)

Dennis, Graham. *Pamber Forest Nature Reserve*; Basingstoke and Dean Borough Council

Dils, Joan (ed). *An Historical Atlas of Berkshire*; Berkshire Record Society (1998)

Dowling, Frank. *The Countess of Huntingdon's Chapels*; MSc dissertation (1992)

Ellis, Georgie. *Ruth Ellis, My Mother*; Smith Gryphon (c1955)

Eveleigh, David J. *The Victorian Farmer*; Shire Publications (1991)

Everand. *The History of Gas Light and Coke Co 1812-1949*; Benn (1949)

Fairman, J.R. *Basingstoke: 150 Years of Railway Progress*; (1987)

Feuillade, John G. *Migration to a North Hampshire Village in the latter half of the Twentieth Century*; Open University project report (1994)

Filmer, Richard. *Hops and Hop Picking*; Shire Publications (1982)

'Fire at Aldermaston House'; *Illustrated London News* (14 January 1843)

Fowler, Simon; Elliott, Peter; Conyers Nesbitt, Roy and Goulter, Christina. *RAF Records in the PRO*; Public Records Office

Freedman, Lawrence. *Britain and Nuclear Weapons*; Macmillan (1980)

Fulford, Michael. *Calleva Atrebatum: a Guide to the Roman Town of Silchester*; Calleva Museum (1987; rev 1995)

Gains, R.A. 'Hampshire's Famous Ghosts'; *Hampshire* (vol 2, no 2, p25)

Gannaway, Norman. *A History of Cricket in Hampshire*; Hampshire Books (1990)

Garlick, V.F.M. *The Newbury Scrapbook*; V.F.M. Garlick (1970)

Gascoine, Bamber. *Encyclopaedia of Britain*; Macmillan

Gascoine, Margaret. *Discovering English Customs and Traditions*; Shire Publications

Gibbons, Thomas (ed). *21 Sermons by the Late Reverend Innes Pearce MA of Tadley, Hants*; London (1763)

Gibson, J.S.W. *Monumental Inscriptions in 60 Hampshire Churches*; Stoneyhall (1958)

Gibson, Jeremy. *Local Newspapers 1750 - 1920*; Federation of Family History Societies (1987)

Goodland, Norman. ; BBC Radio Solent (May 1986)

Griffin, James and Lomas, Tim. *Exploring Local History*; Teach Yourself Books (1997)

Grigg, E.M. *A History of St Saviour's Church Mortimer West End Hants 1856-1958*

Hampshire Archives Group. *Education in Hampshire and the Isle of Wight*; Hampshire Archives Group Publication No 3 (1977)

Hampshire Archivists' Group. *Poor Law In Hampshire Throughout the Centuries*; Hampshire Archivists Group Publication No 1 (1970)

Hampshire Archivists' Group. *Transport in Hampshire and the Isle of Wight*; Hampshire Archivists Group Publication No 2 (1973)

Hampshire Treasures, Vol 2 Basingstoke and Dean; Hampshire County Council (MCMLXXIX)

Hampton, Angela. Bringing Back the Birch; *Hampshire* (May 1998)

Hancock, Robert. *Ruth Ellis*; Weidenfeld & Nicholson (c1958)

Handscomb, Sue. *Tilehurst*; Alan Sutton Publishing Ltd (1995)

Harris, Richard. *Timber-framed Houses*; Shire Publications Ltd (1978)

Hart, Liddell B.H. *History of the Second World War*; Pan Books Ltd (1973)

Harvey, Nigel. *Trees, Woods and Forests*; Shire Publications (1981)

Hastings, Max. *Overlord*; Papermac (1993)

Haycock, Lorna. *History of Chivers of Devizes*; Create Publishing Services (199?)

Headley, Gill and Rance, Adrian (ed). *Pleasure Gardens – The Gardens and Landscapes of Hampshire*; Milestone Publications (1987)

Hey, David. *The Oxford Companion to Local and Family History*; Oxford University Press

Hillbourne, Doreen St. 'The Unknown Knights of Pamber'; *Hampshire* (September 1970, Vol 10, No 11, pp 44-46)

Hillman, Mollie. 'Do You Live in Tadley?'; *Hampshire* (May 1974, vol 14, no 7, p 22)

———————— Tadley Roll; *Hampshire* (May 1974)

Hohler, Major. Various articles in *Wolverton Echo* (1980-81)

Holes, Noel. The First 'William' Pear; *Gardening Illustrated* (15 December 1956)

Hope, Brigadier General J.F.R. *The 3rd (Basingstoke) Battalion Hampshire Home Guard 1940-45*; Brigadier General J.F.R. Hope (1945/6)

Horn, Pamela. District Nursing in Berkshire 1914; *Berkshire Old and New* (No 12, 1995)

———————— *Labouring Life in the Victorian Countryside*; Gill and Macmillan (1976)

Hudson, W.H. Hampshire Days

———————— A Shepherd's Life

Hutchins, Monty. 'A Country Childhood'; *AWRE News* 1983

Industrial Berkshire; Berkshire County Council

Jenkins, J.Geraint. 'Broom-maker of the woodlands'; *Country Life* (17 October 1957)

———————— 'Craft of the Village Rake-maker'; *Country Life* (2 January 1958, pp 22-23)

———————— 'Waning Craft of the Rake-maker' *Country Life* (23 November 1961)

Jennings, Henry. *Heavenly Melodies* (1865)

John, Janet R. *Fairfields School (1888-1979)*; Janet J. John (1979)

Karau, Paul; Parsons, Mike; Robertson, Kevin. *The Didcot, Newbury and Southampton Railway*; Wild Swan Publications Ltd

Kimber, Ernie. *Tadley During My Time and Before*; Private (1983)

———————— *My Story of the Tadley Band and my 75 Years as a Bandsman*

Kightly, Charles. *The Customs and Ceremonies of Britain*; Thames & Hudson

Lacey, Paul. *The Independent Bus and Coach Operators of the Newbury Area 1919 –1932*; Paul Lacey (1985)

Lawson, John and Silver, H. *Social History of Education in England*; (1973)

Lewis, D.T. The Early Years; *AWRE News* (April 1971)

Luffrum, Jean & Williams, Hannah. *The House in Mary Ann's Garden Known As The Shrubbery*; The Platinum Printing Co Ltd

Lunn, George H.. *Tadley Common Methodist Church, Silver Jubilee*; (1982)

Maggs, Colin. *Branch Lines of Berkshire*; Alan Sutton (1993)

Makin, Jenny. Down Your Street – Newtown; *Basingstoke Gazette* (22 March 1999)

Mann, John Edgar. 'Tadley, Gawd elp us'; *Hampshire* (January 1992, Vol 32, No 4, p24)

———————— *Hampshire Customs, Curiosities and Country Lore*; Ensign Publications (1994)

Marks, Laurence. *Ruth Ellis, A Case of Diminished Responsibility*; McDonald (1956)

May, Trevor. *The Victorian Schoolroom*; Shire Publications Ltd (1994)

———————— *The Victorian Workhouse*; Shire Publications (1997)

McGowan. *On the Gypsy Trail*; Romany and Traveller Family History (1998)

Minter, Pat and Searing, Roger. *Tadley Tracks, Tadley Facts*; Private (1982)

Mitchell, Vic and Smith, Keith. *Reading to Basingstoke: Country Railway Routes*; Middleton Press (1994)

Money, W. A Perfect Booke of all the Lands…

———— Various articles; *Transactions of Newbury District Field Club* (Vol IV 1886-95)

———— *A History of Newbury*; Newbury Bookshop & Thames Valley Press (1972)

Morgan, Michael. *Historical Sources in Geography*; Butterworths (1979)

Mortimer History Society. *19th Century Mortimer*; Mortimer History Society (1980)

———— *Mortimer Between the Wars*; Mortimer History Society (1984)

———— *Mortimer Through the Ages*; Mortimer History Society (1994)

Mortimer Local History Group. *Walks Around Mortimer*; Mortimer Local History Group (1998)

Mortimer, Roger. *The History of the Derby Stakes*; Michael Joseph (1961 (2nd edition))

Mortimer West End Rights of Way Committee. *Circular Walks Around Mortimer West End*; Mortimer History Society

Moutray Read, D.H.. *Highways and Byways in Hampshire*; (1908)

Munby, Julian (ed). *Domesday Book* vol 4 Hampshire; Phillimore (1982)

Naxton, M. *The History of Reading School*; (1986)

Newham, Mary Rose. *Notes on the History of the Parish of Aldermaston*; Private (1944)

Nicholas & Co. *The Wilderness, Tadley*; Sale document; (1920)

Norris, Barry. *A Priestly Purpose*; Churchman Publications (1985)

O'Bee, Bob. *Baughurst Parish Council – The Last 100 Years*; Baughurst Parish Council (1994)

Osborne, Keith. *Hampshire Hogheads – The Lost Breweries of the County vol 1*; (1996)

Owen, W. Charles. Crabbed Age and Youth; *AWRE News* (April 1971)

Past Pieces; Basingstoke Archaeological & Historical Society (1992)

'Padworth House'; *Country Life* (September 1922)

Pemberton, Wilf. 'Twilight of the Hampshire Rake'; *Hampshire* (March 1961, Vol 1, No 5, p 29)

Petty, John. *The History of the Primitive Connextion*; (1864)

Pevsner, Nicholas. *The Buildings of England: Berkshire*; (1st edition 1967)

Pevsner, Nicholas and Lloyd, David. *The Buildings of England: Hampshire and the Isle of Wight*; (1st edition 1967)

Phillips, Daphne. *Berkshire: A County History*; Countryside Books (1993)

———— *The History of Reading*; (2nd edition 1990)

Phillips, M. The Site is Chosen; *AWRE News* (April 1971)

Porter, Roy. *Disease, Medicine and Society*; CUP (1995)

Potter, Robert W.F. *Hampshire Harvest*; Phillimore & Co Ltd (1977)

Pounds, Reginald. *Gillies, Surgeon Extraordinary*

Preece, Pat. Osier Growing and Ciltivation in the Kennet Valley Area; *Berkshire Old and New* (No 13, 1996)

Pugh, Peter. *The Manor Reborn*; Cambridge Business Publications (1988)

Railton, Margaret. *Early Medical Services – Berkshire and South Oxfordshire from 1740*; Polmood Publications (1994)

Richardson, John. *Local Historian's Encyclopaedia*; Historical Publications (1993)

Roundabout; Tadley and District Chamber of Trade

Ruston, Gillian A. *100 Years of Progress: Hampshire County Council 1889-1989*; Southgate Publications (1989)

St Hillbourne, Dorothea. 'The Unknown Knight of Pamber'; *Hampshire* (September 1970, Vol 10, No 11, pp 44-46)

Sands, T.B. *The Didcot, Newbury and Southampton Railway*; The Oakwood Press (1971)

Scholfield, Albert. *Baughurst Methodist Church, 1872-1972*; (1972)

Searing, Roger. Tadley; *Reading Midweek Chronicle* (16 Oct 1984)

———— Tadley – the butt of local wags; *Reading Chronicle* (16 October 1984)

Sharp, Mary A. *The History of Ufton Court*; Elliot Stock (1892)

Shrubsall, Dennis. 'Round and About Silchester with W.H. Hudson'; *Hampshire* (January 198?, Vol 20, No 3, pp 35-36)

'The Site Takes Shape'; *AWRE News* (April 1971)

Smallbone, Ken. *James Potter (Quaker)*; Sessions Book Trust, York (1992)

———— Hampshire Parishes: Baughurst (no 29)

Smallbrook, Pamela. *Laundry Bygones*; Shire Publications (1983)

Smallwood, D. Information sheet

Smith, Dilys. *Park Prewett – the History 1898-1984*; Basingstoke & North Hampshire Health Authority (1986)

'Smiths of Baughurst'; *Basingstoke Gazette* (May 1991)

Snow, C.F.F. 'The Art of Besom-making'; *Country Life* (14 April 1944, pp 644-645)

──────── 'A Workshop of the Countryside'; *Country Life* (7 December 1945, pp 1006-1007)

Sparkes, Ivan G. *Woodland Craftsmen*; Shire Publications Ltd (1997)

Stevens. Spotlight on Tadley; *Basingstoke Gazette* (13 January 1992)

Stevens, Carol. Nostalgia; *Pamber Heath Newsletter* (198?-198?)

Suggested Walks in the Parish of Baughurst; Baughurst Parish Council (1997)

Tadley Conservation Area; Basingstoke and Deane Borough Council (1999 draft)

Tadley Womens' Institute. *Tadley WI Scrapbook*; Tadley Womens' Institute (c1950 and 1965)

Tavener, L. Ellis. *The Common Lands of Hampshire*; Hampshire County Council (1957)

Thomson, James. *The Book of Silchester* Vol I and II (1924)

Tighe, M. *A Gazetteer of Hampshire Brewers*; Proceedings of the Hampshire Field Club (vol 27 1970)

Timmins, Gordon. *Aldermaston Spitfires*; Gordon Timmins (1998)

──────── The History Surrounding Heldremanstone Now Known as Aldermaston; Gordon Timmins

──────── *A History of the Village School, Aldermaston*; Gordon Timmins

──────── *Aldermaston the Airfield*; Gordon Timmins

──────── *Aldermaston Decoy Pond*; Private (1999)

Tingle, M.F. *A Gazetteer of Hampshire Breweries*; Southampton University Industrial Archaeology Group (?)

Toogood, Revd R.C. *A History of Bramley*; (1993)

Transco. *From Beach to Meter*; British Gas (1998)

Trigg, John. *Before the Fountain – a View of Victorian Woolhampton and Midgham*; John Trigg

Turner, L Ellis. *The Common Lands of Hampshire*; (1957)

Tute, Warren, Costello J. and Hughes T. *D-Day*; Sidgewick and Jackson Ltd (1974)

'Twilight of the Hampshire Rake'; *Hampshire* (March 1961 Vol 5 p 29)

Vickers, John. *The Religious Census of Hampshire for 1851*; Hampshire County Council (1993)

The Victoria County History of Hampshire; 5 vols and index; (1900-1911)

Vine, P.A.L. *London's Lost Route to Basingstoke*; David & Charles (1968; rev 1994)

Walford, Jill. *The Quakers of Baughurst in the Seventeenth and Eighteenth Centuries*; Jill Walford

Warlan, RN, Lt Cdr Ben (compiler). *Shore Establishments of the Royal Navy*; Maritime Books (1992)

Waters, Laurence. *Railway Centres: Reading*; Ian Allen (1990)

Waugh, Auberon. *Will This Do?*; Arrow (1992)

Wheeler, Dennis. *Regional Climates of the British Isles*; Routledge (1997)

White, W.C.F. *A Gazetteer of Brick and Tile Works in Hampshire*; (vol 24 1970)

Whitehead, R.A. *Wallis & Steevens – A History*; The Road Locomotive Society (1983)

Wilmot, Chester. *The Struggle for Europe*; Collins (1952)

Who Was Who; A & C Black Ltd

Williams, L.F. Rushbrook. *The Church of St Mary the Virgin, Silchester*; (1970s)

Williams, Leon. 'Munich Fifty Years On'

Williams, T. *A History of the British Gas Industry*; OUP (1981)

Willis, Arthur J. (compiler). *A Hampshire Miscellany III, Dissenters' Meeting House Certificates 1702-1844*; Arthur J. Wallis

Willis, Steve and Holliss, Barry. *Military Airfields in the British Isles 1939-1945 part 1 (A -E)*; Enthusiasts Publications (1981)

Willis, Steve and Holliss, Barry. *Military Airfields in the British Isles 1939-1945 (omnibus edition)*; Enthusiasts Publications (1987)

Wilson, Angela (ed). *The Last of the Darby Griffiths; Padworth House in the 1920s*; Padworth College (199?)

Womens' Institute. *The New Hampshire Village Book*; Countryside Books (1990)

Woodley, Charles. *The Golden Age: British Civil Aviation 1950-1965*; Airlife

Wright, A. Brickworks: *A Gazetteer of Brick and Tile Manufacturing Sites in North East Hampshire*; (1980)

Wright, Geoffrey N. *Turnpike Roads*; Shire Publications Ltd (1997)

Wynn, Godfrey. The Five Ages of Ruth Ellis; *Sunday Despatch* (17 July 1955)